COUNTDOWN 1960

ALSO BY CHRIS WALLACE

*Countdown bin Laden: The Untold Story of the 247-Day
Hunt to Bring the Mastermind of 9/11 to Justice*

*Countdown 1945: The Extraordinary Story of the Atomic Bomb
and the 116 Days that Changed the World*

COUNTDOWN 1960

THE BEHIND-THE-SCENES STORY OF THE 312 DAYS THAT CHANGED AMERICA'S POLITICS FOREVER

CHRIS WALLACE

WITH MITCH WEISS

DUTTON

DUTTON

An imprint of Penguin Random House LLC

penguinrandomhouse.com

LIBRARY OF CONGRESS CATALOGING-IN-PUBLICATION DATA HAS BEEN APPLIED FOR.

ISBN 9780593852194 (hardcover)
ISBN 9780593852200 (ebook)

Printed in the United States of America
1st Printing

BOOK DESIGN BY SILVERGLASS STUDIO

To Peter, Megan, Catherine, Andrew, Sarah, and Remick.
I love you. And I'm proud of you.

January 2, 1960
Washington, D.C.

The moment arrived. U.S. senator John Fitzgerald Kennedy of Massachusetts entered the majestic Senate Caucus Room, looking more like a movie star than a politician. He calmed the applause, stepped up to a bank of microphones, and told the world he was running for president of the United States.

After hinting for years, he made it official, surrounded by family members and friends.

He was polished and articulate, a mature but still youthful forty-two. He stood tall and slender, tanned and well-rested after a nearly two-week family holiday in Jamaica. His blue eyes, toothy smile, and neatly tousled hair gave him a healthy, confident appeal.

Jack Kennedy shone in the historic room, dressed in a perfectly tailored pin-striped suit, white button-down shirt, and blue necktie.

He'd picked the perfect place and time to introduce himself to the electorate. The news conference was scheduled for 12:30 p.m. on the first Saturday after the New Year's holiday. It would be a slow news day, so his announcement would get plenty of media attention in the heavily read Sunday newspapers.

And it was no accident that JFK chose the Caucus Room—one of the most impressive places in the nation's capital. Sunlight streamed through three grand windows and sparkled on crystal chandeliers. Corinthian columns and the marble floor gleamed. Kennedy might have appeared young, but the stunning backdrop would quietly convey to voters that he was serious.

The Caucus Room had served as a stage for some of the Senate's most dramatic public hearings: the sinking of the *Titanic*, the Japanese surprise attack on Pearl Harbor, Tennessee senator Estes Kefauver's hearings into organized crime, and Wisconsin senator Joe McCarthy's televised anti-communist crusades.

Standing before the microphones, Kennedy glanced at the text he had prepared on notecards. He lifted his head, took a deep breath, and stared straight ahead.

"I am today announcing my candidacy for the presidency of the United States," he said, in his distinct Boston accent.

Kennedy promised to take the nation into a new decade of global leadership. He laid out a list of challenges facing the United States, with America's relationship with the Soviet Union and Communist China as his campaign's top issue. He warned that the United States had to find a way to end the arms race, which threatened the very existence of civilization.

But JFK didn't stop there. He brought up issues that would become campaign staples. He vowed to reinvigorate American science and education, prevent the collapse of the farm economy, and stop urban decay.

Without missing a beat, he said prosperity must be extended to all Americans, without increasing inflation or unemployment.

If Jack Kennedy was nervous, he didn't show it. The speech flowed. He was firm, direct, and polished from years of practice. He had been running unofficially for the Democratic Party's nomination since 1957. He had traveled all over the United States to introduce himself to voters. He had made numerous speeches and campaign appearances on behalf of Democratic candidates, picking up IOUs along the way as he built his own formidable organization.

But Kennedy knew that many Democratic leaders still thought he was too young, too inexperienced—and Roman Catholic, to boot—to lead the party into the November general election.

That day in the Senate Caucus Room, Kennedy unveiled a new campaign strategy—one that could play to his strengths and cut out the old political bosses.

Before 1960, presidential primaries were minor events. Party leaders settled on who would be the standard-bearer in the proverbial smoke-filled rooms at national conventions. The candidate with the best connections to state and regional political kingpins usually became the nominee.

But Kennedy vowed to flip the script. Bucking tradition, JFK would campaign in primary elections and empower voters—not party bosses—to win him as many delegates as possible.

Kennedy indicated the Democratic primaries were a true testing ground for candidates with presidential ambitions. If he could win over primary voters, they'd follow him in the general election.

It was a gamble. So far, only Hubert H. Humphrey, the liberal Democratic senator from Minnesota, had announced that he was running for president. Senators Lyndon B. Johnson of Texas and Stuart Symington of Missouri were still deciding whether to seek the Democratic nomination.

So, Kennedy challenged any rival to face him in the primaries. He asked, if they couldn't beat him there, how could they defeat Vice President Richard Nixon, the presumptive Republican presidential candidate, in the fall?

Kennedy was confident that his strategy would pay off.

"In the past 40 months, I have toured every state in the Union, and I have talked to Democrats in all walks of life. My candidacy is therefore based on the conviction that I can win both the nomination and the election," Kennedy said.

"I believe that any Democratic aspirant to this important nomination should be willing to submit to the voters his views, record and competence in a series of primary contests," Kennedy said, adding, "I am therefore now announcing my intention of filing in the New Hampshire primary, and I shall announce my plans with respect to the other primaries as their filing dates approach."

John Kennedy announcing his candidacy, January 2, 1960
(Associated Press)

The audience cheered. Kennedy flashed his grin. And when the press asked, following his remarks, Kennedy made it clear that he was running for the presidential nomination of his party—and under no circumstances would he be a candidate for vice president.

Kennedy was hoping to become only the second Catholic to land the Democratic presidential nomination. The first, New York governor Al Smith, lost in a landslide to Republican Herbert Hoover in 1928.

Anti-Catholic bigotry was still alive and strong in the United States. Some voters believed that a Catholic president would be under the control of the Vatican, that church doctrine would influence his decisions. Kennedy knew it would take longer than a single news conference to put that to rest. JFK said he believed the voters' only question should be,

"Does the candidate believe in the Constitution, does he believe in the First Amendment, does he believe in the separation of church and state?"

When the news conference was over, Kennedy's thirty-year-old wife, Jacqueline, smiled as she posed for pictures with her husband. For Kennedy, the day was a good start to what would certainly be a tough campaign. Yes, he was young, but he wasn't lacking in experience. He had served as a U.S. Navy officer. He was a decorated World War II combat veteran, not to mention a member of Congress.

But he had a long way to go to convince voters that he was more than just a handsome war hero with a picture-perfect, and affluent, family. Kennedy would have to show a skeptical nation he had character enough to tackle divisive issues at home, and the gravitas needed to stare down military threats that could destroy the world.

And he had to keep some other things carefully concealed. His personal flaws could easily derail his campaign. So far, he had been successful at keeping his private life and serious health issues separate from his public persona. He had a rare but potentially fatal disorder of the adrenal glands that leaves the body's immune system unable to fight off infection and disease. And he was a philanderer who'd had numerous affairs with staffers, actresses, and others. The question was, how long could he keep the lid on?

COUNTDOWN: **298 DAYS**

January 16, 1960
Miami, Florida

The big twin-engine Convair charter touched down in Miami just after midnight, and Vice President Richard Nixon dragged his weary body out of its folded-up position. His wife, Pat, his staffers, and a few Washington reporters gathered their things.

The candidate yawned, stretched, and put on his game face.

When the cabin door opened, Nixon bounded into the night air. He walked down the boarding stairs, measuring the boisterous crowd waiting for his arrival—at least a thousand of them. Suddenly, he felt a jolt of energy.

"People stay up later here than they should . . . It's almost one o'clock," Nixon quipped to the well-wishers on the tarmac.

Nixon waded into the crowd, shaking dozens of hands, soaking up the excitement. He could have stayed there all night, but his security detail was waiting with a ten-car motorcade to whisk him off to the Roney Plaza Hotel in Miami Beach.

On the way downtown, Nixon sighed and took his wife's hand in his. They were looking at a busy weekend, but that was fine. If he was going to win the White House, he had to do the hard work.

He'd learned a tough lesson in the 1958 midterms. Republicans had suffered massive losses. Nixon told GOP leaders the blunt truth: The Democrats deserved to win. "Republicans worked for two months. Our opponents worked for two years."

No one was ever going to outwork or outhustle Dick Nixon. He had an inner drive for success that he couldn't explain. He was an enigma, even to friends. Nixon was dogged, determined, and ambitious. Yet he could be distrustful, peevish, even paranoid at times.

In private, Nixon was reserved and insecure. He was an introvert in a profession that demanded outgoing, loquacious leaders. In an interview early in his career, Nixon admitted as much to Stewart Alsop, a newspaper columnist and political analyst: "But it is true that I'm fundamentally relatively shy. It doesn't come natural to me to be a buddy-buddy boy. . . . I can't really let my hair down with anyone."

But on the campaign trail, Nixon came alive. At just over five feet, eleven inches tall with a prominent nose and thick, dark eyebrows, Nixon was a skilled and energetic campaigner—a trait that emerged during his first run for public office.

A lieutenant commander in the U.S. Naval Reserve, Nixon had just been released from active duty in 1946 when Republican leaders in his hometown of Whittier, California, urged him to run for Congress.

His opponent was Representative Jerry Voorhis, a popular Democrat who was seeking his sixth two-year term. Democrats had a solid majority in Voorhis's Twelfth Congressional District. So, Nixon knew the GOP wasn't really looking for a viable candidate. They wanted a sacrificial lamb.

But Nixon had other plans. Yes,. he was "absolutely green," but he vowed to win. Nixon was an attorney, and politics seemed like a natural extension of his profession. So, he turned to his wife, Pat: Would she be on board if he ran for Congress? She said yes. They decided to sink $5,000—more than half of everything they had saved—into the campaign.

Nixon's modest nest egg began in the Solomon Islands, where he'd served during World War II. He quickly became known as a card shark at poker and carefully tucked away his winnings for the future.

Nixon was an unlikely gambler. He grew up in a Quaker family where betting was frowned upon. A religion that abstained from any participation in violence, Quakers had been exempted from military service for generations. But after Pearl Harbor, Nixon felt the need to serve his country. How could he sit on the sidelines when his nation was in peril? When he joined, he was twenty-nine years old and working as an attorney for the Office of Emergency Management in Washington, D.C.

When the cards and dice were pulled out, Nixon watched his fellow officers closely, quickly picking up on their strategies and techniques. His disciplined approach came from his poker-playing buddy, a fellow named James Stewart, who offered sage advice: You didn't stay in the game unless you were "convinced" that you had the "best hand."

Nixon took lessons from Stewart, spent hours watching the best players, learning their moves, until "his playing became tops," Stewart said. A former Navy officer said Nixon turned into a brilliant poker player.

"I once saw him bluff a lieutenant commander out of $1,500 with a pair of deuces," James Udall recalled.

He returned home from the war with several thousand dollars in extra cash in his pocket. When he launched his congressional career, Nixon was a conservative Republican, staunch anti-communist—and a big underdog in the race against Voorhis.

But he initiated what soon became the Nixon formula for success, a mix of heavy campaigning and blasting the competition with negative, misleading information.

During the summer of 1946, Nixon painted himself as a "clean, forthright young American who fought in defense of his country in the stinking mud and jungles of the Solomons." Meanwhile, Voorhis had "stayed safely behind the front in Washington."

Nixon was relentless. In a series of five debates across the district, he suggested that Voorhis had connections to communist groups. Soon, people began receiving strange telephone calls from an anonymous caller: "This is a friend of yours. I just want you to know that Jerry Voorhis is a Communist."

In November, Nixon was elected with 56 percent of the vote. It was the start of a meteoric career.

Richard Nixon campaigning, 1960
(UPI/Newscom)

In six years, Nixon went from freshman congressman to vice president, riding the wave of America's anti-communist hysteria. He won his seats in the House in 1946 and the Senate in 1950 by accusing his opponents of being soft on communism.

The U.S. Senate race was especially ugly. His opponent was U.S. representative Helen Gahagan Douglas, who was intelligent, articulate, and attractive. Nixon attacked her character by questioning her loyalty to the United States. He suggested that she had communist sympathies and printed information about her on a "pink sheet" that was distributed at campaign rallies. Nixon called her the "pink lady" because of her Soviet support, saying she was "pink right down to her underwear." Nixon's attacks were rough, even for a political campaign, but they resonated with the electorate, and in the last days of the campaign, some people threw rocks at her car as she left rallies.

Nixon's campaign style didn't change as the years passed. He put his technique to work helping other Republican candidates raise money and win elections across the country. In return, Nixon won the loyalty of GOP leaders from big cities to small towns. Nixon seemed to have the skills to unify his party.

It was no surprise that key Republicans from all over Florida—who called themselves Citizens for Nixon—had planned a series of public events for the vice president and his wife. They had billed the gatherings as nonpartisan, saying everyone, regardless of party affiliation, was invited to meet the Nixons.

But there could be no mistake—these were campaign stops. Comparable events were planned over the next few weeks in strategic spots all over the United States.

Hours before landing in Miami, Nixon had opened his campaign for the GOP presidential nomination by promising a crowd in Gainesville, Florida, that, if elected, he'd continue on the path blazed by President Dwight D. Eisenhower. And why not?

The nation's economy was humming. Eisenhower was still beloved as one of the great American generals in World War II, even after almost eight years in political office. And Nixon was one of the president's most ardent supporters. He had been vice president for those eight years and actively backed Ike's domestic and foreign policy priorities.

Term limits prevented Eisenhower from running again for president, and the most obvious choice to take his place was his loyal wingman. Nixon was the top political figure in the party. Nothing stood in his way, especially after his chief Republican rival, New York governor Nelson A. Rockefeller, announced he wasn't going to be a candidate on December 26, 1959.

But lately, Rockefeller had been hinting he might challenge Nixon for the nomination because he felt the party was headed in the wrong

direction. Nixon was concerned. Rockefeller came from one of the nation's wealthiest families. So, he'd be able to mount a serious campaign.

While Rockefeller never had to worry about money, Nixon knew all
about hard times. His father had opened a small grocery store and gas
station in Whittier, and his family struggled to make ends meet. Nixon's
early life was marked by financial hardship, and he would later tell Eisenhower about it: "We were poor, but the glory of it was we didn't
know it." Still, his family's financial problems left an indelible mark on
his life. He wasn't born into wealth and didn't have family connections
to get ahead. So, Nixon had to study and work hard—and hope for
scholarships.

When Rockefeller realized that a presidential campaign "would
entail a massive struggle" that would keep him from fulfilling his obligations as New York's governor, he decided not to run for the GOP
nomination.

With Rockefeller presumably out, Nixon was no longer just the
GOP's presumptive front-runner for the nomination. Media pundits favored him to capture the White House.

So why was Nixon working so hard so early on the campaign trail?
Maybe he was motivated by the quiet fear that gripped the nation—
Cold War tensions were high between the United States and the Soviet
Union.

The Eisenhower administration had built up a stockpile of nuclear
weapons to deter military threats, but that didn't stop the Soviets in 1957
from launching the first man-made satellite to orbit Earth. Sputnik had
triggered a national conversation about whether America had lost its
edge in math, science, and technology.

And then there was Cuba. In 1959, Fidel Castro, the charismatic
leader of the Cuban revolution, had overthrown Fulgencio Batista, a
brutal dictator with ties to U.S. mobsters. Now it seemed that Castro
had become pals with Nikita Khrushchev, the Soviet premier. A dangerous development 90 miles from America's southernmost shores.

Maybe Nixon was uneasy because of what Rockefeller didn't say.

When someone drops out of an election, they usually endorse another candidate in the race. That's especially true if there's only one candidate left in the contest. But Rockefeller didn't endorse Nixon. He didn't praise him, either.

And the New York governor was emphatic about something else: Under no circumstances would he accept his party's nomination for vice president. In other words, there was no way he'd be on the same ticket with Nixon. As one Nixon staffer put it, "We've just been kicked in the groin."

What did Rockefeller really want? Did he still harbor thoughts and plans for the nomination? Nixon didn't know, but Rockefeller made him uneasy.

And at a time when Nixon should have been excited about his prospects, he also was fighting his own demons.

For years, he had been treated for depression by psychiatrist Arnold Hutschnecker. The doctor was now a vice presidential "adviser," treating him for "stress." Nixon kept it a secret. If the voters knew he saw a shrink, it could be the death knell for his campaign. The American public wouldn't hand the presidency to a man who was mentally ill.

In the end, Nixon was relieved that Rockefeller pulled out of the race and forestalled a costly battle inside the GOP for the nomination. The last thing Nixon needed was more stress.

He even issued a statement. "Gov. Rockefeller has made an excellent impression in the states he has visited in the past few months. People throughout the nation have recognized him as a leader of national and international stature," Nixon said. The New York governor was "destined for continuing leadership in the Republican Party and the nation in the years ahead."

Nixon was sticking to his strategy, staying nonpolitical and statesmanlike as long as possible. On the campaign trail, he'd take every opportunity to champion the administration's policies. He'd tell Americans that Ike was responsible for the "ending of one war, avoiding others."

Nixon would tell the crowds that he'd been right there at the president's side the whole time—and that he had more experience than any vice president in U.S. history. He had made numerous overseas trips on Ike's behalf—fact-finding missions to troubled spots, goodwill trips to struggling nations, and diplomatic visits to prime ministers and kings.

"Experience" was the key word in his new campaign rhetoric that circulated in brochures and was repeated in paid print ads:

> In these times of crisis there's no time for "on the job" training of a new President. Instant decisions are called for the instant he takes office. Only Richard Nixon already has the knowledge and skill required, based on eight years of direct experience.

It noted that Nixon had traveled to five continents and fifty-four countries—"winning friends for the United States."

> He knows the needs of other nations, the attitudes of their peoples, the thinking, and personalities of their leaders. Foreign statesmen have learned to respect him. Firm in asserting America's position, yet skilled in negotiating, Dick Nixon by his judgment and cool headedness in crisis has proved himself able to make the right decisions for America.

Nixon told his staff that he wanted to stay "low-key." He told his campaign not to commit him to anything fancy or formal unless it was mandatory.

He planned to stay in Washington as much as possible, handling most of his appointments from his office in the Senate building. A week earlier, on January 9—Nixon's birthday—Herbert Klein, the vice president's press secretary, had called a news conference.

Klein said Nixon had given the go-ahead to enter his name in the New Hampshire, Ohio, and Oregon primaries. There was no formal statement declaring his candidacy because the media already assumed he was running. Nixon had no national campaign headquarters nor a paid speechwriter. An assistant was handling his trips. At this point, Nixon truly was running a low-key campaign.

So, in Florida, Nixon followed the script, acting more like a statesman than a candidate. During a visit to the University of Florida, he answered questions from a five-man panel on foreign and domestic policies.

"We do have peace, and have the prospect of continuing peace if we do not make major mistakes," Nixon told some ten thousand people inside the university's gymnasium.

In Miami, he told supporters he'd continue building on the programs Ike had initiated.

Behind the scenes, Nixon summed up his potential Democratic opponents. Nixon told his friends that Texas senator Lyndon Johnson would be a tough opponent. Over the years, he'd built a reputation in Washington as being a smart, cagey politician—a legislative wizard.

But Nixon didn't worry about Johnson. He didn't believe Johnson could even get the Democratic nomination—not with his history of heart disease or the South's history of segregation. But Jack Kennedy? That's who Nixon believed would be the Democratic presidential nominee. Kennedy had it all—he was a good-looking, articulate senator who seemed to connect with voters.

But the vice president believed that even with Kennedy's attributes, he was vulnerable like the other potential Democratic candidates. A Nixon pollster had pointed out JFK's liabilities: "youth, inexperience, wealth, and religion."

Johnson and Kennedy would be easy targets in the general election. But Nixon made one thing clear to his aides: A statesman stays above the fray. So, no personal attacks, at least for now. The only question was, how long would he be able to stick to that?

January 25, 1960
Nashua, New Hampshire

On a snowy New England morning, this little town was humming. Massachusetts senator John F. Kennedy was headed here—the first official stop on his campaign for the Democratic presidential nomination.

By dawn, hundreds of supporters had lined its streets, stomping their feet in the snow, trying to keep warm in the subfreezing temperature while they waited patiently for JFK's arrival.

And then, just as Kennedy's motorcade approached the edge of town, the snow let up and the sun broke through the gray—as if the scene had been scripted in Hollywood.

The caravan zipped along narrow streets until it reached a parking area in front of city hall, a three-story redbrick building with six impressive white columns and a bell tower with a statue of a gold eagle perched on top.

When the doors to one of the vehicles opened, there he was, JFK, looking like he had just stepped out of the pages of *Life* magazine. The crowd roared. Kennedy was tall, with a stylish dark wool overcoat that hugged his thin frame. With a strong gust of wind whipping off the Nashua River, which bisected the town, many people wore hats to keep warm. Not Kennedy. He was hatless, yet not one hair on his head seemed out of place.

Kennedy soaked in the applause, grinning at supporters and reaching into the crowd to shake hands. As usual, everything Kennedy did was scripted. It had to be. This was his first day on the trail. Some pundits said it was too early for this kind of campaigning. The Democratic National Convention wasn't until July. The general election wasn't until November. In politics, that was an eternity. So many things could change between now and then. Yet Kennedy felt the need to take charge, control his own destiny. He wasn't going to waste a day.

That's why he was here, in Nashua, on a cold January morning. He wanted to build support—and momentum—so that his candidacy would become a force, a tidal wave that would wipe out his rivals before they got started.

Police escorted Kennedy out of the cold and into the building, up to the third floor, where Nashua mayor Mario Vagge was waiting. So were dozens of other people, who packed the narrow hallways to catch a glimpse of the celebrity senator.

Vagge introduced Kennedy to city workers, local labor leaders, and politicians. Many held signs saying "All New Hampshire Backs Kennedy" and "We're with You Jack."

Under the glare of flashbulbs and television lights, Kennedy shook hands and made small talk.

Meanwhile, John Latvis wondered about the commotion at city hall. The thirty-nine-year-old insurance agent was headed to his downtown office when he noticed more cars than usual near the municipal building. Then it hit him: *JFK*.

Latvis remembered that Kennedy had been planning to visit Nashua. *This must be the day*, he thought. Latvis wanted to meet him. Like so many others, he was fascinated by Kennedy's backstory: During a nighttime patrol in August 1943, Kennedy's small torpedo boat was cut in half by a Japanese destroyer. While JFK was seriously injured, he helped rescue his crew. At one point, despite his own injuries, JFK went to heroic lengths. He swam to an injured sailor, then towed him by a life-vest strap three and a half miles to a small coral island.

Latvis didn't want to miss his chance to talk to Kennedy.

So, he parked his car, found a back way into the building, then walked up the stairs to the third floor. By now, Kennedy was inside the mayor's office, getting ready for the next event on his busy schedule.

When Latvis walked in the room, he heard someone shout, "Who's going to get coffee?"

"I'll do it," Latvis said. He wheeled around and bounded straight to the Yankee Flyer, a diner across the street from city hall. He ordered twelve cups of coffee—and told the waitress that one was for the next president of the United States.

"If they're for the next president, I'll donate them," the diner's owner shouted. Everyone laughed.

When Latvis returned, he placed the cups down on a desk, then handed one to Kennedy. Latvis was especially excited to meet him because they had so much in common. They both had served in World War II. And they both had graduated from Harvard University. Kennedy had an undergraduate degree in government. Latvis, after graduating from the University of Syracuse, earned a master's degree from Harvard Business School.

The encounter didn't last long. Aides told Kennedy it was time for a news conference in the city hall auditorium.

When Kennedy left the mayor's office, Latvis followed. So did Dolly Bellavance, a twenty-year-old in the city clerk's office. Bellavance and her coworkers knew Kennedy had been planning to visit. She had read newspaper stories about him. But he was a politician—and political types were all the same, right?

For Bellavance, though, watching JFK interact with regular people was eye-opening. Kennedy was warm and cordial. Or maybe "charismatic" was the word she was searching for. No one could keep their eyes off him—he was that good-looking. Bellavance's friends giggled and said they weren't going to wash their hands—not after JFK's handshake.

In the auditorium, Kennedy answered a wide-ranging set of questions with comparative ease—from the latest about Fidel Castro's regime in Cuba to which Democrats posed the biggest challenge to the

Massachusetts senator's candidacy. The *Nashua Telegraph* reported he was "poised, surprisingly fast with his answers, and willing to talk about any subject."

But he mostly covered familiar ground, steering the questions to the primaries—the reason, he said, he was in Nashua in the first place.

Politicians must be able to test their candidacy with the people, Kennedy said. He was on the ballot for New Hampshire's March 8 primary—the first in the nation—to prove that he was a viable candidate. That's why he was also running in Wisconsin, West Virginia, and Oregon, with more states to come.

"In this all-important process of nomination, the American people are entitled to a voice. The people of this state—and the people of other states—are entitled to be heard," Kennedy said.

And JFK warned that the old days of choosing presidential candidates were over.

"I regret that more candidates in both parties will not join me here in that discussion, for primary contests not only educate the public—they educate the candidate as well," he said.

After the event, Kennedy exited the building. And Latvis noticed that the crowd waiting outside had grown. It didn't matter whether Kennedy addressed a handful of people or several hundred, he was always the same: Passionate. Articulate.

With the snow beginning to fall again, Kennedy explained that the United States was the great beacon of hope around the world.

"The United States today is the great defender of freedom. If we fail, that cause fails all over the world. If we succeed, the course of freedom succeeds," he said.

For most politicians, the day would have ended right there—he had already been in Nashua for almost two hours. But not for Kennedy. Accompanied by local politicians, police officers, and firefighters, he walked along Main Street, making his way through the cold and snow, followed by hundreds of supporters.

John Kennedy campaigning in Nashua, New Hampshire, January 1960
(John F. Kennedy Presidential Library)

He stopped in stores to talk to shopkeepers and regular folks about their concerns. Yes, many were worried about the Soviets and the threat of nuclear war. But for most people in this city of 39,000, the economy was the main issue.

Nashua's economic growth had slowed. Salaries hadn't kept up with inflation. This was once a thriving textile town. Factories here had churned out shoes, clothing, and other items for generations. But many of those union jobs were being moved in search of cheaper wages. Kennedy made sure to remind the rank and file that he was on their side.

Everywhere Kennedy went, he exchanged handshakes and signed autographs. At one crosswalk, he ventured into the middle of the street to say hello to a traffic cop.

Kennedy dropped into one luncheonette for a ham and cheese sandwich, and another for more coffee—with cream and sugar. He visited a firehouse and posed with the fire chief's hat in his hand (he rarely wore hats). The visit had taken on a parade-like feel, with firefighters sounding their sirens, the fire truck's loudspeaker system blasting music, and police cars flashing their lights. As JFK waded into the crowd, more than one woman said, "Isn't he handsome?"

And then, in front of a paint store, Kennedy spotted his wife, Jacqueline, who had just flown in from New York. They kissed and linked arms. She looked as fashionable as he did, in her bright red overcoat, dark fur hat, scarf, and black gloves.

They walked together, greeting folks waiting in store doorways or workers leaving factory gates. Everywhere they went, they got a hearty, enthusiastic welcome.

"Nashua's never seen anything like this," Royal Dion, the local chairman of the Kennedy for President committee, told JFK as they walked. "If a man wants to be president, he's got to work."

Kennedy didn't need the hint. That's why he was out here, campaigning like it was only a few days until the election. While his potential Democratic rivals were in their Washington offices or resting comfortably in their homes, he was on the road, filling people like Latvis and Bellavance with hope while building a network of supporters who'd volunteer to help his campaign. Now, with Nashua in his rearview mirror, Kennedy knew that kind of support could make all the difference in a tight race, especially with important primaries in the next few months.

COUNTDOWN: **282 DAYS**

February 1, 1960
Greensboro, North Carolina

It was a long mile-and-a-half walk in their Sunday shoes, but the weather was kind to the four freshmen from the historically Black Agricultural and Technical College of North Carolina. Franklin McCain and his dorm mates stopped in front of the F. W. Woolworth store in downtown Greensboro, North Carolina.

It was a busy place, part of a national chain of five-and-dime discount stores. Black people could shop there, but they had to stick to a set of store policies designed to keep them in their place. McCain and his friends traded glances and nods, then stepped past the plate-glass double doors.

The Greensboro Woolworth store was one of the few places downtown where shoppers could have a seat at a lunch counter for a quick meal. At least white shoppers could. Woolworth's lunch counter had a "whites only" policy, just like many other cafés, stores, and retail outlets across the American South.

That's why McCain, Ezell Blair Jr., Joseph McNeil, and David Richmond walked into town that day. They came to create a stir.

McCain wondered if they'd be arrested or beaten. Or something even worse. In a place like Greensboro, anything could happen. Greensboro was the second-biggest city in North Carolina, and white people ruled the town. Jim Crow, a system of laws that legalized racial segregation, codified their racial prejudices.

In 1960, America moved slowly toward racial equality partly because of detours placed along the road to civil rights by southern governors.

Many southern states still refused to abide by the 1954 U.S. Supreme Court ruling ending racial segregation in public schools. The state of Arkansas had tried to defy federal court orders in 1957 to integrate. So, President Eisenhower sent U.S. troops to protect Black students trying to attend class at Little Rock Central High School.

Vice President Nixon was a supporter of civil rights. He had worked on legislation to prevent racial discrimination in federal contracts. And he was instrumental in pushing Congress to pass the Civil Rights Act of 1957 through Congress. The law allowed federal prosecutors to seek injunctions if anyone tried to stop minorities from voting.

Nixon had met repeatedly with civil rights leaders and promoted his administration's record. He knew the Black vote would be important in November.

The vice president had asked prominent Black leaders for advice on how to improve race relations, forming ties with the Reverend Martin Luther King Jr. and Jackie Robinson, who had broken baseball's color barrier in 1947. Meanwhile, Jack Kennedy had been silent about segregation. He had voted for a watered-down version of the Civil Rights Act and refused to condemn southern governors who opposed integration.

But even with Nixon's support and some progress, Black people in the South were not allowed to use the same bathrooms, water fountains, public parks, beaches, or swimming pools as whites. They were only allowed to sit in designated sections of movie theaters. Some restaurants were off-limits, or relegated Black customers to stand-up snack bars or take-out windows.

Franklin McCain was tired of this second-class treatment. Today he was going to fight back, but in a peaceful, nonviolent way.

McCain and his friends had devised their plan the previous night during one of their many "rap sessions"—late-night discussions when they'd talk about current issues and racial inequality. Sometimes they went on until dawn.

The four eighteen-year-olds had met in the fall of 1959, when they moved into the same dormitory. They discovered they could be open and honest with one another about issues that were usually hushed up and kept quiet back home. They didn't hold anything back.

It was during their last rap session that McNeil had expressed his frustration with the slow pace of desegregation. It seemed like everybody talked about ending Jim Crow, but nobody stepped up and did anything to challenge it.

"It's time to take some action now," McNeil said.

The others nodded in agreement. But what kind of action?

They modeled themselves after Reverend King and his nonviolent protests. King had organized a boycott of the Montgomery, Alabama, bus system after a Black woman named Rosa Parks was arrested on December 1, 1955, for refusing to give up her seat to a white passenger. The tactic proved to be a powerful economic tool. More than 75 percent of Montgomery's bus ridership was Black—and an overwhelming majority supported the boycott.

Black men and women walked, carpooled, or found other ways to get around instead of using the municipal bus system. The protests ended after the U.S. Supreme Court prohibited segregated seating on public transit. The boycott lasted 381 days—and provided civil rights activists with a blueprint for social action.

If they could do it in Montgomery, they could do it in Greensboro, McCain said. So that night, McCain, McNeil, Blair, and Richmond challenged one another to do something that would change the nation.

The lunch counter was Joseph McNeil's idea. He'd grown up in Wilmington, North Carolina, but his family had moved to New York City. On his bus trip back to Greensboro after Christmas break, McNeil arrived hungry—and once over the Mason-Dixon Line, a Black man couldn't buy a meal in a southern bus depot.

He suggested to his friends that they should try to order food at the Woolworth lunch counter. If they weren't served, they'd stay. Woolworth was the perfect target. It was considered one of the company's flagship stores. With marble stairs and 25,000 square feet of retail space, the company encouraged Black and white customers to spend money in their store. But McNeil knew Black people were treated as unwelcome guests. He was done with eating his sandwiches standing up in a far corner of the store.

The young men stayed up for hours, meticulously planning the details.

Franklin McCain had grown up following his parents' and grandparents' advice: Get a good education, do good, and fight for your rights. Sometimes that was easier said than done, but Franklin was ready to change the system.

The following day, the teens went to class, regrouped, reviewed their plan, and left campus on foot. It was sunny, with temperatures in the mid-50s—a perfect day for the hike. Along the way, the young men stopped at a pay phone to let some friends know what they were about to do, just in case something bad happened.

The Greensboro Four (L to R: David Richmond, Franklin McCain,
Ezell Blair Jr., and Joseph McNeil), February 1, 1960
(Photo by Jack Moebes / Jack Moebes Photo Archive / www.jackmoebes.com)

McCain wore his Air Force Reserve Officer Training Corps (ROTC) uniform. The others wore their Sunday-best coats, hats, collared shirts, and ties.

They walked together into the store and spread out to make some purchases.

McCain bought a tube of toothpaste, paper, and colored pencils for a homework assignment. His friends made other small purchases. They made sure to get receipts, just to show that Woolworth took their money at one turn but refused to serve them at another.

They stepped over to the lunch counter. McCain was craving a cheeseburger and fries and wanted to chase it down with a cherry soda and maybe a banana split.

It was a big place. Sixty-six aqua and orange pedestal stools with chrome-plated backrests stood along an L-shaped Formica lunch counter. The students moved in silence. There weren't four seats together, so they split up. McCain sat next to McNeil on the far end, Blair and Richmond nearer the entrance.

As they settled into their chairs, they knew they'd crossed an invisible line. Heads turned. The cafeteria went quiet. The clock above the counter showed some time around 4:45 p.m. The store closed at 5:30.

The waitress was white. McCain politely asked her for a coffee. McNeil did the same.

"I'm sorry. We don't serve colored here," she said, directing them to the area where they would be served.

McCain was angry. He knew the lunch counter was segregated, but hearing those words cut him like a knife. McCain was a big, quiet, gentle young man, a chemistry and biology major in the ROTC. He believed in America. He believed in his rights.

McCain knew he had to maintain his composure. But that didn't mean he couldn't challenge her.

"You just served me at a counter two feet away. Why is it that you serve me at one counter and deny me at another? Why not stop serving me at all counters?" McCain asked.

The waitress didn't know how to respond. She walked away from McCain and his friends and simply focused on the white customers. Then she vanished into the kitchen. She'd gone to find the manager.

McCain's eyes met his friends' down the counter. They stayed put. They were going to sit there until they were served or arrested, or until the store closed. This was only the beginning.

Tension was building inside the Woolworth. McCain felt his heart pounding, but he didn't feel afraid. He thought of the many times he'd been called the N-word, how freely whites called him "boy," how many times he'd feared for his life.

He thought of the stories of Blacks who'd stepped out of line and been lynched, the horrible images of Emmett Till in *Jet*, a magazine that provided a voice for the Black community.

A white woman in August 1955 had accused Till, a Chicago teenager visiting relatives in Money, Mississippi, of whistling at her in a store. A few days later, the woman's husband and his half brother kidnapped and tortured Till, dumping his lifeless body in the Tallahatchie River. The men were caught, but an all-white jury quickly acquitted them.

When Till's mother, Mamie, brought his body home to Chicago, she wanted people to see what happened to her son. She told the funeral director, "Let the people see what I've seen." Tens of thousands filed past Till's open casket. A photographer took pictures of the teenager's mutilated corpse. Nearly five years later, those images were seared into McCain's memory.

That's what happened to young Black men who defied orders in the South. Sometimes McCain felt so dispirited he didn't want to live anymore.

But something strange happened at the lunch counter. Yes, McCain felt scared, but he felt transformed, too. He'd stepped up. He was doing right. He had "made a down payment on my manhood" by this simple act of courage. If he went to jail—or if this was the last day of his life—so what? What good was living if you couldn't live free?

McCain realized at that moment that he and his friends were parked in their seats like "a Mack truck." No one was going to move them.

The waitress returned with store manager Clarence Harris. He asked them to leave, but the students refused. A police officer arrived moments later, conferred with Harris, then headed for the young men. McCain's heart hammered when the policeman pulled his baton from its holster. "This is it," McCain said to himself.

The officer paced behind McCain and his friends—back and forth, back and forth—slapping the baton into his palm. He didn't say a word.

It was unsettling, but as long as they didn't cause trouble, as long as they stayed quiet, what could he do? There was no reason to take them in. After all, what did they do wrong?

The officer left the store. Some of the white patrons tossed out racial slurs as they paid and left. But most of the customers just stared.

All but one. An elderly white woman who'd been sitting at the counter got up and headed for McCain, the only young man in uniform. He braced himself for the worst.

The woman sat down next to him and looked into his face. "I'm disappointed in you," she said, loud enough for his friends to hear.

McCain sighed. "Ma'am, why are you disappointed in us for asking to be served like everyone else?"

She paused and replied, "I'm disappointed at you boys because it took you so long to do this."

With that, she got up and left the store. For McCain and the others, it was vindication. This *was* the time to fight to end another vestige of the old South. It *was* the time to push for change—no matter how dangerous. No matter the personal risk.

At 5:30 p.m. the manager scurried back to the lunch counter. The store was closing early, he announced. Everyone, including the students, had to leave. Right now.

McCain gathered his things and walked to the front door with his friends. They realized what they had done. They had simply taken a seat at the counter. They had asked to be served. They had sat there peacefully and quietly. And by doing just that, they had paralyzed the store, its staff, its patrons, and the police, for an entire hour that Monday afternoon.

None of them expected to walk freely out of the Woolworth that day. It seemed much more likely they'd be arrested or injured or even killed. And while they weren't served any food, they knew this was only the first step in a long journey.

Outside, McCain and his friends agreed to return to the lunch counter with even more students. They'd keep coming back until Woolworth and other restaurants ended their discrimination.

The young men headed back to campus in the gathering dark. They had homework to do. And calls to make. Many calls.

COUNTDOWN: **276 DAYS**

February 7, 1960
Las Vegas, Nevada

Judith Campbell had been around plenty of handsome men before, but she couldn't stop looking at Jack, the man in the pin-striped suit, the one with the bright blue eyes.

Judith was a Los Angeles party girl, the well-dressed daughter of a prosperous architect. Bob Hope was just one of the celebrities that were frequent guests at their home.

Her sister was a budding actress, and when Judith was a teenager, she went along to Hollywood parties with her sister's up-and-coming friends from the studios. Judith had even married one of them, but that didn't last.

Jack, the man sitting across the table in the Copa Room at the Sands in Las Vegas, was different. When his eyes met hers, Judith was mesmerized, she wrote years later in her memoir.

He was a politician, and his name was Jack Kennedy. She didn't follow political news, so his name didn't mean a thing to her. She only knew that she was totally charmed.

Since Nashua, New Hampshire, Kennedy had been campaigning full-out, hopping from city to city and state to state. That morning it was Albuquerque. The next big stop was Portland, Oregon. Kennedy and his entourage decided to take a break along the way in Las Vegas, where Frank Sinatra and his "Rat Pack" cronies were performing at the Sands Hotel and Casino.

For Kennedy, it was the perfect place to unwind.

Kennedy and Sinatra had been friends for years. Kennedy's sister Pat was married to actor Peter Lawford, a member in good standing of the Rat Pack.

Sinatra shimmered with Hollywood glamour. The hard-drinking Rat Pack—singers Dean Martin and Sammy Davis Jr., comedian Joey Bishop, and actor Lawford—oozed urbane sophistication.

Kennedy, on the other hand, was serious business. His youthful ease and upright frame emanated political power, congressional corridors, and work that mattered to the world. He and Sinatra saw each other as living an enviable life.

Both also had an appetite for parties and beautiful women.

Sinatra was liberal, an outspoken critic of racism. He often invited Kennedy to join him in Los Angeles and Las Vegas. Kennedy enjoyed hearing inside gossip about stars' romances and scandals. Sinatra, "the king of Hollywood," happily introduced the senator to studio bigwigs, rising young starlets, and shadowy figures who worked in the background.

Judith Campbell and Sinatra had dated briefly. He was a player in Hollywood, and the twenty-six-year-old Campbell was strikingly beautiful, an Elizabeth Taylor look-alike with high cheekbones, dark hair, and piercing blue eyes.

Sinatra kept in touch, inviting her to some of his shows, escorting her to events. He asked her to stay at the Sands while he filmed *Ocean's Eleven*, a movie about a daring group of World War II buddies who plan to simultaneously rob five Las Vegas casinos under the cover of New Year's Eve celebrations.

No one would ever say that Sinatra and the rest of the Rat Pack weren't hardworking professionals. They shot the film during the day and performed onstage at night.

That evening in February, Campbell swept into the cocktail lounge to meet up with Sinatra for predinner drinks. She knew she was looking lean and tanned from the desert sun, and when introduced, she sparkled at Jack Kennedy and his twenty-seven-year-old brother, Teddy.

Judith Campbell
(Associated Press)

At dinner, she sat next to Teddy and across from Jack. She regretted that Peter Lawford and Gloria Cahn, wife of songwriter Sammy Cahn, completed the group. Every time she tried to speak to Jack or his brother, Cahn would interject and make the conversation about her, or Lawford would complain about the grueling shooting schedule—even though the *Ocean's Eleven* film concept had been Lawford's idea.

After dinner they headed to the Copa Room to watch Sinatra perform with Martin and Davis. Judith sat next to Teddy, but wished it was Jack, who was across the table from her.

From the stage at the Sands, Sinatra introduced JFK as "the next president of the United States." The room erupted with applause.

It was a fast-moving show, one laugh after another, with songs in between. Campbell had seen it countless times, so she watched Jack instead.

Poised and witty, he spoke to all the women at the table and made everyone around him feel comfortable. He was affable, but clearly accustomed to being in charge.

After the show ended, Teddy asked Campbell to show him around Las Vegas. She sighed, but said yes.

They traveled along the main strip from one casino to the next, laughing, drinking, and feeding the slot machines. By the time they got back to the Sands, Judith was exhausted.

Teddy walked her to her room. When she opened the door, he stepped inside and sat down on her bed. She knew what that meant. Teddy was nice, but he didn't have his brother's appeal.

He asked her to fly to Denver with him aboard the campaign plane. She didn't know if this was just a come-on or if it was a serious offer—but either way, she wasn't interested. Campbell politely said no, then escorted Teddy to the door.

Judith went to sleep wondering if she would ever see Jack again. Her answer came the following morning. This time, the right Kennedy called her room and asked her to have lunch with him. She didn't hesitate.

Poolside at noon, he said.

Just before noon, she put on a burgundy Kimberly knit dress and headed to the pool. The deck was swarming with photographers and men in suits. Jack Kennedy was there in the middle of the scrum, answering questions. He was holding a news conference.

She sat down in a lounge chair and waited to catch his eye. "Judy, I'll be right with you," he told her. "We're just finishing up."

The reporters turned their heads and took a long look at her. She was a little shocked. "Fine, take your time," she answered.

Kennedy wound up the talk, then swept her off to lunch in Sinatra's hotel suite.

They spent the next three hours together. Judith told him about growing up in the shadow of the "Hollywood" sign, her big family, her love life. She felt at ease with Jack.

Kennedy asked if she was a Democrat or a Republican. She confessed that she didn't know.

"Well, we'll change that," he said.

Campbell recounted his brother Teddy's antics of the night before, including asking her to fly with him to Denver.

JFK laughed. "That little rascal."

No one had mentioned that Jack was married. The "details" emerged during the torrid love affair that followed.

Jack finally said he had to go.

He promised to call.

February 9, 1960
Havana, Cuba

As darkness fell over Havana, Fidel Castro, the Cuban revolutionary turned national dictator, paced in his office. Earlier in the day, 104 people had been convicted by a military court, charged with conspiring to overthrow his government. Generalissimo Rafael Trujillo, the dictator of the Dominican Republic, was behind it. But Castro was no fool. It wasn't just Trujillo who wanted him gone.

Castro had turned the coup attempt into a media triumph. Every tantalizing detail of the attack was described in a nationally televised broadcast. Under the heat of television lights, Castro told the nation how Major William Morgan, a revolutionary firebrand from Toledo, Ohio, had uncovered Trujillo's plan—and then worked as a double agent.

Morgan had convinced Trujillo he had an armed group of Cuban exiles ready to meet up with Dominican soldiers to kill Castro and overturn the Cuban Revolution. But when the planeload of Trujillo's fighters landed at an airstrip in central Cuba, Castro's military was waiting for them. After a firefight, the invaders surrendered.

"All this is part of a great plot," Castro told his people. "This is not only the work of Trujillo. Trujillo is just one phase of the giant conspiracy against the Revolution."

Despite his bluster, the attack unnerved Castro. Yes, he'd stopped this one. A five-man military tribunal had sentenced most of the defendants to thirty years in La Cabaña, a notorious prison on Havana Bay. But where would the next attack come from? And the one after that?

Castro was popular among left-leaning and working-class people across the Caribbean. He was a larger-than-life figure, a lean, ruthless revolutionary with a scraggly beard, fatigues, a Cuban cigar, and a machine gun.

He was a magnificent orator, appealing to Cuban nationalism and Latin American pride. He had captured the imagination not only of Cubans but also of peasants and workers struggling for better lives all over the world.

Long before he seized power from Cuban president Fulgencio Batista, Castro had railed against corrupt dictators more interested in lining their own pockets than in helping their people—dictators like Generalissimo Trujillo, who had ruled the Dominican Republic for more than thirty years. Trujillo tortured and killed anyone who opposed him, but even as he looted the Dominican treasury and brutalized his citizens, he enjoyed the support of the United States. To U.S. conservatives, he could do no wrong. He was virulently anti-communist. He was America's backstop in the Caribbean.

Castro worked hard to do right by his people, but with every move, he seemed to create new enemies. He needed powerful friends to ensure his survival. Maybe that's why he was turning more and more to the Soviet Union.

He scanned the documents on his desk. In a week, another contingent of Russian officials was coming to visit.

Castro swore he was not a communist, but his leftist regime and nationalized economy were too familiar for the USSR to leave alone.

Castro was an unlikely revolutionary. The son of a wealthy farmer, he'd led a left-wing revolution in Cuba. In 1958, his military force, known as the 26th of July Movement, won a string of victories over Batista's military. And on January 1, 1959, Batista fled Cuba—and headed straight for the Dominican Republic. Castro's force of ragtag guerrillas had defeated a nearly thirty-thousand-man professional army.

No Cuban revolutionary leader ever came to power with a greater

Fidel Castro
(UPI/Newscom)

reservoir of goodwill. And as the undisputed decision-maker, Castro had complete authority. He set out to change Cuba's image.

The nation had a raffish reputation as a sunshine and blackjack gambling resort for Americans, forever memorialized in the musical *Guys and Dolls*. Organized crime bosses like Santo Trafficante Jr. and Meyer Lansky had built lavish casinos and hotels on the island, and payoffs from tourism and gambling proceeds had financed Batista's rich lifestyle. But Castro condemned the casinos publicly, saying that American gangsters had more influence over Batista than his own generals did.

Most of the casinos were looted and then closed after Castro seized power, and Cuba's attempts to resurrect the tourist economy collided with Castro's open hostility to the United States.

The mob bosses lost millions of dollars as well as their influence on the island, posing another potential threat to Castro's government—and possibly even his life. But Castro didn't care. Batista's massive corruption had left Cuba a mess. He had a mandate from the people to improve their lives.

Besides, Castro could control internal threats to his leadership. It was the outside forces—especially the United States—that kept him up at night.

At every step, the United States was trying to undermine his leadership. It wouldn't sell him arms. It wouldn't support his reforms. Now it was preparing to cut all sugar purchases, seriously hurting the Cuban economy—as 80 percent of the nation's exports depended on sugar. Without a market, they'd go broke.

In the United States, Cuba was weaving its way into the 1960 presidential campaign. Democratic presidential candidate John Kennedy had criticized the Eisenhower administration for ignoring the crisis unfolding in Cuba and the impact of the USSR gaining an ally so close to Florida.

Trujillo. The mob. Now the U.S. government—through the Central Intelligence Agency, and through economic sanctions. Castro did the political calculus. For his government to survive, he needed help. So when Soviet leaders came knocking, he opened the door.

Castro would meet with Soviet deputy premier Anastas Mikoyan and sign a trade deal that he hoped would help sustain his economy. Cuba would exchange its sugar for Russian fuel.

It appeared that Cuba was on the road to communism. Did America really want that? And what would stop Castro from exporting revolution to other countries in Latin America? That could destabilize the entire region.

At that point, Castro wasn't thinking about revolution. He was focused on hanging on to his power while keeping little Cuba on an upward trajectory. With so many powers opposing him, Castro knew the alliance with the Soviet Union was his only real option.

February 10, 1960
Corvallis, Oregon

John F. Kennedy was shaking hands at lumber mill gates and making stump speeches outside town halls like it was the final day of the presidential race. Since the January launch in Nashua, he'd been going nonstop. In two weeks' time he'd campaigned in more than a half dozen states, including New Mexico, California, North Dakota, and now Oregon.

Kennedy wanted to meet and greet farmers and city dwellers, college students and blue-collar workers. They may have heard his name or seen his face in newspapers or magazines, but the voters really didn't know what the Massachusetts senator stood for. Was he liberal? Conservative? Progressive? He was here in person to let them know.

The stop in Corvallis was part of a two-day swing in Oregon that included a luncheon, a reception, and a chamber of commerce dinner. Everywhere he went, Kennedy attacked the Eisenhower administration for policies he said were hurting average Americans.

And then Kennedy and his entourage headed back to the plane for the next stop in the next town. Yes, it was early, but he had to keep pushing, had to keep attacking. That was the Kennedy way.

At every campaign appearance, Kennedy was on top of all the major issues, thanks to his devoted and talented campaign team. They were intellectuals and political insiders, people who understood policy and backroom politics. They knew all the key people in the critical states.

But JFK knew his most valuable asset was his kid brother, Robert Francis Kennedy, "Bobby," who was a rising politician in his own right.

Bobby had been a crusading attorney, the chief counsel for the Senate Rackets Committee. For more than two years, he had overseen numerous high-profile hearings. The committee found an alarming number of cases where union leaders, corporate managers, organized crime members, and public officials—sometimes in combination, sometimes separately—had cheated rank-and-file union members.

He had focused on the Teamsters union—with some 1.5 million workers and a pension fund of around $200 million (worth over $2.1 billion today)—calling it the most powerful institution in America besides the U.S. government. He called Teamster boss Jimmy Hoffa a crook.

But Bobby's career was cut short when his father, Joseph P. Kennedy, the family patriarch, asked him to run Jack's presidential campaign. And when Joe asked his children to do something, they did it. So, Bobby resigned from the Senate committee. After all, his brother needed him.

Bobby was relentless, tough, well organized, and laser focused on his mission: getting his brother to the White House. Nothing else really mattered.

Bobby didn't wait. He began holding strategy sessions with JFK and their team of advisers. During one in October 1959, Bobby grilled his brother like he was a hostile witness before a congressional committee. "Jack, what has been done about the campaign? What planning has been done? Jack, how do you expect to run a successful campaign if you don't get started?" Bobby asked.

JFK responded by imitating his brother's high-pitched voice and staccato-like delivery: "How would you like looking forward to that voice blasting in your ear for the next six months?"

But JFK knew what his brother could do. Bobby's campaign work was creative, groundbreaking, masterful. It seemed Bobby Kennedy was born to boost his big brother. He knew his business. He'd run JFK's campaigns since his brother campaigned for a U.S. Senate seat in 1952.

Eight years earlier, JFK had challenged incumbent Republican senator Henry Cabot Lodge, a Massachusetts blue blood with a strong record.

Attorney Mark Dalton had run JFK's first congressional campaign in 1946. So, Jack reached out to him again. He agreed and knew it was going to be an uphill battle to unseat Lodge.

Joe Kennedy made it even harder. He kept offering advice—but Dalton didn't seem to listen. Joe wanted him to run a more aggressive campaign.

When Jack said he was going to officially announce Dalton's appointment, Joe blew a fuse. No way. If Joe was spending the money, he'd have a say in who was his son's campaign manager.

Dalton could see the handwriting on the wall. When Jack didn't challenge his father's decision, Dalton resigned. So, who would run JFK's Senate race?

Joe had a good idea who he wanted. He knew Bobby had the skills that JFK needed to make a serious run. He was smart, super-focused, and disciplined. Plus, he was a Kennedy. He knew Jack would need someone he could trust.

Working as an attorney at the Justice Department, Bobby didn't want to take the job. "I'll just screw it up," he said to Kenneth O'Donnell, one of JFK's close advisers. What did he know about running a campaign anyway?

But O'Donnell said Kennedy's campaign lacked discipline and unless they righted the ship, it was headed for "absolute catastrophic disaster."

So, he agreed to do it. His organizational skills quickly emerged. He took care of all the day-to-day details, like planning events, and finding creative ways to promote his brother's candidacy. A team of Kennedy volunteers delivered more than 1 million campaign brochures to nearly all of Massachusetts' homes. And the Kennedy women—his mother, sisters, and sisters-in-law—held tea parties across the state so female voters could meet JFK.

Bobby worked from dawn to dusk to keep the campaign on track.

Yes, he could be caustic at times. And he didn't always play nice in the sandbox with others. But he got the job done. In a year where a Republican, Dwight Eisenhower, captured the White House in a landslide—and Massachusetts by more than 200,000 votes—JFK was elected Senator. He beat Lodge by 70,000 votes. (It didn't help that Lodge couldn't spend as much time campaigning for himself because he was also one of Eisenhower's campaign managers.)

Now Bobby was resurrecting his role. He knew this would be different. This wasn't just one state—it was fifty. He'd have to find new, innovative ways to promote his brother's campaign for the Democratic presidential nomination.

And now, after spending years as a star lawyer in the Senate, Robert was back in the campaign business on John's presidential run. He left nothing to chance and continued creating innovative campaign techniques that would guide a new generation of candidates seeking office.

They had to prepare for the worst. So, Bobby created an instructional guide on how to respond to attacks on JFK's character, religion, health problems, and other issues. Bobby's book didn't deal with his brother's extramarital affairs. Journalists usually didn't touch that subject. If they did now, JFK's campaign would be over.

Bobby knew that his brother's Addison's disease could be problematic. Most people had never heard of it. And Addison's wasn't a simple disease to understand, either. Was it fatal? If not, was it debilitating? Could it affect a person's judgment? What was the treatment? They were all critical questions the public might ask if they knew the person running for America's highest office had it.

The simple truth was if you had Addison's disease, it meant your adrenal glands weren't producing enough of certain hormones—cortisol and aldosterone—that help the body deal with injury or illness. Treatment included boosting the body's supply of the missing hormones. Weight loss, areas of darkened skin, low blood pressure, abdominal pain, and depression were some of the symptoms of the life-threatening disease.

Doctors said stress—physical or emotional—could make the symptoms worse. And that was one of the problems. The presidency was an inherently stressful position. With the threat of nuclear war and other crises, how could you mitigate that? That's why Bobby knew it could never get out that JFK had Addison's. If it did, he'd never get elected. So, if anyone said JFK had the disease, the campaign would just lie. They'd say he had malaria, or a bad back—anything except Addison's.

Jack was a handsome man and Bobby wanted to take full advantage of his brother's good looks. To do that, Bobby used image consultants. And he created a rapid response team that could distribute materials to targeted groups about Kennedy's position on different issues.

With Joe's money and Jack's personality, they assembled a first-rate staff. The Kennedy brothers had no trouble attracting the best operatives. Jack Kennedy was himself brilliant, articulate, self-effacing, someone who could crack jokes with both intellectuals and blue-collar workers. And the Kennedys paid top dollar.

Bobby hired Louis Harris, an influential pollster whose political insights would help guide the campaign. He was among the first political consultants to provide polling services directly to a candidate. Using Harris's polling, Kennedy would often craft messages based on what the surveys told him were voters' concerns.

Ted Sorensen was a key member of the team. The Nebraska attorney was hired in 1953 to work in Kennedy's Washington office. Within a year, he became JFK's speechwriter and one of his closest advisers. Kennedy would call Sorensen his "intellectual blood bank."

With Sorensen, Kennedy developed a distinct style: "short speeches, short clauses and short words, wherever possible" and memorable phrases. Most important, Sorensen said, "the test of a text was not how it appeared to the eye, but how it sounded to the ear."

Kennedy's press secretary was Pierre Salinger, a crusading investigative reporter who'd caught Bobby's attention when Bobby worked for the U.S. Department of Justice. He hired Salinger to work for him on the Senate committee investigating organized crime, then asked him to join

JFK's campaign. It was Salinger's job to get close to the reporters covering Kennedy and the campaign.

"What I want to develop is a good, hard-hitting press operation," Jack Kennedy told him. "You get whoever you need, develop your contacts. You know a lot of newspapermen around this town."

He made it clear he was hiring Salinger only because of his brother Bobby's recommendation.

The Kennedys' youngest brother, Ted, and brother-in-law Steve Smith, who was married to their sister Jean, were also involved. In the beginning, the team discussed the strengths and weaknesses of possible opponents, including Nelson Rockefeller or Richard Nixon. They were forever planning, trying to stay one step ahead.

And they didn't worry about expenses. Joe Kennedy made sure of that. He was worth up to $400 million (over $4 billion today), and seemed willing to spend it all to put his son in the White House. He even bought a plane—they dubbed it the *Caroline*, after JFK's daughter—to help them move quickly from one place to the next. It was a big advantage for the campaign.

But it wasn't only the advisers and money. It was about personality. Jack Kennedy had a captivating blend of confidence, passion, empathy, and relatability. Men and women wanted to be around him. He was educated, cool, with combat credentials, good looks, prestige, and sparkle. Add to all this Bobby's strategic mind, and the campaign was a winner with both men and women voters.

Kennedy's Democratic rivals weren't impressed with his strategy.

Texas senator Lyndon Johnson hadn't disclosed publicly whether he'd run. But he still believed in business as usual and was confident that party bosses at the convention would come through for him.

Kennedy was concerned about Johnson's plans. So, he sent Bobby to Texas to check out LBJ's intentions. Bobby wasn't happy. But he agreed with Jack that it was imperative that they find out—and find out as quickly as possible. Kennedy and his team had come to the realization that in all likelihood they'd also need the support of some party bosses to put them over the top. That's because only sixteen states had primaries and there were only so many delegates to pick up that way. If they fell short, Johnson could swoop in and steal the nomination.

In a meeting at LBJ's Texas ranch, Bobby was all business. He asked Johnson if he was going to run for president. Johnson said he wasn't running and wouldn't endorse a candidate, either. Bobby didn't believe him. At that point, all he wanted to do was get on a plane and head home. But Johnson wasn't about to let him leave. Not yet. First, they'd go deer hunting on his ranch. Bobby didn't want to do it, but he went along. Otherwise who knows how long he'd be stuck there.

Johnson drove Bobby to a tower with a platform on top. High above the hunting grounds, LBJ handed Bobby a rifle. There were deer in the fields below, but this didn't feel right. Bobby aimed at one and fired a shot. He missed and the recoil from the weapon knocked him down.

"Son, you've got to learn to handle your gun like a man," Johnson said.

Johnson got him good this time. But Bobby promised himself that wouldn't happen again. This was no longer just politics. It was personal.

COUNTDOWN: **267 DAYS**

February 16, 1960
Detroit, Michigan

Anyone else but Richard Nixon would have been elated. Public opinion polls showed that if the election were held then, Nixon would win big—no matter who he faced in November.

But Nixon didn't put much stock in polls this early in the election cycle. He hoped his strong numbers meant his strategy, as 1960 campaign reporter and historian Theodore White put it, of "choosing to adopt the nonpolitical posture of statesman" was working. Maybe trips like today's stop in Detroit were paying dividends.

Nixon had just whisked through a grueling twelve-hour day of speeches touting the Eisenhower administration's accomplishments. He had even called for an end to racial discrimination, calling it a moral issue that had sullied America's international reputation.

The one thing Nixon scarcely mentioned was his own candidacy for the Republican nomination. And he didn't attack any of his potential Democratic opponents, either.

Democrats were lobbing more political and personal attacks his way. News columnists were dredging up his past controversies, trying to portray him in the worst possible light.

How long could he stay above the political fray? It wasn't really in his nature. But so far, he had.

It was a precarious political strategy, yet one that Nixon handled adroitly in the Motor City. During a noontime speech at the Detroit

Economic Club, Nixon told the nation's automotive moguls that Eisenhower had kept the nation safe and strong.

"We can and will do whatever is necessary to be sure we have enough [weapons] to destroy (Soviet) war making capability," Nixon said.

And just like Ike, Nixon called for less government control of the economy, saying Americans could place their faith "in the principle that the wellspring of true economic growth is the creative enterprise of free people, free business and free labor."

Nixon looked trim and energetic—he'd lost as much as fifteen pounds. He stood upright, spoke in well-rehearsed truisms. His cool demeanor was a product of long study and planning.

If Nixon had to battle New York governor Nelson Rockefeller for the Republican Party's favor, his advisers predicted GOP regulars would strongly back Nixon. He'd accrued plenty of political equity over his eight years as vice president. He'd campaigned and raised money tirelessly for GOP candidates all over America.

Nixon's dignified statesman image was a vital asset and should be preserved as long as possible, his campaign team advised. He should stick to places and issues where his exposure was chiefly nonpolitical.

So, Nixon cruised through Detroit, looking and sounding presidential. His only candidate moment was when he fielded questions from the media. Cool and unhesitating, Nixon answered every question with easy assurance.

When asked if he foresaw a mudslinging election campaign, he promised he wouldn't indulge in such tactics. If Kennedy was the Democratic candidate, he promised he wouldn't even bring up his opponent's Catholic religion (thereby bringing it up).

Nixon said if religion was to become an issue it would be "personally reprehensible to me. I can think of nothing more damaging to the country."

Nixon wasn't naïve. When the time was right, he could dredge up JFK's inexperience, his health problems, and his extramarital affairs. Much of it was rumor, unfounded conjecture. But at that point, it didn't matter.

For now, he was staying positive, saying he was prepared to stand on his record. "I always hit hard on the issues. I expect my opponents will do the same, but we must distinguish between issues and personalities," he said.

That wasn't always easy. On the issues side, Kennedy leveled relentless attacks on Nixon's promise to continue Eisenhower's policies.

"For I cannot believe that the voters of this country will accept four more years of the same tired politics," Kennedy had said days earlier at a meeting of New York State Democrats.

"Four more years of neglected slums, overcrowded classrooms, underpaid teachers and the highest interest rates in history. And four more years of dwindling prestige abroad, dwindling security at home, and a collision course in Berlin."

As for "personalities," Kennedy wasn't fooled by Nixon's "take the high road" strategy. He reminded supporters of Nixon's mudslinging tactics in past campaigns and said it would be a grave mistake if he tried to "out-Nixon Nixon."

"Merely because Mr. Nixon is noted for personal abuse is no reason for our own campaign to follow suit. Merely because Mr. Nixon is known for his flexible principles, is no reason for ours to change," Kennedy had told an audience in Fresno, California.

Right then, a book about Nixon's life was a bigger threat than the sarcastic senator anyway. *The Facts about Nixon: An Unauthorized Biography*, by journalist William Costello, had been released on January 1 and zoomed to the top of the *New York Times* list of bestselling books.

Costello's work was a frank appraisal of Nixon, an attempt to analyze his personality and potential. Nixon had no basic philosophy, he wrote— the vice president was a fatalist about politics who believed that men do not shape their times but are shaped by them.

"Political positions have always come to me because I was there, and it was the right time and the right place . . . It all depends on what the times call for," Costello quoted Nixon as saying.

A large portion of the book dealt with the dirty campaign tactics he'd used in the past, earning him the unflattering sobriquet "Tricky Dick"—a nickname that had stuck.

When Nixon joined the Eisenhower presidential ticket in 1952, he stepped into the role of hatchet man, leveling vicious attacks against Democrats so that Ike could stay above the political fray.

Nixon wasn't handsome. He was bland and had a perennial five-o'clock shadow. His broad nose and receding hairline made him look older than his age. Some thought he didn't look presidential at all. He wasn't a war hero, or rich. He was the average American—a hardworking, self-made man who was a little socially awkward, but driven to succeed. He shook everybody's hand and said the right words to the camera. And for many Americans, stories of Nixon's childhood and upbringing were fresh news, even after eight years in office.

Born on January 9, 1913, Richard Nixon was the second of five sons in a working-class family that lived in Yorba Linda, California. His parents were Quakers who struggled to make ends meet. They raised him in a staunchly conservative environment that prohibited alcohol or dancing. His father, Frank, had tried his hand at lemon farming, but when the enterprise failed, he moved the family down the road to Whittier and bought the gas station/grocery store.

From boyhood, family members and friends noticed that Nixon was serious, even gloomy. Maybe it was because he had to deal with tragedy at a young age; two of Nixon's younger brothers died before he turned twenty. Nixon worked hard at the family store and studied hard at school. But he was argumentative, distrustful, and competitive. He lacked a sense of humor and was highly sensitive to any criticism.

Nixon resented those from more privileged backgrounds. After he graduated high school, Harvard University offered him a scholarship for tuition, but he didn't have enough money to cover the rest of the costs. His family needed him to help at the store. So Nixon said no to the Ivy League and attended Whittier College, a Quaker school closer to home.

At Whittier, Nixon was elected student body president and played offensive tackle on the football team, which had a distinctly unthreatening nickname: the Poets. Nixon was undersized and got little playing time—one teammate called him "cannon fodder"—but he credited the game and his coach with building his tenacity.

Nixon was an excellent debater, training he had received at the dinner table when he argued with his father about current events.

After graduating from Whittier in 1934, Nixon attended Duke University School of Law on a scholarship. At Duke, he was surrounded by wealth. When he finished law school, Nixon interviewed at several prestigious East Coast law firms, but failed to land a position. Humiliated, he returned to Whittier to practice law.

Nixon blossomed back home. He joined the Whittier Community Players, a local theater group. He went to the casting tryouts for its 1938 production of *The Dark Tower*.

When Nixon walked inside the theater that night in January, he met a "beautiful and vivacious woman with Titian hair. . . ." The new girl was Thelma Catherine Ryan, who had just started teaching at Whittier High School. Nixon was captivated.

Everyone called her Pat, a nickname her coal-miner father had given her because she was born just in time for St. Patrick's Day in 1912.

When she was young, her father left the mines and moved to California to be a farmer. Her mother died of cancer when she was thirteen, so Pat helped raise her four siblings, worked at the farm, and thrived at Excelsior Union High School.

Her father died when Pat was eighteen, but nothing could deter her from her education. She found a way to continue with school, working odd jobs to pay for her tuition, first at Fullerton Junior College and then at the University of Southern California. She graduated with honors and landed a job teaching at Whittier High.

After the drama tryouts, Nixon drove Pat home and asked her out. Pat wasn't interested. "I'm very busy," she said.

But she let him drive her home after each play rehearsal. One night he told her, "You shouldn't say that, because someday, I am going to marry you!"

Pat laughed. Was he joking around? But what Pat didn't recognize was Nixon's determination.

Pat was an outgoing, popular teacher. Nixon was an ardent suitor. He drove Pat on the weekends to her sister's house in Los Angeles. He even chauffeured her to dates with other men and waited till the evening was over to drive her back. He didn't give up.

Months after meeting him at the audition, Pat said she'd give Nixon a chance. He began sending her letters to express his love. He playfully called her his "Irish gypsy."

> Every day and every night I want to see you and be with you. Yet I have no feeling of selfish ownership or jealousy. Let's go for a long ride Sunday; let's go to the mountains weekends; let's read books in front of fires; most of all, let's really grow together and find the happiness we know is ours.

In another, Nixon described himself as "filled with that grand poetic music" in her presence.

A year after they met, Nixon was ready. He had picked the perfect spot: a patch of green high above the Pacific Ocean. And the basket filled with mayflowers in the car? It was just a ruse. Nixon had hidden an engagement ring underneath the white, bell-shaped flowers. When she found it, Nixon asked Pat if she'd marry him. She didn't hesitate. She said yes. And so, they married on June 21, 1940.

The couple settled into Whittier, Pat continuing to teach and Nixon practicing law. After the Japanese bombed Pearl Harbor, Nixon landed a wartime job in the Office of Price Administration in Washington, D.C., but then joined the U.S. Navy. Although he did not achieve the heroics of Kennedy, Nixon rose through the Navy ranks, eventually becoming a commanding officer.

While on active duty, he continued to faithfully write letters to Pat, expressing his love.

This weekend was wonderful. Coming back I looked at myself in the mirror and thought how very lucky I was to have you. . . . I was proud of you every minute I was with you. . . . I am certainly not the Romeo type. I may not say much when I am with you— but all of me loves you all the time.

Before he was deployed to the South Pacific, he made a dinner reservation at the Rainbow Room in Rockefeller Center in New York City. He wanted them to dine "where we can sit with real silver, on a real tablecloth with someone to serve."

His letters to her described the insecurities that plagued him, and his introverted character.

After he left the service, he successfully ran for the congressional seat representing Whittier in 1946. Within a couple of years, they had settled into family life and had two daughters.

In 1948, Nixon made national news when the U.S. House Un-American Activities Committee revealed that domestic communism wasn't some existential threat to developing countries. No, communism was a danger here, to the security of the United States.

The case that catapulted Nixon to national attention centered on Alger Hiss. He had all the right credentials—and connections. A former State Department official, Hiss had attended Harvard Law School, served as a law clerk to Supreme Court justice Oliver Wendell Holmes, and advised President Franklin D. Roosevelt at the Yalta Conference in 1945.

But then Hiss was accused by Whittaker Chambers, a former U.S. Communist Party member, of being a spy who'd passed secrets to the Soviet Union. Hiss was a charming fellow. His stirring testimony forced the House committee to consider dropping the investigation, but Nixon said no. He stood his ground, and fellow senators put him in charge of a committee to investigate whether Hiss was lying.

Through Nixon's persistence, the committee collected enough evidence to charge Hiss with perjury. They included the so-called Pumpkin Papers—materials Chambers testified Hiss had passed to him to deliver to a Soviet spy network. Instead, Chambers stored the materials on his Maryland farm.

It was something out of a spy thriller. Chambers had saved sixty-five pages of retyped secret State Department documents, four pages transcribed and handwritten by Hiss, and five rolls of developed and undeveloped 35mm film. He had wrapped the items in wax paper and stashed them inside a hollowed-out Halloween pumpkin.

Nixon was vindicated. Hiss was found guilty and served three years of a five-year sentence.

That—and Nixon's victory in the U.S. Senate race in 1950—thrust Nixon into the national spotlight.

At the 1952 Republican National Convention in Chicago, party leaders told Eisenhower he should choose the thirty-nine-year-old Nixon as his running mate. Ike believed the party needed to promote young, aggressive leaders, so he signed on.

Nixon was an able congressman and senator, but he was chosen "not because he was right-wing or left-wing but because we were tired, and he came from California," one party leader said later. California was strategic for an Eisenhower victory.

But before Eisenhower and Adlai Stevenson could face off in the November general election, ethical questions surfaced about Nixon. Critics said he had taken $18,000 from a supporter and spent it on personal items.

Now Nixon was in real danger of Eisenhower dropping him from the ticket. But Nixon did something extraordinary that would save his spot—and define his young legacy. He decided to fight the charges using the new untested power of television.

Television was relatively new but exploding in popularity. In just four years, the number of television sets in America had increased from around 350,000 to 15 million in 1952. To reach a wide audience quickly, Nixon would release his personal financial records in a live national broadcast. It was risky. No one knew what Nixon would say, or if anyone would even watch the speech.

Just before the cameras were set to roll, the evening of September 23, 1952, Nixon wasn't sure he could do it. He expressed his fears to his wife, Pat. But she encouraged him.

"'Of course you can,' she [Pat] said, with the firmness and confidence in her voice that I so desperately needed," Nixon recalled in *Six Crises*.

And then, with studio cameras on, Nixon calmly denied the allegations—except one. He said his family did receive a gift—a cocker spaniel named Checkers.

"You know, the kids, like all kids, loved the dog. And I just want to say this, right now, that regardless of what they say about it, we're going to keep it," he said.

Richard and Pat Nixon, 1960
(Library of Congress, U.S. News & World Report Magazine Collection)

Cute little girls and puppies . . . Nixon's speech was seen by a record television audience of 60 million Americans. The Checkers speech seasoned Nixon's political experience and convinced him that "television was a way to do an end-run around the press and the political estab-lishment."

The Nixons kept their dog.

And Eisenhower kept Nixon on his ticket.

"You're my boy," Eisenhower said.

Nixon was Eisenhower's boy in 1952, and the duo was reelected in 1956. But for much of the 1960 campaign, Eisenhower's vice president didn't feel he had the boss's support.

He couldn't get the president to publicly endorse him. Reporters asked the president several times if he supported Nixon's candidacy, and each time Eisenhower declined to comment.

When he wasn't in the White House, Eisenhower lived in a farm-house in Gettysburg, Pennsylvania. The president often invited friends to visit there—but never Nixon. The vice president quietly burned.

"Do you know he's never asked me into that house yet," Nixon griped.

It had been a long road, but now it was Nixon's turn to run for the top spot on the GOP ticket. The Democrats were dominating newspaper and broadcast news coverage with their presidential horse race. Nixon was worried that he was fading into the background, that his campaign would lose momentum. That's why trips like this one to Detroit were so important—he needed to build energy, to keep his supporters engaged and excited. Entering GOP primaries would keep his name in the news.

Nixon also placed himself on the ballot in the New Hampshire, Ohio, Oregon, and Wisconsin primaries. The move was designed to unify Republicans. By putting up a Nixon slate, the states' GOP leaders pledged to work hard to roll up an impressive vote total for the vice pres-ident. If Rockefeller still had any thoughts of entering the race at the last minute, Nixon would have the nomination sewed up already.

Nixon was fed up with Rockefeller's shenanigans. The New York governor's camp was pressing him to declare himself a progressive. That wasn't going to happen.

The "new Nixon" might've been a little more liberal than many of his GOP colleagues on civil rights, but he was a loyal conservative. Nothing was going to change that—especially now, when he had a clear shot to the White House.

Nothing was going to change the fact that Nixon had made a lot of enemies on his climb to the top, either. His closest friends and advisers knew it wouldn't be smooth sailing, and that bad news had a way of breaking at the worst moment. But they hoped for the best and prepared for the worst, praying the Nixon campaign could hang on.

February 20, 1960
Hyannis Port, Massachusetts

Joseph Patrick Kennedy Sr. was restless. In his Hyannis Port, Massachusetts, home, he'd pace, then make calls. When he hung up, he'd pace again until the phone rang. Another call for him. It went on like that for most of the day.

Joe's son was running for president, not him. The old man didn't want to hurt Jack's chances of winning the Democratic presidential nomination. He had worked too hard and spent too much money on his dream to put a Kennedy in the White House. He tried to stay in the background, but that wasn't easy for him. Joe Kennedy wasn't a background kind of guy.

With JFK's emerging popularity, the media spotlight turned to the Kennedy family, especially its patriarch. And bright lights cast black shadows.

But while newspapers ran story after story about the Kennedy wealth and social status, none broke new ground. Reporters mostly rehashed old material.

The Kennedy clan had enough friends in the media to kill or shape stories that might reveal details about the shady side of Joe's character, business dealings, connections, or opinions.

If a journalist got too close to new or damaging information about Joe—or the family—the Kennedy machine shifted into gear. Joe would answer a few questions now and then to clarify the facts on issues that might be used against Jack.

The Kennedys' wealth was a tempting target. When Joe was accused of trying to "buy the election for his son," he told the reporter that Jack could "stand on his own feet."

Joe was protective of his family. And despite his wealth, he wasn't immune to attacks, including anti-Catholic bigotry. When his children were younger, Joe couldn't seem to buy a summer house in upscale communities along the Massachusetts shore, even with all his millions. To rich Protestants, Joe Kennedy and his brood were outsiders. After all, Joe was a Roman Catholic whose father had owned a saloon. There were whispers about how he made his fortune.

After years of searching, he discovered a quaint village with white sandy beaches: Hyannis Port.

So, in 1928, Joe paid $25,000 for a charming house on a private street along Nantucket Sound. By the time he was finished with renovations, he had doubled its size to 9,000 square feet with twelve bedrooms and a wraparound porch.

During wonderful endless summers, the nine Kennedy children called Hyannis Port home. The Kennedys were a tight-knit, privileged family. They'd play touch football in the backyard or swim in Nantucket Sound. Their nights were filled with laughter and excitement.

Maybe it was all those fond memories, but Jack would buy his own house in Hyannis Port in 1956 adjacent to property owned by his brother Robert. JFK's place was near Bobby's cottage and across a broad lawn behind his father's home, looking toward the sound. The three properties composed the Kennedy compound, where Jack and Bobby would return for family gatherings.

"Joe was determined to capture each of the kids himself," Charles Spalding, one of Jack's close childhood friends, told Joe Kennedy biographer Ronald Kessler. "He wanted to be the biggest item in all his kids' lives."

Joe had spent a good part of his life in the public eye. Appointed as the U.S. ambassador to Great Britain in 1937, Joe was initially opposed to the United States joining the war against Adolf Hitler and Nazi Germany. When reporters covering Jack's campaign dug up his father's diplomatic record, Joe reacted angrily. He said he didn't want Jack to be tainted by opponents—"those monkeys" who claimed Joe was an isolationist who, as Scripps-Howard described it, "ran with the appeasement crowd" in London.

"All I was doing was trying to avoid war," Joe Kennedy said.

He didn't "want people to be confusing Jack's views with mine," and said he would not try to influence his son. "Jack will run his own show; he wouldn't want it any other way," he said.

If JFK captured the Democratic nomination, Joe promised to stay on the sidelines. His views were not important, he said.

Still, many Americans had doubts about the old man. Some in the Kennedy camp hoped he'd stay home quietly in Palm Beach, Florida, or Hyannis Port through the campaign. They didn't need any unpleasant surprises in a race that was expected to be very close. JFK couldn't waste valuable time defending—or distancing himself from—his father.

The media pressure was overwhelming at times. Robert Kennedy read stacks of newspapers and magazines every day. He didn't mind the ones that admired JFK and his wife—his campaign had planted a few of those. But lately, Bobby felt like he was playing whack-a-mole—slapping down a story here, a story there.

Theodore White wrote a piece in the *Saturday Review* where he described the impact Joe's wealth had on his son's campaign.

"The drive of the Kennedy campaign, the style and pace of its direction speak of an entirely different personality—of a man who has mastered the cold grammar of power with a toughness of instinct and clarity of analysis that approach remorseless perfection," White wrote.

Kennedy is, of course, extravagantly financed. He can joke disarmingly about his financing—"I received a telegram from my father last night," he quipped at a friendly meeting recently. "It said 'don't buy another vote. I'm not going to pay for a landslide.'" But what is remarkable is not the depth of resources this financing has purchased; it is the precision with which they are organized. For the enormous Kennedy operation has not simply grown; it has been engineered as a machine for the application of power.

Lots of money, and a slick, professional campaign—is that a bad thing? Is this criticism? Joe thought. Joe Kennedy's past was nothing short of lurid, and he'd done some scandalous things right out in public. If this analytic nonsense was the worst they could say, the Kennedys had no worries.

Joe Kennedy with sons Bobby and Jack
(Bettmann/Getty Images)

Stories published in respectable newspapers usually left out—or downplayed—distasteful aspects of Joe Kennedy's life, including his notorious womanizing.

Joe really didn't care what anyone said about him. He only cared about getting his son into the White House. Anything short of that was failure, and failure was not an option—not in the Kennedy household. "We don't want any losers around here," he'd tell his family.

So, how did Joe make his millions? Only Joe knew, and he never talked about his finances, not even with his wife or children. Three years before his son launched his presidential campaign, Joe's wealth was estimated to be between $200 and $400 million. In today's dollars, he'd be a billionaire.

The official Kennedy family biography painted Joe as an American success story. He grew up in a comfortable home. His father, Patrick Joseph Kennedy, started as a common laborer and became a successful businessman, owner of several Boston bars and a liquor importing business. He engaged in local politics and invested heavily in the Columbia Trust Company.

His son Joe attended Boston Latin School and Harvard College, but learned early on that his upper-middle-class standing was still several cuts below Boston's Yankee Brahmin society—old-money families that controlled most of New England's wealth. Joe was a masterful self-starter—and self-promoter. He had skillfully navigated the worlds of high finance and politics to stay a step ahead of his rivals. By twenty-five, he was a Harvard graduate and the youngest bank president in America.

If that wasn't enough, Joe had married the mayor of Boston's daughter, Rose. John F. "Honey Fitz" Fitzgerald was a colorful politician, known to sing a song or two at social events.

Joe Kennedy's shady past may have begun with his father-in-law. In 1918, Fitzgerald decided to run for a seat in the U.S. House of Representatives. Joe Kennedy was his money man in the race to unseat Representative Peter Tague.

Fitzgerald defeated Tague by 238 votes, but an investigation by the U.S. House Elections Committee revealed massive voter fraud. Young Joe Kennedy and other Fitzgerald supporters had recruited Italian immigrants and professional boxers to intimidate Tague supporters. Some Fitzgerald votes were cast by men who lived outside the district, or were soldiers who had been killed in the war. The results were overturned. Tague was reelected.

After leaving Columbia Trust, Joe joined a brokerage house, where he learned to play the stock market. And then in 1923, he went out on his own and made millions during the red-hot Roaring Twenties.

There were lots of ways to make fast money in those days.

The Volstead Act, which banned the importation and sale of liquor in the United States, took effect in 1920, but was finally repealed in all states of the nation thirteen years later. There was no definitive evidence that Joe Kennedy sold booze during Prohibition, but there was enough to show that he did business with people who did.

Joe Kennedy was already in the alcohol business at the start of Prohibition—because of his father's bars and liquor imports. It was the family's bread and butter. According to his biographer Richard Whalen, during Joe's tenth Harvard reunion in 1922, witnesses said Kennedy had a large stock of scotch delivered by boat right onto the beach at a Plymouth hotel. "It came ashore the way the Pilgrims did," one partygoer told Whalen.

Decades later, iconic mob bosses like Frank Costello and Meyer Lansky claimed they made millions by partnering with Joe Kennedy during Prohibition. Lansky told Dennis Eisenberg, his biographer, that one time, his gang hijacked a Kennedy booze shipment, and eleven men were killed in the shootout.

Even if some of his underlings were violent criminals, Kennedy kept his hands clean. In 1927, he jumped into the movie business, where he made millions more—and carried on a scandalous public romance with movie star Gloria Swanson. Joe's financial instincts were uncanny, according to family legend. He cashed out his stocks and bonds only days before October 29, 1929—Black Tuesday, when Wall Street crashed and America plunged into the Great Depression. Was it luck or something else?

Two years later, Joe Kennedy helped New York governor Franklin Delano Roosevelt run for president. FDR trounced Republican president Herbert Hoover, and Roosevelt appointed Joe to run the Securities and Exchange Commission, a newly created agency to regulate the financial markets.

There was more good fortune for Kennedy including a timely business trip to London, England, in late 1933 with Franklin Roosevelt's son James. Joe had created Somerset Importers Ltd., a legitimate liquor import business, following in his own father's footsteps. By the time Joe left London, Somerset had landed the exclusive U.S. distribution rights for two brands of scotch and Gordon's Gin. The agreement was signed just in time for Prohibition's full repeal in December 1933.

While his long-suffering wife, Rose, produced nine children, Joe Kennedy was involved with a string of women, including actress Marlene Dietrich, and had a yearslong affair with his secretary, Janet DesRosiers. His wife knew about his infidelity, but looked the other way. His sons looked—and learned.

Years later, Rose would recall why she stayed. When you marry a man of caliber, you have to accept the good with the bad, she said. Her favorite saying was "God does not give one more burdens than one can bear."

Joseph Kennedy supported Roosevelt in 1932, as well as four years later.

At the end of 1937, Roosevelt named Kennedy ambassador to the Court of St. James, the U.S. representative to Great Britain.

The Kennedy family made a big splash in London society, but darkness was falling across Europe. Perhaps Joe Kennedy could handle Boston gangsters, but he was no match for Adolf Hitler.

Kennedy stood by while the Nazi dictator played English prime minister Neville Chamberlain for a fool during a meeting in Munich. Kennedy was adamant about the United States staying neutral, avoiding war at all costs.

In May 1938, Kennedy began meeting Herbert von Dirksen, the new German ambassador to Great Britain—a Nazi. Kennedy went outside U.S. State Department channels to tell von Dirksen that the president was not anti-German and wanted friendly relations with Hitler, though he didn't understand Hitler's motivation, or philosophy.

Kennedy added that the U.S. media on the East Coast was highly influential in helping shape America's "public opinion" on important issues—and that the press was "strongly influenced by the Jews," according to Kessler.

Von Dirksen went back and told his bosses that Kennedy was as close to an ally as they could get in London.

Two days after Germany invaded Poland in September 1939, England and France declared war on Hitler's regime. With British soldiers and sailors dying in battle, Kennedy continued pressing for America to stay out of the war. His position chafed the British public, politicians, and press.

Kennedy privately did not support Roosevelt's unprecedented run for a third term. But this was one time he made the wrong bet. He underestimated Roosevelt's connection with the American people. After FDR's victory, Joe resigned his post and returned to the United States in November 1940.

But if Joe's feelings about Hitler were compromised, that wasn't true about his oldest son, Joseph Kennedy Jr., a U.S. Navy pilot. On August 12, 1944, Joe Jr. and a copilot were on a secret mission over Normandy, flying in a radio-controlled bomber loaded with explosives. Once the plane was in the air, the pilots would engage the autopilot to make sure it worked, then parachute to safety. When they did, the aircraft would be flown by remote control into the target. By the summer of 1944, the Allies were searching for German V-2 rocket launching sites. It was an extremely dangerous program; just about anything—turbulence, static—could trigger the explosives. Tragically, that's what happened. Joe's plane exploded. Though the exact cause was never determined, speculation was that faulty wiring caused the early detonation that killed Kennedy and his copilot.

Joseph Jr. had been the family star. The old man had groomed him from childhood to someday become the president of the United States. "All my plans for my own future were tied up with young Joe and that has gone to smash," Joe Kennedy said afterward.

Heartbroken, the father found another channel for his grand ambition, handing the Kennedy mantle to Jack. He had the right stuff, his father said—and that meant forgetting about his dreams of being a writer, journalist, or historian. No, he was going to be a politician, and his heroism launched his political career.

Joe stepped away from politics and diplomacy to focus on his son's career throughout the 1940s—proudly sending Jack to serve in the House of Representatives and then the Senate. At least that was the story repeated to press agents. Rumors of Joe's unscrupulous behavior along the way were nothing more than gossip, they said.

But clues about his bootlegging days still trickled out during the 1950s, including in Senator Estes Kefauver's hearings about organized crime.

During one session, the Tennessee Democrat heard testimony about a man named Thomas J. Cassara, who had signed leases to build Miami Beach hotels for known mobsters. Cassara was the accountant. He helped develop a gambling empire that stretched around the world.

According to the testimony, Cassara had worked for Joe Kennedy's Somerset Importers in 1944. In 1946, Cassara was shot "gangland style" in the head.

Kennedy sold Somerset Importers for $8 million months later.

Things happened around Joe Kennedy, and while no one could pin anything on him, there was always talk. He was a powerful man, ruthless, at times unethical. He used people to benefit himself, and to help his children. He'd shown up those people who had put him down—the old Boston Brahmin crowd—to become one of the richest men in the country.

Now the old man's past indiscretions could derail JFK's presidential campaign. Joe expected that Nixon would probably dredge up some of this history. And, of course, Jack had his own liabilities: The women. The bad back.

But Joe had put together a research file of his own about Nixon and wouldn't hesitate to use it at the right moment if the vice president pulled any dirty tricks. Joe may have had some enemies, but he also had a lot of friends. His connections could power his son through the tough primary battles and beyond.

Still, Joe wanted to put a lid on his shady Wall Street deals, antisemitism, and association with organized crime figures. He had a list of responses ready for when the questions came up.

Later in the campaign, when asked about the obstacles that faced his son, Joe sighed. "Let's not con ourselves. The only issue is whether a Catholic can be elected president," he said.

But for now, New Hampshire was just a few days away. After that, Wisconsin and then West Virginia, which would probably be Jack's final hurdle in the primary season. Winning West Virginia—and the general election in November—was going to require some help from Joe Kennedy's "friends."

Unscrupulous politicians. Bureaucrats on the take. Mobsters. It wasn't a pretty picture, but Joe Kennedy was a winner. Winning was everything. He was putting his boy in the White House. There was nothing he wouldn't do.

COUNTDOWN: **247 DAYS**

Dolly Bellavance didn't have to wait for the next day's *Nashua Telegraph* or watch television news to know who won the Democratic New Hampshire primary.

All her friends and neighbors supported John F. Kennedy. They had JFK signs in their front yards. They went knocking on doors, campaigning for him. They handed out brochures touting Kennedy's experience and character. They made phone calls, making sure people got to the polls.

Kennedy had lit up the little town when he chose to kick off his campaign for the Democratic presidential nomination there. Bellavance and her circle were all in for the candidate.

"He's going all the way to the White House," Bellavance told her colleagues in the city clerk's office. They all nodded agreement. Yes. *They just knew.*

They were five young women who spent their days filing documents, finding deeds, and collating city records. Meeting Kennedy in person on that snowy January day had turned them all into enthusiastic Democrats. The father of one of Bellavance's coworkers had signed up as a campaign volunteer.

Politics became exciting and fun. For Bellavance, Kennedy represented hope for the future at a time when the United States' international supremacy was being challenged by the Soviet Union. The politics were complicated, but everybody agreed the players were clearly Good versus Bad, Us versus Them. Bellavance dug into the news with genuine interest now.

The nations were engaged in the Cold War, the phrase coined by English writer George Orwell in the wake of World War II. It was more a fierce political rivalry than actual bloodshed. It was about alliances—some nations supported democracy while others leaned toward communism. And given the arms race between the U.S. and the Soviets, if nations on opposite sides came to blows, it might trigger a nuclear war—which could wipe out mankind.

America and the Soviet Union played elaborate power games, exerting influence over nations big and small, in places all over the globe.

In Southeast Asia, Ho Chi Minh, the leader of the communist forces in North Vietnam, was trying to reunite his nation, but South Vietnam rejected communism. President Eisenhower had just sent more than seven hundred U.S. "advisers" to Saigon to help prop up the South Vietnamese government. The Soviet Union and China stepped in to arm their communist colleague, creating a war of attrition in Vietnam.

The United States was determined to stop the spread of communism at any cost. Leaders believed that if South Vietnam fell to the North Vietnamese, then neighboring Cambodia, Laos, and even Thailand would fall like dominoes under communist control.

For most Americans, this was nothing more than a story buried in the newspaper. Communist intrigue was something that happened on the other side of the world.

But then there was Cuba.

A few days earlier, a French freight ship, *La Coubre*, had exploded in Havana harbor while unloading more than 70 tons of grenades and munitions. Nearly one hundred people were killed, and at least double that many seriously injured.

Cuban president Fidel Castro implied that America was behind it, in a speech that went on for more than two hours at the cemetery where the twenty-seven Cuban dockworkers who died were being buried. Castro said, "We have reason to believe that this sabotage was the work of those who do not wish us to receive arms for our defense." In a show of solidarity, Castro locked arms with Che Guevara, William Morgan, and other revolutionaries as they walked along a Havana street in a memorial march for the victims.

American officials denied any wrongdoing. But everybody knew that Cuba—right at America's front door—was trading heavily with the Soviet Union. And not only for sugar.

The arms race with the Soviet Union was disturbing, and some people were building bomb shelters. But many Americans learned to live with the uncertainty, just going on with their lives.

Bellavance and her friends at city hall focused on their families, faith, and work. This was a happy, prosperous time in Nashua, and for many small cities and towns all over America.

By 1960, over 50 million homes had a television set. Programs like *Perry Mason* and *The Andy Griffith Show* had become part of the fabric of pop culture. Westerns like *Gunsmoke*, *Bonanza*, and *Rawhide* delivered a morality play with each episode, teaching values of honesty and integrity. The heroes were strong, reliable white men who always won over the bad guys.

Movies went upbeat, too. Film noir, a moody genre that ruled in the late 1940s and 1950s, was being replaced by blockbusters like *Ben-Hur*, a story about an aristocratic Roman-era Jew forced into slavery who finds salvation through Jesus Christ.

Top 40 radio was replacing the gritty rock and roll songs of the mid-1950s by Elvis Presley and Chuck Berry with harmonized ballads of true love.

Factories were humming, and there were jobs enough for anyone who wanted to work. And America had a possible president to personify its bright future. John Kennedy was young, handsome, and charismatic. Bellavance and her friends knew that firsthand. Nixon? He was about the same age as Kennedy, but he seemed rumpled and gray. Like America's troubled past, he was best set aside.

Kennedy had spent a lot of time and energy in New Hampshire, even though he knew he was way ahead in the polls there.

A day before the primary, Kennedy gave a speech in tiny Dover, New Hampshire, that summed up the importance of the primary.

"Never was this process of selecting a candidate more important—more meaningful—than it is today. For during the coming year, we will select not merely a party favorite, but a national leader for the fabulous, demanding sixties. We will not merely reward party service—we will choose a man to be the center of activity and energy in our entire governmental system. Only if the parties choose their candidates well—only then will the American people next November be able to select a man equipped with the qualities which our country, and our age, demand," he said.

Democrats had every reason to be confident. Less than two years earlier they had won "tremendous victories in the House, in the Senate and Governors' mansions and State legislatures all over the country."

But the path to the White House wouldn't be easy. "We cannot take victory for granted," Kennedy said, reminding the audience that the Republicans "have all the vast, powerful machinery of government at their command. In addition, they have a great asset and a great campaigner in the current President of the United States."

He gave a backhanded compliment to the vice president.

"And Mr. Nixon, himself, is an experienced political fighter, a skillful campaigner—and a candidate with tremendous backing by large financial interest and by the press," he said. "But—despite these handicaps—despite the great advantages of the Republican Party—the Democratic Party can—and will—win in 1960," he said.

And he criticized some potential rivals for their failure to step up at the primary level.

"I am sorry that there are some members of the Democratic Party who regard Presidential primary contests with indifference," Kennedy said.

"Tomorrow the eyes of the entire nation will be on New Hampshire. . . . Let New Hampshire tomorrow—as it has in the past—signal the rebirth of American will—the restoration of American vision—the beginning of America's time for greatness."

Kennedy's energy paid dividends. New Hampshire voters lined up in large numbers. A surprise snowfall apparently had no effect on the balloting.

When the polls closed, Kennedy had captured a stunning 85 percent of the Democratic vote. There were 43,372 ballots cast for Kennedy—a decisive number of them Protestants.

But Richard Nixon also had a big night. Even though he didn't set foot in the state, he received 65,204 votes in the GOP primary, which topped the 56,464-vote record set by Eisenhower in 1956.

Representative William Miller of New York, chairman of the Republican Congressional Committee, said the primary results "proved conclusively the tremendous vote-getting ability of Dick Nixon."

Maybe, Kennedy thought. He still wondered whether the GOP machine could turn out the votes for Nixon in November. But that was another worry for another day.

In the end, New Hampshire wasn't going to decide the presidential election, or even who became the presidential candidate for either party. But it did show one thing: People were taking notice. They were interested in this election.

And for now, Kennedy had momentum heading into his next big challenge: the Wisconsin primary.

There he'd face rival Senator Hubert Humphrey of Minnesota, who had been campaigning hard in his neighboring state. Humphrey was a familiar face there, a fellow midwesterner.

But the Midwest had never seen a campaign team like Kennedy's, and JFK was set to hit the state hard and fast. If Humphrey could handle a sudden blow, he might stop Kennedy's momentum.

If not, the race might be all but over.

March 29, 1960
Madison, Wisconsin

Hunkered down and freezing in a beat-up campaign bus on the side of a Wisconsin road, Hubert Humphrey could hear the engine of an airplane passing overhead.

It has to be that damn Jack Kennedy, Humphrey thought.

"Come down here, Jack, and play fair!" Humphrey shouted, startling the others on the bus.

It seemed like Kennedy was taunting Humphrey. Everywhere Humphrey campaigned—from small towns to big cities—some smiling, slick Kennedy was already there, shaking the hand of every Democrat in sight.

It was frustrating. Humphrey didn't have Kennedy's charisma or deep pockets. He was a balding middle-aged man with a round face and a high-pitched, squeaky voice. But Humphrey had a ton of credibility. People trusted him. And he didn't give up easily.

The Minnesota senator was a passionate campaigner, an unabashed liberal who'd become a politician because he truly wanted to help people. He felt the government existed to improve the quality of life for all Americans, not just the privileged few. Politics was his calling.

Humphrey's upbringing was the antithesis of his rival for the Democratic presidential nomination. The forty-eight-year-old Humphrey and his three siblings grew up in Doland, South Dakota, a farming community of some six hundred people.

His father was a pharmacist who owned a drugstore in town, while his mother, the daughter of Norwegian immigrants, was a teacher in a little one-room schoolhouse on the prairie, where the temperature stayed in the single digits for a good part of the winter.

The local economy was dependent on small family farms scattered across the sprawling prairies in the eastern part of the state. And like many rural communities, Doland faced serious economic problems long before the Great Depression. Humphrey wrote in his autobiography that "farmers were caught in a vise of high costs and low prices. And drought made life and economic conditions even worse."

Humphrey knew it was a vicious cycle. "As the land and profits dried up, banks began to fail." And when that happens, people have less money to spend in drugstores like the one owned by Humphrey's father.

One of the few Democrats in the area, his father lost his drugstore, then the family home as they struggled with crushing debt. Growing up in hard times, Humphrey learned a lot about people and human nature. During the Great Depression, it wasn't the traditional poor who were in rebellion—but "those who had once had something. Now, they were mad—ready to march, picket, indeed to destroy."

Despite the hardships, Humphrey's parents taught him to keep the faith. His father had lost nearly everything, yet one night, Humphrey recalled his father talking with great passion about the promise of America.

"Just think of it, boys. Here we are in the middle of this great big continent, here in South Dakota, with the land stretching out for hundreds of miles with people who can vote and govern their own lives, with riches enough for all if we will take care to do justice," Humphrey Sr. said.

Maybe that's why Humphrey tried not to lose hope—even in the face of overwhelming odds.

He was influenced by President Franklin Roosevelt's attempts to alleviate the Great Depression with New Deal programs. After graduating high school, he briefly attended the University of Minnesota. When he ran out of money, he went home—to work at the family pharmacy.

A few years later, he attended an intense six-month program at the Capitol College of Pharmacy in Denver. When he completed the program, Humphrey became a registered pharmacist. But by the late 1930s, he was unhappy with his career. So, he returned to the University of Minnesota, earning a political science degree.

After working for several government agencies, he successfully ran for mayor of Minneapolis in 1945. Three years later, Humphrey delivered a passionate speech at the Democratic National Convention about civil rights that openly challenged the segregationists, who wanted to maintain the status quo in the South.

He implored Democrats "to get out of the shadow of states' rights and walk forthrightly into the bright sunshine of human rights." Thirty-five of the nearly 280 delegates from southern states—the so-called Dixiecrats—walked out in protest, but the civil rights platform was adopted by a 71-vote majority.

The speech resonated with Minnesota voters as well, and he found support in the party. He was elected to the U.S. Senate later that year. It was the first time in nearly a century that voters had sent a Minnesota Democrat to the Senate. Humphrey didn't waste any time. When he got to Washington, he became a champion for social issues.

Now here he was, in Wisconsin, the prototypical midwestern state. While it had a diverse agricultural economy with seventy thousand farms, Wisconsin also had large urban and industrial areas. Thirty-two percent of Wisconsin's population was Roman Catholic, the largest percentage in the Midwest.

Humphrey genuinely loved campaigning. He was known to stride into a firehouse and greet firefighters with "How's business, boys? Slow, I hope." Then he'd whip out a card with his qualifications printed on one side and "mama's recipe for beef soup" on the other.

"Try it," he'd tell the firefighters. "It'll give you the vitality of a buffalo."

He wore the underdog label like a badge of honor. What he didn't like was a disadvantage on the campaign trail.

With a week to go until the Wisconsin primary, polls showed the race was close. Kennedy was ahead, but he needed to trounce Humphrey if his heavy-on-the-primaries strategy was going to work.

Kennedy spent two weeks of February in Wisconsin. He woke up early to stand at factory gates at dawn, greeting workers at the shift change. He spent his days crisscrossing the state from county to county, giving speech after speech.

The grueling schedule was taking a toll on his spirits and his fragile health.

Unlike Humphrey, Kennedy wasn't fond of campaigning. It could be physically strenuous for him, especially with his health issues. Even so, when Kennedy emerged from the car, his smile would light up the scene. He shook each outstretched hand with such a natural ease that no one would ever suspect his true feelings.

Wisconsin had nearly 4 million people spread out over a wide area, and the Kennedy clan hit cities and towns with their distinct brand of campaigning. JFK's mother, Rose, and brothers Robert and Ted were featured at campaign receptions with coffee and cake. His sisters Eunice Kennedy Shriver, Jean Kennedy Smith, and Patricia Kennedy Lawford fanned out across the state, meeting and greeting voters in small towns and rural areas, touting their brother and happily taking questions about their family.

Everywhere the Kennedys went, they were followed by reporters, and voters. Lots of people had seen their faces in newspapers and magazines. They were celebrities.

But it wasn't all clear sailing for Kennedy. The days were long and the weather was brutal. And some people in the crowds questioned his candidacy.

Campaign aides Kenneth O'Donnell and David Powers described it as "that winter of cold winds, cold towns and many cold people."

At one stop, an old woman approached Kennedy with some advice. "You're too soon, my boy," she scolded JFK. "Too soon."

Kennedy knew what she meant: He was too young to run for such an

John and Jacqueline Kennedy, campaigning in Wisconsin
(Photo courtesy of the Telegraph Herald, Dubuque, Iowa)

important office. But whether it was his ambition, his health, or two of his siblings dying in plane crashes—Joe Jr. in 1944 and Kathleen "Kick" in 1948—he felt he had no time to waste.

"No. This is my time. My time is now," he said.

JFK knew the Wisconsin primary wouldn't be nearly as easy as New Hampshire, where Humphrey wasn't even on the ballot. But thanks to Robert Kennedy's steady management, Jack Kennedy's campaign was a sophisticated operation. His ads were slick and professional, and the voters who saw Jack and Jackie Kennedy on television turned out to see them in person. They were bright lights in a dull, dark season.

The Kennedys cultivated an image as a wholesome American family. They had a young daughter and Jacqueline was pregnant.

And in an appealing media coup, their radio and television commercials featured Frank Sinatra singing a somewhat awkward rewrite of his hit "High Hopes"—with lyrics tailored to the campaign:

Everyone is voting for Jack
'Cause he's got what all the rest lack
Everyone wants to back—Jack
Jack is on the right track
'Cause he's got high hopes
He's got high hopes

Humphrey knew that defeating Kennedy in Wisconsin would strike a heavy blow against the momentum JFK was counting on. Pundits agreed. Several said that if Kennedy didn't walk away with a decisive victory in Wisconsin, he might well not get the Democratic presidential nomination on the first ballot. And the longer the voting went on at the convention, the more likely it was that Kennedy would fade and another candidate would emerge—maybe someone like Adlai Stevenson, who had lost two presidential elections to Dwight Eisenhower, or Texas senator Lyndon Johnson.

But Humphrey wasn't thinking about the Democratic National Convention. He was worried about today, in Madison and Beloit and Oshkosh. He was worried about all the attractive Kennedy siblings and JFK's increasingly famous wife combing the counties for votes.

At one point Humphrey wrote of the onslaught, "I felt like an independent merchant competing against a chain store."

Humphrey and Kennedy were both drawing big crowds—sometimes in the same places but at different times. They'd trudge through the slush on Main Street to shake hands. They kept things civil, but that was beginning to fray: The Kennedy camp was hitting Humphrey with smear tactics, a technique designed to deflect attention from Kennedy's "Catholic problem."

After the Japanese attack on Pearl Harbor, Humphrey tried to enlist but was rejected three times, twice by the Navy and once by the Army, due to color blindness and other physical ailments.

The Kennedy team whispered that Humphrey was a draft dodger. They saturated the state with campaign workers and attack ads. Humphrey's campaign was old-fashioned by comparison; he spent only a little more than $100,000 on flyers, placards, and his rickety bus in Wisconsin. No one could say how much money Kennedy spent. His old man had pumped in at least $1 million up to this point, and his aides raised more by selling hundreds of lapel pins shaped like PT boats, a reminder of Kennedy's heroics during World War II.

As the primary drew closer, the fighting got edgier. Anti-Catholic pamphlets circulated, and the Kennedy camp suspected Humphrey. But Humphrey thought it might be the Kennedys, as a way to fire up Catholic voters and make sure they went to the polls.

It wasn't a fair fight.

Humphrey and his wife, Muriel, were average-looking people with no Hollywood connections. They had no private airplane—just a bus with a broken heater. The candidate and his crew were known to spend nights on the bus, parked along country roads on the way to the next campaign event.

But the Minnesota senator was committed.

"Beware of these orderly campaigns, they are ordered, bought, and paid for. We are not selling corn flakes or some Hollywood production," he warned his supporters. Everyone had to make their choice "on more than how we cut our hair or how we look."

Kennedy had charm, was the point, but Humphrey had passion. Kennedy's plane might beat him to the next location, but Humphrey had the better message, and a stronger legislative record.

In the end, he believed that the message was what mattered. Humphrey promised to stay optimistic, no matter how ugly the Wisconsin fight became. He would stay in the race.

But the ugliness hadn't even begun.

March 27, 1960
Miami, Florida

Frank Sinatra had asked Judith Campbell to fly down to Miami to see him open at the fabulous Fontainebleau Hotel.

The Fontainebleau? The Fontainebleau was trendy, one of the biggest, most luxurious hotels in Miami Beach. The hotel stood on Millionaire's Row, right on the oceanfront. Its lobby was a 17,000-square-foot jewel box, furnished with French antiques. It stood on six acres of formal gardens copied from Versailles. Stars like Elvis Presley, Bob Hope, and Lucille Ball went there to soak up the Florida sun.

And Sinatra would be there with his crew. Campbell instantly said yes.

Campbell wasn't attracted to Sinatra. They'd had a fling, that's all, and he was vain enough to ship her across the country just to have a pretty girl on his arm.

Sinatra was entertainment royalty, an A-list celebrity. With his baritone voice, his smooth, effortless phrasing, and his impeccable sense of style and acting chops, Sinatra was a living legend. Campbell knew she'd have a good time.

Everyone knew his story: He was born in working-class Hoboken, New Jersey, son of Italian immigrants. He came of age just as sound technology—radio, film soundtracks, and recordings—made music accessible to the masses.

After touring the country in a vaudeville group and then landing a solo gig as a singing waiter, he got a series of breaks: He landed a job as the lead singer for trumpeter Harry James's band in 1939, then joined the Tommy Dorsey Orchestra before leaving for a solo career.

By the early 1940s, the slender young singer released a string of favorites and amassed a rabid fan base. Seemingly almost overnight, Sinatra was everywhere. With his movies, radio shows, concerts, and records, he had become a pop culture phenomenon.

But by the 1950s, Sinatra was fading as a heartthrob. And America was on the cusp of a new sound: rock and roll. Sinatra's career began to stall. The genre was so new—with electric guitars, walking basslines, raspy saxophone solos—no one knew what to call it. It wouldn't be long before Elvis Presley would walk into Sun Studio in Memphis, Tennessee, or Chuck Berry would perfect the distinctive guitar sound that would become the staple of every rock guitarist in the future.

It wasn't only his music that was hurting Sinatra's career, it was his behavior. Tabloid journalism was exploding. Stories about the entertainer's decadent lifestyle, anger issues, and shady friends sold those glossy magazines on racks inside drugstores. Then Sinatra made a surprise comeback—fueled in part by his role in a 1953 film based on the bestselling novel *From Here to Eternity*.

Sinatra won the Academy Award for Best Supporting Actor for his portrayal of Angelo Maggio, a street-smart Army private who befriends a shy recruit—and reluctant boxer—in the weeks leading up to Pearl Harbor. Sinatra's dramatic turn was in line with antihero roles being embraced by rising young method actors like Marlon Brando and James Dean. The same year he won an Oscar, Sinatra signed a record deal with Capitol Records, and with a new arranger, began releasing hit singles and albums again. Soon, Sinatra was bigger than ever as he made edgier movies like 1955's *The Man with the Golden Arm*, about a drug-addicted musician.

The Rat Pack rose to fame in the late 1950s, when Sinatra inherited an all-star posse from Humphrey Bogart—a group of the coolest cats in the entertainment world. They performed separately or together, and drank and caroused all night long.

Rat Pack member Peter Lawford married Patricia Kennedy, Jack's sister, in 1954. Lawford introduced his brother-in-law Jack to Sinatra, and the two men immediately hit it off. They were bright shining stars in the center of their own universes. Sinatra was hip, cool, an entertainment icon. JFK was JFK. When Kennedy walked into a room, the gravitational pull was palpable. But both men had dark sides. At times, they were reckless and self-centered. Maybe it was because they knew they were protected by fixers and unscrupulous characters. They were also close in age: Kennedy was forty-two, Sinatra forty-four. The politician and the crooner bonded over beautiful women, expensive cigars, and gossip. Kennedy loved Hollywood chatter. Sinatra knew Kennedy's predilections. So, when they partied together, the singer made sure he took care of his pal—whether it was with a starlet or an aging Hollywood sex symbol. You never knew who'd show up to one of their wild soirees, which rotated between Las Vegas and Lawford's Santa Monica home— or any place in between.

The men were also in sync politically. Sinatra donated to Democratic candidates and became close friends with party leaders, including Eleanor Roosevelt. He was ahead of his time in fighting against racism and segregation.

In fact, Sinatra landed a special Academy Award in 1946 for his short film released the year before, urging Americans to end racial and religious bigotry. The singer comes across a boy being bullied because of his religion, breaking it up with a message preaching tolerance.

The first step, Sinatra says, is seeing how everyone essentially bleeds the same, and that, in the end, they were all Americans.

The lyrics of the film's song, "The House I Live In," are a powerful reminder that diversity and freedom are what makes America great.

What is America to me?
A name, a map, a flag I see
A certain word, democracy
What is America to me?

The house I live in
A plot of earth, a street
The grocer and the butcher
And the people that I meet
The children in the playground
The faces that I see
All races and religions
That's America to me.

Sinatra sang "The House I Live In" throughout his career, and sometimes at political gatherings like a 1956 Democratic Party rally in Hollywood. The singer put his career at risk at times when he refused to play clubs and hotels that discriminated against Blacks.

While Sinatra was progressive on social issues, he was no saint. He grew up among organized crime figures, and they'd helped him out at different stages in his career. Sinatra was unapologetic about his friends, saying he'd hang around with people he liked—even if they had questionable reputations. He and his Rat Pack pals sang at mob wedding celebrations and performed at nightclubs and casinos owned by gangsters.

What Sinatra didn't know was that the Federal Bureau of Investigation had followed him for years and knew about his Mafia connections.

It's not clear if Jack Kennedy knew about that, but his father certainly did. Joe Kennedy did the political calculus: With Sinatra's connections to A-list celebrities and major organized crime figures, he could potentially play a substantial role in his son's campaign.

Joe Kennedy, an old hand when it came to Hollywood stars and the film business, knew the Rat Pack network. Joe believed Sinatra and his crowd could be turned into a potent fundraising, vote-getting machine.

The Rat Pack were legends, Hollywood box office gold. They made a lot of money for the Las Vegas nightclubs.

Peter Lawford may have been the connective tissue between the Rat

Pack and Kennedys. But it was Sinatra and JFK's friendship that took center stage. And it was Sinatra who introduced Kennedy to Judith Campbell.

On March 7, the night before the New Hampshire primary, Campbell recalled spending the night with Jack at the Plaza Hotel in New York. He had been calling her regularly for a month.

She hadn't meant to fall in love with the man. What if the public found out? She sighed. *Why am I doing this?* And why was *he* doing this? He had a beautiful wife, with a young daughter and a new baby on the way.

Campbell didn't know the details about Kennedy's womanizing, but she'd heard that Jack was seeing other women besides her. Was he really having an affair with Marilyn Monroe? Who else was he making love to? How did he find the time, energy, or rashness to bed so many women, and in the middle of a presidential campaign?

His behavior was so reckless, so careless; the Kennedys seemed to have their own set of rules, Campbell thought. He just didn't think he'd get caught, especially with the media on his side. Meanwhile, his sexual appetite was ramped up by his regular cortisone shots for his back. And his behavior was indulged by his close friends, who were willing to find him partners.

Campbell would later discover it was a family tradition, something he had picked up from his father. Still, it stunned her.

Now in late March, when Jack called that night, Campbell told him about her planned trip to meet Sinatra in Miami. He seemed jealous. He wanted to know how long she'd be there. A few days? A week? She'd have her own room, right?

Campbell didn't ask him who might be sharing his hotel room. She marveled at his nerve—and him a married man!

"Have a good time, and I'll try to call you every day," he told her. "Don't forget we have a date in Washington very soon."

The call ended. She cradled the receiver and smiled. She always felt better after talking to Jack. When they were alone, she had his full attention. He listened. He made her feel special. He was kind and gentle—and a wonderful lover.

Sinatra was Jack's friend. If the singer was asking her to travel to Miami, maybe it was somehow related to Jack's campaign.

She had to get ready. While she packed, she thought about how hard JFK had been campaigning in Wisconsin, how focused he was. He shared everything with her. They talked about politics, religion, and what it all meant.

No man had ever had such long, heady conversations with her. She was falling for him. There was probably nothing she wouldn't do for him. Nothing. And that worried her.

Judith spared few details of the trip in her 1977 memoir, *My Story*. In the morning, she flew to Miami. The next evening, Sinatra had made all the arrangements so she could see his show. He asked Campbell up to his suite. "We'll have cocktails while I finish getting ready for the show," he said.

When Campbell arrived, only two other people were in the room: Sinatra's valet and a man introduced as Joe Fish. (She didn't know that Joe Fish was an alias for Joseph Fischetti, a cousin of the notorious gangster Al Capone.)

She wrote, "Frank was in a good mood. As I came into the room, he held out his arms and crooned, 'A pretty girl is like a melody.' Then he went 'boom, boom, boom' rotating his hips like a stripper."

Drinks were poured. While Frank joked, his valet whisked lint from his suit and brushed his shoes to a high shine. He straightened Sinatra's tie and tucked a folded handkerchief into the tiny breast pocket.

They headed to the auditorium. "I watched the show from the wings. In those days Frank was magnificent. There is no other way to describe what he did on that stage. He would snap his fingers, sing a couple of bars, and the whole audience would fall under his spell. It was like watching mass hypnotism. Women would stare glassy-eyed while their burly husbands furtively brushed away tears as Frank took them on a sentimental journey." Sinatra had planned a celebration for his final per-formance at the Fontainebleau. Campbell decided to go, and go in style. She wore an ice-blue cocktail dress with shoes and handbag that matched. She had a custom necklace of crystal-blue beads. And off she went to Sinatra's bash.

The French Room was jammed with beautiful people. Sinatra swanned through the crowd, greeting everyone with his wide smile. Joe Fish tugged at Sinatra's sleeve. "Hey, Frank, look who's here," he said.

Sinatra turned his head and smiled and motioned her over. "I want you to meet a good friend of mine, Sam Flood."

They weaved through the crowd. Sinatra made the introductions. Campbell offered her hand to the man, but he did not shake it. Flood held it between his two hands and gave it a little squeeze. "It's a pleasure, Judy," he said.

Flood was middle-aged with a medium build, ruddy complexion, and penetrating dark eyes. Nothing remarkable. Maybe a little creepy. He didn't let go of her hand.

"Do you mind if I say something, Judy?" he said.

"Not at all—I think," she replied.

He laughed. "You're far too beautiful to be wearing junk—excuse me—I mean costume jewelry. A beautiful girl like you should be wear-ing real pearls and diamonds and rubies."

The man released her hand finally, and Campbell tried to blend in to the crowd. She knew plenty of the people there, she laughed and min-gled, but the entire evening, no matter where she was in the room, Flood watched her. He had a little smile on his face every time she glanced at him. He wasn't handsome, but he was very sure of himself. She noticed a muscular man was always by his side, watching Flood's every move. She later learned it was his bodyguard.

The next day, Campbell's friend Betty Winikus invited her to dinner. Campbell said yes, but told Winikus she had to catch a plane at 10:00 p.m. She couldn't stay long.

Dinner was at a suite at the Eden Roc hotel. Winikus met Campbell at the door. Seated at the table, rising when she entered the room, was that man, Sam Flood.

Her friend had set her up.

Campbell didn't know what to think. They had drinks. Winikus did most of the talking.

Flood was inquisitive. He asked Campbell about her family, her life and ambitions. She said she was single, an aspiring artist. He said he was a widower, a businessman. At the end of the dinner, Flood asked if it would be all right if he called her.

"Yes, that's fine," she said.

She surprised herself with her answer. She'd only just met Flood, but she actually enjoyed his company. He was calm and low-key—so much more mature than her usual companions. From the way people catered to him, she knew Flood was obviously a "man of 'position,'" she wrote.

And there was the bodyguard, standing now right outside the door. Only someone really important has a personal bodyguard, she thought.

After dinner, Campbell went back to the Fontainebleau to get her luggage. When she stepped up to the front desk to check out, Flood handed her a piece of paper. It was the hotel bill—and it was marked "Paid."

Campbell was stunned. Why did he do that? She insisted on paying him back. She wrote a check and forced him to take it. She made him promise that he'd cash it.

He flashed a wide smile and said he would. He wheeled around, walked out of the lobby, and disappeared into the night. It was a strange end to a wild week in Miami.

The man would never cash her check, but then, Sam Flood was not his real name. He was Salvatore "Sam" Giancana, head of the Outfit—an organized crime network based in Chicago.

COUNTDOWN: **223 DAYS**

April 1, 1960
Greensboro, North Carolina

The Black students who sat down at the whites-only lunch counter two months earlier had made a big splash. The Reverend Martin Luther King Jr. kept tabs on what was happening there as a great wave gathered force.

The morning after Franklin McCain, Joseph McNeil, Ezell Blair Jr., and David Richmond made their stand, twenty-seven students took seats at the same five-and-dime in Greensboro, North Carolina. Their food orders were also ignored.

The protest grew. Five days after it began, more than one thousand students arrived at Woolworth on a busy Saturday. Those who could not sit at the counter formed picket lines outside.

They used nonviolent resistance to draw the nation's attention to segregation and to build support for their cause. The lunch-counter movement had quickly spread beyond Greensboro. Now, by April, young Black people were sitting down at segregated eateries in fifty-five cities in thirteen southern states. As the sit-ins continued, more than forty were arrested—mostly for misdemeanors like trespassing, disorderly conduct, or disturbing the peace, and national media coverage brought the civil rights movement into living rooms all over America.

Meanwhile, the scope of the protests had widened. It was no longer just about integrating lunch counters. Demonstrators aimed to end all racial segregation in public places. In Petersburg, Virginia, more than one hundred students entered the public library through the "Whites only" front door and took all the open chairs. When the library reopened days later, a smaller group came back to do the same; eleven were arrested.

But as the "electrifying movement" took hold, King saw the opposition was growing louder—and violence was a language it spoke fluently. Protesters in many places were confronted by whites shouting racial slurs. They were often harassed and assaulted. In many places, the situation grew tense and dangerous. But the majority of the protesters knew they had to stay in control—and nonviolent—for the movement to succeed. They faced police guns, tear gas, arrest, and jail sentences. Even in the face of danger, these protesters continued to sit down and demand equal service.

The new activism was "initiated, fed and sustained by students," King told supporters a week later at Spelman College in Atlanta. "This struggle we are going through today is not to benefit the Negro race only, but will save the souls of America in the sight of other nations of the world."

When King spoke, Blacks and many whites listened. Black leaders stood up against segregation in the United States, but King was the face of the civil rights movement. He was America's preeminent advocate of nonviolence and social justice. Despite threats to his life, he kept pushing for integration and equal rights.

King's rise was meteoric. Five years earlier, he was a little-known pastor at a Montgomery, Alabama, Baptist church. Events beyond his control thrust him into the national spotlight, while his upbringing and faith helped him navigate the sudden fame and the heavy responsibility.

Born in Atlanta, Georgia, King was raised in a home centered around Southern Black Protestantism. His father and grandfather were Baptist preachers. His great-grandfather, brother, and uncle were all pastors. So, it only made sense that someday he'd follow in their footsteps.

His father, the Reverend Martin Luther King Sr., was the successful pastor of the Ebenezer Baptist Church, and his mother, Alberta, provided a loving family environment for their three children.

But they couldn't shield young Martin and his siblings from the blatant racism that permeated Atlanta and the entire South. Years later, King Jr. would recall a trip with his father to a downtown shoe store.

When they walked inside, they sat in empty seats at the front of the store. And that's when a young white clerk approached and murmured politely, "I'll be happy to wait on you if you'll just move to those seats in the rear."

His father replied, "There's nothing wrong with these seats. We're quite comfortable here."

"Sorry," she said, "but you'll have to move."

By now, his father—the son of a sharecropper—was furious. "We'll either buy shoes sitting here, or we won't buy shoes at all."

King Sr. could tell the clerk wouldn't help them. So, he grabbed his son's hand and stormed out the door. King could still remember walking down the street with his father as he muttered, "I don't care how long I have to live with this system, I will never accept it."

Young Martin resented segregation, calling it a "grave injustice." But his parents' love guided him through difficult years and made him optimistic about the future.

America's racial problems "were a social condition rather than a natural order." She could protect her children by instilling in them a sense that they "must never allow it to make me feel inferior," King wrote in his autobiography.

His family lived on Auburn Avenue, Atlanta's bustling "Black Wall Street." It was home to some of America's largest and most prosperous Black businesses and churches in the years before the civil rights movement.

Even so, King felt keenly the prejudice then common in the South. King attended Morehouse College in 1944 as an early admission student when he was only fifteen. After graduation, he spent the next three years at Crozer Theological Seminary near Chester, Pennsylvania, a predominantly white institution. There he encountered Mohandas Gandhi's philosophy of nonviolence and honed the speaking skills that later made him famous.

King was working on his doctorate at Boston University in 1952 when he met Coretta Scott, a native of Alabama who was studying at the New England Conservatory. A year later, they married.

In 1954, King became the pastor of the Dexter Avenue Baptist Church in Montgomery, when he led a boycott that integrated the city's buses. He capitalized on the success to help organize the Southern Christian Leadership Conference. It gave him a base of operations throughout the South and provided him with a national pulpit.

King, his wife, and their four children had just moved to Atlanta, where he became co-pastor at his father's church. But he devoted most of his time to the Southern Christian Leadership Conference and civil rights, declaring that the "psychological moment has come when a concentrated drive against injustice can bring great, tangible gains."

Meanwhile, the college students in Greensboro were putting King's nonviolence principle to the test.

Joseph McNeil felt the admiration of some in the community but the anger of others. Still, they knew that if they fought back, they would give away the moral high ground. They leaned on one another and pushed forward.

What puzzled the Greensboro protesters was that many of the church leaders in the city—both Black and white—didn't speak out right away against the injustice. They looked the other way, or didn't take them seriously. Ezell Blair Jr. knew that many people "figured we were just four dumb black freshmen students out on some kind of prank."

But they had teachers who instilled in them that you have to stand up for what's right. The four young men met with Woolworth officials about how to resolve the issue. For McCain that was easy: Just integrate the lunch counter.

The businessmen tried to make it complicated. An attorney for the retail giant suggested the company build "a comfortable facility, but downstairs someplace, for Black folk to eat at." The restaurant, he said, would be "as nice as, or, in fact, a little bit better than what the white people have there now."

The protesters were insulted. The talks broke down.

King knew they needed help. The preacher called together a conference of college students from the North and South to discuss strategy. They formed the Student Nonviolent Coordinating Committee. Along with the Congress of Racial Equality, founded in 1942, they became the main grassroots organizers of future sit-ins, protests, and marches.

King urged students and activists to train people to fill the jails rather than post bond or pay fines. This tactic "may be the thing to awaken the dozing conscience of many of our white brothers."

He called for whites to support the students. And he asked the government to do the same. King had hoped national politicians, including the presidential candidates, would express their support for the peaceful protests. Neither Kennedy nor Nixon had that kind of backbone—not with an election on the line.

The civil rights leader was disappointed, but he wasn't surprised. The U.S. Supreme Court's 1954 ruling outlawing segregation in public schools had drawn a backlash from southern Democratic leaders.

On the campaign trail, Kennedy didn't mention segregation or civil rights for fear of losing southern support.

King wondered out loud just what Kennedy stood for. Why was he running for president? What motivated him? He offered JFK a chance to define himself, show his courage. Instead, Kennedy ran from the issue.

Kennedy admitted privately that he hadn't known many Black people in his life. He was born into a privileged, wealthy Massachusetts family. He attended white schools and had few Black friends. The Navy was still segregated when he'd served in World War II.

Kennedy had spoken with Black people on the campaign trail, but they were often entertainers or athletes. He had never met Martin Luther King Jr., nor any other civil rights leader. It didn't seem worth the risk.

In 1960, more than 85 percent of the U.S. population was white. A large percentage of Blacks had never voted. Many lived second-class lives in a nation that was supposed to be a beacon of liberty and democracy to the world.

Yet, Kennedy played both sides. At the 1956 Democratic National Convention, segregationist George Wallace escorted his sister, Eunice Kennedy Shriver, to address the Alabama delegation.

John Temple Graves, a noted segregationist and national newspaper columnist for the *Birmingham Post-Herald*, praised JFK, calling him a better alternative to labor leader Walter Reuther or Vice President Richard Nixon. Graves wrote that Kennedy might be the "living antithesis of Earl Warren," the chief justice of the U.S. Supreme Court who penned the majority opinion in *Brown v. Board of Education*. In response, JFK sent Graves a thank-you note.

Even more telling, Kennedy in June 1959 invited segregationist Alabama governor John Patterson and his aide Sam Engelhardt Jr., the racist leader of a white supremacist group founded to combat integration, to breakfast at his Georgetown home. After the meeting, Patterson enthusiastically endorsed Kennedy's presidential bid, outraging Black leaders.

At this point, Blacks felt more at ease with Republicans—the party of Abraham Lincoln. Eisenhower wasn't perfect, but at least he had sent federal troops to Little Rock, Arkansas, to enforce the Supreme Court ruling integrating public schools.

King knew he'd have to push politicians to do the right thing. He would call them out on their willful blindness and silence.

Maybe, at some point, they'd come around.

COUNTDOWN: **218 DAYS**

April 5, 1960
Milwaukee, Wisconsin

The polls had been closed for an hour. John Kennedy sipped chicken noodle soup in his hotel suite, watching the early primary returns trickle in. So far, Senator Hubert Humphrey had a slim lead.

Kennedy wasn't concerned. The reports were from rural farming counties, Humphrey strongholds. No need to worry. Not yet.

But others in the third-floor suite at Milwaukee's Pfister Hotel were anxious. The polls all had Kennedy winning Wisconsin, but the real question was: By how much? Would it be a landslide or a nail-biter?

After New Hampshire, it seemed that Kennedy had all the momentum. And with the money JFK spent in the state, this had the earmarks of a blowout. Anything less would be considered a disappointment.

Wisconsin was the first real test for Kennedy—the first time he'd face a serious challenge. For weeks, JFK and Humphrey had waged an all-out war. Kennedy had the looks, the money, and the organization. What Humphrey had was heart and passion.

Humphrey later wrote that he knew Jack's "well-financed campaign was filled with beautiful people." His campaign had been a slog—"no match for the glamour of Jackie Kennedy and the other Kennedy women." Humphrey was lucky to "get a couple of dozen folks to coffee parties in a farm home or in a worker's house . . ." in an urban area. Meanwhile, "the Kennedys, with engraved invitations, were packing ballrooms in Milwaukee."

"Mink never wore so well, cloth coats so poorly," Humphrey wrote.

Of all the Democratic primaries, Wisconsin was the one where people could vote for candidates of either party. Would Republicans cast ballots for Humphrey to help him win because they believed Nixon would have an easier time against the Minnesota senator in the fall? Could a big Kennedy win prove he was really a national candidate? No one wanted a long, drawn-out battle. So, would delegates in other states commit to the winner of the Wisconsin primary to prevent a prolonged primary contest that had the potential to weaken the party?

New Hampshire didn't much care about Kennedy's religion, but his Catholic faith played more of a role in the Midwest. Ads had appeared in local weekly newspapers throughout Wisconsin pushing Protestants to vote for Humphrey.

Kennedy finished his soup and was feeling more optimistic. Updated returns had pushed him ahead of Humphrey. If he could win at least seven of the state's ten congressional districts, he'd be writing Humphrey's political obituary. If not, the battle for the Democratic presidential nomination would head back to the trenches.

Family and friends milled around the Kennedy suite. But John's brother and campaign manager, Robert, was at the communications center. He was exhausted. He had thrown everything he could at Humphrey, who didn't have the money to run a similar media-driven campaign. Humphrey had attacked Kennedy for spending too much money, calling his campaign "the most highly financed, the most plush, the most extravagant in the history of politics in the United States."

Kennedy countered him simply, explaining that campaigns were expensive. His money allowed him to reach voters in innovative ways. In one of his first ads in Wisconsin, JFK relaxed in a chair with a globe and a nameplate reading "Senator John F. Kennedy" on a nearby table.

Kennedy looked comfortably into the camera and introduced himself to Wisconsin voters.

"The Wisconsin primary has had a great tradition stretching back to the days of Governor La Follette in 1905, who helped design this law in order to permit the people of this state, as well as the people of other states, to participate in the selection of their presidential nominee," Kennedy said.

He had traveled all over America—and Wisconsin—and during that time, he said, "I've come to have an image of Americans as courageous, confident and persevering. It is with that image that I begin this campaign."

It was short, sweet, and unique, and beamed directly into voters' living rooms via television.

Humphrey didn't have money for anything but a scrappy whistle-stop and newspaper campaign, attacking Kennedy's position on just about every issue.

He slammed JFK for being the only Democratic senator not to have voted to censure former Wisconsin senator Joe McCarthy, whose conduct as chairman of the Senate's Permanent Subcommittee on Investigations brought shame to the entire body. McCarthy was notorious for bullying witnesses who testified before the committee, which was investigating communist activity in the United States. McCarthy was a close friend of JFK's father, Joe Kennedy, himself a fervent anti-communist. McCarthy also was a frequent guest at the Kennedy compound in Hyannis Port, Massachusetts.

Again, Kennedy replied simply. He'd been in the hospital when the Senate voted on McCarthy.

Humphrey pointed out that Joe Kennedy contributed money to the Eisenhower-Nixon ticket in 1952.

"Hell, he's a businessman. He gave to everybody," JFK said about his father.

When there were insinuations that JFK's brother Robert was "buying votes" in Wisconsin, JFK snapped. "Do you know how many voters there are in Wisconsin? I know we're rich, but not that rich. [Humphrey] talks about me, about my family, about my friends, the only thing he won't discuss are the issues. Son-of-a-bitch," Kennedy told members of his campaign team.

Robert Kennedy left the bickering to the candidates and focused on crafting his brother's media image. John's charisma and good looks appealed to a new generation of voters. Kennedy campaign ads were sharp and professional, and the voters who saw him on television longed to meet him in person. Old Joe Kennedy loved seeing the magic work.

"We're going to sell Jack like soap flakes," he boasted.

It looked like the work was paying off. As he watched the television news reports, Kennedy knew he was well on his way to winning the primary. The room lit up with cheers.

At the end of the count, Kennedy collected 476,024 votes to Humphrey's 366,753, or almost 57 percent of the ballots. Kennedy tried to spin the results. Six out of ten districts was a victory, he said, and "anything else would be gravy."

But the race was uncomfortably close. Kennedy captured the districts with large Catholic voter blocs. Humphrey's districts were predominantly Protestant.

With the primary victory, Kennedy took a measured—but not conclusive—step toward the Democratic presidential nomination. If JFK had won more decisively, the cash-strapped Humphrey might have surrendered right there.

But Humphrey said he wasn't ready to give up on the Democratic contest—much to the disappointment of the Kennedy camp.

Describing Wisconsin as "a sort of warmup," Humphrey said he'd "be very much alive, politically" in the next primary: West Virginia.

"I don't feel injured by the results here. I feel, in fact, encouraged. Another week here and we might have won it," he said.

As the campaign moved on, the West Virginia primary on May 10 would be a bone-crushing showdown. The rural coal-mining state was approximately 95 percent Protestant. Kennedy's religion was becoming a cutting-edge issue.

Before the Wisconsin primary, polls suggested a sizable Kennedy lead over Humphrey in West Virginia. But that lead disappeared overnight.

Some advisers urged Kennedy to skip West Virginia. His father agreed. West Virginia, he said, "is a nothing state and they'll kill him over the Catholic thing."

But JFK wanted to confront the religious bigotry issue head-on. If he didn't call it out soon, the shadow would follow him for the rest of the election season.

No, JFK had to overcome anti-Catholic prejudice, or he might as well quit now. Humphrey might pull ahead of him, or maybe the political bosses would make a backroom deal and nominate Lyndon Johnson—or somebody else.

Eunice Kennedy Shriver watched the evening unfold in the hotel room. She thought her brother must have been overjoyed about winning the Wisconsin primary, but he seemed almost dejected.

"What does it all mean, Johnny?" Eunice asked him.

"It means that we've got to go to West Virginia in the morning and do it all over again. And then we've got to go on to Maryland and Indiana and Oregon, and win all of them," he said.

That night, Jack Kennedy came to the hard truth: All the flash and cash in the world wouldn't hand him the Democratic presidential nomination. He was heading down a long, grinding road.

April 6, 1960
Washington, D.C.

While the Democrats monopolized the spotlight in Wisconsin, the Republican candidate stood back and waited. Richard Nixon had entered the Republican primaries, but he hadn't spent a single day campaigning. In Wisconsin, where voters could vote for anyone in either party, he'd finished well behind Kennedy and Humphrey.

The primaries didn't mean a thing, really. Nixon didn't have any competition. It was a matter of racking up votes—seeing how many of the party faithful would turn out when nothing was at stake.

Nixon landed 339,383 votes in Wisconsin, lower than President Eisenhower's total in 1956. But back in Washington, Nixon described his voter turnout in the Wisconsin primary as impressive.

He sent a telegram to Wisconsin GOP leaders. "Observers agree that our vote was surprisingly large in view of the fact that there was no contest for Republican delegates and that I did not campaign in the state," Nixon wrote. "We can now plan and work with renewed confidence for a Republican victory in Wisconsin in November."

Nixon didn't mention the furious last-minute publicity bump the party had laid on to boost his showing. Just for the sake of appearances, Republicans spent hundreds of thousands of dollars to saturate the electorate with political advertising. They bought ads in newspapers and on radio and television. They produced pro-Nixon buttons, pamphlets, and brochures. No one was surprised at Nixon getting fewer votes in the Republican primary than either Kennedy or Humphrey in the

Democratic contest. But if they hadn't banged the drum to turn out Republicans, it would have been a humiliation.

A mediocre third-place finish, a candidate who didn't campaign . . . Nixon knew there were people who felt the party could do better with someone else. And New York governor Nelson Rockefeller was still being discussed as a possible GOP presidential candidate.

Rockefeller had already said he wouldn't seek the nomination, but Rockefeller was a politician. He had the same upper-class polish and charisma as Jack Kennedy, and even deeper pockets. Perhaps most important, he was able to articulate his own vision for America's future— unlike Nixon, who was running on Eisenhower's coattails.

But Nixon did have an advantage. He had assembled a first-rate campaign team. He had started putting his group together in December 1958 during a meeting at the Key Biscayne, Florida, home of his close friend Charles "Bebe" Rebozo, a banker who had known Nixon since he was a young congressman in the late 1940s.

Old friends like Jack Drown, a magazine distributor from Southern California, and Ray Arbuthnot, a California rancher, were there. So were the top advisers: Robert "Bob" Finch, a savvy California attorney; Leonard Hall, former chairman of the Republican National Committee who'd lost the Republican primary for governor of New York to Nelson Rockefeller; and Herbert Klein, his longtime press secretary. New staffers included H. R. Haldeman and John Ehrlichman, who were young and aggressive.

Finch and Hall were in campaign managerial positions. Nixon would listen to their advice. But in the end, Nixon made all the big decisions himself. After the GOP took a beating in the 1958 midterm elections, and it was unclear what Rockefeller would do, they urged Nixon to hold off committing himself to policy positions until the New York governor made up his mind.

If the vice president had to battle Rockefeller for the nomination, his advisers believed he'd win because of all the fundraising and campaigning Nixon did for GOP candidates. They owed him.

Still, party leaders who worked for years with Nixon asked themselves why he was running for president. What motivated him? What did he want to accomplish? Who was he? So far, Nixon hadn't been able to put his views, goals, and vision into words.

An April 18 *Denver Post* editorial laid out the concern. The editorial board called for Nixon to step aside for Rockefeller, who was the "most attractive Republican candidate.

"Instead, Republicans are sitting around telling one another that Richard Nixon is the certain nominee; that he has such a firm and unchallenged hold on the party's machinery that no one can dislodge him; that the party has no choice but to try to make Nixon acceptable to the electorate on the platform of 'Peace and Prosperity.'

"This is the stuff that political defeat is made of."

The editorial board said Nixon might make a good president, but he was essentially riding "on Eisenhower's coattails." And the vice president looked lackluster when compared to the two "appealing candidates" vying for the Democratic presidential nomination, the paper noted.

"But they should face the uncomfortable fact that Nixon is not the type to inspire fervid enthusiasm among uncommitted voters who will determine the outcome of the 1960 race. It may be that he is lacking in that vague quality called 'personal magnetism.' It may be that he simply does not impress people as being of presidential caliber."

Influential Washington columnist Drew Pearson piled on, saying Rockefeller wouldn't stay in the background.

"Unless he can be talked out of it, Gov. Nelson Rockefeller will begin next month to set forth his views on major issues in a series of speeches that will be highly critical of Vice President Nixon," he wrote.

"For the plain truth is that Rockefeller dislikes and distrusts Nixon . . . [who] lacks the vision to lead the nation into the surging new era which the Space Age is opening up."

Pearson said Rockefeller believed Nixon "is so obsessed with what he is against that he is incapable of constructive, forward leadership."

Nixon, Pearson wrote, had tried to divert the Rockefeller threat by offering him the vice presidential slot, or the keynote speaker's spot at the Republican National Convention.

So far, Rockefeller had rebuffed Nixon's offers.

Nixon wasn't thrilled by the Rockefeller development, but what could he do? The primaries were already underway, and he didn't think Rockefeller could stop his momentum.

But some GOP insiders argued that the vice president didn't have momentum. The Democrats had it all. Nixon was just plodding along in their shadow.

Other newspapers called Nixon's poor showing in the Wisconsin primary a harbinger of things to come.

"Nixon and the Republicans may brush off Tuesday's results with the conclusion that an uncontested primary does not generate much enthusiasm, and the fact that Nixon made no direct appeal to Wisconsin voters," according to the editorial board of the state's *Racine Journal Times*.

"But the fact that the Vice President wasn't even able to top the second-ranking Democratic candidate is bound to set Republicans wondering about these old 'Nixon-can't-win' stories. What happened in Wisconsin Tuesday must be counted as a setback for Nixon's ambitions to go to the White House."

The latest Gallup poll had Kennedy leading Nixon by 53 percent to 47 percent. But Nixon shrugged it off, attributing the results to Kennedy's "blaze of national publicity."

This was a bad week for Nixon. *That's politics,* he told himself. Some weeks were good, others difficult. The main thing was to stick to your plans and keep moving forward. The vice president might not have been actively campaigning in the primaries, but he was working behind the scenes to shore up support.

Would it be enough to stop Rockefeller? If it wasn't, Nixon knew it could open a wound that might not heal in time for the November election.

April 7, 1960
Washington, D.C.

One thing Judith Campbell thought Jack Kennedy enjoyed about her was the easy way she moved among the glamorous, rich, and famous. He listened intently on the phone as Campbell told him about Frank Sinatra's behavior during the Miami trip. JFK prompted her for details: What did she wear? Who did she meet?

She mentioned how Sinatra had introduced her to a funny little man named Sam Flood, who seemed to be infatuated with her. He was sending her roses every day, dozens of yellow ones.

Kennedy said he knew Sam Giancana. "Oh, is that his real name?" she asked.

It was, but his name didn't mean a thing to her. JFK, his brothers, and his father were all well acquainted with Giancana. The FBI was, too.

Momo Salvatore "Sam" Giancana was a mob boss, the leader of the Outfit, the Chicago branch of the American organized crime network brought to power by the legendary gangster Al Capone.

Giancana was a prototype Mafia don. A troubled teenager from the wrong side of town, Giancana started as a driver for mobsters. By twenty, Giancana was a suspect in several murders.

In the early 1930s, the Outfit was going through a transition period. Al Capone was in federal prison for tax evasion and mob leaders were trying to fill the void, creating a perfect opportunity for an ambitious thug like Giancana.

As he rose in the organization, it seemed that he was involved in every profitable criminal enterprise. He was arrested in 1939 for bootlegging and, after spending a few years in jail, Giancana picked up where he left off. Using sheer terror, Giancana took over Chicago's highly profitable "numbers rackets."

By the mid-1950s, Giancana controlled not only illegal gambling operations, but prostitution rings and drug trafficking. He made mob families millions a year. Maybe that's why the Outfit's top boss, Anthony "Joe Batters" Accardo, stepped down so Giancana could take over. If he didn't, he might get whacked, too.

Sam Giancana
(Bettmann/Getty Images)

Following the death of his wife, Angeline, in 1954, Giancana liked to hobnob around town with beautiful young women on his arm. Judith

Campbell was his type. Her involvement with Sinatra and Kennedy sharpened her appeal. Giancana followed politics closely, and kept a collection of politicians in his pocket.

Even though Kennedy's father had met "Sam Flood" many times as he built his Chicago real estate portfolio, Joseph Kennedy didn't do much business with Giancana.

That was about to change.

Since Campbell met Giancana at the Fontainebleau, he had called her several times a day. She learned to enjoy the mobster's attention. She found Giancana had a hearty laugh and a good sense of humor. He always took a light and positive tone with her.

Meanwhile, Jack was calling to remind her about their "date" in Washington the following day. Meet up in the city, dinner at his house in Georgetown. Stay there together overnight. Campbell sighed. Yes, she remembered. He had reminded her about the rendezvous countless times.

She confirmed she'd be there.

When she went to the airport the following morning she picked up a few newspapers before boarding the plane. On the flight, she read all the way to Washington, scanning for items about Kennedy and the Wisconsin primary.

She was thrilled that Jack had won, but knew he hadn't delivered a knockout blow. Humphrey was still a viable candidate. At least that's what the pundits were saying.

She tried to relax, but by the time she arrived at the Sheraton Park Hotel in Washington, she felt strangely jumpy. Maybe it was because she was about to stay in the same house where JFK lived with his wife. Jackie was out of town for a few days, so Kennedy was free.

But she felt a little better after she opened the door to her hotel room and was greeted by a dozen red roses—courtesy of Jack.

She got comfortable, then called one of Kennedy's secretaries, Evelyn Lincoln, for instructions. Lincoln had made the hotel reservation for her. She knew all about JFK's affairs and was the go-to person for Campbell.

They had developed a cordial, friendly relationship over the phone. Lincoln told Campbell to take a cab to Jack's house in Georgetown at 7:30 p.m.

Campbell glanced at the clock. It was late afternoon. She knew she could take her time getting ready. So, she took a shower, then donned a black knit suit and a new mink coat she had bought in New York City. When her taxi pulled up to 3307 N Street in Washington's tony Georgetown section, he greeted her at the front door.

"You look fantastic," he said.

They weren't alone at the house.

A tall man sat in the living room. Jack introduced him as an old friend, a railroad lobbyist. Campbell felt shaky. Not only was she in Jacqueline Kennedy's house, but also another person knew about their affair. Sooner or later, it would get out, right? She didn't want to think about that.

They had drinks and made small talk before they sat down to cold soup, meat, and potatoes. Campbell listened as Kennedy and the lobbyist discussed the next primary in West Virginia. They said if Humphrey won, Jack would still stay in the race. But Kennedy said it could lead to a deadlocked convention, opening the way for party bosses to ram through someone like Lyndon Johnson. If Kennedy won, that was it. Game over.

After they finished, they had an after-dinner drink. Jack finally escorted the lobbyist to the door. Years later she recounted her conversation to investigative reporter Seymour Hersh, and said that when JFK returned, he asked her for a favor: Could she set up a meeting with Giancana? She said yes, but wasn't sure if she should ask why. Kennedy answered: It was for his campaign.

There was one more thing. He lifted a satchel and asked if she'd mind taking it to Giancana by train.

Again, she didn't hesitate. "Not at all."

"But I want you to know what's in it," he said. And when he opened the bag, there it was, bundles of hundred-dollar bills, as much as

$250,000. Her heart raced. She later told Hersh that she asked Kennedy if it was safe carrying so much money.

Kennedy said it was. Someone would be following her. And JFK said he wouldn't force her to do it. She could turn him down.

But Campbell wasn't going to say no to Jack. If he thought it was important, then it must be. And that meant one thing: He trusted her. She would do it.

Kennedy told her to give the bag to Giancana, but then stopped. He didn't want to tell her anything more. He didn't want to involve her too deeply. By carrying the money, she'd be in deep enough.

Still, the cloak-and-dagger stuff was exciting. Campbell felt part of something important.

Why did Giancana need the money? She didn't know—and she didn't ask.

But decades later, Sy Hersh and other journalists would discover the answer. A few months earlier, Giancana had reached an understanding with Joe Kennedy. The Chicago Mafia would help out with the 1960 election. Now the Kennedy campaign needed Giancana's help in West Virginia.

Kennedy couldn't win the primary just by shaking hands at factory gates or making speeches to garden clubs. No, the Kennedy campaign needed people to distribute millions of dollars to sheriffs, poll workers, preachers, and mayors all over West Virginia to win the primary and seal the Democratic nomination. Kennedy needed preachers to get up in the pulpit and urge their congregations to support him. They needed election officials to put Kennedy's name on the top of crowded ballots, and law enforcement to remove competitors' election signs from stores and yards.

But how could they move all that cash without being observed? That's where Giancana's expertise came in. He and others on the Kennedy payroll knew which palms to grease.

Why would Giancana want to help Kennedy? Maybe it was because of Cuba. Fidel Castro had overthrown Cuba's dictator in January 1959, but instead of founding a democracy there, Castro had gone commie and cozied up to the Soviet Union.

America's crime families, deeply committed capitalists, weren't thrilled with Castro. They had millions of dollars tied up in Havana's lucrative casinos. When Castro took over, he had shut down their gambling houses and nightclubs.

The Mafia bosses wanted Castro gone—and maybe JFK could make that happen. They also wanted the Justice Department—and Kennedy's brother—to ease up on organized crime investigations. But for any of that to happen, Kennedy had to win.

What Campbell knew that night in Georgetown was that she was helping Jack. That's all that mattered. For the rest of the night, Kennedy didn't say another word about the mission. Instead, he turned his attention to romance.

He gave Campbell a tour of the house. When they got to the master bedroom, Kennedy put his arms around her, then sat them both on the bed. He "was almost immediately amorous."

When was Jack not amorous? While Campbell didn't know how many women he had been with in his life, the FBI had a good idea. It had kept a file on JFK's escapades since the early 1940s, when he'd dated Danish beauty queen and journalist Inga Marie Arvad. In the mid-1930s, as a freelancer, she had interviewed Adolf Hitler.

She and young Kennedy, a naval officer, had a torrid affair that was monitored by FBI director J. Edgar Hoover. Someone had tipped off the FBI that she was not only a married woman but potentially a German spy, too. After months of surveillance and wiretaps, the FBI had nothing but audio of two lovers talking about their lives.

Hoover personally relayed the information to Joe Kennedy. So, the old man pulled some strings and had his son transferred from Washington to Charleston, South Carolina.

Joe tried to make sure that his son stayed out of trouble—especially with women. Anything that could hurt his son's political future was his business.

Still, here was Jack, taking enormous risks, having affairs with multiple women. Campbell's wasn't the only name in his little black book. So far, the public didn't know about his indiscretions.

But why was he risking everything to cheat on his wife? Not even his closest friends could explain it. Maybe it was the thrill? Maybe he was a sex addict? Maybe it was because Kennedy wanted to live life to the fullest, knowing the future wasn't guaranteed, especially with constant concerns about his health. And maybe the risk was calculated: The Kennedys had a network in place to deal with any issue that might come up.

That night Campbell and Kennedy made love in the same room—the same bed—he shared with Jackie. Campbell knew that.

She'd later recall that she loved Jack's possessiveness. After they made love, he didn't want to let go. She said she'd lie with his arms around her, and she'd rest her head on his chest—listening to the beat of his heart as they talked for hours.

Campbell slipped away in the morning, climbing into a cab with satchel in hand. Kennedy was already making plans to see her again, maybe in a week or so.

Pushing away the dark morning-after thoughts, Campbell was a little afraid. She knew she had to get out of this mess sometime soon. But not now. It was all too intoxicating.

COUNTDOWN: **192 DAYS**

May 1, 1960
Washington, D.C.

Richard Nixon was stunned. A U-2 spy plane had been shot down over the Soviet Union. So far, President Eisenhower hadn't disclosed the incident to the American people. The president was waiting to see if the pilot, Francis Gary Powers, had survived.

While worried about Powers's safety, Nixon knew this could become a big campaign issue. Democrats had accused the Eisenhower administration of failing to stop the spread of communism. So had New York governor Nelson Rockefeller, who said nations all over the world were turning to the Soviet Union—not America—for economic and military help.

Eisenhower and other world leaders had hoped the Geneva Summit in 1955 would lead to an arms control agreement. But Soviet premier Khrushchev balked when Ike proposed allowing each country to fly over the other to inspect their nuclear facilities and launchpads.

Khrushchev said Eisenhower's "Open Skies" plan was another way for the United States to spy on the Soviet nuclear arms program. He claimed the Soviet Union had developed intercontinental ballistic missiles—a weapon capable of hitting targets in America.

Thus, the U-2 spy plane. It was a special high-altitude aircraft that could fly above 70,000 feet, out of reach of Soviet radar—or so U.S. officials thought.

Flying over another country's airspace without permission was a risky proposition. It was considered an act of war. So, if the United States was going to do it, it was critical for the spy planes to be undetectable. Up until now, they had been. The U.S. Central Intelligence Agency ran the reconnaissance program. The spy plane's first mission was on July 4, 1956. It flew undetected over Moscow and Leningrad before returning safely to its base. So, the secret flyovers continued.

But there was always the danger that something like this could happen, creating an international crisis. That's why Eisenhower had to personally approve each mission. But that limited the number of flights. So they had to be high-value missions.

Even before Powers's spy plane was hit, the secret flyovers were becoming more dangerous. It appeared that Soviet radar had actually detected the planes. So, the Russians were starting to deploy surface-to-air missiles around their nuclear sites.

Powers's mission was to fly over 2,900 miles of Russian airspace. His spy plane would take off in Pakistan north over western Russian and land at an airbase in Norway. But somewhere along the route, less than halfway through, his U-2 was picked up by Russian radar and shot down by a missile in the Ural Mountains.

Did Powers eject and parachute to the ground? The United States didn't know. And if he landed safely, was he captured?

At first, U.S. officials told Soviet leaders a whopper: The U-2 was a weather plane on a routine flight. The oxygen delivery system malfunctioned, and the pilot blacked out and drifted over Soviet airspace.

The Soviets knew it was a cover story. They had recovered the plane mostly intact, including the aerial spy-camera system.

The American public knew nothing about spy planes. But now the secret program would be exposed. Eisenhower would have to own up to Americans that he had authorized the project. He'd have to explain that without an "Open Skies" agreement, such surveillance flights were necessary to help keep the nation secure. The president would continue the program—even after this disaster.

Wreckage of U-2 spy plane piloted by Powers
(Bettmann/Getty Images)

But first, he had to find out if Powers was alive. CIA director Allen Dulles told the president that the pilot probably didn't survive. Still, they couldn't be sure. And if Powers did make it, Eisenhower would have to find a way to get him out of Russia, without losing too much face.

Nixon knew that a spy plane and an imprisoned American pilot would spell big trouble on the campaign trail. He had tied himself so closely to Eisenhower that he'd have to accept the bad with the good.

He also knew how difficult Khrushchev could be—from personal experience. A year earlier, Nixon had engaged with the Soviet premier in the "kitchen debate" over which form of government was better for the people—capitalism or communism.

When the United States and Soviet Union agreed to set up exhibitions in each other's countries, it was supposed to show how the other side lived. The hope was these kinds of cultural exchange events would ease tensions and improve relations between Russians and Americans.

When the Soviet exhibition opened in New York in June 1959, the

Russians focused on Sputnik and space-age technology, farm machines, and art.

The U.S. exhibition showcasing the best of American free enterprise was scheduled to open to the public in Moscow's Sokolniki Park on July 25.

The day before, Nixon served as Khrushchev's guide. As they strolled through exhibits, Nixon explained how the items had made life easier for average Americans. When they stopped, they'd often engage in impromptu exchanges about their economic and political systems. Some of the most intense ones took place in the model of a suburban home.

When they reached the home's model kitchen, Nixon stopped Khrushchev.

"I want to show you this kitchen. It is like those of our houses in California," said Nixon, pointing to the dishwasher.

Khrushchev wasn't impressed. "We have such things."

"This is the newest model," the vice president said. "This is the kind which is built in thousands of units for direct installations in the houses. In America, we like to make life easier for women."

"Your capitalistic attitude toward women does not occur under Communism," Khrushchev said.

"I think that this attitude towards women is universal. What we want to do, is make life more easy for our housewives," Nixon said, adding, "This house can be bought for $14,000, and most American [veterans from World War II] can buy a home in the bracket of $10,000 to $15,000."

Nixon touted the fact that any steelworker in the United States could buy the house. "They earn $3 an hour. This house costs about $100 a month to buy on a contract running 25 to 30 years," he said.

Khrushchev noted that Russian steelworkers—and even peasants— can afford to spend $14,000 for a home. But in the Soviet Union, they built homes that last longer. "Your American houses are built to last only 20 years so builders could sell new houses at the end. We build firmly. We build for our children and grandchildren," he said.

"American houses last for more than 20 years," Nixon said. "But even so, after twenty years, many Americans want a new house or a new kitchen. Their kitchen is obsolete by that time . . . The American system is designed to take advantage of new inventions and new techniques."

But Khrushchev replied that Nixon's "theory" was wrong. "Some things never get out of date—houses, for instance. Furniture, furnishings—perhaps—but not houses. I have read much about America and American houses . . . and I do not think that this exhibit and what you say is strictly accurate."

"Well, um . . ."

"I hope I have not insulted you," Khrushchev said.

"I have been insulted by experts," Nixon said. "Everything we say [on the other hand] is in good humor. Always speak frankly."

But then their conversation turned more serious. Khrushchev said if you were born in the Soviet Union "you were entitled to housing." But in America, Khrushchev said, "if you don't have a dollar you have a right to choose between sleeping in a house or on the pavement."

Journalists couldn't get enough of the exchange. They continued to follow the men after they left the kitchen. Nixon and Khrushchev kept talking about the competition between their nations in every aspect of life.

When the vice president conceded that the Soviets might be ahead in the development in "the thrust of their space rockets," Khrushchev interrupted, "No, in rockets we have passed you by."

At times, the exchanges were heated, especially when they went back and forth about nuclear weapons. Nixon told Khrushchev that his constant threats of using nuclear missiles could lead to war. But there were other moments where it seemed like they enjoyed themselves.

"You're a lawyer of Capitalism. I'm a lawyer for Communism. Let's kiss," Khrushchev said.

The debate was front-page news in America. It showed that Nixon could stand toe-to-toe with the Soviet leader and added to his credibility when he touted his experience on the campaign trail. He had it; Kennedy didn't.

Richard Nixon and Nikita Khrushchev in the "kitchen debate," July 24, 1959
(UPI/Newscom)

But that was then, and this was now.

Nixon hoped he could contain the political fallout from the spy plane incident, and that Nelson Rockefeller, who had been hinting about entering the presidential race, wouldn't pounce on the opportunity. This might prove to be just the kind of opening that the ambitious New York politician-prince had been waiting for.

COUNTDOWN: **191 DAYS**

May 2, 1960
Charleston, West Virginia

At first glance, things looked great for Jack Kennedy. He'd won in Wisconsin and swept four of the five primaries that followed.

But it would take more than his charisma, war record, and good looks to put Kennedy over the top in the West Virginia primary. It was one of the most Protestant states in America. Only some 5 percent of the state's 1.9 million people were Catholic. So, if JFK could win here, he could win anywhere. At least that was the theory.

To overcome that challenge, Joe Kennedy didn't have just money to offer. He had a vast network of contacts, back channels, and IOUs.

Things looked great early on. In December 1959, Jack Kennedy's pollster, Lou Harris, said he was winning the state by 70 to 30 percent over Humphrey.

But things started shifting after the Wisconsin primary. And when Robert Kennedy flew into Charleston, West Virginia, to get a feel for the Democrats there, he discovered a big problem.

At a meeting with campaign volunteers at the Kanawha Hotel, Bobby asked for a frank assessment of his brother's chances. It didn't take long to find out the truth: his brother's campaign was in deep trouble because of his religion. Almost overnight, voters had discovered JFK was not a Protestant, and that's when Kennedy's lead began to evaporate.

Bobby Kennedy panicked. "He seemed to be in a state of shock. His face was as pale as ashes," recalled Kenny O'Donnell, a campaign adviser. Bobby called his brother in Washington and urged Jack to negotiate with

Humphrey, to ask the Minnesota senator to immediately withdraw from the West Virginia primary.

Jack quickly reminded Bobby of the positive Lou Harris poll. "It can't be that bad," he said.

It was. "The people who voted for you in the poll have just found out you're Catholic," Bobby said.

JFK paused, then told his brother to come back to Washington. They'd find a way to deal with Humphrey.

And so, Kennedy operatives began a hard drive to force Humphrey out of the race. Humphrey refused to withdraw. Why should he, just as the momentum had shifted? New polls showed him ahead: 60 percent of the electorate said they'd vote for him, while 40 percent said they backed Kennedy.

The numbers encouraged Humphrey to keep going. Other Democrats who'd been waiting in the wings for a Kennedy stumble were on alert, too. Pundits speculated that if Humphrey won West Virginia, it could lead to a deadlocked Democratic National Convention. And if that happened, the choice would fall to the party bosses. Maybe they would choose Lyndon Johnson, or Senator Symington of Missouri—or even an old familiar face, Adlai Stevenson.

Kennedy was in the tough spot he always knew would come sometime during the Democratic primaries.

West Virginia was the place where Kennedy had to crush Humphrey. Winning the state would put JFK in the fast lane to the nomination. Lose, and his road to the White House would become a dreary slog. After his years of planning and hard work, someone like Johnson might saunter in and steal the prize.

Kennedy kicked his West Virginia campaign into high gear. He drew big crowds in small places. He crisscrossed the state, talking to coal miners and steelworkers, seeing poverty like he had never witnessed in the United States. He met families whose children stayed home from school because they didn't have food to eat or clothes to wear.

West Virginia's economy depended on coal, but mining jobs were disappearing. In 1950, more than 120,000 residents were coal miners. By 1960, the number had dropped to 40,000. In more than a third of the state's fifty-five counties, at least 15 percent of families received some kind of government assistance.

Kennedy dialed up his passion on poverty and low-income economic issues. That was usually Humphrey's territory, but politically, the men had a lot in common. Both advocated for raising the minimum wage, additional job training programs, and government-sponsored health care.

But Kennedy had a ten-point plan to expand economic opportunities and relieve suffering, while stimulating the coal industry at the same time. And he was going to promote it at every campaign stop in West Virginia.

Kennedy was truly moved by the poverty he witnessed in parts of the state, and emotional about what needed to be done. One of his proposals was using America's "huge food surpluses . . . to feed hungry people." Another was channeling more federal money into West Virginia.

At a campaign stop in Charleston, Kennedy told his supporters that the federal government had to do more to help—and they had to do it now. "Jobless men and hungry families can't wait for long run plans to work out—they want to eat every day, not just in the long run," Kennedy said.

But that wasn't enough. At the same time, the government had to work on permanent solutions to "the deep-rooted causes of these economic troubles," Kennedy said. "The depression in West Virginia—and it is just that—has gone on far too long."

Kennedy used a medical analogy to drive home the point. "When a man is bleeding, you first stop the flow of blood. But you also go on to heal his wound," he said.

Joe Kennedy's money paid for publicity. The Massachusetts senator's name and face were everywhere—in newspapers, magazines, on television, billboards, and buses. That wasn't enough. The campaign wanted to capitalize on JFK's good looks and promote his accomplishments at the same time. So they produced a short film, which reminded voters about his heroics during World War II. Then they bought broadcast time to show the documentary on television stations. But it was unclear whether the song and dance would translate into votes. It felt like more help was needed.

West Virginia had a long, dark history of corruption. Shady election deals were a way of life in the state—a way for the powerful to choose who would hold public office, and make a lot of money at the same time.

A shark like Joe Kennedy felt right at home in those murky waters. He knew that political bosses in each county—usually the sheriff—sold their services to the highest bidder. He just had to find ways to get money to the right people without drawing attention.

In West Virginia, candidates who contributed the most money to political bosses in each county—usually the sheriff—were "slated," meaning their names appeared on sample ballots given out to voters. Sometimes, a candidate's attempt to get slated for a particular position would turn into a bidding war.

County power brokers were paid as much as $3 for every vote they delivered. They said many voters lived in rural areas and didn't have a ride to the polls, so the bosses hired buses and jitneys to haul them there and back. Their kickback was said to cover the voters' transportation costs.

Humphrey witnessed the stunning corruption. When a campaign adviser explained slating to him, Humphrey was appalled. His campaign didn't have money to pay bills let alone political bosses.

Before speaking at an event in Franklin, a judge approached Humphrey. He said he supported the Minnesota senator, but that didn't matter. Humphrey was going to lose.

Humphrey was a little puzzled. Even though JFK was blanketing the state with advertising, Humphrey was still doing well in the polls.

And while Humphrey's campaign barely had enough money to cover expenses, he was drawing large, enthusiastic crowds.

The judge said none of that mattered. "Kennedy is going to be slated and he is going to carry the state," he said.

The judge's words shook Humphrey and made him more determined to win the primary.

The Kennedy campaign didn't limit itself to the old tried-and-true schemes. This campaign was about religion, so Joe Kennedy enlisted an old friend, Richard Cardinal Cushing of the Archdiocese of Boston. Cushing had officiated at Kennedy's marriage to Jacqueline Lee Bouvier in 1953 and had baptized several of Joe's brood. The two men devised an ingenious plan where the tithes and offerings of Boston Catholics would go to pay off Protestant preachers and pastors all over the Mountaineer State.

The plan was simple. All the cash donated by the faithful of the Catholic Archdiocese of Boston during a particular Sunday would be quietly passed to Joe Kennedy. Joe would then write a check to the archdiocese that would more than cover the amount collected in the Boston churches.

Joe could then infuse his son's campaign with untraceable cash, while taking an enormous tax deduction for his "charitable donation."

Joe and Cushing then decided which ministers in key parts of West Virginia should receive "offerings" of $100 to $500 (about $1,000 to $5,000 today) in exchange for urging their flocks to support JFK.

(Years later Humphrey would write that Cushing told him how he and Joe sent money to West Virginia clergy, saying, "It's good for the church. It's good for the preacher, and it's good for the candidate.")

The candidate, of course, was Jack Kennedy, who was fighting for his political life. At the beginning of the West Virginia campaign, JFK's speechwriters were warned not to mention religion. He wanted to avoid the topic to focus on policy issues. But in the last two weeks, his campaign abandoned its defensive stance. No, it was time for a new campaign strategy, especially with some Protestant clergy questioning the loyalty of America's Catholics.

JFK began responding more forcefully to questions about his religion. Instead of avoiding the subject, he attacked it head-on—sometimes with righteous indignation.

At a speech at Bethany College, a Disciples of Christ school, a heckler asked how JFK could reconcile being a Catholic—under orders from the pope—and president.

"I don't take orders from above. I am going to go to church where I want, regardless of whether I'm elected president or not," Kennedy said.

"What is objectionable," the Associated Press reported, "was action by the State to make church conformity compulsory."

One of the first times JFK addressed the issue was during a campaign event in Morgantown. "Nobody asked me if I was a Catholic when I joined the United States Navy and nobody asked my brother if he was a Catholic or a Protestant before he climbed into an American bomber plane to fly his last mission," he said.

At an American Society of Newspaper Editors luncheon in Washington on April 21, Kennedy complained that newspapers gave too much attention to his religion in the Wisconsin primary. And they were doing it again in West Virginia. "I do not speak for the Catholic Church on issues of public policy—and no one in that Church speaks for me," Kennedy told the group.

West Virginia voters "had hardly given the issue a thought until they read in the newspapers that it was an issue in the campaign," Kennedy said.

"There are many serious problems in that state—problems big enough to dominate any campaign. But religion is not one of them. I do not think that religion is the decisive issue in any state. I do not think it should be," he told the newspaper editors.

JFK's message was clear—and broadcast all over the country on the evening news: How dare you doubt my loyalty to the United States?

The next day, newspapers not only ran front-page articles about his speech, but they began writing editorials, too.

"Sen. John Kennedy, the Massachusetts Catholic, obviously has decided he cannot soft-pedal the religious issue in his campaign for the Democratic presidential nomination," the *Chattanooga Daily Times* board wrote. "He has become almost brutal in his efforts to dredge it up, to dissect it in full public view, and, hopefully, to bury it once and for all.

"His tightly controlled and yet intensely emotional statement to the American Society of Newspaper Editors on Thursday was perhaps the frankest statement ever made on the subject by a major candidate under similar circumstances . . . There was not a single question when he finished, but there was tremendous applause . . . Religious intolerance should have no place at all in a free and democratic society's political processes, but the truth is it continues to live in narrow minds and small souls, ready to dictate the possessors' actions in all fields."

But the West Virginia campaign continued to grow uglier. Kennedy issued a statement to the media, saying Humphrey had attacked his integrity and distorted his record. The news release added that if Humphrey was nominated as the Democratic presidential candidate, Nixon would be the next president of the United States.

Now the gloves were off. Humphrey hit Kennedy for his lavish spending. But Humphrey's campaign was scraping for cash. As they did in Wisconsin, Kennedy's glamorous family and friends fanned out over the state. So did Joe Kennedy's bagmen.

Logan County political boss Raymond Chafin told a Kennedy campaign operative he needed "thirty-five." He meant $3,500, but the courier brought him $35,000. When he called the Kennedy team to report the error, he was told to keep the money and put it to good use, so Chafin spent it all.

Another Logan County political operative, Claude "Big Daddy" Ellis, received $50,000. He joked that Kennedy didn't buy West Virginia, "he just rented it for a day."

Other stories spread around the state about corruption. Massachusetts congressman Tip O'Neill, who had taken over Jack Kennedy's old congressional seat, said a successful real estate man from Boston made the rounds of sheriffs' offices in critical counties to deliver a Kennedy sales pitch. He gave one sheriff up to $5,000, and promised great things for West Virginia if Kennedy was elected—and a cash bonus for the sheriff if Kennedy carried his county.

It was a good time to be a West Virginia county sheriff. Several enjoyed weekends of glitzy gambling at Paul "Skinny" D'Amato's 500 Club in Atlantic City, paid for by Sam Giancana.

Meanwhile, Kennedy's pal Frank Sinatra was moving mysterious bags of cash around.

"If you want to see what a million dollars in cash looks like, go into the next room, there's a brown leather satchel in the closet, open it. It's a gift from the hotel owners for Jack's campaign," Rat Packer Peter Lawford told Sammy Davis Jr. But Davis declined, saying there were some things "you don't want to know."

Sinatra seemed to enjoy his bagman gig. He had an actor friend retrieve a satchel from his car one day and had the man peek inside. It was filled with hundred-dollar bills wrapped in plastic. Sinatra said it was organized crime money for JFK's campaign. "Don't worry about it. There's more where that came from," he said.

It was a big problem for Humphrey, who saw his lead slipping in the polls. If that wasn't enough, Kennedy then trotted out Franklin Delano Roosevelt Jr., whose father was credited with helping save the state during the Great Depression. A Kennedy supporter, FDR Jr. stumped for Kennedy in the Mountaineer State. He spoke passionately about JFK's qualifications and finished by asking where Humphrey was during World War II.

Reporters all over the state began writing stories about FDR Jr.'s allegations that Humphrey was a draft dodger. Those claims were inaccurate. And Kennedy denied putting Roosevelt up to saying that, but it didn't stop Roosevelt from repeating the insinuation at other campaign events.

Meanwhile, Kennedy was sharpening his own attacks. At one rally, JFK told supporters that Humphrey should just drop out of the race. There was no way he'd get the nomination. The only reason he was still in the race, Kennedy said, was to stop him. Or maybe it was to help

Lyndon Johnson. "If Johnson and the other candidates want your vote in the November election, why don't they have enough respect for you to come here and ask for your vote in the primary?" he asked.

With so much at stake, Kennedy and Humphrey attacked each other instead of addressing the issues. Humphrey was the champion of the common man. He had labor union support and Protestant beliefs. West Virginia should have been his stronghold, but Kennedy threw up one obstacle after another. Humphrey, known as "the Happy Warrior," started turning bitter.

"I can't afford to run through this state with a little black bag and a check book," he told a crowd outside a courthouse in Kingwood. "I can hardly afford to drive around in that bus, much less buy an airplane."

His family hadn't seen him in weeks. He had raided the savings account for his daughter's wedding to pay for campaign printing bills.

The candidates' bare-knuckle attacks just days before the primary could only mean one thing: West Virginia was still up for grabs.

COUNTDOWN: **186 DAYS**

May 7, 1960
Washington, D.C.

It seemed all Vice President Richard Nixon had to do was sit back and watch while Kennedy and Humphrey battled it out in West Virginia for the Democratic vote. Nixon, the Republican heir apparent, got little news coverage. He was a lame-duck vice president in a lame-duck administration. No one took any interest.

To the public, Nixon appeared confident. But he was worried—not because of the Democrats. No, he was concerned Nelson Rockefeller might use the U-2 spy plane debacle to move a step closer to running for the GOP presidential nomination.

The Soviet Union had just announced that the spy plane pilot, Francis Gary Powers, was alive and uninjured. Apparently he had ejected and parachuted to safety.

In the pursuit of détente, Soviet premier Khrushchev said he'd consider releasing Powers—if Eisenhower apologized for the spy plane program. Otherwise, Powers would undergo a trial for espionage. Ike refused to issue a formal apology to the Soviet Union.

All this back-and-forth played into the hands of Rockefeller, a staunch anti-communist. Rockefeller was making speeches, blaming the Eisenhower administration for the rise of global communism—meaning the Soviet Union. He said communists were making inroads all over the world.

Rockefeller said the United States should form a Western Hemisphere economic union through the United Nations, and America should give NATO—the North Atlantic Treaty Organization—oversight of its nuclear arsenal. NATO was created after World War II, when the Soviets were installing puppet regimes in Eastern European nations that had been conquered by Germany. NATO was designed to halt the Soviet Union's westward expansion. An attack on one of the NATO nations would be considered an attack on all of them.

Rockefeller insisted his speeches were not criticizing the administration. Journalists—and Nixon—were skeptical.

But Rockefeller had support. Some Republicans were pushing Rockefeller to jump into the race. They believed he was progressive enough, had enough charisma—and, more important, enough money—to counter a possible John F. Kennedy campaign.

Kennedy's old man was rich, but his fortune was small change compared with the legendary Rockefeller wealth. And although Nelson's last name had been synonymous with his grandfather John D. Rockefeller's ruthless business tactics, later generations created major philanthropic institutions and movements, from the Rockefeller University (originally the Rockefeller Institute for Medical Research) to the New York City community gardens movement.

Nelson had been an art collector and president of Rockefeller Center in New York City before he took his first federal job in 1940. He was a Republican in a Democratic administration, proof that he could work across the aisle—something the GOP could use in the 1960 presidential contest.

He was affable and poised, with a broad, international view, the popular choice of progressive Republicans. The "Let's draft Rockefeller" rumors were for real.

One such movement had just begun in Maine. Attorney Henry Fuller, a Rockefeller classmate at Dartmouth College, placed a full-page advertisement in the *Portland Evening Express* calling for "Republicans anxious to draft Rockefeller" to write him letters to gauge their interest.

"I've had an excellent response," Fuller said, adding, "You know as well as I do that Vice President Nixon has absolutely no appeal to the uncommitted vote . . . or the independent vote. No Democrat would ever vote for Nixon."

Without support from these "swing voters," it would be nearly impossible to win the presidency, he said. Fuller predicted that Republicans in other states would follow his lead.

Rockefeller was coy. When asked about his plans, Rockefeller said, "Dick Nixon has been a very good friend of mine for many years. He has done an absolutely superb job as vice president."

But asked if he would support Nixon, Rockefeller simply stated he wouldn't support any candidate before the convention.

Rockefeller was a problem, Nixon thought. But there was truth in what he said about the Soviet Union. Just look at Cuba. Fidel Castro was clasping hands with the communists. Nixon understood that was probably the only way Castro could save his regime, since the United States was on the verge of severing diplomatic relations with Havana.

But right now, the spy plane incident—and Rockefeller's next move—concerned Nixon more than Castro or Cuba or anything else on the campaign trail.

Rockefeller and Kennedy belonged to different political parties. But both had been hammering the administration on the missile gap, saying the United States had failed to keep up with the Soviet Union.

They charged that the United States had fallen behind the Soviet Union on just about every front, including math, education, and science.

Kennedy promised a tough stance against the Soviet Union and international communism. The United States had not kept apace with the growing Soviet military. He warned of the Soviets' growing arsenal of intercontinental ballistic missiles and pledged to revitalize American nuclear forces.

He proposed a range of programs to try to stop the spread of communism, including a buildup of conventional weaponry to give the nation's military more flexibility.

Rockefeller was saying the same thing. Not a good sign for Nixon's campaign. After all, he was part of the administration that was under fire from both sides.

Time and again, Eisenhower said there was no missile gap. But now he had to defend America's spy plane program. This was a sensational development.

Ike said publicly he was upset over the Soviet reaction to the U-2 incident, insisting its mission over Russia wasn't a "provocative act." He said the United States needed to gather intelligence on Soviet weapons so they wouldn't be caught by surprise. "No one wants another Pearl Harbor," he said.

Nixon agreed with Eisenhower and defended reconnaissance flights over the Soviet Union. "The United States cannot afford any gap in its intelligence," he said during a TV interview.

The vice president didn't know how it would play out on the campaign trail. But he was confident that the American people would back Eisenhower.

Nixon just hoped that he could contain the fallout, and that Rockefeller would honor his promise to stay out of the presidential race.

But Nixon knew that in politics, anything could happen.

COUNTDOWN: **183 DAYS**

The green country outside Washington, D.C., spooled out below the *Caroline*, John F. Kennedy's private Convair 240 aircraft. The candidate was headed home as West Virginia voters headed to the polls.

JFK leaned back in his seat and closed his eyes. The plane was a smart idea. He could hop from one campaign event to another. It certainly gave him an edge over poor old Hubert Humphrey, who traveled in that sad bus. And if JFK won West Virginia and everything went as planned, Humphrey would be gone. Then Richard Nixon would be his only obstacle to the White House.

But it was too early to think about that. West Virginia was on Kennedy's mind. He had spent the last few days making speech after speech until he finally lost his voice altogether. It wasn't the first time he suffered from laryngitis on the campaign trail. His doctor ordered him to stop talking.

So, Kennedy had taken to writing notes on legal pads or scribbling on the back of envelopes or any paper he could find at his desk toward the back of the plane. That section of the *Caroline* was off-limits to reporters who traveled with him.

Janet DesRosiers was one of the few people who had access. She had been his father's secretary—and mistress—for nearly a decade. When Joseph Kennedy hired her, she was a beautiful twenty-four-year-old—a perfect target. She was tall, with green eyes, brown hair, and long legs.

After ending her affair with Joe, DesRosiers took a job in aircraft sales, but kept in touch. Joe contacted her in late 1959 to buy the Convair 240 for Jack's campaign—and to have her come aboard as the plane's stewardess and Jack's airborne "Girl Friday." She said yes.

Now DesRosiers traveled with the Kennedy entourage, providing food and drinks for the senator and whatever reporters, campaign workers, or family members flew with him.

Jack Kennedy wasn't sleeping with her—but that didn't mean he didn't try. Early in the campaign, he'd handed her a napkin with the message "Don't you think it's about time you found me attractive?" She rejected his advances.

The pair shared their own kind of intimacy. DesRosiers occasionally massaged JFK's tired shoulders, neck, and feet—just like she'd done for his father. She stood by with legal pads or notebooks so he could communicate without speaking. And he wrote little notes to her, commenting on his day, the people he met, and the women whose company he enjoyed.

DesRosiers was a skilled secretary. She would sit with Kennedy at his desk on the plane, taking dictation and clearing away the crumpled notes Kennedy scrawled during telephone calls and discussions.

She kept them. Years later, presidential historians enjoyed these enlightening snippets of political gossip, speech ideas, and just a bit of braggadocio: "I got into the blondes."

Kennedy needed rest. West Virginia had been exhausting. He had planned a quiet evening at his Georgetown home with Jackie. His friend Benjamin Bradlee, a journalist with *Newsweek*, was coming over with his wife for dinner.

Hubert Humphrey was just as drained. The weather was dreary and wet—like Humphrey's mood.

The campaign had opened wounds that would take a long time to heal. Humphrey's reputation had taken a major hit. His positive, upbeat personality had taken a bitter turn. The primary season should have been about the issues, but instead he'd been dragged down into something personal, ugly, and grubby. He could do nothing about it now. Tonight he would know.

At the Kennedys' house, the couples finished dinner and headed to the movies to pass the time. Bradlee was surprised when Kennedy took them to the Plaza Theatre, a place that often showed racy movies. The night's feature, *Private Property*, was about a sex-crazed woman who falls in with violent gangsters. A strange choice, Bradlee thought. After the movie, they headed back to the Kennedys' house and waited for the election results.

No one knew how it would turn out. Some predicted Kennedy would win—but it would be close. If that happened, Humphrey would stay in the race. If Humphrey won, Robert Kennedy knew his brother's race was over. Not even their father's money would be able to save JFK's campaign.

When the early returns started coming in, it was clear that Humphrey was going to lose. The only question was by how much. Would it be another Wisconsin or a landslide?

They didn't have to wait long. Kennedy trounced Humphrey—61 percent to 39 percent. His resounding victory proved a Catholic could carry a predominantly Protestant state. Of course, nothing was mentioned in the media about the Kennedy campaign's shady tactics.

When Kennedy got the call from his brother, he let out a loud cheer, despite the damage to his voice, and opened a bottle of champagne.

Humphrey spent the evening in misery. He decided to concede defeat and withdraw from the race for the Democratic presidential nomination. He would go back to Minnesota and focus on his Senate reelection.

Humphrey simply could not compete with Kennedy's deep pockets. Humphrey spent $25,000 for the entire West Virginia primary. Kennedy spent $34,000 on television ads alone.

Kennedy was jubilant. He told reporters that West Virginia proved that voters were interested in the issues. Maybe his victory would go a long way in dispelling the notion that a Catholic couldn't win the presidency.

This wasn't a state with many Catholics. No, this was a state that was overwhelmingly Protestant—and he still won big.

Now only one real contender remained: Lyndon Johnson. The Texas senator had not campaigned in a single primary. He trusted the old-fashioned backroom politics that always worked for him.

And Lyndon Johnson was a powerful old pol with his own bag of dirty tricks.

May 14, 1960
College Park, Maryland

Florence Kater was a decent, God-fearing woman. She was fed up with Jack Kennedy's hypocrisy, sick and tired of the wholesome family-man image plastered on billboards and TV screens.

She knew better. Jack Kennedy was a low-down adulterer, a slap in the face to good Catholics everywhere. It was her duty to show her proof to the world, to shout out the dirty truth.

But few wanted to know. Kennedy himself had shooed her away, and threatened her husband's government contractor job. She sent dozens of letters to the media, as well as competitors' campaigns. Her "proof" was not very convincing. No one followed up.

So when a "Kennedy for President" rally came to the University of Maryland, Florence Kater turned up with a poster-sized blowup of the "damning photograph," ready to do battle in public.

Kater's frustration dated back two years, to July 1958. She and her husband, Leonard, rented out the upper floor of their town house to Pamela Turnure, a pretty young receptionist who worked in Senator Kennedy's D.C. office.

The Katers were pleased to have an agreeable, trouble-free tenant upstairs in their quiet home in a leafy suburban neighborhood.

But they were soon disillusioned. Late one night, Leonard noticed Senator Kennedy paying a visit upstairs. He didn't leave until early the next morning.

Leonard didn't think anything of it. But then it happened again. The senator kept coming back.

The Katers were suspicious. The visits couldn't be work related—not at those hours. They assumed the worst.

The Katers were proud Irish Americans and strict Catholics who had supported Kennedy's rise to power. But the senator's apparent immorality—and Turnure's participation—was deeply offensive to them.

The Katers needed proof. So they placed a tape recorder to listen in on Turnure's apartment and soon had audio tapes of a man and woman having sex.

The Katers didn't do anything with the tapes.

Florence Kater confronted Turnure with her behavior, and the young woman agreed to move out.

She found a new house a few blocks away. Florence was anxious to know if the affair was still going on. So on July 11, 1958, she and her husband decided to stake out the new apartment.

Florence said they'd hoped to shock Kennedy by taking photos, to rattle him from his infidelities and convince him to be faithful to his wife. She never wanted to harm anyone.

Just like clockwork, there he was! Kennedy went into Turnure's house. And at 1:00 a.m., Kennedy sauntered back out. The Katers approached him. Florence told him he should be ashamed of himself. Leonard, camera in hand, clicked a frame. JFK shielded his face with a handkerchief, but the Katers had the shot they wanted. He knew they were onto him. They waited to see if his behavior would change.

But the Katers misjudged Kennedy. He wasn't chastened. He was angry.

A few days after they'd snapped the photo, Kennedy stopped the Katers on the street and scolded them. Waving his index finger in their faces, he told them his whereabouts were none of their business and issued a warning: If they didn't stop harassing him or repeating their lies, Florence's husband might find himself on the unemployment line.

Florence Kater, filled with righteous conviction, said no. She wasn't going away. The senator should know better. He should have some morals. She said he was a disappointment to her.

If Kennedy was angry then, he was livid after Florence sent copies of the photograph—along with a letter detailing Kennedy's extramarital affair—to fifty journalists and influential politicians in Washington and New York.

Sure, the photo was blurry and Kennedy's face wasn't clearly visible. Florence didn't have experience sending news stories to reporters. But there were millions of devout parishioners in America who would agree that Kennedy's adultery disqualified him from the White House. Voters ought to know, she thought. He was unrepentant. She was duty bound to tell America what she knew.

Polls by Lou Harris showed that Kennedy's image as a family man was central to his presidential run. Voters believed that JFK was a faithful husband with an attractive wife and cute young daughter. Kater's story could destroy his career.

So Kennedy sent in his "fixer," according to reporter Sy Hersh.

A former FBI agent, James McInerney was a no-nonsense kind of guy. More important, he was discreet. Joe Kennedy would call him when there was potential trouble. McInerny paid the Katers several visits, each time with the same message: Stop trying to distribute the photograph—or else.

Most surprising of all was the media reaction to the Katers' mass mailing. In the weeks that followed, not a single outlet responded. No one took it seriously. Maybe Kennedy quashed it, they thought, or paid off the editors. Maybe they'd painted Florence as a religious kook. And then there was the unwritten rule that Washington reporters didn't delve into public figures' private lives.

Still, even if no one else wanted to know the truth, they'd gotten Kennedy's attention.

Florence was fired up with righteousness. If the news media wouldn't cooperate, she wasn't going to shut up. This was too important. She had to stand up, take this to the public, and personally show the world that

Kennedy was cheating on his wife—confront them with the question: Is this tomcat the man you want in the White House?

And that's why she was here, at the University of Maryland rally, with her signpost. She wanted to show people that Kennedy was a womanizer. She made her way inside the noisy university gymnasium, jammed with four thousand students who had turned out to hear Kennedy talk about the upcoming Maryland and Oregon primaries. After that, he was on the road to Los Angeles—and the Democratic National Convention.

Kennedy had been racking up wins. By the time he got to the convention, he'd have all the delegates he needed to be nominated on the first ballot.

Earlier in the day, JFK had been greeted by big, enthusiastic crowds at several stops throughout the state. During one rally, Kennedy had told the audience the presidency should be a "place of moral leadership—the place for setting the unfinished business of the country before the people."

Kennedy was confident. There was a "new sureness in his bearing, a new ring to his sentences that were not in evidence in his previous appearances here," a *Baltimore Sun* reporter wrote.

Screaming women treated JFK like a rock star. "I want to touch him," one young woman shrieked.

At the University of Maryland, students were energetic, laughing at every joke and applauding every campaign promise.

The big victory in West Virginia, Kennedy said, had buried the Catholic issue "eight feet underground. Now it is possible to discuss the one great issue—the Presidency itself," he said. The crowd cheered.

From her place on the gymnasium floor, Florence Kater raised her sign and heckled Kennedy. But she was quickly drowned out.

The crowd took up the chant: "It looks like Tricky Dick. It looks like Tricky Dick," and security guards took Kater by the elbow and escorted her out of the gym.

Didn't these people realize this charlatan wasn't who he said he was?

He was betraying his family, insulting his faith, taking advantage of a young woman. Didn't they care about his wife, Jacqueline?

Kater sighed. Scripture is full of stories of truth-tellers whose warnings were ignored. She decided to head home. Maybe this was the wrong venue. Maybe someone would listen at the next rally. She promised the Lord she'd keep trying. History was on her side.

Florence felt a flicker of hope when she saw the next edition of *The Washington Star.* Mention was made of a heckler in the audience at the university rally, and the following day photographers knocked on the Katers' door. They said the Kennedy campaign told them the picture she was carrying was a fake created by Christian zealots.

They wanted to know her story—where did they take the photo? Who was involved? Florence Kater was excited to tell it all. They seemed to believe her. Maybe this would be her big break.

But the interview came to nothing. Kennedy had too much power in D.C. Weeks went by. Florence Kater knew she'd tried her best and done the right thing. She put away her posters, tapes, and photos.

COUNTDOWN: **150 DAYS**

June 12, 1960
Washington, D.C.

The Republican National Convention was a month and a half away, and New York governor Rockefeller was playing political games. Rockefeller had said at the end of 1959 that he wasn't a candidate for the Republican presidential nomination. He wouldn't challenge Nixon for the nomination. But that was then. For months, Rockefeller had been reconsidering his position, thanks to two new advisers: Emmet Hughes, a speechwriter who'd recently left the Eisenhower administration, and Henry Kissinger, a Harvard government professor who was Rockefeller's chief foreign policy adviser.

Now Rockefeller was running a shadow campaign, hoping to be "drafted" at the convention by popular acclaim as the Republican nominee instead of Nixon.

Rockefeller knew it would take a miracle to pull it off, but snatching the nomination away from the vice president was still possible.

Wendell Willkie had managed it twenty years earlier. A few weeks before the 1940 convention he had zero delegates. He was an attorney, the president of a power company. After Republicans heard him eloquently criticize New Deal programs, Willkie skyrocketed to national prominence. Wendell Willkie for President clubs sprouted up all over the country—and that groundswell of support led to Willkie landing the Republican presidential nomination. No matter that Franklin D. Roosevelt trounced Willkie in the general election.

Rockefeller was throwing shade on President Eisenhower's record. His defense policies exposed the United States to danger, Rockefeller said—but his real target was Nixon. The governor said the vice president had never clearly expressed his views on important issues.

The American people have the right to know from Nixon "precisely where he stands. I have stated my position on the questions I have posed. I invite the vice president to state his," Rockefeller said.

Only Rockefeller knew why he was taking this route. His attempts to capture the nomination had created confusion just when the GOP was trying to foster unity.

A few days earlier, Rockefeller had breakfast with Eisenhower at the White House. He spent most of the meal attacking Nixon, but afterward he disclosed details in a news release that touted his pet initiatives: federal aid for education, medical assistance to the elderly under Social Security. The list went on and on—like he was on the campaign trail, barnstorming in another city in another state, trying to drum up local media attention.

Eisenhower felt used. He didn't want his name attached to any Nixon-Rockefeller electioneering. Rockefeller clearly relished the "spoiler" role and loved to needle the humorless vice president.

Nixon was the odds-on favorite for the Republican presidential nomination. It was standard practice for Republican governors to endorse the heir apparent, but Rockefeller refused to follow tradition. Rockefeller said he was waiting for Nixon to "articulate his vision of America."

Rockefeller's people didn't think Republicans could beat the Democrats just by running on President Eisenhower's record. They wanted the party to adopt a more liberal platform.

The governor had big money and plenty of support. A few delegates might spark a "Draft Rockefeller" movement, and that might spread like wildfire. He could ruin everything for Nixon.

Back in January, Nixon hadn't minded answering queries about his potential rival. "Nelson and I have been friends for a long time," Nixon the statesman had said, over and over. "We both want the same thing: A Republican in the White House."

But by June, Nixon was growing peevish, weary of the uncertainty. Was Rockefeller in? Was he out? What did he want?

Meanwhile, Rockefeller told the world he was worried about the United States. The nation was in crisis. A U-2 spy plane had been shot down over the Soviet Union. A summit in Paris between U.S. and Soviet leaders had been scuttled because of fallout from the crisis. Communists were gaining a foothold in the Western Hemisphere—and Richard Nixon didn't have the skills to lead the nation, or inspire the world.

A few days after his breakfast meeting with Ike, the governor phoned Eisenhower at the White House.

He told the president he was thinking of throwing his hat in the ring and asked for his advice on whether he should run.

Eisenhower hesitated. If the New York governor challenged Nixon, it could divide the party. Ike understood that Nixon wasn't easy to like. Hell, he had spent eight years working with him. By now, he knew his vice president's strengths and weaknesses. Personality wasn't one of Nixon's selling points. But the president was a good judge of character. And he saw how hard Nixon worked on behalf of the administration and GOP candidates around the country. As he told a cabinet official, Nixon was gaining exposure and people were looking up to him.

So, Ike used a little psychology. He reminded Rockefeller that he had quit the race once before. And even if Rockefeller could get someone to put his name up at the convention, did he really think he had a shot?

Eisenhower told Rockefeller that if he tried to wrestle the nomination away from Nixon, it would divide the party. Maybe even cost the GOP the White House in the fall. And that, Ike said, would hurt the New York governor's reputation in the party. He could become a pariah.

He trusted Nelson's common sense. He didn't want Rockefeller to hurt his standing within the party. And Eisenhower reminded Rockefeller of something else. If by some chance Nixon lost in November, Rockefeller would be the favorite heading into 1964.

Rockefeller thanked Ike for his counsel, but he knew he had to decide this on his own. He appeared on morning talk shows and assured everyone that he was a loyal Republican and that he was not trying to block Nixon's nomination.

But, he said, the presidency was the most important job in the land. If he was drafted by the convention, he'd run.

Nixon was furious. Rockefeller was ready to undermine his candidacy, and he had powerful supporters.

L. Judson Morhouse, chairman of New York's Republican Party, argued that Rockefeller had widespread national appeal. He urged New York's ninety-six delegates to stay uncommitted. He said the New York governor had to run.

New York Republican senator Jacob Javits challenged Nixon to prove "that his thinking is modern and forward looking, and is not rooted in a stand-pat attitude."

The New York Times said Rockefeller's attack "is as clear and unequivocal a declaration of his candidacy . . . and the platform on which he is running as it is possible for him to issue without actually using the words themselves."

Rockefeller's more cynical supporters believed that his only goal was to weaken Nixon enough for him to lose in November and clear the way for his own presidential run in 1964.

It was a lot of hot air and "maybe," but Nixon took it seriously. He had to address Rockefeller's criticisms. Until he did, he'd be hounded by the media. So, during a campaign stop in Camden, New Jersey, Nixon held a news conference. He told reporters that he sharply disagreed with Rockefeller's view that the vice president hadn't articulated his positions on important issues.

And then he dropped a bombshell. He invited the New York governor to publicly meet with him to have an in-depth discussion about his views. Was Nixon challenging Rockefeller to a debate? At least that's what the broadcast journalists at the news conference thought. Several jumped at the opportunity to host it. They quickly offered their studios for the event.

The following day, Nixon was greeted with a standing ovation when he walked into a breakfast session of the Republican National Committee.

He talked to them about the possible impact the internecine drama would have for the GOP. Nixon said party unity was the key to keeping the White House.

"We have ahead of us the fight of our life," Nixon told the group. "We will win if we are united. We will lose if we are divided. I hope we can discuss the issues and disagree without being disagreeable."

Nothing worthwhile ever comes easy; Nixon knew if he stuck to his plan and minimized the drama, maybe Rockefeller would flame out. All would be well, he told himself.

COUNTDOWN: **127 DAYS**

July 5, 1960
Washington, D.C.

John Kennedy was still a senator for Massachusetts, but he let his legislative duties slide while he campaigned for president. Meanwhile, Lyndon Johnson, the Senate majority leader from Texas, zealously showed up for work each day in Washington, even as he calculated his own run for the White House.

Johnson took his time. He focused his strategy not on the primaries but on the Democratic convention. He set the gears turning in the spring and watched his support slowly take shape. While Kennedy battled it out with his rivals, Johnson played the statesman.

Newspaper columnists and editorial boards agreed that Johnson was Kennedy's biggest threat. The old fox knew how to block an early Kennedy nomination.

In the beginning of June, the editorial page of the *Orlando Evening Star* said, "We find it significant that Kennedy's strength has been shown in primaries in which he had little real opposition, or at least not the kind of opposition which could be given by a forceful conservative such as Lyndon B. Johnson."

The paper declared that no Democrat could win the presidency without the support of the South.

The *Orlando Evening Star* was one of nineteen newspapers that backed Johnson for the Democratic presidential nomination. In 1960, that was a significant boost to any candidate.

"The times call for a man who has demonstrated qualities of leadership, who has experience and judgment, a man of vitality and courage, and patriotism that rises above partisanship," one editor wrote.

Another added that "Lyndon Johnson, in our opinion, has those qualities to a greater degree than any other potential nominee in his party."

Johnson basked in the praise. It enticed him to announce a presidential run.

"He [Johnson] has hesitated to do this [announce], perhaps because he is not completely sure in his own mind, but more likely because there has been extremely urgent business in the U.S. Senate, and that he felt his duty to the country was to stay in Washington and work, rather than to devote his time to a personal campaign," the *Orlando Evening Star* gushed in another editorial.

Kennedy's strategy was to campaign and win the primaries, and it worked. By one estimate, Kennedy already had 698 delegates of the 761 needed to capture the nomination. Johnson had 449, though—when he wasn't even an official candidate.

"Considering that Sen. Johnson has made no campaign, has not even announced, we think this is remarkable," the *Orlando Evening Star* noted.

The newspaper said they believed the real contest wasn't between Kennedy and Humphrey or Senator Stuart Symington or Adlai Stevenson. No, Johnson was the man to beat.

"We think Lyndon Johnson can win, therefore, if the South remains united, there are solid reasons why we should back Senator Johnson," the newspaper said. "He is a Southerner. He is a leader, a conservative, a man interested in preserving the rights of states. He is capable and experienced, a man with executive and legislative abilities."

Johnson's friends pushed him to enter the race.

Speaker of the House Sam Rayburn, another Texan, worked behind the scenes for Johnson. Rayburn's influence reached into almost every congressional district represented by a Democrat. Johnson was the only politician who could stop Kennedy, Rayburn said.

A strange thing started to happen. Despite all of Jack Kennedy's campaigning and Bobby's direction, with all of Joe's money, power, and influence, a powerful coalition began forming around Johnson.

Maybe it was the fact that some in party leadership didn't think Kennedy could win in the general election. Or maybe it was the long-term relationships that Johnson had developed over the years. But something was happening.

Columnist David Lawrence said a battle was brewing behind the scenes over who would land the Democratic presidential nomination.

"The public generally isn't aware of the struggle," he wrote. "The results of the inside fighting, moreover, are not always visible to the naked eye. But the tacticians working vigorously on behalf of Senators John Kennedy and Lyndon Johnson are playing their respective trump cards with all the resourcefulness known to politicians."

And Lawrence discovered that "more and more state leaders, especially members of Congress on the Democratic side, are saying privately that they believe the country will be much more likely to elect a man with the maturity and legislative experience of Sen. Lyndon Johnson than to take a chance on the youth and relative inexperience of the Massachusetts senator."

With the wind at his back—and little time before the convention—Johnson in late June visited six states to gauge his strength. The reality was he had been making these kinds of campaign-style stops over the last two months. At every stop, he didn't lay out his vision for America. No, Kennedy was his target.

New York Times political columnist James Reston noted that Johnson was "doing what he rarely if ever does: he is attacking his Democratic opponents personally."

Johnson brought up Kennedy's response to the U-2 affair—Kennedy had said the president should apologize to the Soviet Union for the debacle. Johnson had jumped on that gaffe at the Washington State Democratic Convention in late May.

"I am not prepared to apologize to Mr. Khrushchev, are you? I am not prepared to send regrets to Mr. Khrushchev, are you?" Johnson shouted to the cheering crowd.

For Johnson, this could be his last chance to run for president. He was a fifty-one-year-old man who had a heart attack in 1955. He did the math. If Kennedy served two terms, Johnson would be sixty when JFK left office. Hell, Johnson didn't know if he'd still be alive at sixty.

Maybe that's why Johnson had embraced the "stop Kennedy" movement. Some political leaders had anointed Kennedy after the West Virginia primary. That rubbed some Democrats the wrong way—especially the ones who believed Nixon would crush Kennedy.

Besides, delegates were the name of the game. And with the reach of political leaders in key states, Johnson had been adding more delegates every day. Rayburn predicted he'd have five hundred by the time he arrived in Los Angeles for the convention. In that scenario, he'd be short by 269 votes.

And as the convention neared, Johnson continued gathering support from more newspapers.

"In his role as majority leader, Lyndon Johnson has displayed a caliber of statesmanship sorely needed in Washington these days," the editorial board of West Virginia's *Wheeling News-Register* wrote. "Senator Johnson has resisted the temptation to resort to political sniping, to practice obstructionist opportunism for the purpose of partisan advantage."

Ads even ran in the liberal *New York Herald Tribune*: "Senator Johnson is unquestionably a man of stature, a master of political statecraft and of compromise, a wizard at the maintenance of unity among warring and divergent forces."

Such praise could go to a man's head, but Johnson kept his feet on the ground. He knew a presidential bid would be a hard battle. Had Kennedy already gained too much momentum? Was Johnson too late to the game?

Slowly, the answer became obvious. His old friend Representative Tip O'Neill of Massachusetts was already pledged to Kennedy on the first ballot. But when Johnson asked O'Neill if he'd consider supporting him on the second ballot, O'Neill's response felt like a gut punch. Forget about a second ballot, he told Johnson. Kennedy had already locked up the magic number.

Johnson was stunned. While he was back in the Capitol doing the country's business, JFK had been collecting delegates.

But if he was going out, it would be in a blaze of glory. Johnson announced his candidacy on July 5. The convention would officially start on July 11.

Not much time to do anything except cause chaos. And that's what Johnson's team did. Back in Washington, John Kennedy ignored the Johnson announcement. He knew it was too little, too late. Johnson was about to discover his old smoke-filled room had been aired out and filled up with Kennedy delegates.

COUNTDOWN: **122 DAYS**

July 10, 1960
Los Angeles, California

The Democratic National Convention was only one day away, and Kennedy was facing a tough audience—six thousand people, most of them Black—crowded into a hot auditorium.

JFK had few Black friends, and not a single top aide on his campaign was Black, but it was time to address this important constituency. If he wanted to win in November, he'd have to bring the Black vote into his coalition.

The throng was gathered for a rally by an influential civil rights group.

Reverend Martin Luther King Jr. was at the National Association for the Advancement of Colored People event in Los Angeles's Shrine Auditorium, as were other leaders of the civil rights movement.

The crowd was surly. They wanted Democrats—and everyone else in the nation—to know they were finished with business as usual.

Many were from the Deep South, where they knew they could be lynched for looking at the wrong person the wrong way. Blacks all over America were finished with casual, systemic racism.

No more segregation. No more bigotry. No more prejudice. No more waiting for a better moment. Blacks didn't want handouts; they wanted to get ahead. They needed better schools, teachers, housing, job opportunities. . . . But how could things ever change if they couldn't vote for candidates who'd represent them?

The people in the audience wanted leaders who would support their fight to change the system. No more status quo. They wanted to hear words of encouragement. They wanted to hear that a new day was on the horizon.

Kennedy's civil rights record was abysmal. For years he had done almost nothing to sponsor legislation that would curtail discriminatory practices in the South, or anywhere else.

Kennedy had lashed out against religious bigotry aimed at Roman Catholics, but that was self-serving, as he was a Catholic himself.

JFK seemed to have little empathy for the plight of Blacks in America. The only Blacks in his orbit were gardeners, maids, or drivers. Kennedy lived in a lily-white world.

And the hypocrisy of some of his causes showed.

Kennedy was outspoken in trying to help people escape oppressive communist regimes. But he was silent when American Blacks spoke out against racist governments at home.

He had met with some prominent Black civil rights leaders during his campaign. He was polite but nervous, rarely making eye contact. They noticed. Jackie Robinson said Kennedy was clearly uneasy around Blacks.

Kennedy was careful to never openly criticize southern state segregation. He thought he couldn't afford to lose the support of white voters.

Since February, Black students all over the South had been trying to desegregate restaurants through sit-ins at whites-only lunch counters. But so far, Kennedy had been silent about the protests.

What did Kennedy believe? No one knew. But civil rights had clearly never been a political priority for Kennedy—until now.

Kennedy had to score enough Black votes to capture the White House. But to some civil rights advocates, it seemed he was more willing to meet with segregationists than with Black leaders. They pointed to that breakfast with Alabama governor John Patterson and his friend Sam Engelhardt Jr., the leader of a racist group. That certainly didn't play well with Black leaders.

Kennedy had met with Reverend King. The pair had breakfast only a few weeks prior at Joe Kennedy's New York City apartment. (The visit had taken place after Black leaders criticized JFK for the breakfast with the Alabama segregationists.) King described the June 23 meeting with Kennedy in a letter to U.S. Representative Chester Bowles of Connecticut, the chair of the Democratic platform committee.

King and Bowles were good friends. He had publicly supported the civil rights leader during the Montgomery, Alabama, bus boycott.

King described his meeting with JFK as "fruitful and rewarding."

King believed Kennedy had "a long intellectual commitment" to civil rights, but hadn't yet developed "the emotional commitment."

"I have no doubt that he would do the right thing on this issue if he were elected president. Of course, I am sure that you have been a great influence on Mr. Kennedy at this point," King wrote in a letter to Bowles. A former ambassador to India, Bowles had reached out to King to urge him to travel there to study Gandhi's nonviolent tactics—even offering to introduce him to the right people.

"It may interest you to know that I had very little enthusiasm for Mr. Kennedy when he first announced his candidacy," King said, adding that he changed his mind after he learned that JFK had asked Bowles to serve as a foreign policy adviser.

"I said to myself, 'If Chester Bowles is Mr. Kennedy's adviser he must be thinking right on the major issues,'" King wrote.

In the letter to Bowles, King also listed what he thought should be the major planks in the Democratic Party's civil rights platform.

King urged that "the 1954 Supreme Court Decision be explicitly endorsed as morally right and the law of the land and that a forthright declaration should be made that the racial segregation and discrimination in any form is unconstitutional, un-American and immoral."

One of his other suggestions was among the most important: That the party endorse the spirit and tactics of the sit-ins as having the same validity as labor strikes.

"These are just some of the things I think are quite significant. I know that most of them would be strongly opposed by the South, but I think they are important enough to at least reach the discussion stage," King wrote.

Now it was time for Kennedy to fill in his blank slate and make the case for why he should be the next president of the United States—and how he'd help Blacks on their journey to social justice.

This wasn't the usual Kennedy crowd, filled with adoring white fans. No, these people were upset at being shut out of the American system. They felt Kennedy didn't take them seriously—and maybe they were right.

When his name was announced, the Massachusetts senator took a deep breath, pushed himself up from his chair, and smiled and waved to the audience as he walked slowly to the podium. He was dressed in a dark blue suit, white button-down shirt, and tie. His hair was neatly brushed to the side.

He walked amid a loud chorus of boos. The catcalls were so loud and long that Clarence Mitchell Jr., an NAACP official, had to intervene.

"Stop it. Stop it, please," he said, adding that they needed to show Kennedy respect.

Kennedy understood why they were booing. He knew he had to win them over. His campaign depended on it.

Kennedy said this was a critical time in American history. He warned that the nation faced issues that would shape America for generations, including civil rights. Kennedy rarely touched civil rights issues on the campaign trail—especially in the South, where segregation was a way of life one hundred years after the Civil War.

But on this day, he did. JFK said he didn't want "second-class citizenship for any American anywhere in this country." Kennedy said they had to find a way to turn America into a "society in which no man has to suffer discrimination based on race into a living reality everywhere in our land. And that means we must secure to every American equal access to all parts of our public life—to the voting booth, to the schoolroom, to jobs, to housing, to all public facilities including lunch counters," he said.

Kennedy paused to scan the audience. They were Black and white and brown, carrying signs that said "Support a Strong Civil Rights Plank," "Judge by Character Not Color," and "We Want Freedom Now." But their eyes weren't wandering around the auditorium. No, they were locked on Kennedy, listening closely to every word.

"The next President of the United States cannot stand above the battle engaging in vague little sermons on brotherhood," he said. Instead the White House needed to use all its power to protect voting rights and end discrimination in schools.

He was on a roll. He had captured everyone's full attention.

"To be sure, there will be protest and disagreement—but if the end result is to be permanent progress instead of frustration, there must be more meetings of men and minds. And the place to begin is the White House itself, where the Chief Executive, with his prestige and influence, should exert firm and positive leadership," he said.

When JFK ended his speech with a promise to end segregation, the crowd went wild. They cheered him, a stark contrast to the boos heard when he'd first stood before the microphones.

After Kennedy, King took the stage. He had been pushing for the Democrats to strengthen the party's civil rights stand. Once again, King spelled out the devastating impact segregation had on Black people's lives. It had to end. It had to end now.

"We want to be free. We are struggling to save the soul of America," King declared.

And he turned his attention to the young people, the future of America. He praised the brave students who had started the sit-ins, risking their freedom and their lives for social justice.

"They have taken the deep groans and passionate protest of their elders and turned them into a force patterned after the Gandhi movement," King said. "We will continue the sit-ins until the national government begins its stand-up for justice."

Now the crowd was on its feet.

"We have a determination to be free in this day and age," King told the crowd. "We want to be free everywhere, free at last, free at last, free at last."

The audience cheered itself hoarse.

Kennedy wondered if King would endorse him, if the passion in the auditorium would translate into votes. Placing a strong civil rights plank in the Democratic platform might do that, but it would anger southern whites. Lyndon Johnson would make the most of that.

Kennedy was back on the high wire. There were only a few more days until the delegates voted. Could he keep his balance that long?

COUNTDOWN: **121 DAYS**

July 11, 1960
Los Angeles, California

The sidewalks outside the Memorial Coliseum in Los Angeles crawled with reporters, photographers, and fans, all waiting for the limousines to deliver the next load of celebrities to the Democratic National Convention.

Inside, the music was loud, the colors bright. This wasn't just a big night for politics. Some of the country's most famous entertainers would open the event with music, dance, jokes, and glamour.

The 1,521 delegates, die-hard Democrats sent from every corner of America, could rub elbows with Frank Sinatra and the Rat Pack. Hollywood stars Tony Curtis, Janet Leigh, Lloyd Bridges, and Shirley Mac-Laine arrived to an explosion of flashbulbs. Singer Nat King Cole brought his trademark cool. All crowded in to show their support for Kennedy.

Sinatra would open the event. Then the delegates would get down to business: choosing the Democratic Party's presidential nominee—the one who would, likely, challenge Vice President Nixon in November.

Of those 1,521 delegates, some 700 were pledged to support John F. Kennedy. That afternoon, he was around 60 votes short of the magic number: 761.

Throughout the day, JFK, his brother Robert, and all in the Kennedy camp worked feverishly, making calls and personal visits—anything to lock up those last delegates.

Johnson's team feared he was too far behind to catch up, but he wasn't going to step aside quietly. He didn't like the Kennedys. He'd dug up some dirt, and he wasn't willing to keep it to himself. He didn't have much time, but if he could sow enough doubt and do enough damage, maybe his situation would change.

Just before the convention opened, he had India Edwards, co-chairwoman of Citizens for Johnson, drop the first bombshell. If the public found out the truth, they might turn on JFK. They wouldn't want a sick man carrying the nation's nuclear codes or staring down Nikita Khrushchev.

The Johnson campaign told any delegate who'd listen that Kennedy wasn't physically fit to be president. The accusation was so serious that Bobby Kennedy jumped in and personally addressed the issue.

"JFK does not now have, nor has he ever had, an ailment described classically as Addison's disease," Bobby Kennedy said. "Any statement to the contrary is malicious and false."

In Kennedy parlance, that meant a lawsuit for any journalist who repeated the allegation. But Edwards was telling the truth; JFK had Addison's disease. Everyone in Kennedy's inner circle knew that. So, Bobby took an extraordinary extra step to make sure reporters didn't touch the story.

The Kennedy campaign released a June 11 letter, saying JFK was in excellent health and that his strenuous primary campaign proved it. It was signed by Eugene Cohen, an endocrinologist who had been treating Kennedy, and Janet Travell, JFK's personal physician.

Coincidentally, days before the convention, Dr. Cohen's New York City office was burglarized. Nothing was missing except patient records filed under "K." Had the burglars been looking for Kennedy's medical records? They had intentionally been filed under another letter.

Few journalists touched the Addison's disease story. The ones who did downplayed it. Bobby's rapid-response team had pulled another miracle.

Then Johnson threw another bomb—this one involving the old man.

Johnson reminded the public that Joseph Kennedy, while he was ambassador to Great Britain in the late 1930s, had cozied up to Adolf Hitler.

"I never thought Hitler was right," Johnson told Washington State delegates at the convention.

Yes, it was old news for historians. And Joe had already rewritten that part of his life. But Johnson didn't care. Most of the American public didn't remember—or didn't know—details about Joe Kennedy's time as U.S. ambassador.

Bobby Kennedy took a page from his counterattack playbook. He talked about Johnson's own health issues—a massive heart attack that nearly killed him. So, was LBJ really healthy enough to become president? Would the stress kill him in office?

When Johnson surrogates complained, Bobby exploded. Really? Johnson said JFK was dying and his father was a Nazi sympathizer, but they were complaining about this?

And at that moment, on the eve of the vote to nominate a presidential candidate, Johnson realized that his last-ditch efforts to discredit JFK and derail his campaign had failed. No one could successfully challenge Kennedy. Not Adlai Stevenson or Senator Stuart Symington of Missouri. Kennedy's early, cover-the-primaries approach had worked. So did his father's more old-fashioned tactics.

By the time Sinatra stepped on the stage to open the convention, all LBJ could do was enjoy the show. Now Johnson, the powerful Senate majority leader, was nothing more than another delegate, waiting for a roll call that would anoint Kennedy as the Democratic presidential nominee.

Johnson was pissed off. He didn't like JFK or any of the Kennedy clan—especially that young punk Robert Kennedy. The feeling was mutual. Johnson had not only tried to humiliate Bobby again, like back on the Texas ranch when the recoil from the hunting rifle knocked him to the ground, but he attacked RFK's family. That was unforgivable—and Bobby would remember that for the rest of his life.

Up front, "Old Blue Eyes" called out each star as they took the stage to a wall of applause. But when Sinatra announced Sammy Davis Jr.'s name, some southern delegates booed and jeered.

Davis was the consummate entertainer, a singer, dancer, comedian, and television personality. But Davis was a Black man engaged to Swedish actress May Britt, a white woman. Their relationship was an outrage to southern racists. In 1960, marriage between whites and Blacks was still illegal in thirty-one states.

The insult angered Sinatra, who years before had won a special Academy Award for that short film that promoted racial and religious understanding. After the booing subsided, Sinatra draped his arm over Davis's shoulder.

"Those dirty sons of bitches," he told his pal. "Don't let 'em get to you."

Sinatra then stood on the stage, alone, in front of those delegates—some of whom had just booed his friend because of his race—and sang a heartfelt, moving rendition of "The Star-Spangled Banner."

This was another moment that pointed to the deep racial and political fissures in America. Nearly a century after Appomattox, the South was still segregated. Democratic leaders there did everything to protect the status quo, the Jim Crow laws that treated Black people as second-class citizens. But Democratic leaders in the North wanted to end segregation. The two sides often clashed in Washington, especially over civil rights legislation.

Davis's humiliation at Democratic hands didn't end there. The couple had planned to wed that October. But the Rat Pack and the Kennedy family had become synonymous. Peter Lawford was married to JFK's sister and Sinatra was always around. Pictures of Davis marrying a white woman so close to the November election could cost JFK votes in the South. At least that's what worried Joe Kennedy. So, through intermediaries, he asked Davis to postpone his wedding until after the election.

The catcalls at the convention were just more of the same. "What can you say when people boo you?" Davis told reporters. "I don't know why they would want to do a thing like that. I flew all the way here from Boston just to spend two days and do what I could to help out."

JFK didn't offer any public words of comfort to Davis. Even as the Democratic convention was underway, he had someone else on his mind: Judith Campbell.

They hadn't seen each other for a month, although they talked almost every day. She'd done everything Jack had asked: meeting up at hotels, carrying satchels of cash to Sam Giancana, waiting by the telephone for his calls.

Kennedy hoped his invitation to the convention would cheer up Campbell, who'd been sick. A doctor had removed an ovary and she needed rest.

Not only was Sam Giancana still calling, but so was Jack. And now here he was with the eyes of the world on him, taking more risks—even though, like Addison's disease—disclosure of his private life could cost him everything.

Campbell was excited to see Jack. Kennedy had invited her to dinner at Puccini's, one of Sinatra's favorite restaurants. She questioned the idea—there were so many reporters around.

She was right, of course. Instead, JFK invited her to suite 744 at the Biltmore Hotel, which he said was under Peter Lawford's name, but if anyone asked she should tell them she was looking for Kenny O'Donnell.

When she arrived, she knocked on the door, but no one answered. She was angry. Here she was, standing in the hallway where people could pass by and see her. She'd had enough. Campbell turned around and went home. When she got there, Jack called. He begged her to come back. It was a mistake, he said. He didn't hear her knocking.

She turned around and drove back to the hotel. And this time when Campbell knocked, Kennedy answered. When she walked into the room, everyone excused themselves and left. But a woman stayed behind. She was tall and thin, in her late twenties, with brownish hair and sharp features. She smiled at Campbell and then ducked into the bathroom.

Kennedy apologized to Campbell. He looked into her eyes. With a sly grin, he suggested they celebrate with something special. The three of them—Jack, Campbell, and the girl in the bathroom—should jump into bed together. Kennedy wanted to have a threesome.

Campbell was outraged. "You have your nerve!" she shouted.

But Kennedy didn't seem to get it. "I hope you're not angry with me," he said.

Angry? Yes, she was angry. But she was also embarrassed and terribly hurt.

"I can't tell you how sorry I am. I think you're reacting too strongly to it," JFK said.

She stopped him right there. "I'm tired and I want to go home."

"Will you call me when you get home?" he asked.

"No," she said. "I want to go home and think this over."

Judith Campbell considered the last few months. She was in love with Jack Kennedy, possibly the next leader of the free world. At the same time, she was falling for Sam Giancana, one of the most dangerous mobsters on the planet. One wrong move, and something really bad could happen to her.

Back at home, in the quiet of her kitchen, Campbell poured herself a big Jack Daniel's and drew a hot bath.

When her phone rang, she took a sip of whiskey and slipped into the steaming water. The phone rang and rang until, like white noise, it faded into the background.

COUNTDOWN: **119 DAYS**

July 13, 1960
Washington, D.C.

J. Edgar Hoover had seen it all. There was nothing new in the documents stacked on his desk. After decades as the FBI's founding director, he knew even the most respected man has dirty secrets.

Presidents came and went as the years passed—Calvin Coolidge, Herbert Hoover, Franklin D. Roosevelt, Harry S. Truman, and Dwight D. Eisenhower. But J. Edgar Hoover seemed to go on forever.

It wouldn't matter who won the 1960 presidential election. Hoover knew he'd probably still be sitting in the same chair at the same desk, with his folders full of sensitive information.

Hoover was sixty-five years old. Civil service rules said he should retire, but Hoover didn't want to leave. With all the information he'd collected on key people over the years—some legal, some not—he wouldn't have to.

Nobody in Washington would risk Hoover leaking damaging information about their personal life to the media. He could destroy their careers, and he enjoyed all that power. Like a dictator in a third world country, Hoover was director for life, or as long as he wanted to be. He was either going to die in that chair or retire on his own terms.

Stocky, strict, and humorless, with a crew cut and a perennial frown, Hoover was a by-the-book lawman who'd circumvented the law only when it was to his advantage.

He never married, and some people wondered if he was gay. Hoover was careful and crafty. He planted stories with the right people at magazines and newspapers about how he was still trying to meet the right woman. It worked, or at least the chatter died down. No one was going to question the masculinity of America's top cop, the ultimate G-man.

Hoover used everything the FBI had on hand, from surveillance techniques and wiretaps to informants who would shadow even those not suspected of crimes. The agency focused as much on noteworthy Americans—civil rights leaders like Martin Luther King Jr. and politicians like JFK.

The seven-page Kennedy memorandum on his desk didn't contain any information that the FBI chief didn't already know about JFK.

Hoover was sphinxlike as he thumbed through the documents disclosing Kennedy's "immoral behavior."

The file on JFK's sex life reached back to World War II and Inga Arvad, a former Miss Norway suspected of being a Nazi spy. She was having a torrid affair with the young naval officer. Their fling was captured on FBI surveillance tapes as early as 1942.

In 1951, word was Kennedy had been engaged, and possibly secretly married, to a striking Polish immigrant named Alicia Darr. Joe Kennedy took care of that with a timely application of cash.

Other rumors followed. Kennedy just couldn't stay away from women—even after he married socialite Jacqueline Bouvier.

Maybe that was true. But Hoover knew that a woman named Florence Kater was waging a battle to disclose Kennedy's carousing to the public. The list of women's names in his "active" file included Marilyn Monroe (who had an FBI file of her own), young interns in his office, and Judith Campbell.

The new memorandum was prepared by an agent to summarize "pertinent available data concerning Kennedy in view of strong possibility he will be Democratic candidate for President."

Hoover stared at the words at the bottom of the first page:

"Allegations have been received concerning immoral conduct on the part of Kennedy and hoodlum connections of Kennedy."

Hoodlums? Organized crime.

More information to fatten the Kennedy file.

Hoover and Joseph Kennedy held each other in mutual respect. Joe Kennedy was a successful businessman, a strong capitalist, and an enemy of communism. Over the years, they had sent each other complimentary letters. But Hoover viewed the sons of his old friend in a different light.

The memorandum he was reading also described Kennedy's relationship with Frank Sinatra and his Mafia pals, as well as his potentially fatal illness that he kept hidden from the American public.

The report referenced some of the candidate's "immoral" peccadillos, including an "illicit relationship with another man's wife during World War II." And it mentioned that JFK was "compromised with a woman in Las Vegas," referring to Judith Campbell. If that weren't enough, the report noted that "Kennedy and Frank Sinatra have in the recent past been involved in parties in Palm Springs, Las Vegas and New York City."

Not tea parties. Sex parties.

As one agent put it, JFK was "a very bright man with a very immoral background."

This was just the tip of the iceberg, the memo alleged. "In the interest of brevity, no effort is made to list these allegations in full detail."

JFK's behavior might have been unscrupulous, but Hoover had no legal authority to bypass laws and spy on Kennedy. The files on his desk were ammunition, savings for a rainy day.

Hoover believed that the president of the United States should be a man of dignity and upstanding morality. But he also believed that the nation's chief executive should be in debt to J. Edgar Hoover.

He knew he could afford to be flexible where presidential dignity and morality were concerned. When the time was right, he'd let JFK know he had the sensitive information. The public didn't need to know anything. At least, not yet.

COUNTDOWN: **118 DAYS**

July 14, 1960
Los Angeles, California

It was just after midnight, but John F. Kennedy couldn't sleep. A few hours earlier, he had been selected by delegates to be the Democratic presidential nominee.

It was a powerful night. Minnesota governor Orville Freeman gave the main nominating speech, calling JFK a "proven liberal" who can win, but bring the party's platform to life.

All told, the names of nine candidates, including Lyndon Johnson, had been placed before the convention. But when the voting started, it took only forty-five minutes for the delegates to give Kennedy the nomination—on the first ballot.

The final count: 806 votes for Kennedy, 409 for Johnson, 86 for Stuart Symington, just under 80 for Adlai Stevenson, and just over 140 for a handful of others.

Kennedy supporters all over the nation let out a collective cheer. He did it. Yes, he still had a long way to go. But securing the nomination was half the battle.

JFK should have been celebrating, too. Instead, he was in his ninth-floor suite at the Biltmore Hotel, pondering his next move. He had to pick his running mate before the convention closed in less than twenty-four hours.

Philip Graham, publisher of *The Washington Post* and close friend to both Kennedy and Johnson, had been urging Kennedy to consider LBJ. Congressman Tip O'Neill had approached JFK with the same suggestion. Kennedy told them that of course he'd want Johnson.

But Kennedy was being disingenuous. He didn't like or trust Johnson— especially after LBJ lobbed hand grenades at his family. Besides, he doubted Johnson would even consider the position. Why would he? He was the Senate majority leader, one of the most powerful positions in the United States. Why would he trade that for a position that John Nance Garner, who served as vice president under FDR, said was worth less than "a pitcher of warm piss."

Kennedy was certain Johnson would say no. But JFK calculated it would be a gracious gesture to offer him the position anyway. Maybe it would build goodwill and Johnson would actively campaign for the ticket in Texas. The Democrats certainly needed to carry that state to win the presidency in the fall.

So before he went to sleep, he called his secretary, Evelyn Lincoln, and when she was not immediately available, dictated a note to her husband, Abe:

Dear Lyndon. If it is agreeable with you I would like to talk to you in your room tomorrow morning at ten [signed] Jack.

Kennedy called Lincoln to see if the note had been delivered to Johnson's suite. It had been, setting JFK's plan in motion.

Bobby Kennedy knew his brother would ask Johnson to join the ticket. No one hated Johnson more than Bobby. And like JFK, he was positive that Johnson would turn down the offer.

To make sure, JFK sent Bobby to Sam Rayburn's room sometime around 3:00 a.m. They knew Rayburn would advise Johnson against running with Kennedy. Better to plant that seed early. The seventy-eight-year-old Rayburn was sleeping when Bobby knocked on his door. So, he was a little grumpy when he turned the knob and saw Robert Kennedy standing in the hallway. Bobby didn't waste any time.

"We want Lyndon to run for vice president and we want you to persuade him to accept," he said.

Rayburn was pissed off that Bobby would wake him that early, and for that reason. When Bobby left, Rayburn called Lyndon and advised him to say no to the Kennedys. Rayburn's advice meant a lot to Lyndon. The old man was Johnson's mentor, a real friend in a place where you couldn't trust a soul.

Meanwhile, JFK was having second thoughts. What if Lyndon accepted? At 8:00 a.m., he called Johnson's seventh-floor suite.

Lady Bird picked up the phone.

Jack Kennedy told Lady Bird he wanted to talk to her husband. She turned to Lyndon, who had been sleeping, and handed him the telephone. "It's Senator Kennedy and he wants to talk to you."

Still not fully awake, he muttered yes a few times into the receiver, then hung up. Lady Bird asked Lyndon what Kennedy wanted. Kennedy was coming to the suite to offer LBJ the vice presidency.

She was excited, but Johnson told her not to say a word to anyone. Nothing was set in stone.

So, Lady Bird jumped out of bed and started tidying up the messy suite. Meanwhile, Johnson began calling his closest advisers.

Democratic Party strategist Jim Rowe argued that Johnson had the power where he was, but the Texas senator said, "Power is where power goes."

Before the convention, Johnson had said on *Meet the Press* that he'd never consider running as vice president. "Most vice presidents don't do much," he said.

Still, Johnson began to weigh his options. If he refused and Kennedy won, JFK might push for another Senate majority leader. He knew the Kennedys didn't trust him, especially after what had happened when he'd attacked their family. But if he accepted, it would raise his national visibility. So, if Kennedy lost, not only would LBJ probably remain in the senate, he'd be the front-runner for the Democratic presidential nomination in 1964.

Maybe most important, the vice president was just a breath away from the top spot. Jack Kennedy was relatively young, but Johnson was aware he was not a healthy man. Johnson was one of the few people who knew Kennedy really had Addison's disease. He knew that JFK could have a stress-related flare-up at any time and that it might become fatal. Maybe Johnson wouldn't have to wait eight years after all.

As Kennedy was getting ready for the meeting, his brother-in-law and campaign adviser, Sargent Shriver, told JFK that he had gotten a signal from a Johnson supporter that the Texas senator might accept the offer to be the running mate.

Kennedy ignored Shriver. Instead, he told Evelyn Lincoln he was heading to Johnson's suite.

Meanwhile, the media was staked out by the elevators, watching for politicians as they tried to figure out Kennedy's choice for vice president. To avoid the eyes of the media, Kennedy sneaked down the back stairs from his suite on the ninth floor to Johnson's on the seventh. No one was camped outside Johnson's room because the press believed he wasn't being considered for the ticket.

When Johnson heard a knock, he greeted Kennedy at the door. And when the Massachusetts senator walked inside, LBJ congratulated Kennedy on his victory. Several of Johnson's close advisers were in the suite, including John Connally, who had become one of the Texas senator's most trusted political operatives.

Jack didn't waste any time. He asked Lyndon if he'd be his vice president. Johnson responded with an answer that shook Kennedy. "Yes," Johnson said.

Kennedy's heart hammered. Johnson said there were still some issues that had to be hashed out. He said he wouldn't accept JFK's offer unless he had Rayburn's blessing. Meanwhile, Kennedy said he'd have to talk to labor and liberal leaders, too.

JFK said he'd call back in a couple of hours. When Kennedy left the suite, he walked up the stairs to his room. Bobby could tell by the look on his brother's face the news wasn't good.

John and Robert Kennedy conferring at the Democratic National Convention, July 1960
(Time & Life Pictures)

"He wants it," Kennedy said.

Bobby panicked. Their plan had backfired. Now they had to find a way to get him off the ticket. Nothing had been announced. Maybe they had time.

So, for the next few hours, politicians used the back stairs to relay messages between the two camps. For Johnson, his allies had to persuade Rayburn that this was a good move for the Texas senator. If they couldn't do that, Johnson would decline.

But then the unthinkable happened. Several of Johnson's allies managed to convince Rayburn that it was a good idea. They said their common enemy was Richard Nixon, not the Kennedys. And Johnson gave the Democrats the best chance of defeating the vice president in November.

"Do you want Richard Nixon to be president of the United States?" Hale Boggs, a Louisiana congressman, asked Rayburn.

Rayburn sighed. Lyndon Johnson had to do it. He told Boggs to get Kennedy. So, Boggs hustled up the back stairs to JFK's suite. A few minutes later, Jack Kennedy and Kenneth O'Donnell entered Rayburn's suite. Everybody waited in another room while Kennedy and Rayburn talked alone.

And that's when Rayburn had a heart-to-heart with Kennedy. He told JFK that he had been against Johnson accepting the spot on the ticket. But now, after he had time to think about it, he felt differently. He said, "I am in the twilight of my life," and "Lyndon is only approaching the summit of his. I am afraid I was trying to keep him in the legislative end where he could help me." But Rayburn said he could see that Kennedy needed him more. So, Sam said he was giving Lyndon his blessing.

When Kennedy got back to his suite, he broke the news to his brother and their advisers, and they were enraged. Years later, Robert Kennedy would say the offer was made as a courtesy. No one believed he'd say yes.

But now they had to deal with the fallout from labor leaders and liberals. And they didn't take the news well.

A group of major union bosses, including United Auto Workers president Walter Reuther, had arrived at Kennedy's suite with suggestions about who JFK should name as his running mate. Johnson was not on the list. But then Kennedy broke the news: He had already picked Johnson. They were upset and knew the rank and file would be, too.

Kennedy faced his first major test as the Democratic presidential nominee. His plan had turned into a disaster. He knew Johnson had to go or his supporters would be in an uproar.

So, JFK decided to send Bobby to break the news to Johnson. The younger Kennedy didn't mind being the hatchet man. By now, RFK and Johnson despised each other. As Joe Kennedy once said, "When Bobby hates you, you stay hated."

When Bobby arrived at Johnson's suite at about 1:45 p.m., Rayburn answered the door. Johnson was in another room with Lady Bird. Bobby asked to meet with Johnson, but the Texas senator said no. He wouldn't meet with him.

Meanwhile, Phil Graham called JFK to see what was going on. Kennedy said liberals and labor were angry about his choice. But so was Graham—about JFK trying to renege on the offer.

Kennedy was in a real bind. If he kept Johnson on the ticket, he risked losing the labor vote. And more Blacks would move to the GOP column. But if he pushed Lyndon off the ticket, he'd alienate the South. If he had just not reached out to Johnson in the first place—everything would be going smoothly.

JFK had no choice. He picked up the phone and called Johnson. He asked the Texas senator again if he wanted to join the ticket and Johnson said yes. There was no turning back now.

Or was there?

Bobby was going to try one more time. When he got to Johnson's suite, Rayburn, Connally, and Graham were there. Bobby pleaded with Johnson to withdraw. Labor was unhappy. The party would be split in two, and Nixon would win. Was that what Johnson wanted?

The Johnson team was beyond angry. Why was Bobby there, not his brother? Was JFK too scared to tell Johnson in person? What the hell was going on?

Rayburn was particularly mad. He was Johnson's mentor. He knew this was Johnson's time to walk in the sun before it was too late. This was just a chicken shit thing to do.

Maybe, but Bobby was determined to get his way. He told LBJ if he declined his brother's offer, maybe he'd be appointed as chairman of the Democratic National Committee.

Bobby knew that would tick off Johnson. But when he stared at LBJ, he didn't see an angry man. No, he glimpsed a man who had been hurt, a man on the verge of tears.

"I want to be vice president," Johnson said.

Meanwhile, Graham called JFK and asked him why Bobby was back in Johnson's suite. Kennedy said he hadn't had a chance to tell his brother about his recent conversation with LBJ. Graham handed Bobby the phone and JFK broke the news.

The vice presidential chaos was over. Outfoxing Bobby Kennedy boosted Johnson's insatiable ego, but even that couldn't totally overcome the sting of resentment. That weasel had made him beg for the vice presidential nomination. He'd never forget Bobby's treachery.

A few days after the convention, Pierre Salinger, Kennedy's press secretary, asked him why he had picked Johnson. Kennedy recited some of the facts that had been in a news release explaining the choice. But then Kennedy stopped and looked at Salinger. "The whole story will never be known. And it's just as well that it won't be," Kennedy said.

End of conversation. Kennedy never elaborated about the cryptic remark.

John Kennedy and Lyndon Johnson—the 1960 Democratic ticket
(Library of Congress, U.S. News & World Report Magazine Collection)

JFK's secretary, Evelyn Lincoln, would later tell British journalist Anthony Summers that J. Edgar Hoover and Johnson conspired to make sure LBJ got the spot.

The FBI director and Johnson lived on the same block. She said they were close. Hoover shared information with Johnson about Kennedy's private life, including his womanizing and illnesses. She said Johnson was using that as clout, and Kennedy was angry about it.

Lincoln later told investigative reporter Seymour Hersh of finding Jack and Bobby in a deep conversation early on the morning of July 14.

"I went in and listened. They were very upset and tried to figure out how they could get around it, but they didn't know how they could," she told Hersh.

Eventually, Kennedy found a way of dealing with Johnson, telling his adviser Kenny O'Donnell, "I'm forty-three years old. I'm not going to die in office. So, the vice presidency doesn't mean a thing."

With the convention almost over, it was time for Joseph Kennedy to slip out of town. He'd been lying low in Beverly Hills, watching the action from film star Marion Davies's 29,000-square-foot mansion. His and Davies's friendship went way back to her glory days in the 1920s, when she'd sparked a more than three-decade relationship with newspaper mogul William Randolph Hearst.

Joe kept out of sight, but he still pulled strings for Jack and Bobby. All Joe needed was a telephone line and a scratch pad to get things done. When Joe Kennedy called, people picked up the phone.

He knew JFK would roll to victory on the first ballot. He believed Lyndon Johnson was an excellent choice for vice president. He'd pushed for him, telling his son that in a few weeks the people now shouting for blood would call it a brilliant move. It didn't matter if Jack wanted someone else on the ticket.

JFK listened to his father. Maybe he's right, Jack thought. He hadn't been wrong yet. Bobby stayed mad, but Jack calmed down.

Joe would be on the road before Johnson and Kennedy made their acceptance speeches. With his son ready to launch his general election campaign, he had a lot of meetings to set up, a lot of cash to spread around and promises to buy.

As for Texas, Joe knew "Landslide Lyndon" would take care of business. It seemed the Texas politician had a way of making sure tight elections turned in his favor.

Voter fraud was part of Texas lore. In fact, two of Johnson's races had played a big role in that narrative. When Johnson ran for the U.S. Senate in 1941, he was initially ruled the winner. But it was overturned the next day when more votes were discovered.

Johnson wouldn't let that happen again. In 1948, when LBJ tried again for the Senate, he first had to win the Democratic primary against Governor Coke Stevenson. Johnson lost by around 120 votes.

Then out of the blue, a day later, election officials in Jim Wells County discovered box 13, a ballot box full of uncounted votes.

When the new votes were tabulated, Johnson beat Stevenson by eighty-seven votes. He beat the GOP Senate candidate later that year, catapulting him to national attention.

Joe knew election fraud was easy. You just needed the right people in the right places, and enough money to pay them. Precinct captains, registrars, security guards—people with access to ballot boxes, voting machines, election rolls. To move big numbers of votes you needed politicians who controlled cities, or the Mafia boys who ran major labor unions from the shadows—forcing members to vote for certain candidates. It wasn't cheap. There was a world of people out there waiting for Joe Kennedy, most with their hands out.

So, Joe headed east. This election was going to be close. If there was going to be a Kennedy in the White House in 1961, Joe had better get started.

Jack Kennedy was drained. He had worked so hard to win on the first ballot and then gotten such fierce blowback for choosing Lyndon Johnson. Soon he'd have to stand up before the convention and present Johnson's nomination to the crowd.

Party conventions are made of promises and compromises, but Kennedy's choice of vice president left the liberals feeling double-crossed. They had managed to get a plank calling for the end of segregation included in the platform. But nominating a southern good old boy for VP undermined everything they'd worked for, they said.

Top labor leaders were shocked, too. George Meany, the president of the American Federation of Labor and Congress of Industrial Organizations (AFL-CIO), called a meeting with dozens of his colleagues. In the end they agreed to trust Kennedy's decision. They couldn't abandon him now—not with Richard Nixon on the horizon.

Newspaper editorial boards, especially in the South, were shocked for a different reason, thinking Johnson and the Democrats had sold out their values—pro-segregation. The Charleston, South Carolina, *News and Courier* said the Texan had "embraced the 1960 party platform, including the harshest racial plank in history."

It continued, "The South has lost on every count at Los Angeles. The radical forces in control of the Democratic Party planned it that way. Unless South Carolina Democrats devise some escape hatch for the November election, a straight out vote for Nixon is the only alternative for loyal, patriotic citizens."

July 15, 1960
Los Angeles, California

The one thing that remained was Kennedy's big acceptance speech. The Democratic National Convention was ending.

After all the buildup and drama and excitement, the candidate was feeling deflated. He knew he should be happy, but today he just wasn't his usual cheerful self.

But this was a new beginning. He could end the convention on a high note. He and his speechwriters were crafting an address that would fire up the delegates—and millions of people watching at home—to go out and help him get elected.

Bobby Kennedy, reaching again for the extraordinary, had scheduled the speech for late afternoon at the big, wide-open Los Angeles Memorial Coliseum. Most speeches were delivered in closed arenas. This would be a sunny, exciting ending to the raucous convention. It would feel more like a pep rally before a football game than a dull campaign speech.

JFK liked the idea. He only hoped he could muster the energy to pull it off. Kennedy was a good communicator. He usually spoke in a clear, concise manner, with dignity and verve.

He felt the pressure. This had to be perfect. He was the first Roman Catholic to run for the presidency since Al Smith. Forget about all the people in the stands—he knew millions would be watching him at home on their televisions. For many, this would be their first chance to see him live. He needed to make a good impression.

Plenty of them were skeptical of his ability to do the job. Black leaders were still fuming about his choice of Lyndon Johnson. They felt that Kennedy had sold them out, a sentiment expressed by Jackie Robinson in his column in the *New York Post*.

Robinson said the Democratic Party's civil rights plank and goodwill built by JFK during the convention were negated by Johnson's place on the ticket. Choosing Johnson was nothing more than a "bid for the appeasement of Southern bigots."

He said JFK was willing to "ruthlessly gamble with the rights—and the very lives—of millions of Southern Negro Americans in order to satisfy his own personal ambition."

Kennedy felt the sting. He needed to carry a majority of the Black vote to win in November.

Kennedy's speech had to contain the right combination of optimism about America's future and concern about the nation's current trajectory.

The 1960s were here. Would America look or feel the same in ten years? Would technology improve daily life—maybe cure diseases like cancer? What about civil rights? Would nearly a quarter of the nation still be segregated? Would relations between the Soviet Union and United States improve, or would the world order topple into nuclear disaster? Would there even be an America in ten years?

After the warm-up speakers were finished, he was introduced. Showtime.

Kennedy walked to the podium, blinked at the bright lights, and relaxed into the applause. Behind him, a huge American flag hung from a rafter. He seemed confident in his usual blue suit, white shirt, and blue tie. His face was tanned, and his wide smile showed off his perfect white teeth.

He thought the setting would energize him, but his body felt lethargic. He'd had to up the medicine dosage.

JFK took a deep breath. He thanked party leaders for their help. And he said, "With a deep sense of duty and high resolve, I accept your nomination."

A mighty roar came up from the crowd of sixty thousand people.

When the noise died down, he hit the key issue head-on. He said the Democratic Party was taking a risk "by nominating someone of my faith," but he assured the public that he'd "reject any kind of religious pressure or obligation that might directly or indirectly interfere with my conduct of the Presidency in the national interest."

When it came to deciding who to vote for, his religion was irrelevant, Kennedy said.

His eyes scanned the audience. He talked about how difficult it would be to campaign against a man "who has spoken or voted on every known side of every known issue."

But Kennedy said the election was more than that. He wasn't just running against Richard Nixon. No, he was running to improve the lives of Americans who had been left behind. He told the crowd they were the farmers who lost their land and unemployed miners and textile workers. They were the elderly without health care and families "without a decent home" or enough food.

". . . [T]hey all know that it's time for a change," he declared.

He said it was time to think of the future. He said it was a new world—one with weapons able to wipe out civilization. But he felt optimistic about the future, as a new generation was ready to take over from the old.

That new generation would lead the nation into a New Frontier—one that would be tasked with trying to solve so many of the world's problems. "I am asking each of you to be pioneers on that New Frontier," he said.

Kennedy added that the New Frontier offered not a set of promises, as did the New and Fair Deals, but a "set of challenges."

Kennedy left no doubt that his would be a hard-hitting campaign to capture the White House. He attacked Nixon and Eisenhower's administration. And he said voters would reject Nixon because he "did not measure to the footsteps of Dwight D. Eisenhower." When he finished, his speech received a thunderous ovation.

The crowd loved it.

Richard Nixon wasn't impressed.

The Republican candidate watched Kennedy on television in his Washington, D.C., home. He criticized the speech—from the "literary language" to his "rapid delivery." It didn't help that JFK looked tired.

But Nixon knew that none of that mattered. The man on the screen had the looks, charm, and money Nixon didn't have.

Nixon was in for the fight of his political life.

COUNTDOWN: 109 DAYS

July 23, 1960
New York City

The vice president climbed into his limo and rolled down the deserted Manhattan streets toward the airport. It was three thirty in the morning. Nixon was exhausted.

He hadn't thought the road to the Republican National Convention in Chicago would pass through upper Fifth Avenue, but New York governor Nelson Rockefeller was determined to have his say.

Rockefeller had welcomed Nixon to his luxurious New York City residence, a triplex with thirty rooms on the building's top floors, with sweeping views of Central Park. During a lamb chop dinner in the apartment, Nixon pitched the idea of the governor joining the ticket. He laid out his ideas for making the vice presidency more important than it had been in the last administration. But Rockefeller said no. Then after dinner, the governor spent hours detailing his vision for the party, its platform, and the presidency. The convention was only days away.

Nixon needed time to process all the demands coming in from everyone. He wanted to hear what his advisers had to say. His acceptance speech wasn't even written yet. And he hoped he'd talked Rockefeller out of any plans to threaten his nomination. But Nixon knew he had to resolve this fight with his top rival inside the GOP before he could fully turn his focus to the November election.

Nixon felt in his bones that the race between him and Kennedy would be tough and tight. He also felt he would prevail. He had many

years of experience—and that really mattered to voters, especially in
these uncertain times.

Still, Nixon felt anxious. Kennedy was ready to launch his now trademark media-blast campaign, while the vice president was trying to
patch things up inside his own party. How could his rivalry with Rockefeller remain unresolved—and so close to the Republican National Convention?

Nixon had tried everything. He and the governor had sent flurries of
private messages through intermediaries, and found they were close on
some issues but far apart on others. Rockefeller and the more liberal
wing of the Republican Party wanted a federal health-care plan for senior citizens. The conservative wing said no, that Republicans were
about dismantling Big Government, not expanding it. Nixon had to find
a way to satisfy both sides. And Rockefeller continued to play games.

He still hadn't endorsed Nixon. What the hell was he waiting for?
Nixon knew the answer.

Rockefeller was holding out hope—or maybe even planning for—the
"Draft Rockefeller" movement to emerge from the shadows at the convention.

Nixon supporters had tried leaning on Rockefeller. Indiana governor
Harold Handley surprised Rockefeller at an event and handed him a
petition pledging to support Nixon for the GOP presidential nomination. The petition had been signed by a large batch of Republican governors but not Rockefeller. The New York governor handed it back
unsigned. "You're some kind of artist, aren't you?" Rockefeller said and
smiled.

Meanwhile, Rockefeller had insisted that the platform committee in-
corporate some of his proposals, including a $3.5 billion increase for
nuclear arms control and federal health insurance for Americans over the
age of sixty-five.

While Rockefeller was making demands, Nixon's inner circle—
Leonard Hall, Bob Finch, and Herb Klein—had been working behind
the scenes to ensure the vice president had the votes for his platform and

presidential nomination. That way, if Rockefeller complained or jumped into the race, it wouldn't matter.

But that wasn't good enough for the vice president. Nixon realized that ignoring Rockefeller's demands could lead to a damaging floor flight over the platform at the convention. They needed unity, not warfare. The "Rockefeller thing has to be worked out," Nixon wrote in a memo.

The time had come for a face-to-face meeting. When it came to campaign decisions, Nixon didn't trust anyone except himself. So, without consulting any of his campaign advisers, Nixon flew to New York with his military aide, Major Donald Hughes, to meet with Rockefeller privately.

With both men so meticulous, driven, and detailed-oriented, it projected to be a long night. They didn't disappoint. Rockefeller and adviser Emmet Hughes went through the platform differences with Nixon point by point. It took more than six hours until they had reached a détente.

Rockefeller was satisfied. So was Nixon—just to have it settled. They called the agreement "the Compact of Fifth Avenue." That was the governor's idea, just in case there were any doubts about who had been the driving force. Rockefeller issued a news release disclosing details of the settlement. Nixon did the same hours later when he returned to Washington.

To Nixon the meeting was no big deal. It was a move to resolve differences. That's all. And Nixon told reporters that they agreed more than they disagreed. They both wanted strong economic growth and an increase in defense spending. Both favored a civil rights plank. But they disagreed on a few things, including health care for the elderly.

As far as Rockefeller joining the ticket? No, that wasn't going to happen, Nixon said.

The deal headed off a high-profile fight at the convention, but some conservatives in Chicago were shocked and angry about the agreement. They discussed starting another party with Senator Barry Goldwater of Arizona as the presidential candidate. He was a rising star in the conservative movement. He advocated for overturning the Supreme Court's

Brown v. Board of Education school desegregation decision—calling it a states' rights issue. He pressed for a "right to work" plank so that employees who didn't want to join unions wouldn't have to.

What really ticked off Goldwater was he had talked to Nixon the previous morning, and Nixon didn't say a word about flying to New York to meet with Rockefeller. Who was more important: Governor Rockefeller or conservative Republicans?

Nixon shrugged. Politics. That's all it was. Everyone had an opinion. The end result of the late night in New York City was the blessed assurance that Rockefeller was happy with a kingmaker role and wouldn't cause trouble at the convention. He wasn't going to throw his hat into the ring at the last minute. Problem solved.

As soon as everyone arrived in Chicago, the whining and sniping would be lost in the roar of applause.

COUNTDOWN: **107 DAYS**

July 25, 1960
Greensboro, North Carolina

The F. W. Woolworth Company store in Greensboro had lost $200,000 (over $2 million today) in sales since February 1, the day four Black students from the Agricultural and Technical College of North Carolina sat down at the whites-only lunch counter and tried to order food.

They weren't served. And their simple action had helped trigger sit-ins and boycotts at other segregated restaurants and stores in Greensboro and all over the South. Hundreds of Blacks were arrested in dozens of cities for trespassing.

Reverend King praised the students for their nonviolent protests. And while the presidential candidates from both parties all but ignored the demonstrations, King kept bringing the issue to the public's attention through a series of speeches and rallies.

Clarence Harris, manager of the store where it all started, saw how this would play out. The Greensboro mayor's Advisory Committee on Community Relations had recommended that stores sell merchandise and food to all customers, Black and white. Now Harris had 200,000 more reasons to change store policy. Woolworth had lost a large amount of money because Blacks—and some whites—were boycotting the store.

That morning, he asked four of his Black employees to have lunch at the counter. They sat down quietly and placed their orders.

And so, with little fanfare, the Greensboro F. W. Woolworth's store was desegregated.

The young men whose protest sparked the movement weren't there to see it happen. Franklin McCain, Ezell Blair Jr., Joseph McNeil, and David Richmond had been informed of the decision, but they were on summer vacation from school.

The months of protest, the growth of the movement, and the pressure of sudden fame had brought the four young men closer together. If they were asked to speak to a civil rights group, they decided which of them would go to spread the gospel of integration through peaceful protest.

They still had much to do just in Greensboro. Only a handful of restaurants and facilities agreed with the mayor's recommendation. So, they'd have to continue to pressure businesses there. Not an easy thing to do when you're a full-time student.

McCain had come to North Carolina's A&T College to get an education. That was his central mission. With the protests, he had to continually remind himself why he was there—and what his future could be if he studied hard. But how could he give up protesting for study when so many Blacks were being humiliated?

Blair felt the pressure, too. Before he sat down at the lunch counter for the first time, he checked with his parents, both of whom were working for the public school system. He feared reprisals against them.

He told them he was going to do something that would "change things in Greensboro, maybe the nation," and asked, "Will you support me?"

His mother said yes. "As long as you don't do anything that's going to bring disrespect upon the family or yourself."

Now Blair felt comfortable about what he was doing.

Even though Blacks could now be served at Woolworth's lunch counter, the Greensboro Four knew it was only the beginning.

They had started a movement, but they weren't finished. Their long-range goal was getting Congress to pass a bill that would make equal access mandatory in all places of public accommodation throughout the United States.

But such a bill would need to be signed by the future president, and the presidential candidates' voting records and positions on civil rights were far from stellar. Southern Black voters had little faith in either Senator Kennedy or Vice President Nixon.

So, McCain, McNeil, Blair, Richmond, and thousands of others promised to keep pushing, to risk their lives for equal rights—and to vote for candidates who were willing to stand up for them.

COUNTDOWN: **104 DAYS**

July 28, 1960
Chicago, Illinois

I t was a great night to be Richard Nixon.

He'd held steady, worked hard, followed all the rules to get here, and everything ran as smooth and neat as a silk pocket square. Unlike at the Democratic National Convention, there was no drama at the GOP event. All possible distractions had been tucked away well in advance.

Nixon's preconvention meeting in New York City with Nelson Rockefeller had worked. Nixon wasn't going to select him as his running mate, and Rockefeller said he didn't want to be vice president anyway. Nixon agreed to put a few liberal planks in the Republican Party platform, and so sidetracked a possibly chaotic "Draft Rockefeller" movement.

Party conservatives like Senator Barry Goldwater of Arizona hadn't liked the liberal planks—one of which called for the removal of the last vestiges of segregation. They complained, but for the sake of party unity, they came around.

On civil rights, though his record wasn't strong, Nixon was more liberal than Kennedy. He'd worked to bring Black voters into the party and closely watched the sit-ins that had spread across the nation. The vice president could see that segregation was coming to an end in the United States.

In 1957, in the wake of *Brown v. Board of Education*, Eisenhower had sent the 101st Airborne into Little Rock, Arkansas, to protect the first Black students to integrate Central High School. Eisenhower and Nixon had discussions and meetings with Black leaders, including Reverend King.

Baseball great and newspaper columnist Jackie Robinson was one of Nixon's most avid supporters. Nixon had supplied Robinson with copies of his civil rights votes and positions. Robinson, in turn, wrote glowing stories about Nixon.

Even though Ike hadn't publicly supported Nixon's campaign to become the GOP presidential nominee, he had given the vice president more high-profile work to do.

In May, Nixon appeared on David Susskind's television show to defend America's U-2 flights. He said the president was justified in using the spy planes to gather data on Soviet missile capabilities.

Some supporters were worried that Nixon hadn't actively campaigned in the primaries. But he didn't care. Nixon said he didn't want to start campaigning early and run out of gas.

He had been through this before, twice with Eisenhower at the top of the ticket. He knew this time it would be more grueling since he'd be the presidential nominee. There'd be a lot more pressure. So, it would be more important to conserve his energy to be strong at the end of the campaign.

Nixon's calm, cool statesman strategy, adopted over the past six months, had worked well. He stood back, maintained a dignified, gaffe-free silence, and let the Democratic convention occupy the media machine.

Nixon felt good when he arrived in Chicago for the GOP convention—steady and focused. Now it was all about his campaign.

He was winnowing his list of possible running mates. He considered his friend from Michigan, Representative Gerald Ford, who had served six terms in Congress and had plenty of credibility. But in the end, Nixon turned to Henry Cabot Lodge Jr., the U.S. ambassador to the United Nations.

Lodge was a third-generation Massachusetts official who had crossed swords with JFK before. Like Kennedy, he was sharp, handsome, a Harvard grad with a family fortune, and a decorated hero of World War II. Lodge had been in politics since 1932. He ran for the U.S. Senate in 1936 as a Republican and won, but resigned in 1944 to serve in the army. He retired as a lieutenant colonel and was elected again to the Senate in 1946. But in 1952, he lost his seat to a young Democrat named Kennedy.

Eisenhower befriended Lodge during the war in Europe. After the loss to Kennedy, Ike smoothed the ex-senator's ruffled feathers by appointing him ambassador to the United Nations.

As the GOP convention opened, Ike campaigned actively for Lodge, who was one of Nixon's biggest supporters. The vice president never forgot how Lodge had praised him after the Eisenhower-Nixon ticket was reelected in 1956. "You have confounded your enemies, impressed the circle of your friends, and stand as a public figure of real stature before the nation."

As the U.S. ambassador to the United Nations, Lodge had to counter Soviet narratives. And his latest salvo was perfectly timed. With the Soviet Union proudly displaying pieces of the U-2 spy plane in Moscow, Lodge showed up at a UN Security Council meeting with some evidence of his own.

It was a wooden carving of the Great Seal of the United States. It looked like something that would be displayed in a hunting lodge or mountain cabin. But this was a gift to the former U.S. ambassador to the Soviet Union in 1945, a thank-you, of sorts, for being Russia's ally in World War II.

Lodge said the Soviets shouldn't complain too hard, because they'd just found a listening device planted in the wood carving that had been hanging in the U.S. ambassador's residence in Moscow.

Soviet foreign minister Andrei Gromyko remarked that Lodge had shown the council "a prop," something used for a play. But Lodge snapped, "It's not out of any play. It's out of the Soviet Union."

When Nixon asked Lodge to run for vice president, he said no.

But Nixon was relentless. People voted for the top of the ticket, and Nixon had the lead, with Lodge as a counter to Kennedy: urbane, articulate, blue-blooded.

The convention opened on Monday, July 25 at Chicago's International Amphitheatre. Compared with the Hollywood razzle-dazzle the Democrats had enjoyed, the GOP affair was dull indeed.

President Eisenhower addressed the delegates and the nation on the second night. Millions tuned in to his speech, where Ike recalled the last eight years of success stories. He said he had kept America at peace, and the economy rolling.

Eisenhower noted that America had achieved "unprecedented prosperity," adding that more Americans were employed with "higher wages, and more take-home pay than ever before in our history." But for that to continue, he said, the country had to continue his administration's policies.

Although Eisenhower didn't say Nixon's—or Kennedy's—names in his speech, Ike made it clear earlier in the day that the vice president was the one to lead the nation over the next four years.

His support came in a telegram, parts of which Nixon read to reporters. The telegram said Nixon had Eisenhower's "blessing to speak freely and frankly" expressing "your views" about the nation's future.

"To your hands I pray that I shall pass the responsibility of the office of the presidency—and will be glad to do so," the telegram said.

It was the first time the president had given Nixon such a ringing public endorsement.

Now, on the final evening, it was Nixon's turn. It was Nixon's party. He swept his party's presidential nomination in a unanimous vote.

Rockefeller gave the introduction. The vice president was "a man of experience, capacity, vision and judgment on whose behalf all of us are united."

He predicted that Nixon would "succeed Dwight D. Eisenhower."

Nixon wasn't listening. He stood behind a curtain backstage, scanning his speech. He had put a lot of time and thought into what he was going to say to the American people.

Over the last few months, Kennedy had been particularly rough on him. He'd said Nixon was old, tired, and incompetent. That you couldn't trust him. Outside his relentless pursuit of communists—there was a communist under every rock and behind every tree—what did Nixon really stand for? Nixon was an old fogey, dowdy, behind the times.

Nixon knew the attacks were only politics. But he wanted to show everyone a different Richard Nixon. It was 1960, the beginning of a new decade of the twentieth century. Nixon wanted to do something more than sling mud at his opponent. He decided he'd stay on the high road. He wrote his speech to be positive and uplifting—a first for the man widely known as "Tricky Dick."

He walked out from behind the curtain with a big smile, accompanied by his wife, Pat, who wore a big white carnation and a double strand of pearls with her bright green dress. The Nixons smiled and waved as

Richard Nixon accepting the Republican nomination
(Library of Congress, U.S. News & World Report Magazine Collection)

they strode across the stage, shook hands with a few of the delegates, and greeted their daughters, Patricia and Julie, and Nixon's mother, Hannah, near the front of the stage.

"We want Dick! We want Dick!" the crowd chanted over and over.

When the thunderous applause died down, Nixon's family moved to chairs on the side of the stage, leaving the candidate alone in the spotlight.

For much of his political career, Nixon had felt insecure—almost unloved—by the public, and even his party. But now, here he was, standing before thousands of people—and they were cheering for him. The love in that room was palpable. And he wanted the delegates and the American people to know it.

He casually removed a handkerchief from inside his suit jacket, wiped the sweat from his brow, and put it away. He thanked the audience—and the nation—for showing such warmth toward his wife, daughters, and mother, and to him.

Nixon said he was genuinely humbled by their affection. Now it was time for him to earn it. Campaigns were long and hard. He only prayed that in the months ahead he'd be worthy of their trust and support.

Nixon had prepared notes for his speech and occasionally glanced at them. He covered the usual subjects: national defense, the economy. But these were his words and beliefs. He wasn't parroting his boss, the general, Ike. No, these were Nixon's thoughts and policies—although on the surface they didn't sound much different from Eisenhower's. He pushed for strong defense spending to thwart the Soviet Union and global communism.

Nixon was calm, sometimes animated, but always in control. He praised Rockefeller and Goldwater, his political rivals on the left and right—he'd need their support in the coming days.

He touted the administration's accomplishments, but said he wanted more than the status quo. He wanted to build on Eisenhower's record.

But Nixon wanted to focus on something else. He warned that the next president would face unprecedented challenges, then used an analogy to show what would be waiting for the new commander in chief on his first day in office.

"One hundred years ago, in this city, Abraham Lincoln was nominated for President of the United States. The problems which will confront our next President will be even greater than those that confronted him. The question then was freedom for the slaves and survival of the Nation. The question now is freedom for all mankind and the survival of civilization," he said.

The next president, Nixon said, will not only have to deal with bellicose communist leaders like Nikita Khrushchev, but with communism itself. He reminded the American people that the goal of communism is to spread its system of government all over the world. They want one system, where there will be no liberty or freedom.

And he had a message for Americans about Khrushchev's boastful rhetoric: "When Mr. Khrushchev says our grandchildren will live under communism, let us say his grandchildren will live in freedom. When Mr. Khrushchev says the Monroe Doctrine is dead in the Americas, we say, the doctrine of freedom applies everywhere in the world."

And then he made a promise—one that would end up pushing him to his limits. He said he had been asked by reporters which states he would focus on in the campaign. He said his answer was "In this campaign we aren't going to concede any states to the opposition. I announce to you tonight, and I pledge to you, that I, personally, will carry this campaign into every one of the fifty states of this nation between now and November the eighth.

"And in this campaign I make a prediction. I say that just as in 1952 and in 1956 millions of Democrats will join us—not because they are deserting their party, but because their party deserted them at Los Angeles two weeks ago."

In the end, he said, going back to Lincoln for inspiration, "A hundred years ago Abraham Lincoln was asked during the dark days of the tragic War between the States whether he thought God was on his side. His answer was, 'My concern is not whether God is on our side, but whether we are on God's side.'

"My fellow Americans, may that ever be our prayer for our country, and in that spirit, with faith in America, with faith in her ideals and in her people, I accept your nomination for President of the United States."

The speech was a rousing success. Even his opponents liked his high tone. "If Richard M. Nixon can come as close to appealing to the general public as he wowed the Republican convention, his Democratic opponent John F. Kennedy has his work cut out for him," wrote Merriman Smith, a correspondent for United Press International.

"Now, Nixon is engaged in the greatest fight of his career," said Arthur Edson of the Associated Press. "Once again, since there are more Democrats than Republicans, he must convert a minus into a plus," he said.

Some reviews focused on his physical appearance. "The vice president had only the slightest trace of make-up for the TV cameras and his blue-black beard, although freshly shaved for the evening, still stood out prominently," one reporter wrote.

Another was more sarcastic. "[A]t the end of his speech, the assembly rose to sing 'God Bless America.' The nominee knew the words and sang so lustily that the very volume of his own voice seemed to make him quiver."

Afterward, Nixon's daughter Patricia complimented her father in backhanded teenager style: "Daddy, don't misunderstand me, because I mean it as a compliment, but your speech was hardly boring at all," she said.

At the end of the night, Nixon was one step closer to his dream. He was the official Republican nominee.

No one could say how it would all turn out. Nixon was a relentless campaigner. Kennedy had charisma—and his father's money and network of illicit connections.

Both candidates had secrets that could derail their campaigns and their careers. Both sides suspected the other knew about their unsavory habits or defects.

They had an unspoken understanding. Nixon and Kennedy both had enough personal information to destroy the other's campaign, maybe his party.

Who would be the first to blink?

COUNTDOWN: **95 DAYS**

Fidel Castro had no choice. The United States was constantly trying to undermine his government, and the time had come for drastic action. American leaders needed to learn to stay out of Cuba's affairs.

For six months, the United States had been punishing Castro for strengthening his ties with the Soviet Union. When Cuba needed help, the Soviets stepped in. In February, they agreed to a five-year deal to buy tons of sugar, while providing oil, grain, and other help. The United States retaliated with an embargo, blocking the sale of oil, arms, and guns to Cuba.

When the Soviets shipped oil to the island, U.S. petroleum companies in Cuba refused to refine it. When Cuba and the Soviets established diplomatic relations, Washington turned up the heat a little more.

Castro knew this couldn't go on much longer. The Soviets were defending his regime, while the United States wanted to destroy him. Neither nation cared much about Cuba's best interests. Castro felt like a bone tossed between two big dogs.

It was time for a bold move.

In early August, more than fifty thousand young men and women were gathered in Havana for the Latin American Youth Conference. Castro had been ill. He was still running a high fever, but the young revolutionaries were counting on him to show up. It was the perfect platform for his special announcement.

Castro put on his iconic olive-drab fatigues and military hat and headed for the stadium. His aides helped him to the stage.

A podium, a microphone, and the Cuban flag were all he needed. Castro stood for a moment, basking in the cheers of thousands of followers.

Then Castro told them the news: All American-owned assets in Cuba were now the property of the nation, including the Cuban Electric Company, a subsidiary of the American and Foreign Power Company of New York, valued at $300 million.

The audience shouted out with joy. Castro smiled through his scraggly beard. The power company was just the start. The Cuban Telephone Company, two oil refineries, and thirty-six American-owned sugar mills—and all their properties, worth about $770 million—all became the property of Cuba.

The speech energized Castro, but his handlers hurried him back to his residence. He was clearly still feeling woozy.

Castro was playing a dangerous game. But with Soviet protection, Castro could finally take provocative action against America for exploiting Cuba's resources and mistreating its people.

Only hours later, another shot was fired across the Cuban horizon. This one came from another powerful quarter: the island's Roman Catholic hierarchy.

Liberal Catholics had formed an important part of Castro's revolution, but the nation's Catholic hierarchy and the revolutionary movement were at odds. Seizing the goods and businesses of others was clearly not Christianity in action. Hours after Castro's big announcement, the Cuban Catholic archbishop warned against "the increasing advance of communism in our country."

It was the church's first official criticism of the steadily increasing Soviet influence on the Castro regime.

Castro and his ministers made plain that they stood firmly with Russia as an economic and military ally—regardless of what the United States and Latin American governments might think. Foreign Minister Raúl Roa played coy, saying the Soviet Union's offers of help didn't mean it was exporting communism, or trying to gain a foothold in the Western Hemisphere.

The Eisenhower administration knew that was a lie. The Soviets had found a partner nation that posed a clear threat to America's national security.

Eisenhower distrusted Castro and was wary of his relationship with Soviet leader Nikita Khrushchev. Earlier in 1960, Eisenhower had signed off on a plan by the CIA to train Cuban exiles to invade their homeland. They assumed the Cuban people and military were fed up with Castro and would rise up to support the invasion. The ultimate goal was creation of a noncommunist government friendly to the United States. It was a gamble—just like the U-2 spy plane program. High risk, big reward. But what if the invasion failed? The fallout could only increase the growing antagonism between the United States and Cuba—except now Castro had Soviet protection.

Most Americans hadn't been spending much time thinking about Cuba. Ever since the casinos closed, the island nation had moved even further off their radar.

It was late summer and many people in the United States were at the beach or in the mountains, traveling cross-country with their families.

All three major TV channels were full of news about the presidential race between Kennedy and Nixon. The baseball pennant races were in full swing. As usual, the Yankees were on top of the American League with sluggers Mickey Mantle and Roger Maris leading a powerhouse lineup. And in the National League, the Pittsburgh Pirates were in first place, with the Milwaukee Braves four games behind.

At the movies, Alfred Hitchcock's *Psycho* was a huge box office hit. On TV, audiences at home were into Westerns like *Gunsmoke*, *Wagon Train*, and *Have Gun—Will Travel*.

Castro's seizure of American businesses made the front pages of most major newspapers, but the story didn't gain a lot of traction.

Americans didn't care about Cuban sugar mills and were still wrapping their heads around Soviet posturing. Meanwhile, they had other things on their minds.

August 7, 1960
Hyannis Port, Massachusetts

Most voters didn't start paying attention to presidential elections until after Labor Day. But Joe Kennedy couldn't wait.

After both party conventions wound up, the pollsters went to work—and it was good news for Nixon. The latest Gallup poll showed him with 53 percent of the vote and Kennedy with 47 percent. Most pundits predicted the race would be tight, but Nixon would win.

Not Joe Kennedy. He had worked for more than a decade to make sure Jack would live in the White House.

He'd used all his power and connections to push his son to the front of the line. He hadn't done all that work so Jack would lose now. As Joe had said, "We don't want any losers around here. In this family, we want winners . . . Don't come in second or third—that doesn't count—but win."

There was no second place—there were only winners and losers. Second place? You're a loser. And Jack was the cream of the crop, born to take first place. Jack Kennedy had more than good looks—he had all the intangibles that made a winner.

Now the old man was working harder than ever, crushing every rumor about his son. Joe had been doing that kind of thing for years.

Some in the Nixon camp—and others outside, including J. Edgar Hoover—had heard rumors about the women, and the hush money. Years later, Cartha "Deke" DeLoach, one of Hoover's trusted lieutenants, disclosed that the FBI director was stunned by Kennedy's behavior. The agency had thick files on Jack going back two decades that involved "immoral behavior" and allegations of "sexual misconduct."

Every day it seemed that something else came up: Jack's health record. A reckless romance with a starlet, or that girl from his office, or the call girl . . . Joe took care of those, while family members and loyalists promoted Jack's public persona: a healthy, devoted family man with a loving, supportive wife.

How long could Joe plug the leaks before the dam burst? It was a rhetorical question, of course. The press wasn't going to expose Jack—not with Joe and his fixers around.

But Joe was realistic: Despite Jack's charisma, he knew his son needed a boost to defeat Nixon in November. So, he continued to call on a motley collection of characters who helped him funnel money to the right people in the right states.

Unions were strong in 1960; 30 percent of all workers were in organized labor. But some unions were corrupt, run by Mafia figures who skimmed money from dues and pension funds.

As the leader of Chicago's Outfit, Sam Giancana had a grip on the Teamsters union and its president, feisty Jimmy Hoffa. Hoffa hated JFK and his brother Bobby, but Giancana was the boss. His words were law in organized crime circles.

Giancana wasn't fond of Bobby, either. It hadn't been long since the punk had grilled him before a Senate subcommittee investigating organized crime. When Giancana smugly refused to answer questions, Bobby replied, "Are you going to tell us anything, or just giggle? I thought only little girls giggled."

That didn't matter. Joe Kennedy realized Giancana could help him put Jack in the White House, so he'd started pulling strings. During the primaries, Giancana's men had spread money around in West Virginia, a critical victory in JFK's journey to the Democratic presidential nomination.

Now Joe needed Giancana's help again. Giancana could be most effective in big industrial cities in the Northeast and Midwest—especially Chicago. If Kennedy captured Illinois, it would be checkmate. So, Joe reached out.

Could Giancana get out the vote in mob-controlled unions in Chicago and other parts of the country? Giancana said yes, believing his support would commit the new Kennedy administration to going easy on organized crime in the coming years.

Joe saw the mob involvement as an investment. He didn't gamble. He only bet on sure things—events he controlled through manipulation or payoffs. That's how he'd made millions in the stock market and the liquor and real estate businesses.

He also had another ace up his sleeve: Chicago mayor Richard Daley.

Daley ran the Chicago Democratic Party machine—an operation that controlled tens of thousands of lucrative city jobs that he doled out to reward supporters. He was allied with the city's largest labor unions. He told members how to vote and they followed orders. His precinct workers controlled the voter rolls; they knew who voted and for whom. When a voter died, he was often still listed as an eligible voter. Sometimes, the dead were known to vote in Chicago.

Daley had promised to go all out for JFK, a fellow Irish Catholic.

So, with Giancana and Daley on board, Joe figured the Chicago returns would offset Nixon votes from more rural parts of southern Illinois. That could make the difference in a battleground state.

Texas was another key state, but Joe knew Lyndon Johnson had it under control. If the vote was close in Texas, the senator could pull a few tricks to win.

Hoover stepped lightly. Johnson was the Senate majority leader, and he could—and would—make Hoover's life miserable if he knew the FBI was investigating him. And Hoover liked Johnson. He didn't go after his friends.

Joe Kennedy's reading of the national election map was still just a theory, but with this head of the family, theories had a way of turning into reality. He still had to make more phone calls to his minions around the country.

It was going to take more than money to win this election.

August 24, 1960
Washington, D.C.

A fter a fast start following the convention, Richard Nixon ran into trouble that threatened his momentum.

He zipped across the United States—Seattle, Washington, to Portland, Maine. Then, on the seventeenth of August in Greensboro, North Carolina, Nixon had headed to a nighttime rally at the War Memorial Coliseum. A cheering crowd had surrounded his car, and as he got out, he smacked his knee hard into the edge of the car door. It hurt like hell, but it didn't slow him down. It was President Eisenhower's slam that hit him hardest.

His campaign was in full damage-control mode—thanks to an off-the-cuff remark by no less than his boss.

Everything had gone smoothly for Nixon since his nomination. He was on his way to fulfilling a campaign promise to visit all fifty states. He was answering the accusation that no one knows what Nixon stood for by releasing "study papers," including one called "The Meaning of Communism to Americans" and another called "The Scientific Revolution." Nixon said he supported creating programs and agencies to help cure diseases and unlock some of the secrets of the universe.

Like Senator Kennedy, Nixon had been balancing his presidential campaign with his legislative duties. In the middle of the month, lawmakers were called back to Washington for a special session of Congress.

As the president of the Senate, Nixon had to be there. No one really wanted to be in steamy-hot D.C. in the middle of August.

The Washington press corps was waiting for him.

Eisenhower had been coy for months about how hard he was willing to work for Nixon's election. Ike was popular with Americans. After eight years in office, he had a 65 percent approval rating. Republican leaders were anxious to have him campaign for Nixon.

Reporters had dogged Nixon about the president's reticence. At a news conference in Newport, Rhode Island, he was asked, Will the president campaign for him? "Did you get any clear indication as to the extent of the President's participation in the campaign to come?"

Nixon said he knew but that Ike should disclose that information. But Nixon said Eisenhower would be an asset because of his popularity. "I will only say that he is vitally interested" in helping with the campaign, Nixon said.

By the middle of August, Ike was on board, despite any misgivings he might have had. Nixon had been a loyal vice president. More important, Eisenhower was determined not to hand the keys to the White House over to Kennedy. Ike believed that JFK didn't have the experience or maturity to run the country.

How much could he campaign? Eisenhower would be seventy years old in October, and he had a history of heart problems. Republican leaders didn't want to exhaust him, but they didn't want to underuse him, either. Eisenhower was clearly a campaign asset. He could get Republicans to the polls.

After discussing the issue with GOP leaders and the Nixon campaign, the president agreed to appear in up to ten motorcades to energize the base and help organize Volunteers for Nixon, a group that would raise money for the vice president's campaign.

With Congress in session, Eisenhower had presented scores of proposals to Capitol Hill, including new civil rights legislation. He knew there was little chance that any of his measures would pass. The Democrats controlled both the House and Senate. It was political one-upmanship, a way for the president to show the public that the Democrats were the problem in Washington. If they wanted health care for seniors, they couldn't blame the GOP for standing in the way. Democrats held a majority in both houses. So, what were they doing?

Eisenhower decided to clarify that point at a press conference.

"I don't know why the complaints," the president said. "[Democrats] have the majority—such great majorities. They can do anything they want to, if they get together."

Nixon had been touting his time as the number two man. His many years in government were one of his campaign's central themes.

Sarah McClendon of the *El Paso Times* asked the president to talk about some of the executive decisions Nixon had participated in.

Eisenhower reminded her that executive decisions were in the president's domain. That's it. But he noted he had plenty of advisers and they all got a chance to weigh in on the issues.

The news conference was over. But as Eisenhower was leaving the podium, Charles Mohr from *Time* pressed him with one last question. He wondered if Eisenhower could give an example of a major idea, a suggestion that Nixon might have made that the president used to help come to a decision.

Ike interrupted him, quipping, "If you give me a week, I might think of one. I don't remember."

It was offhand, snide, and snappy: a perfect headline.

"Give Me a Week" was front-page news. It became a punch line for comedians. Not the kind of publicity that Nixon wanted at this stage of his presidential campaign. One Democrat replied it was "obvious that Mr. Nixon's contributions were so slight that the president could not recall a single one."

Nixon was flummoxed. At a last-minute news conference in Detroit, where he had just addressed the Veterans of Foreign Wars, he was asked about Ike's put-down.

Nixon was peeved, but professional. The commander in chief consults with cabinet members before making key decisions. But in the end, the president is ultimately the decider, he said.

Nixon hoped that was the end of it.

The sting faded with time. But just as his campaign was getting back on its feet, Nixon took another blow.

September 5, 1960
Washington, D.C.

R ichard Nixon couldn't believe his luck. Bad luck.

First it was that drama with Rockefeller, and then having to cut a deal with the party liberals.

And then, right when Nixon was basking in the praise for his convention speech, there was Ike, saying he needed a week to remember anything significant the vice president had contributed to his administration.

Now here he was—on Labor Day, no less—stuck in a hospital bed at Walter Reed Army Medical Center. The knee that he'd banged against a car door in North Carolina had become unbearably painful by month's end. Doctors discovered a lump had formed under his skin, a dangerous infection called *hemolytic Staphylococcus aureus*.

He'd be laid up for at least a week, maybe two. Instead of flags and bunting and stump speeches, he spent his Labor Day writing a statement that celebrated American workers:

"We have great production, high standards of working and living but America's strength is beyond those, the strength represented in the vigor and integrity and independence of American unions, in the institution of free collective bargaining in which workers and management establish the pace of economic advance."

Nixon was being treated with antibiotics. He had to stay off his feet so his knee could heal. His press secretary, Herb Klein, told the media that Nixon "continues to be in excellent physical condition."

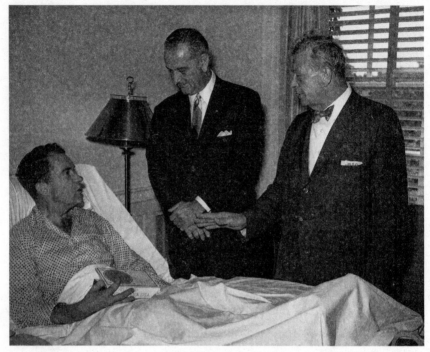

Richard Nixon visited by Senate leaders Lyndon Johnson and Everett Dirksen
(Associated Press)

But GOP leaders were whispering loud: What if Nixon's condition deteriorated? What if he couldn't campaign? If his recovery dragged on, the Republican National Committee might have to choose a new nominee, and soon.

Nixon wouldn't let that happen. He'd follow his doctors' orders. He'd come back stronger than ever. But losing two weeks in a tight campaign was serious. A long list of speaking appearances was already wiped out.

If everything went right, Nixon said he'd resume his campaign on September 12 with a six-day, 9,000-mile swing through fourteen states. That would show the public that he was back on his feet.

The political landscape was shifting. Nixon couldn't afford to lose any more ground to Kennedy.

And JFK was a politician to his bones, taking full advantage of Nixon's misery. Kennedy was zigzagging all over the country in his private airplane, showing up in places that were considered GOP strongholds.

All Nixon had to counter Kennedy's attacks on the campaign trail was Henry Cabot Lodge Jr., his vice presidential candidate. But Lodge wasn't as aggressive a campaigner as Nixon was. He didn't like the routine of meeting and greeting voters. In fact, sometimes Lodge seemed to have trouble staying awake at events. He'd take long naps after lunch, and he refused to make campaign appearances at night.

If Kennedy got a big bump in the polls, it might be time for Nixon to abandon his "clean and upright" electioneering pledge. Nixon knew all too well that muckraking could work wonders.

Detroit, Michigan

Jack Kennedy was on fire. He was on a swing through union-rich Michigan on Labor Day, conjuring up images of the old Franklin D. Roosevelt New Deal coalition.

In Detroit's Cadillac Square, sixty thousand people heard Kennedy rip into the Eisenhower administration for failing to promote economic growth, for high interest rates that hurt the "working man."

The Massachusetts senator said the administration's policies had cost a family of four $7,000 during the Eisenhower presidency. That meant less money a worker had for "an education, or a new house, or a rainy day or his old age."

The GOP slogan "You never had it so good" meant little to the nation's four million unemployed, he said.

"For the last eight years, we have had a government frozen in the ice of indifference. . . . We must recapture the spirit of Franklin Roosevelt and start moving forward on the unfinished business facing this country," he declared.

He said he stood strongly on the side of organized labor.

"The goals of the labor movement are the goals of all Americans and their enemies are the enemies of progress. The man and party who

John Kennedy in Detroit on Labor Day
(*Library of Congress*, U.S. News & World Report *Magazine Collection*)

oppose a decent minimum wage also oppose decent wages for our teachers. The man and party who oppose medical care for the aged have no more compassion for the small farmer or the small businessman, or hungry families in the United States or around the world. That kind of man—and that kind of party—likes things the way they are," he said.

And JFK made the strongest civil rights speech of his career, declaring his desire to end racial discrimination everywhere: in schools, homes, and churches—and at lunch counters.

He daringly stated his support for the sit-in strikes, like the one that started with the four Black college students in Greensboro, North Carolina, and spread across the nation.

His comments in the Motor City were intended to appeal to the United Auto Workers, whose sit-down strikes in the late 1930s led to higher wages and better working conditions.

"I want every American free to stand up for his rights—even if he has to sit down for them," he said.

His visit to Michigan energized Democratic leaders across the state. It was like that everywhere Kennedy campaigned. He wasn't just a politician. No, he was a celebrity, a movie star.

Michigan governor G. Mennen "Soapy" Williams gushed about Kennedy's charisma in towns throughout the state. "At the state fair, policemen tried to keep [JFK] from mingling in the crowd and shaking hands, but he did it anyway," Williams said. "The way people swarmed to him, grabbing his hand and wanting his autograph and storming his car—why, he proved he's a bearcat at campaigning."

With Nixon sidelined with his knee injury, Kennedy knew this was the time to crank up the razzle-dazzle, build his support, press his advantage. He might not get a chance like this again.

COUNTDOWN: **60 DAYS**

Jack Kennedy's campaign was carefully planned, precise and meticulous, thanks to his brother Bobby, his manager. There was no question who was in charge. Bobby controlled everything—and Jack liked it that way. All JFK had to do was show up and make speeches.

Bobby Kennedy knew the Republicans had assembled a formidable campaign team. But RFK always seemed to be one step ahead. His cutting-edge campaign strategy used market analysis and image consultants. He had pollster Lou Harris track JFK's daily progress.

Always looking for an edge, Bobby had recently hired a speech expert to help his brother improve his campaign delivery by relaxing his throat and taking deeper breaths.

Bobby Kennedy understood that the race to the White House was a marathon. He knew he'd have to work long hours over the next ten weeks to get his brother elected—and he expected others to do the same.

At times, Bobby could be blunt and abrasive—and he didn't care who he offended. His life revolved around Jack. It was filled with campaign schedules and strategy sessions. Nothing else seemed to matter—and Bobby thrived under the pressure.

Even as he trampled over others in his own pursuits, Bobby had noted at the Democratic convention that his brother had to mend some fences. Many liberals had been less than enthusiastic about Jack before he became the nominee. They had been downright disenchanted after he selected Lyndon Johnson as his running mate.

Former first lady Eleanor Roosevelt had openly criticized Jack for failing to cast a censure vote against Joseph McCarthy, the Red-baiting senator from Wisconsin. Taking direct aim at JFK's book, *Profiles in Courage*, she said he should have displayed "a little less profile and a little more courage."

To help gain her backing, JFK called and visited her, assuring her of his support for traditional liberal causes. Jack went to Hyde Park, New York, in August to speak at the twenty-fifth anniversary of the signing of Social Security into law. Eleanor's husband, Franklin Roosevelt, had fought vigorously to create Social Security during his first term in the White House.

"For millions of Americans, with that one stroke of the pen, their insecurity and fear were transformed into hope—their poverty and hunger were transformed into a decent life—their economic degradation was transformed into a chance to live out their days in the dignity and peace they had so richly earned," Kennedy said.

Bobby knew Jack also had to win the support of former president Truman, who had backed Missouri senator Stuart Symington for president. Truman openly despised Joe Kennedy. And just before the Democratic convention, he'd raised concerns about JFK's qualifications for the presidency.

When the question of Jack's religion came up, Truman took a shot at Kennedy's father, quipping, "It's not the *pope* I'm worried about, it's the *pop*."

But after JFK charmed the former president at the Truman Presidential Library in Missouri in late August, he came around.

At a news conference, Truman was his usual cantankerous self. When asked by a reporter, "What just took place?" Truman responded, "We have accomplished enough to win the war, that is all. Isn't that enough?"

Now Truman was actively campaigning for Jack.

Even with all the work there was to do, the biggest problem for Robert Kennedy was containing his contempt for Lyndon Johnson. He was unhappy with Johnson's presence on the ticket but determined to make the most of the unlikely political marriage.

Bobby couldn't stop thinking about Johnson calling their old man a Nazi and saying out loud that Jack had Addison's disease. That was more than politics; those were deeply personal attacks. Bobby stored them away, along with his bitter memories of his visit to Johnson's ranch.

"We put that son-of-a-bitch on the ticket to carry Texas," he said. He didn't want Johnson campaigning together with his brother. He wanted him barnstorming in the Deep South, assuring Democrats that JFK was no liberal, that they didn't have to worry about his religion.

LBJ was determined to show he could be an asset to the ticket. Privately, he told his protégé, John Connally, how devastating it would be to lose in Texas. It was a matter of political pride.

But Johnson had to prove he could deliver more than his own state. The entire Democratic South was at stake. Voters there worried that the party had become too liberal—some states were on the verge of slipping into the GOP column. Johnson spoke their language. He could talk them off the ledge.

Bobby hoped he wouldn't need to see Johnson again until the end of the campaign. But he was getting good feedback about Johnson's speeches in the South, so he sent him an encouraging note. "We are getting outstanding favorable reaction to your speeches, wherever you go," Bobby wrote.

But the Texas senator was feeling left out. He noticed that Nixon and Henry Cabot Lodge Jr. were making joint appearances. So how come the Kennedy campaign wasn't doing the same with him?

Johnson was just one more plate for Robert Kennedy to keep spinning. And if Johnson felt ignored now, the worst was about to come.

COUNTDOWN: **58 DAYS**

September 12, 1960
Houston, Texas

A few days before, a group of righteous men of God, 150 Protestant ministers, rose up at a Washington gathering and demanded Kennedy renounce his Catholic beliefs. He would not be free of being ruled by the church otherwise, they stated.

Jack Kennedy heard their concerns. No matter what he said or did, some voters were convinced that a Roman Catholic could not be trusted, and therefore could not be president.

He'd thought the big win in the West Virginia primary had put the issue behind him. At a speech before the American Society of Newspaper Editors in April, Kennedy stated his position clearly. He wanted no votes solely on account of his religion. Instead, every voter should cast their ballot for the man they believed would make the best president.

Not every voter saw things through his idealistic lens.

The ministers' blatant bigotry took Kennedy by surprise.

Some advisers told him to let it pass by, not to dignify it with a response.

But a few days later, he was invited to address the Greater Houston Ministerial Association. The group was mostly Republicans, out to embarrass or entrap Kennedy in religious arguments. But it was a great opportunity to address the issue head-on, in public. Kennedy accepted the invitation.

On his way to Houston, the candidate would make campaign stops in San Antonio, El Paso, and Lubbock. He'd meet with key Democratic Party leaders to shore up support in the Lone Star State.

Baltimore, Maryland

Richard Nixon had been released a few days earlier from Walter Reed and was raring to get back in front of his supporters.

At Friendship International Airport near Baltimore, President Eisenhower wished Nixon "Godspeed" before the vice president and running mate Henry Cabot Lodge Jr. flew to Indianapolis on the first leg of a long campaign swing across America.

The send-off took place inside an airport hall, as heavy rains from the fringes of Hurricane Donna lashed D.C. Eisenhower said the hurricane was "a good omen." He recalled a lucky rainstorm in Abilene, Kansas, where he launched his own campaign in 1952.

Neither Ike nor anyone else mentioned Eisenhower's "give me a

Richard and Pat Nixon campaigning in Indianapolis
(Library of Congress, U.S. News & World Report Magazine Collection)

week" comment. And Nixon didn't mention Kennedy's name in his brief comments.

He continued to tie himself to Eisenhower, saying that under Ike, "we have kept the peace for America . . . extended freedom throughout the world." A Nixon administration would keep to the high standards Eisenhower set during his two terms in the White House.

Nixon said he'd still visit all fifty states, because "no state should be conceded, and none should be taken for granted."

That seemed like a risky strategy when the vice president had been sidelined for two weeks, and still walked with a limp. The latest polls showed he'd lost significant support.

Gallup now had Kennedy with 53 percent of the votes, Nixon at 47 percent. The race kept seesawing back and forth. Three weeks earlier, Nixon had 53 percent of the votes to Kennedy's 47 percent.

In other campaigns, this would be the moment to let slip some ugly truths about Kennedy.

Nixon was tempted, but he'd made a promise. He wanted to show the American people that there was a new Richard Nixon. He was a statesman, not a junkyard dog.

What Nixon needed was a savvy adviser to focus his energy on battleground states. Winning such a tight contest was all about the Electoral College, not the popular vote.

But there was no big-picture visionary on staff. Nixon wrote his own speeches, made up his schedule, even handled seating plans. The stress of juggling so many tasks often left Nixon worn out when the rallies finally started, especially late in the day. But that was the way Nixon wanted to run his campaign.

El Paso, Texas

Kennedy touched down in Texas and made his way to an El Paso breakfast. This was LBJ country. Johnson was in the neighborhood and would be there, but he was ticked off that Kennedy was going to make a major address to the religious association and he wasn't invited to go along. In Texas. His home state.

Johnson believed he should've been invited. He'd been proving his worth to the campaign, with stops and speeches all over the state. But John Singleton, Johnson's campaign coordinator, answered first to Bobby Kennedy.

And the Kennedy team pretty much left Johnson alone to run his own campaign—as long as he stayed in the South. Nothing north of the Mason-Dixon Line.

Johnson knew the Houston speech was the real reason JFK was in Texas. It was the most important event of the day—maybe the entire campaign—and he'd have to watch it on TV. It was humiliating for the man who was supposedly the most powerful politician in the state.

At the El Paso breakfast, Texas political leaders knew that Johnson was jealous, and wanted to see how he'd handle being upstaged. When Johnson walked to the podium, he made only a few brief remarks, unlike usual—when he'd puff and blow about America, the Alamo, and JFK's qualifications—before suddenly introducing him to a crowd.

But Kennedy was ready—and knew how to defuse the tension in the room. He moved slowly to the microphone and quipped about the quick intro, "I was just relaxing to hear Lyndon Johnson make a 15- or 20-minute speech here this morning. I can see it will be a hard day for me."

Everyone laughed. Johnson smiled, but wouldn't forget the slight.

Houston, Texas

It was indeed a long day. Kennedy and Johnson appeared together in several cities before JFK headed to a downtown Houston hotel for the ministerial association meeting. It was hot and humid, but Kennedy, with his deep tan, looked comfortable. The Kennedy campaign had decided to buy airtime to broadcast his remarks in television markets all over Texas. They wanted to saturate the airwaves with the candidate's message.

The meeting opened with a prayer. The Reverend Herbert Meza, the association vice president, said the program was motivated by the religious issues in this campaign.

"The fact that the Senator is with us is to concede that a religious issue does exist," he said, before introducing Kennedy.

Kennedy was prepared. He believed in the power of words to change minds and win votes. As he stood at the lectern, he glanced at the crowd before him.

He knew this was a make-or-break moment for his campaign. Could he finally put the religious issue to rest?

Kennedy took a deep breath, then thanked the group for inviting him. He reminded them of the serious issues facing the nation—hunger, poverty, "old people who cannot pay their doctor bills, the spread of Communist influence, until it now festers 90 miles off the coast of Florida." Yet those issues were being overshadowed by the so-called religious issue—whether the pope and church doctrine would influence his decisions as president.

Kennedy said he believed in a complete separation of church and state. No Catholic bishop or other church authority should tell a Catholic president how to do his job. At the same time, he believed in an America where no Protestant minister should tell his congregation how to vote. Kennedy delivered a direct challenge to Protestant clergy who had already preached against electing a president who was Catholic.

He reminded the ministers that many of their own religious groups had been persecuted in the past for their beliefs.

"For while this year it may be a Catholic against whom the finger of suspicion is pointed, in other years it has been, and may someday be again, a Jew—or a Quaker—or a Unitarian—or a Baptist. . . . Today I may be the victim—but tomorrow it may be you," he said. "I believe in an America where religious intolerance will someday end."

He continued, "This is the kind of America I believe in—and this is the kind I fought for in the South Pacific, and the kind my brother died for in Europe. No one suggested then that we might have a 'divided loyalty,' that we did 'not believe in liberty' or that we belonged to a disloyal group that threatened the 'freedoms for which our forefathers died.'"

As he roared to a close, he said, "I am not the Catholic candidate for President, I am the Democratic Party's candidate for President who happens also to be a Catholic. I do not speak for my church on public matters—and the church does not speak for me."

And finally, "If I should lose on the real issues, I shall return to my seat in the Senate, satisfied that I had tried my best and was fairly judged," he said.

But if he lost because of his religious beliefs, "then it is the whole nation that will be the loser, in the eyes of Catholics and non-Catholics around the world, in the eyes of history, and in the eyes of our own people."

It was a masterful performance. Kennedy was eloquent and struck the right tone. Afterward, he fielded questions from the audience, including ones that asked about possible Vatican interference.

Again, Kennedy was direct. He said he'd made it clear that clergy had the right to direct religious life, but not government policy. If elected, his first responsibility was to the people of the United States. The Vatican would have no influence in his administration.

For some, that still wasn't enough.

Max Dalcke, president of the Gulf Coast Bible College and pastor of the First Church of God, asked Kennedy about protecting religious freedom in South America and beyond: "If you are elected president, will you use your influence to get the Roman Catholic countries of South America and Spain to stop persecuting Protestant missionaries?"

Kennedy didn't hesitate. "I would use my influence as president of the United States to permit, to encourage the development of freedom all over the world. One of the rights which I consider to be important is the right of free speech, the right of assembly, the right of free religious practice. And I would hope that the United States and the President would stand for those rights all around the globe without regard to geography, religion." The crowd cheered.

By the end, he wasn't sure how many of the ministers he had won over. He was realistic. He had already learned you couldn't erase religious bigotry with one speech. But at the very least, he hoped that it would no longer be a troubling campaign issue.

The Kennedy campaign printed more than five hundred thousand copies of his remarks and distributed them to clergymen—mostly Protestant clergymen—around the nation. It was another smart move by a team that always seemed to be one step ahead of Dick Nixon.

September 14, 1960
New York City

"Handsome Johnny" Roselli stared at the man across the table at the Plaza Hotel restaurant. In his line of business, he didn't often meet men as well dressed as he was, but Robert Maheu, a former FBI agent, was a fixer these days, a man with big connections. Both men apparently knew it paid to look sharp.

Maheu was a freelancer, currently the middleman between the CIA and an assortment of mob kingpins. And at lunch, Maheu made Roselli an offer that he knew the gangster couldn't refuse.

Maheu said he was working for a client who represented several "international business firms which were suffering heavy financial losses in Cuba as a result of Castro's actions."

His client was "convinced that Castro's removal was the answer to their problem" and was willing to "pay a price of $150,000 [over $1.5 million today] for its successful accomplishment."

Roselli moved his head a little closer. Had he heard the guy right? "Removal" of a foreign leader? Christ! Kill Castro. For a lot of dough.

Was this a setup? It sounded really risky.

His gut reaction was not to get involved.

But Maheu was persuasive—one of the reasons the CIA's Office of Security had called on him. He wouldn't give up until he had Roselli on board.

Maheu was smart as a whip and a master salesman, a natural for black ops. Born in Maine, he joined the FBI in 1940, a year before the United States entered World War II.

During the war, he posed as a Nazi-sympathizing Canadian and infiltrated New York's German American Bund, passing disinformation to spies who were eventually arrested.

In 1947, Maheu left the FBI to become a private detective. The CIA was his principal client, giving him steady work on clear-cut assignments—dirty work the agency could not officially be involved in.

The CIA work won him contracts with billionaire Howard Hughes, an aviation giant and Hollywood mogul who had gone into luxurious seclusion, mostly in Las Vegas. In the late 1950s, Maheu worked for Hughes, intimidating blackmailers, tailing men who romanced Hughes's actress girlfriend, and collecting information on business rivals.

Maheu had met Roselli, the Chicago mob's front man in Las Vegas, through Howard Hughes. An impeccably well-dressed ladies' man, Roselli had a long history with organized crime.

Roselli was like a character from a mob movie. His family emigrated from Italy to the United States when he was six years old.

Roselli dropped out of junior high and drifted to New York and then Chicago, where he fell in with bootleggers and mafiosi. He gained their trust. They sent him to Los Angeles in the 1930s to help develop the Chicago family's gambling and labor rackets.

He was a good-looking guy who dressed like a movie star, with his slicked-back hair, tailored suits, and sunglasses. But he was no actor. Roselli was a real-life gangster in Hollywood. And his mob credentials gave him a shady cachet; he moved easily among the Los Angeles social set.

But he pushed his luck, and in 1943 he was convicted of extorting money from movie studios and theater chains. He spent four years in prison. Once free, he started over in Las Vegas, just then emerging as a gambling mecca.

Eventually Roselli became Chicago's head fixer in Las Vegas, but his bosses lost confidence in him. They sent him back to L.A. to do lesser work.

That's where he was when Maheu called.

Roselli knew Maheu had some kind of special contract with the CIA. And Maheu knew Roselli had deep ties to the mob.

When senior CIA officer Richard Bissell, who had developed the U-2 spy plane program, put together a "sensitive mission requiring gangster-type action," he knew where to find real gangsters for the job.

The Mafia could fulfill the mission and provide the CIA with a credible cover story. Castro had closed down their profitable Cuban brothels and casinos. If things went wrong and the assassins were killed or captured, the media would accept that the Mafia was acting on its own.

The CIA brass gave Bissell's plan the go-ahead, according to since-released CIA files, and Maheu was hired to organize the plot. Maheu told CIA officials he knew someone he thought was a "high-ranking member of the 'syndicate'": Roselli. Maheu said if Roselli was in fact a member of the mob, "he undoubtedly had connections leading into the Cuban gambling interests."

Bissell asked Maheu to put the plan in motion.

That's why these two "businessmen" were lunching in the hotel restaurant, apparently negotiating important matters. But things were at an impasse. Roselli's body language said he didn't want any part of this deal.

According to a CIA memo among the released files, Maheu pressed him, saying it was Roselli's "patriotic duty" to help get rid of the communist dictator.

Roselli thought about it for a moment. Maybe this job could get him back into the good graces of the bosses in Chicago—and one boss in particular.

"I have to run it by somebody first," Roselli said.

"Who?"

A man named Sam, he said, "who knows the Cuban crowd."

Maheu nodded.

"One thing," Roselli said. "I don't want any money. I don't think my people would want money for this, either."

Maheu smiled to himself. He'd hooked his fish.

This was a top secret operation, he told Roselli, and they needed to move quickly. As they rose to leave the restaurant, Maheu had one more thing to say, the most important thing: "The U.S. government is not involved."

Roselli nodded. He understood the significance. And so would his boss.

COUNTDOWN: **51 DAYS**

September 19, 1960
New York City

Finally, after weeks of speeches, handshakes, and baby kissing, something had happened that might end the Kennedy-Nixon deadlock.

The communists had landed in New York City, and suddenly, both candidates had a new brick to throw.

It wasn't exactly an invasion. Soviet premier Nikita Khrushchev had arrived on the *Baltika*, a Soviet ocean liner, to address the United Nations.

Cuban dictator Fidel Castro was also in town for the meeting. He and Khrushchev had greeted each other on the UN assembly floor with a giant bear hug.

The United Nations treaty gave Khrushchev and Castro freedom to move on American soil while on business for the global peace organization.

Perhaps the American people didn't feel the impact of the UN meeting, but Richard Nixon saw an opportunity to contrast his years of foreign policy experience with JFK's relative beginner status.

Both candidates had finished up the summer crisscrossing America, speaking in big cities and small towns. The polls said they were in a dead heat. Every day mattered.

Their campaigns tried everything to sway the news cycle. At every stop, they appealed to local newspapers, television stations, and news radio outfits to show up and focus on their candidate. The newspapers and airwaves were full of bombast, but for weeks, nothing had moved the needle in one direction or the other. Both campaigns looked forward to the first of four televised debates. Then, if a candidate stumbled, the media could leap on it and maybe create a bump in the polls.

The campaigns were breaking new ground. This was the first time the nominees of the two major parties in a presidential election would square off on live television. It was the most high-profile series of American debates in a century.

The last time a political face-off drew so much attention was in 1858, when Democratic senator Stephen Douglas of Illinois took on Republican Abraham Lincoln. They debated seven times in a Senate campaign that focused on expanding slavery into new U.S. territories.

Douglas was reelected, but the national exposure catapulted Lincoln to prominence. Two years later, Lincoln landed the GOP presidential nomination and the White House.

No one knew how many people would tune in to the Nixon-Kennedy debates. Pundits predicted tens of millions of Americans would, and that could make the difference in a tight race.

The first debate was scheduled for September 26, in a Chicago television studio. Until then, both candidates had to keep grinding it out on the campaign trail.

Nixon, looking for a fresh angle of attack, used Khrushchev's visit to put a new edge on his basic critique of Kennedy, who had suggested in May that Eisenhower apologize to Khrushchev for the U-2 spy plane debacle.

Kennedy was "naïve," Nixon said.

"We have responsibility in avoiding resort to statements which tend to divide America, which tend to disparage America, and which in any way would encourage Chairman Khrushchev and his fellow dictators to believe that this nation, the leader of the Free World—is weak at will, is indecisive, is unsure of and hesitant to use her vast power; is poorly defended, is held at bay by imperialistic communism, is divided in opinion on world affairs, believing that the majority of mankind hold her in disdain," Nixon said at a campaign stop in Scranton, Pennsylvania.

It was a maneuver meant to put Kennedy on the political hot spot, now that a Soviet ship was docked in New York Harbor, and Cuban dictator Fidel Castro was wrangling with his hotel in Harlem over the bill.

Eisenhower and Khrushchev had been scheduled for an important summit meeting in Paris on May 16, but when the spy plane was shot down on May 1, all hopes of mutual goodwill crashed along with it. Khrushchev lashed out at Eisenhower for refusing to condemn the spying and halt further reconnaissance. It was the end of the hopes of many in both countries who'd thought a period of "peaceful coexistence" might be on the horizon.

After another broadside attack on Kennedy in Fort Wayne, Nixon flew to Louisville and picked up the same theme, hoping that it would stick.

"When you're dealing with a dictator, you must never make concessions without getting something in return because that is not the road to peace. It is the road to surrender or even to war," he said.

When asked if he was suggesting that Kennedy was surrendering to the Soviet Union, Nixon backed off, still managing to get in the point about experience. "Absolutely not," he said at a press conference in Springfield, Missouri. "Mr. Kennedy didn't know what he was espousing."

Time and again, Nixon said the U.S. military and economy was first in the world. He appealed for supporting the president.

"We know the regimented communists will march, lockstep, through the United Nations, hanging desperately together to avoid hanging one another separately. There will be, on their part, no deviation," Nixon said the next day at a stop in Michigan.

Kennedy didn't keep silent. He fired back, saying that "personal attacks and insults" would not halt communism, or win the November election.

The danger to the nation lay in denying its shortcomings and perils rather than "continuing to speak up for a stronger America," Kennedy said.

"It's not naïve to call for increased strength. It is naïve to think that freedom can prevail without it," he said.

He said those who "held back the growth of America for the past eight years will be rejected this November."

And so ended another day on the campaign trail. Back and forth they went, but neither gained any ground.

The debates were only a week away. And that would make all the difference.

September 25, 1960
Miami, Florida

When the CIA's man stepped off the plane in Miami, Organized Crime was waiting at the gate in a natty pin-striped suit, ready to do America's dirty deeds.

Robert Maheu didn't have to wait long after his meeting with Johnny Roselli in New York. Roselli was a true-blue patriot, pleased to go to work for America. Yes, Roselli said, his boss would meet with Maheu in Miami.

Maheu booked a flight.

On the tarmac, Roselli smiled, shook Maheu's hand, and helped him with his bags. Roselli was pumped up.

"Where are we going?" Maheu asked.

"The Fontainebleau," he said.

That figured, Maheu thought. The place was over-the-top, a destination for upscale tourists and a hangout for gangsters. Back when Al Capone was at the height of his power, he spent his winters in Miami, and his crew followed. It made sense, with the Cuban casinos only about 230 miles south across the Caribbean.

The men made small talk on the drive to the hotel. Maheu enjoyed the views of the ocean, sky, and art deco buildings in every shade of pink. They parked at the Fontainebleau and headed inside. Roselli led his man past the tourists, bars, and gift shops and into the Boom Boom Room, a swanky restaurant with a performance stage.

Maheu smiled—he'd seen this place on television, back in the spring.

Frank Sinatra had hosted Elvis Presley, who had just been discharged from the Army. It was schlock, but plenty of fun.

The mobsters clearly were out to impress.

Two men were waiting at the table. Roselli waved and headed in their direction.

The men stood to greet them, and Roselli kissed each on the cheek—the old-school way of showing respect to the boss.

Roselli introduced Maheu to Sam Giancana and Santo Trafficante Jr.

Maheu knew who they were. These two controlled almost all the rackets east of Chicago.

Trafficante was just as powerful as Giancana. With his thin build, receding hairline, and thick horn-rimmed glasses, Trafficante looked like an accountant, but he was a stone-cold killer.

When his father died quietly in 1954, Trafficante took over his Tampa-based operation. Gambling was big, but Trafficante Jr. was expanding into narcotics smuggling and distribution. He was keenly interested in killing Castro. He'd lost tens of millions when the Cuban strongman seized power.

Maheu didn't waste any time. He sat down, ordered a drink, and pitched his idea to the bosses.

Giancana listened for a few minutes before stopping Maheu. He was "only going to be the back-up man," he said. If they agreed to cooperate, Trafficante and Roselli would be the point men. Trafficante was fluent in Spanish, so he could serve as a translator to possible recruits.

Over lunch, they discussed the "who" of this assassination. It wouldn't be hard to find a Cuban to kill Castro. Just about anyone in the exile community would volunteer, but they had to find someone who could get close enough to Castro to do the job. He never went anywhere without his machine-gun-toting revolutionaries.

Maheu said the CIA wanted Castro dead as soon as possible. He didn't mention that the agency was coordinating an invasion by Cuban exiles to overthrow Castro. If the dictator was simply removed, they could scrap the expensive invasion.

Giancana knew it would take time to develop a plan and, more important, find the right person to pull it off, but it was an exciting diversion. He was in.

Roselli was ready to fly to Cuba himself and start shooting commies. He was a fiercely patriotic man, or as Giancana said, "Wave a flag and Johnny will follow you anywhere."

Trafficante was quiet but clearly engaged.

Maheu smiled to himself. His bosses would be happy.

The mobsters had their own motivations for eliminating the dictator. Aside from revenge for their lost millions, they believed they could reopen their casinos once the revolutionary leader was out of the picture. Things would go back to where they were before.

And they also believed that cooperating with the government in such a high-risk venture would earn them a kind of "get out of jail free" card that would keep the FBI off their backs as they pursued their dark business at home.

What Roselli, Giancana, and Trafficante didn't know was that this was a covert operation. The FBI had no clue about the CIA's plot, so FBI surveillance of the organized crime leaders and their operations would continue.

Maheu had his own blind spots. He didn't know Giancana was working on behalf of Kennedy's campaign, persuading labor union associates all over the country to campaign legally—and illegally—for Kennedy.

Giancana thought things through and came to a realization. He might be an uneducated thug, but he was now in an unprecedented position to shape the 1960 election. If they killed Castro before November, it would show that the Eisenhower administration had been working behind the scenes to eliminate a communist threat—and Richard Nixon would reap all the benefits.

If they waited until after Election Day, Kennedy could claim that the administration hadn't done anything to remove the Cuban leader from power, or stop Soviet advances in the Western Hemisphere.

The possible scenarios were mind-boggling.

Now that Maheu had successfully recruited the gangsters, they moved on to the "how." Giancana said there was a better, more discreet way of doing the job than using a gun.

At later meetings there was discussion about the possibility that the CIA could furnish "some type of potent pill," and they could come up with a plan to place it in Castro's food. Giancana threw out the name of a "prospective nominee," a former Cuban official who'd been taking kickbacks from the mob and "still had access to Castro." The man was in financial trouble, Giancana said.

That was an interesting idea. Handlers from the CIA would be in touch with them soon, Maheu said.

With a deal in place, the former G-man rose from the table. He told the group he'd still be involved in the planning, recruitment, and execution of the plot. There was no time to waste. He had to get on the phone and talk to his bosses.

He had to get this plan underway before anyone changed their minds.

COUNTDOWN: **44 DAYS**

September 26, 1960
Chicago, Illinois

A s darkness fell over Chicago, a limousine turned toward the entrance of the WBBM-TV television studio, where the first of the presidential debates would take place.

Richard Nixon rode in the back, his hands full of question cards and notes. He was prepared. He was a skilled debater from childhood, when he'd hashed out the issues of the day at the dinner table with his dad. He'd served on the debate teams in college and law school, and they'd prepared him well for world-class deliberation.

It was Nixon who held his own against Khrushchev in the so-called kitchen debate in Moscow in 1959. And Nixon knew how to use television. Hadn't his Checkers speech in 1952 saved his political career?

Nixon had drilled down on the facts, arguments, and counterarguments for both sides of the top issues. He could then develop his own position, anticipate his opponent's, and avoid errors of fact or logic.

Most important, he knew to keep calm and composed, maintain eye contact, use hand gestures, and stand up straight.

Nixon, however, was still feeling the effects of his knee injury. He had emerged from the hospital at least ten pounds lighter—and hadn't regained the weight. To make matters worse, the vice president had recently battled the flu. He was still weak. But instead of resting before the debate, he made a campaign speech.

It didn't matter that he felt physically run-down and low—or that his gaunt face and pale complexion made him look, as Don Hewitt, who directed the debate for CBS, described it, "like death warmed over." He knew he had this debate in the bag. Besides, his psychiatrist, Arnold Hutschnecker, had advised Nixon how to stay calm under pressure.

The car rolled to a stop. An assistant opened the door. Nixon stepped into the warm evening—and slammed his barely healed knee into the edge of the car door. He clutched his leg in pain—and could barely stand.

Nixon's longtime media adviser, Ted Rogers, saw Nixon's face turn white. But the vice president waved away his aides' helping hands. He was okay, he said. He wouldn't let this get to him. He'd fight through the pain. Tonight was too important.

Clearly it wasn't a good start to the evening.

There were plenty of people who thought Nixon should skip the debates, that they would only give Kennedy more visibility. But backing down wasn't an option. Nixon wasn't a quitter. This was the most anticipated political event of the presidential campaign, and Nixon was sure he was up to the challenge.

The idea of broadcasting presidential debates had taken hold months earlier—well before Nixon and Kennedy became their parties' candidates.

It took congressional action to make it happen. Section 315 of the Federal Communications Act of 1934 required broadcasters to allow political candidates equal time to present their views. Democrats and Republicans would have to share the debate stage with third-party candidates, and the events would drag on for hours—unthinkable within the tightly programmed TV format.

Congress passed a resolution to suspend the rule in late July, and Eisenhower signed it on August 24.

Television had brought new awareness and enthusiasm to the political process. In 1950, around 10 percent of the nation's families owned a television. Now, in the fall of 1960, more than 90 percent of American families owned at least one set, a total of some 50 million TVs. The average American watched four to five hours of television every day.

And the Kennedy-Nixon face-off had the potential to be riveting. Both were experienced debaters. In fact, they had squared off long before, in 1947, when they were first-term members of the House of Representatives.

During their early days in Congress, they were appointed to the Education and Labor Committee.

In April 1947, they traveled by train to McKeesport, Pennsylvania, to debate the pros and cons of the Taft-Hartley Act, a law designed to significantly reduce the power of organized labor. The legislation would prohibit certain kinds of strikes and give workers the option of joining a union instead of forcing them. It had already passed the House and was before the Senate.

A coal-and-steel town of about 45,000 people outside Pittsburgh, McKeesport was the perfect location to debate the issue. The United Steelworkers, one of America's most powerful unions, was based in Pittsburgh.

A civic group sponsored the debate at the Penn-McKee Hotel. They picked Nixon and Kennedy because they were considered rising stars in their respective parties. No surprises. Nixon spoke in strong support of the bill; Kennedy was opposed. Most of the pro-union crowd seemed to favor Kennedy, who'd later admit that Nixon won that debate: "The first time I came to this city was in 1947, when Mr. Richard Nixon and I engaged in our first debate. He won that one, and we went on to other things."

After the debate, they headed to a local diner, where they bonded over burgers and baseball. Then they dashed off to the train station to catch the eastbound midnight train to Washington. They shared a compartment and had to flip a coin for who got the lower bunk; Nixon won that, too. Thirteen years later, they were together again on the debate stage, this time competing for the most powerful office in the world.

In midsummer, just before the start of the GOP convention, Robert

Kintner, the president of NBC, had approached them about a debate, saying he'd reserved up to nine hours in prime time for a series of presidential debates. Would Kennedy be interested?

"I know the decision was made in 15 to 20 minutes that we should send a telegram to Kintner saying we accepted," Salinger recalled. "The feeling was, we had absolutely nothing to lose by a debate with Nixon. In fact, if we accepted right away, we put Nixon in a position where he had to accept."

For Salinger, it seemed like the perfect offer at the perfect time. Kennedy had been campaigning hard. People might have tuned in for his speeches, or noted his face on the covers of many magazines, but most "average Joe" Americans still didn't know what Jack Kennedy stood for. The debates would introduce him to a new audience, the prime-time TV viewer. Since there were only three networks—no cable television yet to dilute the audience—the debate would saturate the airwaves.

And TV brought JFK another advantage. Just standing up next to Richard Nixon would show the world that it was Kennedy who looked like a statesman—and Nixon a politician.

The timing was perfect. Kennedy was on top of his game, sharpened by the campaign stops and stump speeches. People could feel his passion. His campaign ads were like nothing ever seen before, and the Rat Pack was out in full force, keeping the Kennedy image in the spotlight.

He looked and sounded physically fit, even if he owed that to special injections from Max Jacobson, a doctor to the stars, whom author Laurence Leamer described in *The Kennedy Men* as "a wondrous doctor who gave his patients magical vitamin injections that contained, among other things, the blood of young lambs." Kennedy had been on the verge of collapse when his friend Charles Spalding told him about Jacobson, whose Manhattan waiting room was full of celebrity patients like Eddie Fisher, Truman Capote, and Johnny Mathis.

Kennedy paid a visit to the doctor in early September, complaining that his muscles felt weak and his energy was low. Jacobson injected JFK with a mixture of amphetamines, steroids, and vitamins. It gave Kennedy the boost he needed for his Houston speech to the group of ministers. A second shot promised to give him an edge in Chicago.

Meanwhile, Republicans weren't sure about televised debates. But Kennedy had already agreed to participate. What would the public think if Nixon said no? Besides, Nixon enjoyed a good debate. He was confident in his ability.

Nixon didn't run the question past his advisers. He just said yes. It was another example of the vice president making important campaign decisions on his own, without consultation, like the New York meeting with Nelson Rockefeller and the pledge to campaign in all fifty states.

His aides were flummoxed. Advance man H. R. Haldeman recalled that he didn't believe Nixon was physically ready for the debate.

"I was concerned because I knew he . . . looked bad physically and was in bad health. He was not in good physical shape and, therefore, not good mental shape, I didn't think. He wasn't ready to do the job in the debate," he said.

But Haldeman didn't help Nixon by not scheduling time to meet with Ted Rogers in the days leading up to the debate.

Originally a producer for television shows like *The Lone Ranger*, Rogers had been with Nixon since his Senate race in 1950. On the day of the debate, Rogers didn't see Nixon until 4:30 p.m. And when he did, he was stunned at the vice president's appearance.

Still, Nixon felt that he could handle Kennedy. JFK didn't have *his* experience, *his* skills. Nixon believed he'd win, and it wouldn't be close.

The format had been settled in advance. The candidates would stand alone, without advisers, without a studio audience.

Howard K. Smith of CBS would serve as the moderator, opening and closing the program. At the outset, each candidate would have eight minutes to state his case, with a coin flip deciding who'd go first.

Then for about forty minutes, a panel of television journalists would ask questions. Each candidate would be allowed three minutes for his reply, after which his opponent would get a minute and a half to respond. This debate would be limited almost completely to domestic affairs.

This was another Nixon miscalculation. He believed the audience for the debates would build—so that viewership would peak later. At the third debate, the focus would be on foreign policy issues, Nixon's strength. What he didn't realize was the first debate would have the biggest impact on voters' perceptions—and domestic issues were in Kennedy's wheelhouse.

The networks selected no newspaper reporters for the panel. And only those who'd traveled with the campaigns could attend the live event—and they had to watch the action on monitors from an adjacent studio. The networks predicted that between 50 and 80 million people would watch the first debate.

NBC would handle the second one on October 7, and ABC would carry the last two on October 13 and October 21.

Robert Kennedy knew the debates would play to his brother's on-camera poise and good looks. Hiring a professional media consultant was paying dividends. TV viewers were already used to seeing Kennedy on their screens.

The Nixon campaign was optimistic, too. Press secretary Herb Klein knew Nixon felt he could debate anyone. And if the vice president avoided the debates, he'd be "hounded by it by the hostile press."

The first debate was scheduled for a Monday night. Kennedy arrived from Cleveland, Ohio, the day before and stayed at the Ambassador East Hotel in Chicago.

Ted Sorensen, Richard Goodwin, and Mike Feldman, Kennedy's "brain trust," had prepared fifteen pages of relevant facts and probable questions. On Monday morning, they held a question-and-answer session with Kennedy: What was the latest unemployment rate? What were Nixon's ideas for improving schools? It was light and easy. No tension.

They helped Kennedy with his eight-minute opening statement, but in the end, JFK rewrote it.

Kennedy headed to a gathering of the United Brotherhood of Carpenters union, then returned to the hotel for a nap. According to Theodore White in *The Making of the President 1960*, when he got up around 6:30 p.m., he was refreshed and ready to go. He read the cards with facts and figures that Sorensen, Goodwin, and Feldman had prepared for him. He ate dinner on his own, and put on a dark blue suit and white shirt and dark tie. Then he headed to the studio.

Meanwhile, Nixon had spent most of the day with only his wife, Pat, alongside him. As usual, Nixon took it upon himself to do just about everything. His advisers had urged him to get to Chicago early the day before the debate so he could rest. Instead, his limo pulled in at night, and he was running a fever—the lingering effects of the flu.

Nixon's advisers had suggested he cancel his appearance the day of the debate before the carpenters union—hell, they were pro-Kennedy, and Nixon needed time to prepare. But Nixon went anyway. By the time he returned to his hotel room just after noon, he was exhausted.

Nixon locked himself in his suite and pored over campaign issues and questions he might be asked by the panelists. He took a telephone call from Henry Cabot Lodge Jr., who urged the vice president to go easy, to try to free himself of the "assassin image" he had built up over the years.

On the way to the television studio, Rogers, his media adviser, suggested just the opposite. He said Nixon should come out swinging. Like a good boxer, he said, Nixon had to hit Kennedy hard from the beginning.

But Nixon could hear Lodge's voice in his head. This was a different Richard Nixon. Maybe he could put an end to "Tricky Dick."

Rogers was worried. The vice president didn't look well. Worse, he didn't seem to grasp how stressful things were going to get.

When Nixon struck his bad knee on the door of the limousine, Rogers winced.

Once inside the studio, Nixon and his men looked around the set. The background was light gray—and Nixon's blue-gray suit blended into the backdrop.

Nixon was sitting in a chair beneath a microphone for a sound check.

When Jack Kennedy walked in, cool, slim, and tanned, Nixon stood to speak to him. He struck his head against the microphone, and the amplified impact boomed through the studio.

Maybe Nixon should have gone home then and called it a night. Things only got worse.

Producer Don Hewitt asked Kennedy if he needed makeup, and he said no. Nixon also refused the offer, but Hewitt could see that was a problem. Nixon looked tired. He had a five-o'clock shadow that he was trying to conceal.

As Kennedy headed to the set, his brother Bobby whispered some advice: "Kick him in the balls," he said, with a mischievous smile.

The candidates stood in their places and took deep breaths while the moderator, Howard K. Smith, sat down behind a desk. The red light went on. It was showtime.

The studio was strangely hermetic, with a handful of panelists and technicians, and the candidates standing in a pool of light. But outside,

First presidential debate, September 26, 1960
(UPI/Newscom)

70 million viewers were watching in homes, churches, or bars—wherever there was a television set. It was the largest TV audience for a political event in history, to that point. The debates had preempted *The Andy Griffith Show* on CBS, the network's most popular series. Millions more listened on radio.

Kennedy went first; and while the debate's focus was supposed to be on domestic issues, JFK weaved the Soviet threat to the United States into his opening statement. He was unhappy, he said, with the way things were going in America.

"Are we doing as much as we can do? Are we as strong as we should be? Are we as strong as we must be . . . ? I should make it very clear that I do not think we're doing enough, that I am not satisfied as an American with the progress that we're making," he said.

Nixon challenged that in his opening statement. He said the nation was on the move, that it had racked up more progress in numerous fields in the Eisenhower administration than under former president Truman.

Kennedy stayed on the offensive. The bright lights didn't help Nixon. He was sweating. He looked tired and ill. He had circles under his eyes.

"My God, they embalmed him before he even died," Chicago mayor Richard Daley said at the time.

During the debate, Kennedy emphasized the differences between himself and Nixon. He hit on his main campaign themes: American economic growth needed to be increased. Teachers were poorly paid. The elderly could not support themselves on their Social Security checks. Kennedy hammered at the Eisenhower administration's failures, while Nixon touted its successes.

But it was more than that. It seemed that Nixon was too polite. He'd often preface his answers by saying he agreed with the Massachusetts senator.

When a reporter asked Kennedy why people should vote for him when Nixon said he was too inexperienced for the job, JFK pointed to the fact that he had served in Congress the same length of time as Nixon—nearly fourteen years. "So, our experience in government is comparable."

Besides, he said, the questions that counted were the programs the two advocated and the records of the two political parties.

Staring straight into the camera, JFK reminded the audience that the Democratic Party had supported and sustained important programs that helped the people.

John F. Kennedy at the first debate
(Associated Press)

"Mr. Nixon comes out of the Republican Party. He was nominated by it. And it is a fact that through most of these last twenty-five years the Republican leadership has opposed federal aid for education, medical care for the aged, development of the Tennessee Valley, development of our natural resources. I think Mr. Nixon is an effective leader of his party. I hope he would grant me the same," Kennedy said.

Nixon had a chance at rebuttal and passed it up: "I have no comment."

It wasn't only Nixon's answers, or nonanswers. It was the way he looked and acted on camera. There were times he seemed uncomfortable. He used a handkerchief to wipe sweat off his face. Was he nervous?

Was it the hot lights of the studio? Was it his fever? Viewers wouldn't have known about that.

By contrast, Kennedy seemed at ease. He'd stare into the camera, making it feel like he was talking directly to people in their living rooms. Meanwhile, his rival would often look off to the side to address various reporters. To television viewers, it felt like Nixon was trying to avoid eye contact with them.

Sander Vanocur of NBC News brought up Eisenhower's "give me a week" comment of a few weeks earlier, about Nixon's apparent lack of contributions to his administration.

Nixon was annoyed—he felt Vanocur had raised the question to hurt his campaign. He said the president was probably being "facetious when he made the remark." He said he had advised Eisenhower on many issues, but in the end, the president made the decisions.

Nixon at debate
(Associated Press)

Kennedy responded that the real issue was "which candidate and which party can meet the problems that the United States is going to face in the '60s."

In his closing statement, Nixon said he concurred with Kennedy that "the Soviet Union has been moving faster" than America in terms of economic growth. But that was because they started "from a much lower base."

And Nixon said he agreed "completely" with Kennedy that "we have to get the most out of our economy."

"Where we disagree is in the means that we would use. . . . I respectfully submit that Senator Kennedy too often would rely too much on the federal government, on what it would do to solve our problems, to stimulate growth," he said.

Nixon predicted that JFK's programs would lead to higher prices for average Americans—and "people who could least afford it—people on retired incomes, people on fixed incomes."

"It is essential that a man who's president of this country certainly stand for every program that will mean for growth. And I stand for programs that will mean growth and progress. But it is also essential that he not allow a dollar spent that could be better spent by the people themselves," he said.

When it was Kennedy's turn, he spoke directly to viewers with more passion than at any time during the debate: If you feel America is headed in the right direction, you should vote for Nixon. But if you don't, you should vote for me.

"I don't want historians, ten years from now, to say these were the years when the tide ran out for the United States. I want them to say these were the years when the tide came in; these were the years when the United States started to move again," he said.

At the end of the debate, Nixon greeted Kennedy. But in full view of the still photographers, Nixon jabbed his finger into Kennedy's chest as if he were "laying down the law about foreign policy or communism," Kennedy recalled.

The image was not of a commander. No, it was more like a schoolyard bully. In fact, throughout the entire debate, Kennedy came across as an energetic leader, while Nixon appeared old, tired, and stuffy.

The debate succeeded in erasing, in one night, the stature and experience advantage Nixon had enjoyed throughout the campaign. Kennedy had appeared to be the vice president's equal. In debate one, Kennedy bested Nixon because he was more relaxed and more in command of the issues, and because he didn't look sick or sweaty.

When it was over, Henry Cabot Lodge Jr., who was watching in his hotel room in El Paso, Texas, with several reporters, including Tom Wicker of *The New York Times*, made a harsh instant analysis about the man on the top of their ticket: "That son of a bitch just lost the election," he said.

September 27, 1960
Washington, D.C.

Richard Nixon sat quietly on the edge of his hotel bed. The trajectory of his campaign had changed in just a few hours. Nixon had been confident heading into the debate. But now he knew that Kennedy had pulled it off. He'd won the debate—at least on style points. JFK didn't just look better; he'd transformed Nixon into a tired, less-imposing figure.

To most viewers, Kennedy emerged from the contest as a world leader—someone who could handle Soviet premier Khrushchev and stop communist aggression.

What had happened? Nixon knew the answer. He had been sick and refused to admit it. He didn't rest. Yes, he'd banged his bum knee on his way into the studio. That certainly didn't help. But he couldn't blame his poor performance just on that.

No. His opponent was more prepared, more aggressive on the issues. Kennedy had set the tone and led the debate, beginning to end.

It didn't help that the studio lights showed no mercy.

Nixon's family and friends said he looked so gaunt and tired they were worried about his health.

His inner circle was crushed, and some began pointing fingers. H. R. Haldeman blamed Herb Klein for allowing the press too much access to Nixon before the debate.

"Richard Nixon did not look his usual self because he was not in top shape," Ted Rogers said about the vice president's performance.

Other Nixon advisers were stunned by his appearance. He wasn't wearing makeup and, with his pale skin, circles under his eyes, and "perpetual five-o'clock shadow," that only made it worse. He did use Lazy Shave, a powder to hide his five-o'clock shadow, but it didn't work.

But Nixon's problems transcended makeup. Time and again, he perspired so much that he'd pulled out a handkerchief to wipe his face. To viewers, it looked like he couldn't handle the pressure of the big moment. His Lazy Shave was streaked with sweat by the end of the hour.

Nixon had a fever, and a sore leg. By all accounts, he should have stayed in bed. So, why didn't he cancel his appearance? Was he worried about the way it would look to the public if he bailed out at the last minute? He didn't say. When Nixon accepted his party's nomination, he was the odds-on favorite to win the White House. And why not? He had national name recognition and was a heavyweight on the world stage. Two months earlier at the Republican National Convention, he'd given the speech of his life—one that even his critics praised. Although engaged in a Cold War, the United States was at peace. Despite what JFK said on the campaign trail, the economy was strong.

Now in his hotel room, Nixon mentally rewound and replayed the debate again and again, trying to make sense of what had happened.

Forget about cosmetics. That was just one of many mistakes the vice president made heading into the debate. Nixon realized that he had been overconfident and had underestimated his opponent. It didn't matter that he was still battling the flu. It didn't matter that he was weak and tired. It didn't matter that his leg still hurt. No, he knew he'd still beat Kennedy.

In the final analysis, Nixon didn't do enough preparation. A few hours in his hotel room. That's all he thought he needed. After all, Kennedy was a lightweight. Nixon? He was the debate king.

And he'd listened to bad advice. He wanted the public to see the new Richard Nixon. The statesman. Tricky Dick was gone forever. So, in an attempt to shed his "assassin image," Nixon wasn't aggressive. He agreed more than disagreed with his opponent. He didn't counterpunch. That— along with appearance—only made him look weaker.

Supporters wondered what had happened to the old Richard Nixon, the relentless politician who'd kept punching and punching until his opponent hit the canvas. That's the Nixon they wanted to see.

Instead, *this* Richard Nixon played by Marquis of Queensberry rules, while Jack Kennedy, the spoiled little rich kid from Massachusetts, was the street fighter, landing one body blow after another. A little longer and the moderator might have stopped the fight on a TKO.

Kennedy knew what he had to do. This wasn't a traditional college debate in front of judges who kept score. No, this was more like a sporting event—the World Series or, years later, the Super Bowl. Kennedy understood the power of television—and that it was more about being seen than heard.

His long grueling primary fight had prepared him well for the debate. Kennedy's campaign team had produced countless slick TV commercials featuring Jack Kennedy. So, he was comfortable under the bright studio lights.

And when it was time, Kennedy looked straight into the camera and ignored Nixon. Voters believed that JFK was talking to them. In the end, they were the real judges.

And what they saw was a young, handsome, articulate man who seemed to genuinely care about them. The photogenic Kennedy knew he had to be crisp and sharp and look his best. So, he showed up in Chicago well-rested and sporting a new tan.

For many potential voters, the debate was the first time they'd seen Kennedy live. They might not vote for him, but they were certainly talking about him the next day at the watercooler or in the backyard.

They already knew Nixon. He was old hat. You either loved or hated him. And it seemed that he had been around forever. And that evening, under the bright studio lights, it looked like he had aged overnight. He couldn't blame that on the Lazy Shave. No, in his hotel room, he knew he should have prepared more. He should have rested instead of addressing the carpenters union. Was he going to get any votes there? But Nixon being Nixon was stubborn and impetuous. He made critically important decisions on the spur of the moment. And last night's one might cost him the election.

Theodore H. White, who was working on a book that would revolutionize campaign reporting, saw the debate this way: "Mr. Nixon was debating with Mr. Kennedy as if a board of judges were scoring points. He rebutted and refuted, as he went, the inconsistencies or errors of his opponent. Nixon was addressing himself to Kennedy—but Kennedy was addressing himself to the audience that was the nation."

In the end, Nixon was the conservative candidate. He'd fought his debate in the settled, old-school style, and those who listened via radio said that Nixon was the clear choice.

But Kennedy's people had gone for the TV audience—all 70 million of them.

Now, a day after the debate, no one wanted to take responsibility for the fiasco. Nixon's doctor, Malcolm Todd, didn't pull any punches.

"You looked weak and pale and tired on TV because, in fact, you are weak and pale and tired—even though you don't feel that way at all, in your mind," he said. "We have to lighten up the schedule, get more food into you, and get you up to par before the next debate." The doctor put Nixon on a new regimen: a milkshake with each meal, plus one more in mid-afternoon, for the next two weeks. By the second debate, the vice president put on five pounds.

Nixon shook his head. Todd was right. Makeup. Bright lights. Television cameras. If it wasn't for his fever, he'd have handled Kennedy. No one would be talking about Lazy Shave.

Meanwhile, the Kennedy camp was ecstatic. Of course Jacqueline Kennedy was biased, but she praised her husband's performance. Six months pregnant and watching from their house in Hyannis Port, Massachusetts, she said, "I thought my husband was brilliant."

Good thing Nixon still had three debates left to redeem himself. Maybe there was still time to turn things around. No one knew how seriously the debate had damaged Nixon's campaign. But the vice president acknowledged that he had to find a way to recover, and fast. It would be difficult to make another first impression. Nixon could see the energy in Kennedy's post-debate rallies. It was still early, but with a little more than five weeks until Election Day, JFK was drawing bigger crowds—louder, younger, and more enthusiastic.

Meanwhile, Nixon's campaign was stuck in a low gear.

The day after the debate, Nixon realized he needed to do something drastic to get his campaign back on track. Otherwise, he'd be looking for a new job in a few weeks.

So, Nixon turned to his psychotherapist, Arnold Hutschnecker, who had been treating him since 1952. By 1960, their therapy sessions had reached a point where the doctor was "drawing psychological portraits" of other candidates for Nixon, including JFK.

Hutschnecker described Kennedy as a handsome, charismatic man's man, according to *The Gumshoe and the Shrink*, David L. Robb's book that detailed the doctor's relationship with the vice president.

Hutschnecker said that Kennedy had a "constant need to prove his masculinity and his courage" to a "hard-driving power-hungry, ruthlessly determined and overly aggressive father."

The doctor closely watched the debate and then offered Nixon advice on how to use psychology to win the next one. "Many undecided voters will be less affected by what someone says and more by how it is said," he wrote in a note to Nixon after the debate. "They must be reached and stirred . . . Often it is the heart (that) decides the issue and not the head."

Good advice. The only question was whether Nixon would take it.

COUNTDOWN: **26 DAYS**

October 14, 1960
New York City

Alabama governor John Patterson needed to see Jack Kennedy as soon as possible, in private. The future of his presidential campaign was at stake. At least that's what the governor told Kennedy's advisers.

Patterson had been an ardent JFK supporter since 1959, when the candidate had won his vote over breakfast at the Massachusetts senator's Georgetown home.

Patterson was only thirty-nine years old, way too young to be a governor, but his privileged life was straight from the pages of a Hollywood script. Like Kennedy, Patterson had served in World War II. He was a lieutenant assigned to General Eisenhower's London staff.

Once home, he earned his law degree from the University of Alabama and went into the family law practice in Phenix City, Alabama, working with his father, Albert Patterson.

His father ran for state attorney general in 1954 on a platform of cleaning up the sleazy brothels and gambling joints that catered to soldiers at Fort Benning in Georgia and had turned his town into "Sin City, USA."

Albert Patterson won the Democratic nomination to become the state's top cop. But he was gunned down in June 1954 before the election.

John Patterson had little interest in politics, but Alabama Democratic Party officials pressured him to run for attorney general in his father's place. He won.

In his first year in office, John Patterson called in the National Guard and drove the racketeers out of Phenix City. With an eye to moving up to governor, Patterson pandered to white voters with a court order to bar the NAACP from operating in Alabama.

By the 1958 gubernatorial election, Patterson was Alabama's toughest segregationist. Ku Klux Klansmen papered the state with his campaign posters. In the primary, Patterson easily defeated George Wallace, who at the time was a circuit court judge and was viewed by many white voters as a racial moderate. After losing the election, Wallace said that he had been outmaneuvered on race, and vowed to never let it happen again.

In late 1959, General Reid Doster of the Alabama National Guard asked for a closed-door meeting with Governor Patterson. He brought along a senior official from the CIA.

The United States needed Alabama's help to deal with Cuban leader Fidel Castro, Doster said. Cuba was aligning itself with the Soviet Union, and that could spell trouble for the United States and its allies.

If the governor agreed, the Alabama Air National Guard would help train an army of Cuban exiles now assembling in Guatemala. Once they were ready, the exiles would invade Cuba and overthrow Castro and his communist cronies.

Patterson was skeptical. This didn't sound right. He pumped the men with questions. "Does the old man know about it?" Patterson asked, referring to his former boss Eisenhower.

"Yes. He's on board," Doster assured him.

The governor took a deep breath. If Eisenhower was behind it, how could he say no? Yes, Patterson was a Democrat, but he admired the president. He'd seen up close how confidently Ike had coordinated U.S. operations in Europe during the war.

Patterson agreed to let them use the National Guard. And every time Doster returned to Alabama, he'd travel to Montgomery to keep Patterson apprised. About 350 Alabamians were involved in the top secret training program.

Sometime in early to mid-October, Doster visited the governor.

It was getting close, the general said. The Cuban rebels were ready.

"Any morning now, you are going to read in the morning newspaper that . . . we've invaded Cuba," he told Patterson.

The governor's heart hammered with the same possibility that had struck Sam Giancana. Whatever happened could have big implications for the race for president.

After Doster left, Patterson sat by himself in his office, trying to decide what to do. If he told Kennedy what he knew, he'd be violating national security. But this information was too important to keep secret. JFK had to know. His political future was riding on it.

If a successful invasion was launched and Castro was overthrown, Richard Nixon's campaign would get a huge boost. The race was neck and neck, and if Nixon could boast that his administration had eliminated one of America's greatest national security threats, it would swing the election to the Republicans.

If the invasion didn't come until after the election, Kennedy would benefit. He could amp up his call to invade Cuba and overthrow Castro. That position would play well with conservatives—especially in Florida—who thought the United States should be doing more to undermine Castro's regime.

Patterson knew what he had to do. He reached out to Steve Smith, Kennedy's brother-in-law and campaign finance manager, and said he had to meet with JFK.

"It's very important that I see him," Patterson said. It was a national security issue, something he couldn't discuss over the phone. "I'll meet him anywhere, anytime," Patterson said.

After a pause, Smith gave him instructions. Kennedy would meet the governor the next day at the Barclay Hotel in New York at 9:00 p.m.

Now there was no turning back. The next morning, Patterson packed his bags and headed to New York. He was waiting in a private conference room at the hotel when Kennedy walked in. Patterson quickly got down to business.

He prefaced his comments by asking Kennedy never to repeat what he was about to tell him. It was a matter of national security.

Kennedy agreed. Patterson disclosed to JFK everything Doster had told him.

The CIA was using Alabama National Guard troops to train Cuban exiles for the attack. The guard would provide logistics for the invasion and help train pilots. Somehow, they had turned a ragtag group of exiles into a full-scale fighting force—complete with air support.

But the most important piece of information was this: the invasion was "imminent and if it occurred before the election I believed Nixon would win."

Patterson noticed that Kennedy didn't express any emotion.

Kennedy already knew some of the information. CIA director Allen Dulles and Eisenhower had disclosed to Kennedy, as the nominee, that something was planned for Cuba, but they didn't divulge any details. Patterson had just given Kennedy the missing pieces.

The meeting ended. The men got up and shook hands. Kennedy again promised not to say a word. But after Patterson left the hotel, Kennedy knew this information was too important to keep completely under wraps. Since Nixon was a member of the administration, he probably knew, too.

His campaign had to take advantage of the inside information. This had the potential to be a game changer.

Kennedy hadn't taken a strong position on Cuba. But now he'd work Cuba into his stump speeches. He'd argue that overthrowing Castro was the only way to stop the potential spread of communism in Latin America.

All of a sudden, Cuba had become a potential political liability for Nixon. Kennedy, always on Nixon's left, would take a tough public position to his right.

It was time for Castro to die.

COUNTDOWN: **15 DAYS**

October 25, 1960
Rockford, Illinois

The campaign was getting nastier and nastier. Although Richard Nixon had promised to refrain from mudslinging, he and his surrogates had started bringing up dark rumors from Jack Kennedy's past. More and more, Nixon was talking about Kennedy's wealth, that he was trying to buy the election.

Pennsylvania Republican senator Hugh Scott noted that JFK had missed a quarter of the Senate's 1,189 votes since taking office in 1953. "This is no job for a playboy," he said.

Nixon and his supporters had to do something because they sensed that Kennedy had the momentum. And at this point, nothing seemed to slow JFK down.

Nixon knew what had gone wrong in that first debate in Chicago, but the vice president thought he had won the next two debates. Why wasn't that resonating with voters?

After the debacle of the first encounter, Nixon heeded the advice of Louis Seltzer, the editor of *The Cleveland Press*, who told the vice president to come out swinging. "You are the most effective when you are on the attack. Tomorrow night with Kennedy on TV, take him on. Take the offensive first, with the gloves off."

When Nixon arrived in Cleveland for the second debate on October 7, he was ready to roll. He'd analyzed the first debate and recognized his mistakes.

The format had changed to Nixon's benefit. Opening and closing statements were eliminated. Each candidate had two and a half minutes to respond to a question; his opponent had one and half minutes to rebut.

Nixon's team would make him look better, less sickly. The backdrop would be more of a brownish color, not gray. There was no pre-debate small talk. It was all business. They didn't meet until thirty seconds before airtime. The second debate could focus on any issue in the campaign. Nixon was confident and articulate from the first question to the last.

When asked about a comment Kennedy made comparing the loss of Cuba to the loss of China, Nixon didn't hesitate. He said he didn't agree that Cuba was lost. And yes, China was gone, but that was the fault of the prior administration, not his.

"Now I'm very surprised that Senator Kennedy, who is on the Foreign Relations Committee, would make such a statement as this kind. . . . I don't think this kind of defeatist talk by Senator Kennedy helps the situation one bit," Nixon said.

Throughout the debate, the vice president was on the offensive. A journalist brought up the Massachusetts senator's comments that the United States should apologize to the Soviet Union for the U-2 spy plane program.

Nixon said Eisenhower owed no apology to Nikita Khrushchev. America should continue its surveillance of the Soviet Union. He harked back to the Japanese surprise attack on Pearl Harbor.

"We lost three thousand American lives on December 7, 1941, because the U.S. military didn't know what the Japanese had planned. We cannot afford an intelligence gap," Nixon said, adding that the United States would continue its spy program.

Six days later, Nixon and Kennedy met for the third debate, which focused on Nixon's strong suit: foreign policy. And television technology gave the debate a gee-whiz new format: a split screen, with the moderator in Chicago, Nixon in Los Angeles, and Kennedy in New York. The men appeared to be in the same room, thanks to identical soundstages.

The main topic of that debate was the islands of Quemoy and Matsu, located between Taiwan and the Communist Chinese mainland.

Kennedy maintained that the United States should exclude Quemoy and Matsu from its Far East line of defense. They were strategically indefensible and were not essential to the defense of Taiwan, he said.

Nixon pounced on Kennedy's answer, saying the islands were too important to Taiwan's security to fall under the control of Communist China.

Kennedy had to backtrack.

Nixon said Kennedy's answers demonstrated his inexperience. Furthermore, Nixon pointed out, Kennedy had used notes during the debate, which was against the rules.

Reflecting on the debate, it felt good to score some points, but something worried Nixon about his rival. Kennedy had suddenly become a hawk on the Cuba question. Kennedy had remained silent about Cuba for months. But suddenly at every campaign stop, JFK was suggesting the United States train Cuban exiles to overthrow Castro's regime. Castro was a menace, Kennedy said. He had to go—or he'd spread revolution to other Latin American countries.

Nixon had been pushing to oust the Castro regime since the middle of 1959. He agreed with Kennedy's position, but couldn't say so, not while the CIA was doing exactly what Kennedy suggested. Nixon knew his first responsibility was to protect the secrecy of the operation.

Clearly someone at the CIA had leaked the secret, and Kennedy was carelessly flogging the highly sensitive information to score political points. Nixon wondered: Who would have been so careless with national security?

Somehow, Kennedy seemed to know the details. He was going to use them against Nixon, knowing the vice president was sworn to silence.

"It was a program . . . that I could say not one word about," Nixon would later recall in his 1962 memoir *Six Crises*. "The operation was covert. Under no circumstances could it be discussed or even alluded to. Consequently, under Kennedy's attacks and his new demands for 'militant' policies, I was in the position of a fighter with one hand tied behind his back."

Nixon felt that Kennedy was jeopardizing the project. But Kennedy had no plans to stop pushing Nixon and giving his own campaign leverage everywhere he could.

Kennedy's good looks, charm, confidence, and sense of humor covered up a ruthless ambition. His campaigns were filled with big money, smears, and bribes. He lied about his health and took risks with women. When it came to the race, he told one thing to voters in the South and another to the electorate in the North. The ends justified the means.

And so it was with Cuba. Alabama governor John Patterson had told him about the Cuban invasion plan, and Kennedy was going to take it as far as he could. Cuba became his best weapon. He only hoped that the exiles didn't invade the island until after the election.

Kennedy went all in. In a statement for Scripps-Howard newspapers, Kennedy suggested that America should take an active role inside Cuba, saying, "The forces fighting for freedom in exile and in the mountains of Cuba should be sustained and assisted."

The fighters could overthrow Castro and ultimately "bring communist rule to an end," he said.

And Nixon could only do one thing: push the CIA to launch the Cuba invasion before the election. Originally, the invasion was set for September, but the anti-Castro exiles weren't ready. With only two weeks left until the election, there was still no date for the invasion.

Nixon was impatient. The invasion had to happen soon or he might well lose. The Americans who wanted to remove Castro from power—and there were plenty of them—would vote for Kennedy, who had become the hard-liner.

Kennedy continued his scorching rhetoric on the campaign trail, in stump speeches as well as news releases. It seemed that every day, he sharply criticized Eisenhower and Nixon for the administration's handling of the Cuba crisis. Communism was moving into the neighborhood—unless the United States took action, Kennedy said.

He said that Castro was training small groups of revolutionaries on the island, who'd then fan out and foment rebellion across Latin America.

Indeed, that was a plan that Castro had discussed at length with Ernesto "Che" Guevara, a charismatic revolutionary himself. An avowed Marxist, Che was an Argentine doctor who abandoned his profession to help Castro overthrow Batista.

Kennedy didn't know those details. But armed with insider information, JFK continued to advocate for an invasion that was already planned. And that, in turn, could jeopardize the operation.

JFK said Castro had transformed Cuba into a "militant communist satellite." And Kennedy made an eerie prediction: With support from Moscow, Castro would soon have the potential to launch missiles to American shores.

And two days before the last debate, Kennedy misled the public by saying Cuban freedom fighters had gotten virtually no support from the United States. Nixon lost it. No support? The damn CIA was training an exile army to overthrow Castro.

Nixon bit back his anger and kept the nation's secrets.

The United States was barred by international law from providing any assistance to Cuban exile groups, he said. Kennedy's proposal was probably "the most dangerously irresponsible recommendation that he's made during the course of the campaign," Nixon responded on the campaign trail, adding that any assistance to the anti-Castro rebels would cause the United States "to lose all our friends in Latin America."

In his book *Six Crises*, Nixon expressed frustration at Kennedy. "For the first and only time in the campaign, I got mad at Kennedy—personally. I understand and expect hard-hitting attacks in a campaign. But in this instance, I thought Kennedy, with the full knowledge of the facts, was jeopardizing the security of a United States foreign policy operation. And my rage was greater because I could do nothing about it."

On October 21, 1960, American viewers once again gathered around their televisions for a debate between Nixon and Kennedy, the fourth and final.

In his opening statement, Nixon said the big issue facing Americans was "How can we keep the peace?" He said the Eisenhower administration did that.

Cuba was the real threat to peace, Kennedy shot back, making sure Americans knew his position: the United States needed to help the insurgents take back their country from Castro. "I look at Cuba, ninety miles off the coast of the United States. In 1957 I was in Havana. I talked to the American ambassador there. . . . He warned of Castro, the Marxist influences around Castro, the Communist influences around Castro," he said, adding, "Can any American looking at the situation in Latin America feel contented with what's happening today . . ."

When the moderator asked Nixon about Kennedy's suggestion to help insurgents in Cuba, Nixon responded as diplomatically as he could.

"Our policies are very different," he said—and Kennedy's policies were "dangerously irresponsible."

"In effect, what Senator Kennedy recommends is that the United States government should give help to the exiles and to those within Cuba who oppose the Castro regime," Nixon said. "We would probably be condemned in the United Nations, and we would not accomplish our objective," he said.

Both men made their points clear. They left nothing on the table. Voters would go to the polls soon. Kennedy had two more weeks of slick ads and dirty tricks. And the possibility of a big swing toward Nixon would be in the hands of an exile army, the CIA, and the Alabama National Guard.

COUNTDOWN: **13 DAYS**

October 27, 1960
Atlanta, Georgia

D r. Martin Luther King Jr. needed help—and fast. He was in a notorious Georgia prison on a dubious charge. Anything could happen to him.

His wife and supporters knew that, too. But in Georgia, with a governor who'd promised to maintain segregation, a Black man in prison didn't count for much.

King's supporters called out to politicians, including presidential candidates Jack Kennedy and Richard Nixon, but so far, they'd heard nothing. Helping a civil rights leader could be politically costly—especially in the South.

King's dilemma had begun in May. King and his wife, Coretta, had hosted bestselling novelist Lillian Smith for dinner. Her books dealt with the consequences of segregation in both Black and white communities. For a white woman in Georgia, that was dangerous. It was even more dangerous for a Black man to be seen with a white woman in a car. But after dinner, King drove Smith to Emory University Hospital, where she was being treated for breast cancer.

Before he got there, King was stopped by a DeKalb police officer. He gave King a ticket for driving with expired tags, but also issued a $25 fine for driving in Georgia with an out-of-state license. King had moved to Atlanta, Georgia, from Montgomery, Alabama. He had a valid Alabama license, but he hadn't yet applied for one in Georgia and it had been over the ninety-day requirement to get one, by less than a week.

In September, King paid the fine and presumed the matter was closed. He was unaware that he was on one year's probation. And, more important, if he violated the terms, he could be sentenced to a year of labor in a work camp, better known as a chain gang.

On October 19, King was arrested with thirty-five others for participating in a sit-in at Rich's department store in Atlanta. The protesters, mostly college students, were trying to desegregate a restaurant inside the store, the Magnolia Room.

The sit-in was part of similar protests at other stores, including F. W. Woolworth, S. H. Kress, and McCrory's.

King refused to post bond. He promised he'd would stay in jail for a year if necessary. The demonstrations would continue, he said, "until something is done."

Appearing before municipal judge James Webb, King said, "We are welcome at all counters but the lunch counter."

King was taken to the Fulton County Jail and charged with misdemeanor trespassing. But then DeKalb County came calling. Officials there said King had violated the terms of his probation by taking part in the sit-in.

King was tried by Judge J. Oscar Mitchell on October 25. The tiny courthouse was crowded with supporters. They wanted to watch the proceedings because they didn't trust the system, and rightfully so. The trial didn't take long; Mitchell found King guilty of failing to have a Georgia driver's license, a misdemeanor. He sentenced King to four months on the chain gang.

The Black community was outraged. How could he be sentenced to four months of hard labor for a misdemeanor? Coretta Scott King, who was six months pregnant, was scared about her husband's safety while he was in prison.

In the South, bad things seemed to happen to Black men in jail. Many had just disappeared over the years. And as the leader of the national civil rights movement, King would be the perfect target for some racist prison guard.

She watched in horror as her husband was taken from the courtroom, his hands cuffed behind his back. As he left, King recalled the terrors of southern "justice," where scores of Black men were plucked from their cells and never seen again.

In the closing weeks of the campaign, the candidates avoided talking about civil rights issues. They knew it would be a tight election and they feared alienating potential white voters in the South.

Still, Nixon had just been endorsed by Martin Luther King Sr., "Daddy King," the leader of Ebenezer Baptist Church. King Sr. knew that Nixon would call his son frequently seeking his advice on issues, and he believed that the vice president would be supportive of civil rights. During the second debate, a reporter noted that Nixon and Kennedy had accused each other of avoiding questions of race when they campaigned in the South. So, how would they address these issues if elected president?

Nixon touted his role in spearheading civil rights legislation, including a measure that would give federal prosecutors the power to stop states from using tactics to prevent Blacks from voting.

Then the vice president spoke passionately about the negative impact of segregation on Black families. Nixon said he had listened to Black mothers as they tried to explain to their children why they could shop in a store but not sit at a lunch counter.

"This is wrong, and we have to do something about it," he declared.

Nixon called segregation a national problem. With the president's power and moral leadership, he said he'd use the bully pulpit to find a solution.

But now both Nixon and Kennedy knew that King's life was in danger—and that the region was a tinderbox.

The Atlanta sit-in King had participated in was part of a well-organized citywide event with picketing and demonstrations at other stores. And the protests had sparked intense reaction from hate groups. The Ku Klux Klan called on white organizations to counter the demonstrations. The Klan urged the governor of Georgia to call out the National

Guard to protect white residents against what it described as "the advancing Negro race."

The Black community was "threatening to take over our businesses and the city of Atlanta," and the KKK offered to lend a hand in stopping the protests.

So far, the demonstrations had been peaceful, but Atlanta mayor William Hartsfield knew that if the Klan took an active role, it would be like pouring gasoline on the fire.

As soon as King and the students were arrested, the mayor tried to broker a truce between Black leaders, student representatives, and business owners.

Tensions were rising in the city. While King and the other defendants were in court, Black students picketed the police station with makeshift signs. Judge Webb warned that any further demonstrations would be punished.

National media arrived on the scene, and Atlanta hit the front pages and the evening news. Black people all over the nation were pleading with both candidates to do something. King's arrest and sentence were grossly unjust. He had a valid driver's license. He just hadn't gotten a new one within ninety days of moving there.

Then King's case took another, even more disturbing turn. On October 26, the civil rights leader was transferred to the rural Reidsville state prison, a notoriously dangerous place for Black convicts. King wrote a letter to his wife, saying, "This is the cross that we must bear for the freedom of our people."

Many expected Nixon to speak up for King. He was the candidate who'd recently touted his civil rights record. Jackie Robinson even visited the vice president and pleaded with him to get King released. But Nixon did the political calculus. Yes, he was opposed to segregation. But if he got the civil rights leader out, he'd lose his chance of possibly taking some southern states from the Democrats. And in a race this tight, that could mean the difference between winning and losing. Nixon remained silent.

Robinson came out of his ten-minute meeting with "tears of frustration in his eyes." Complaining bitterly, he told William Safire, a Nixon speechwriter, "He thinks calling Martin would be 'grandstanding.'" Robinson was so distraught he declared, "Nixon doesn't deserve to win."

Meanwhile, Kennedy remained silent, too. He'd pushed for a plank in the Democratic platform to end segregation, but he rarely spoke about the issue on the campaign trail. How could he, when he'd picked a southern Democrat to be on his ticket?

Meanwhile, Coretta King turned to a friend. She asked Harris Wofford Jr., a law professor at Notre Dame, for his help in trying to secure her husband's release.

Wofford said he would, then talked to Louis Martin, a Black newspaper publisher who had been helping the Kennedy campaign reach out to Black communities. Together, they came up with a plan.

Wofford called Sargent Shriver, Kennedy's brother-in-law who had been advising JFK on civil rights issues.

He asked if Kennedy could talk to Coretta, who was worried about her husband's safety. A simple call would show that JFK cared about her ordeal.

Shriver said he'd talk to Kennedy about it. At the time, Shriver was in Chicago with the campaign. He knew JFK was at an airport hotel, ready to head to another stop in another city. So, he had to move fast. Shriver jotted down Coretta's telephone number and headed to the hotel.

When Shriver arrived, other advisers were talking to Kennedy. Shriver knew they'd tell JFK to say no. So, he waited until they all left and then broached the subject with him.

While Kennedy rested for a bit before traveling, Shriver began his sales pitch. He warned that King's life was in danger. He had been transferred to a notorious prison.

But it didn't seem like Kennedy was really paying attention. So, Shriver took a different approach, one he knew would appeal to Kennedy's sense of right and wrong. He told JFK that he'd be showing sympathy to a pregnant woman whose husband's life was in danger.

Now he had JFK's attention. He stopped what he was doing and listened to a few more details. Then Kennedy stopped Shriver. He had heard enough. It was a spur-of-the-moment decision. JFK said yes, he'd talk to her. He had Shriver dial King's number for him. When she answered, Shriver introduced himself, then handed the telephone to JFK.

Kennedy talked to her for only a minute and a half. He expressed his sympathy and concern about her husband's well-being and offered to help in any way he could. After he hung up, Kennedy didn't think twice about the call. He had already moved on.

When Bobby Kennedy found out, he was furious. He yelled at everyone involved for taking such a risk, saying it had just cost his brother the election. When voters in southern states discovered that JFK had called Martin Luther King Jr.'s wife, that was it, he said. The race was over. They'd vote for Nixon.

But once he calmed down, even Bobby knew he'd have to fulfill his brother's promise to Coretta. So, Bobby started calling the right people in the right positions.

And like magic, on October 27, after nine perilous days in jail, King was released on bail by the judge while his attorneys appealed his sentence.

When King was released, he told reporters that Kennedy was responsible for getting him out of prison. "For him to be that courageous shows that he is really acting upon principle and not expediency," King said.

King's father, who had been a Nixon supporter, led a mass celebration at the Ebenezer Baptist Church. He said he changed his mind. And he urged Black voters to back Kennedy. JFK's team moved quickly to capitalize on his endorsement. They included it in a campaign pamphlet praising the Kennedys' intervention, which appeared in Black churches around the nation on the Sunday before the election.

Blacks had been supporting Democrats in national elections for years. It started with the Great Migration, which began in the early 1900s, when some 6 million Black people moved from the South to other parts of the country for jobs and to escape racism. When they did, they were able to vote without death threats or being turned away from the polls. Blacks who lived in the North, especially in big cities like New York, Chicago, and Philadelphia, had become politically active, leading the fight for desegregation.

In 1952, nearly 80 percent of Black voters supported the Democratic presidential ticket. But in 1956, Republicans made a concerted effort to reach out to Blacks—and it worked. Almost 40 percent voted for Eisenhower. Nixon had hoped that he could increase that number in this election. But now the polls showed that Blacks were starting to move toward Kennedy.

The Kennedy phone call and Nixon's silence gave Kennedy a big advantage among Blacks. And if the election was as close as pundits were predicting, maybe their vote would swing the tide in Kennedy's favor.

King Jr. said as much when he delivered his next sermon at Ebenezer Baptist Church. He drew from the second book of Revelation, including the verse, "You have persevered and have endured hardships for my name, and have not grown weary."

He'd continue to press for civil rights, while the candidates would continue to fight for every vote. With Election Day so close, there would be no rest for the weary.

COUNTDOWN: **12 DAYS**

October 28, 1960
Havana, Cuba

B eing a dictator is hard, stressful work. Fidel Castro's bluster and bombast played well at home, but it seemed the rest of the world just wanted him dead.

The Americans were after him. His people in Miami had filled him in on the latest: An invasion force was coming. Cuban exiles would land somewhere on the island, set up a beachhead, and move inland.

Similar rumors had circulated ever since Castro seized power from Batista. But the earlier threats were just rumors, the dreams of homesick exiles killing time in South Florida bars. Hundreds of ruling-class Cubans had grabbed their assets and hightailed it to Florida as soon as the shooting started. They settled in there and stewed, reminiscing about the good old days of casinos and kickbacks.

This time the chatter was different. This time there were details: More than a thousand exiles had gone to Guatemala, where they were being trained by the U.S. military. The group had parachutes, bomber support, and high-grade weapons.

Castro and his Soviet counterparts scrambled to locate the exile army so they could monitor its movements. If the Cubans could find out where the exiles were landing, they could pin them on the beach and destroy them with heavy artillery.

And that would show Eisenhower, Nixon, Kennedy, and every anti-Castro U.S. clown that Castro was not another Batista—a cowardly dictator who'd flee Cuba rather than fight for his nation.

Castro watched American TV. He'd noticed how the presidential election rhetoric had ratcheted up. Kennedy had become an anti-Cuba hard-liner now, who said he'd help Cuban insurgents overthrow Castro's government. Nixon was less bombastic, but no different from Kennedy.

And Castro knew that even if the insurgent army came to nothing, the United States was not going to leave Cuba and Castro in peace. The Americans would do anything to oust him. He had a big target on his back.

Castro had no reason to keep America's secrets. He announced to the nation that an army of Cuban expatriates was preparing for a large-scale invasion of the country—an attack sponsored by the United States.

U.S. warplanes were concentrated in Guatemala to help insurgents invade Cuba, he said. To meet the threat, Cuba was activating thousands of civilian militiamen and equipping them with arms shipped in from behind the Iron Curtain.

Everyone knew the plan. This had to be an embarrassment to Eisenhower. Maybe now the Americans would back off, Castro thought.

But U.S. reporters were skeptical about a possible invasion. John Pennekamp of the *Miami Herald* wrote, "There is no indication that mercenaries or soldiers of fortune have yet appeared in the anti-Castro forces. . . . That the United States has no aggressive inclination toward Cuba has been apparent from the start."

Reports of an invasion force being trained in Guatemala were false, said García Gálvez, Guatemala's ambassador to the United States.

Others believed that Castro might stage a fake invasion in hopes of smoking out the anti-government underground.

He'd done that a year earlier, when William Morgan, an American who'd fought in the Cuban revolution, made believe he'd help Dominican Republic strongman Rafael Trujillo overthrow Castro. The ruse worked. When Dominican troops landed at a rural Cuban airport, Castro's men were waiting. In the aftermath, Castro rounded up everyone involved.

But Castro could no longer depend on Morgan.

After successfully rooting out the Dominicans, Morgan had tried to raise his own army to seize power from Castro. He was disillusioned that the Cuban leader had turned to the Soviet Union. He believed Cuba should be a democracy, not a dictatorship or a Soviet satellite. He was tucked away now after being convicted of treason, and was awaiting execution by firing squad.

Castro turned his ire on America. He'd created consternation by seizing American-owned factories and businesses, and now there were concerns he would drive the U.S. Navy out of its base at Guantánamo Bay, on the eastern end of the island.

The base was emblematic of the long, complicated history between the United States and Cuba.

Cuba was a colony of Spain from the moment Christopher Columbus came ashore. Cubans had periodically fought for independence. And after the Spanish-American War in 1898, it became a separate nation—and the United States signed a treaty with the new Cuban government to set up a naval base at Guantánamo Bay. The land would technically remain Cuban territory, but America would have complete political control over the area.

Now Castro was threatening to take back Guantánamo. The United States declared it would defend the base.

Castro enjoyed creating chaos and consternation. He criticized Kennedy and Nixon for making Cuba the core of their election campaigns. He assured both candidates that their invasions and policies would fail.

In reality, provoked by Soviet influence in Cuba, America could invoke the Monroe Doctrine—a policy that warned European powers to keep out of Western Hemisphere affairs—as an excuse to invade Cuba.

The wild card, however, was the Soviet Union. What would Soviet premier Khrushchev do if America flexed its muscles and moved on Castro? It could lead to a showdown between the two nuclear superpowers—one that could threaten the world.

Castro didn't want to think about that. He just wanted America to stop meddling in his nation's business.

And at that moment, meddling in Cuba was a politically charged American issue. Nixon pushed Eisenhower and the CIA. When would the insurgent army move? Nixon saw them as his ace in the hole.

Training guerrilla fighters takes time. That was understood. But the CIA and military had been working with the men for nearly ten months. Some of the insurgents already had experience in the Cuban military. It shouldn't be taking this long, Nixon thought.

The vice president knew nothing of Sam Giancana's poison-pill plot, and the mobster was in no hurry to carry out the CIA mission. Giancana knew Kennedy had a better chance of winning if they waited until after the election to hit Castro. And they still hadn't found anyone who could get close enough to Castro to do the job.

Meanwhile, Kennedy kept hammering away at Nixon's record. He said Nixon and the current administration were warned repeatedly by U.S. officials that communists were now in charge in Cuba, but instead of taking action, they did nothing.

In a statement Kennedy made the week before, he harked back to Nixon's 1955 visit to Cuba and Batista, its corrupt dictator then. Nixon's "only reaction was to praise 'the competence and stability' of the Batista dictatorship which was, even then, threatened by Communist activities," Kennedy said. The vice president had not called for any change in policy.

"Mr. Nixon saw nothing wrong in Cuba—he made no recommendations for action. He did not warn America that danger was growing and, as a result, the Communists took over Cuba with virtually no opposition from the United States," he said.

Again, Kennedy pushed for supporting "anti-Castro forces in exile, and in Cuba itself, who offer eventual hope of overthrowing Castro."

But with only eleven days to go before the election, would it happen?

COUNTDOWN: **11 DAYS**

October 29, 1960
Danville, Illinois

Richard Nixon loved riding the rails. There was something magical about old-fashioned whistle-stops, crisscrossing the country, stopping at flyspecks on the map, connecting with voters by delivering fiery speeches from the back of a train. Nixon did it in his two vice presidential campaigns. Now he was doing it again, but this time, Nixon was on top of the ticket. Six days earlier, the "Victory Train" had rolled out of Washington, D.C., loaded with campaign staffers, lapel buttons, Pat and Dick, and about one hundred journalists. They were barnstorming in small towns and cities across Pennsylvania, West Virginia, Ohio, Michigan, and Illinois. Even though time was growing short, Nixon decided against stopping in the big cities in battleground states. Instead, he chugged slowly toward Chicago.

The Victory Train tour turned out to be a great idea. Somewhere on that grueling trek, Nixon snapped out of his funk.

Speaking from the train's rear platform, Nixon didn't offer new programs to lower unemployment, help families buy new homes, or send their children to college. Instead, the vice president shared stories of his own life and struggles—and attacked Jack Kennedy's pie-in-the-sky proposals that he said would spell disaster for America's economy and prestige.

The trip was a change for Nixon, who had started his road to the White House as the senior statesman, heir apparent to popular President Eisenhower.

He was the status quo, the calm, experienced leader who promised the same policies that made the Eisenhower era one of peace and prosperity.

Kennedy offered "a new frontier" and cutting criticisms.

But nothing seemed to change the polls. By mid-October, Dick Nixon was living under a cloud.

On October 16, Nixon had met with his advisers and vice presidential pick at the Statler Hotel in Hartford, Connecticut, for an emergency planning session. His mood had been as gloomy as the cold, wet Sunday. They still had one more debate—on October 21 in New York City—and three hard weeks of campaigning to go before Election Day.

Leonard Hall, Bob Finch, and other key advisers discussed how they would handle the final stretch of the campaign.

This was an important session. They needed a plan to get them across the finish line. Although polls showed the race was a dead heat, momentum was shifting toward Kennedy, especially since he'd started banging the war drums on Cuba.

That wasn't even the Nixon team's top concern that day. Lodge had told a minority group that if elected president, Nixon would appoint a Black man to the cabinet.

Lodge had been cultivating Black voters, but the campaign advisers warned him not to mention the minority cabinet appointment again. It was too big a risk. Gaining a few more northern Black votes wasn't worth alienating many more southern whites.

They also settled whether Nixon should fulfill his campaign pledge to visit all fifty states. Or rather, Nixon did. He was still coping with his knee injury. Everyone would understand if he scrapped the plan. Nixon needed to focus on seven key battleground states, ones that could swing the election. But Nixon said no. He'd made the promise, and he was going to keep it.

As the meeting ended, the advisers said if Nixon wanted to win the election, he needed to wage a more aggressive campaign. Voters needed to see more of the old Tricky Dick, the pit bull who ripped his opponents for their lack of patriotism.

But Nixon already had plans to do that—in his own way. After the last debate, he would do the whistle-stop tour. Nixon enjoyed campaigning by train. It allowed him to meet voters in small towns and midsize cities. He felt comfortable to speak without notes from the train's rear platform, typically in front of enthusiastic crowds.

When the staff meeting ended, Nixon kept campaigning, stopping in a handful of cities over the next two days, with smaller stops along the way. He was still feeling low when he checked into the presidential suite of New York's Waldorf Astoria Hotel.

He was just in time to witness John F. Kennedy's triumphal entrance to New York on October 19. The city's Democratic leaders had arranged for a massive ticker-tape parade to welcome Kennedy to town. The Democratic presidential nominee rode from the tip of Manhattan Island to city hall through an early fall snowstorm of torn paper, streamers, and ticker tape, and a noontime crowd estimated at 1 million people.

Nixon and Kennedy were in town for the fourth debate, but their first stop was the Alfred E. Smith Memorial Foundation Dinner, which raised money for Catholic charities in the New York Archdiocese. The white-tie event honored Smith, the former New York governor who was the first Catholic nominated for president by a major party. Nixon and Kennedy were the guests of honor, sharing the dais with Francis Cardinal Spellman.

Since the charity's inception in 1945, the hosts had usually given serious, long-winded speeches. Nixon delivered a discourse on the role of religion in society, but Kennedy chose a lighter touch. He poked fun at his rival and himself as he touched on the day's issues.

Kennedy said that Cardinal Spellman was the only person who could "bring together amicably at the same banquet table, two political leaders who are increasingly apprehensive about the November election, who have long eyed each other suspiciously, and who have disagreed so strongly, both publicly and privately: Vice President Nixon and Governor Rockefeller."

And he continued with the jokes: "I think the worst news for Republicans this week was that Casey Stengel [the successful Yankees manager] has been fired. It must show that perhaps experience does not count."

The speech was a barrage of one-liners, a razor-sharp stand-up routine, one knee-slapper after another. Nixon was steeped in misery.

And Kennedy reminded everyone that if elected, he would not consider campaign contributions as a substitute for experience when appointing ambassadors.

"Ever since I made that statement, I have not received one single cent from my father," Kennedy said.

That's why Nixon had so looked forward to the train trip through the Midwest. Maybe the whistle-stop tour was a way of getting his campaign back on track. It was time for him to go on the offensive.

As the sixteen-car train cut through hills alight with brilliant foliage, Nixon felt himself start to relax. A crisp autumn chill was in the air.

He didn't preach to the crowds. He talked to them about his own small-town roots, to show the people he was really one of them. In Marietta, Ohio, Nixon reminded five thousand voters that his father grew up in the state. When the Marietta High School Chorus offered a tune, Nixon said it made him think about his own high school musical education. He'd played piano and violin.

Then he brought up how important this election was to average Americans. This was a different era. At the turn of the century, what happened in Washington really didn't affect most American daily lives. But Nixon said things had changed. Now what the president does would have a big impact on them. That's why, he said, it was imperative to elect the right person to the office.

He pointed to stores in the town square. As his eyes scanned the crowd, he said he noticed housewives. He noted they were probably here to do the shopping. Nixon said he had sympathy for what families were going through. "I also see all of the housewives here who will be doing shopping, trying to meet the family budget. And you should know that as you vote this November, two weeks from today, you will be deciding what the prices will be for what you buy in those stores—in the grocery store, in the clothing store, in the drugstore," Nixon said.

Then the vice president got to the point: If the Democrats implemented all the programs in their party platform, housewives would see the price of food and goods go up, possibly as much as 50 percent, as they had when the country was last led by a Democratic president, Harry Truman.

Furthermore, the Soviet Union was expanding aggressively. The arms race, nuclear weapons, the Cold War were all too grave for inexperienced leadership.

And he warned that America's prestige was at an all-time low because of negative statements Kennedy had been making during the campaign.

Nixon was animated. He took a jab at Kennedy's promise of creating a "new frontier" of domestic, social, and economic programs. He said what they're selling is the same old song and dance that left Washington in such a mess when Eisenhower took office in 1953. And he poked fun at the Kennedy campaign theme. Forget about crossing frontiers. You can't do that in "an old jalopy."

Nixon said there were new frontiers to cross, but they were in space exploration, technology, and science.

"So, I say, yes, there are new frontiers, new frontiers here in America, new frontiers all over the universe in which we live. But the way to cross those new frontiers is not through weakening Americans, but to remember how we crossed the old frontiers and who did it. Do you remember? Pioneers, with individual spirit, with faith in themselves; not thinking that they were a second-rate, second-class people, but thinking that they were the best in the world—and that's what we are today. And I'm tired of hearing our opponents downgrade the United States and let our enemies abroad have the benefit of it by what they say," Nixon said to supporters in Marietta.

At another stop, Nixon told of how his father died at age seventy-seven with $3,000 in medical bills. And how his mother would get up at 5:00 a.m. so she could bake pies to sell at the family grocery store to help earn money for her sons' educations.

Then, in Centralia, Illinois, he disclosed how his older brother wanted a pony for his birthday. His father said it would cost $75. So they held a "family council," where they explained to his brother the hard economic facts of life. If they bought the pony, they wouldn't have enough money to pay the grocery bill. They weren't going to have enough money to pay the clothing bill. In the end, they decided against the purchase. It was a hard decision, but the right one, Nixon said.

Nixon delivered similar messages in more than forty small towns, villages, and hamlets. He went to places like Parkersburg, West Virginia; Johnstown, Pennsylvania; Chillicothe, Ohio; Monroe, Michigan; and Danville, Illinois.

It was solid Republican country where it was easy for him to channel the old Richard Nixon. At each stop, he sharpened his attacks on his opponent.

Nearly everywhere the people roared encouragement as he countered the Kennedy campaign theme: "All of this yakking about America with no sense of purpose, all of this talk about America being second-rate—I'm tired of it and I don't want to hear any more talk about it."

And as the week went on, *Time* magazine quoted Nixon as saying the campaign "is beginning to run in a great tide in our direction."

It wasn't all smooth sailing. In Michigan, Nixon was heckled. At one point, someone threw eggs and tomatoes at him. Others screamed profanities at his wife. His press secretary, Herb Klein, called them "goon squads," arranged and sent in by the opposition. By the end of that day, Nixon clenched his fist and snapped, "I've been heckled by experts and we'll take care of you."

In Danville, one of the train tour's final stops, Nixon woke up rasping and coughing. His voice was hoarse. He should have stayed in bed, but Nixon vowed to keep going.

"They threw a few tomatoes and eggs at us yesterday. But let me say this: I have been through a few hecklings, and a few tomatoes and eggs aren't going to stop me either," he told a crowd of several thousand Danville residents.

With a grin, he looked out at the crowd assembled in the fog around the rear platform of his train. No eggs or tomatoes here. "If there are any in this crowd who want to do it, just try it and see," he dared.

At least at this stop, no one did.

COUNTDOWN: **7 DAYS**

November 2, 1960
New York City

resident Eisenhower was a seventy-year-old man with a bad heart. If he had good sense, he'd be on a golf course somewhere down south.

But the sun shone bright on New York City, and Ike smiled with confidence as the open-air motorcade rolled down Broadway. The crowd was massive, the cheers were deafening, just like they were for JFK's ticker-tape parade two weeks earlier. This wasn't Eisenhower's campaign, but it felt like he was running for reelection.

Eisenhower knew he shouldn't be risking his health this way. Word was his wife, Mamie, and his White House physician had both advised against it.

But the president was tired of Kennedy's attacks on his administration. He was tired of Kennedy saying America had lost its way. And he was sick of JFK himself, who Ike believed didn't have the maturity or experience to run the country.

It was time for Eisenhower to step up and campaign for Nixon, even if it was risky. Time was running out.

Nixon had hoped that Eisenhower would take a more active role by this point, but hadn't asked the president to help.

Eisenhower was still immensely popular. He was a war hero, the supreme commander of the D-Day invasion, who'd opened a second front in Europe during World War II. He was the former president of Columbia University. His campaign slogan in the 1952 presidential election fit his personality: "I Like Ike." Who didn't?

For the most part, Eisenhower had stayed clear of the presidential race. Four days after the GOP convention, Nixon had met Ike in Newport, Rhode Island, for a planning session. Eisenhower told Nixon then that he'd do anything to help with his election.

Eisenhower advisers at the meeting believed Nixon should firm up the GOP base, while Ike would campaign to help snare independent voters—dissatisfied Democrats who'd helped him win the presidency in 1952.

Eisenhower would make so-called nonpolitical trips around the country to tout how the nation was thriving under his administration. "Peace and prosperity" would be Ike's theme.

But Nixon didn't take Ike up on his offer. He decided to keep running the campaign his own way.

As August faded into September, the vice president still hadn't asked Ike to help. And on September 26, he stole Ike's spotlight.

Nixon knew Eisenhower was addressing the Golden Jubilee Dinner of the National Conference of Catholic Charities on September 26. It was an important event. Yet, Nixon was glad the first presidential debate was scheduled that same day, ensuring that Ike's speech would get less coverage.

By early October, the president could see that Kennedy had the momentum, especially after the first debate. Eisenhower had been wondering why Nixon waited so long to hit back against Kennedy's disparaging remarks about his administration.

By mid-October, Eisenhower was fed up. The thought of Jack Kennedy in the White House infuriated him.

The president believed Nixon's campaign needed a jolt—and he was just the one to deliver it. So at the end of the month, Ike embarked on a weeklong, nearly 7,000-mile tour of the United States. Detroit was where he first got a good look at how divisive the campaign had become.

Someone traveling with the campaign came across a pamphlet there called *Liberty or Bigotry*, produced by the United Auto Workers union. On one side of the page was a drawing of the Statue of Liberty, on the other was a Ku Klux Klan figure, and the question being posited "Which do you choose?" The message was clear: If you opposed JFK, you must be a bigot.

Ike was so upset at the images that he used his speech to attack UAW president Walter Reuther for producing what he called "malicious propaganda."

From Detroit, Eisenhower flew to Minneapolis–St. Paul, then to California and Texas, and back to Washington. In Minneapolis, he urged voters to reject "fear-mongering people who peddle gloom."

Eisenhower was energized by the road trip. As soon as he got back to the White House, he was raring to go again.

And Nixon, utterly exhausted, had finally asked him for help. With time running short, Eisenhower and Nixon met at the White House on October 31, along with their advisers. Over squab hash, the men mapped out the last week of the campaign.

In a dramatic intervention, the president would appear in Pittsburgh,

Nixon and Eisenhower campaigning in New York City
(Library of Congress, Toni Frissell Photograph Collection)

Cleveland, and New York and throw the full weight of his personality and popularity behind Nixon.

Days later, and less than two weeks after JFK's own ticker-tape parade there, Eisenhower and Nixon rolled down Broadway in Manhattan under a stream of ticker tape and confetti. Both the NYPD and Governor Nelson Rockefeller estimated a crowd of more than 2 million New Yorkers lined the parade route to give a tumultuous welcome to Eisenhower, Nixon, Lodge, and Rockefeller.

It was a political blitzkrieg. The team spoke at several locations in and around the city that day, and that night, in the New York Coliseum, Ike and Nixon appeared before a crowd of ten thousand people.

Eisenhower took the gloves off. He praised his administration's accomplishments, including building a strong economy. In foreign affairs he noted he'd ended the Korean War.

That was proof America wasn't weak, Eisenhower said. No, Kennedy's remarks just revealed his inexperience.

He bristled at Kennedy's claim that the United States was "standing still." He ridiculed the senator's lack of experience and called his claims that America was falling behind "irresponsible."

The president called Nixon and Lodge men of maturity with proven records. He went after Kennedy's domestic agenda, noting the nation's economy was "immeasurably stronger" than it had been when he took office in 1953, and the years since "have been the brightest in our history."

As far as America's international prestige was concerned, Ike said, hundreds of thousands of people each year tried to come to America, defecting from communist-controlled states. To people around the world, the United States more than ever represented freedom, democracy, and hope.

When Nixon took the podium, he couldn't stop smiling. He tried to speak several times but was interrupted by applause and cheers.

"This is the greatest day in the campaign," Nixon declared.

It could have happened sooner, if Nixon had only asked.

November 4, 1960
Chicago, Illinois

After a buildup fit for a circus, thousands of screaming fans packed into Chicago Stadium for the main event. The Democratic Party was putting on a daylong political spectacle.

Chicago was critically important to Jack Kennedy's election chances, and the city was ruled by a man whose support could well push this tight election Kennedy's way.

Mayor Richard Daley had pulled out all the stops. He'd arranged an impressive torchlight parade honoring Kennedy and Democratic candidates for statewide offices. On a cool, rainy night, a million people lined the two-and-a-half-mile parade route from Grant Park to the stadium to hear marching bands and cheer the region's beauty queens waving from decorated floats. Representatives of the city's fifty wards, Cook County townships, and labor unions marched in the procession.

Kennedy needed the vote of every person he could get along the parade route—and then some—if he was going to win Illinois's 27 Electoral College votes.

If the parade wasn't stirring enough, NBC was broadcasting Kennedy's speech nationally—paid for by Daley and the Cook County Democratic Party.

Daley, himself an Irish Catholic, was proud of Kennedy. That Kennedy was able to not only capture the Democratic presidential nomination but also have a legitimate shot at winning the office was a pivotal moment in American history. It wasn't too long ago that anti-Catholic bigotry would have held back leaders like Kennedy and Daley.

Daley was one of the nation's most powerful politicians, but Kennedy's candidacy meant the Irish had finally arrived. Anything was possible. On the last weekend before the election, Daley made sure JFK knew that Chicago had his back.

Kennedy's motorcade snaked down South Michigan Avenue and along Madison Street to the stadium. JFK scanned the vast crowd cheering and waving their "Kennedy for President" placards.

The size of crowds at JFK events had grown exponentially in the past weeks. For many, like twenty-year-old college student Paul Green, politicians were stodgy old men—wizened like Truman or bald like Eisenhower.

Kennedy headed up a new generation of leaders. He was young and cool. He easily articulated his vision for America's future—with programs like the Peace Corps—that made young people want to get involved in government. That's why Paul had waited for eight hours to get into the arena to see Kennedy speak.

Big crowds didn't necessarily translate into big Election Day turnouts, but tonight was something special. Twenty-six thousand supporters filled Chicago Stadium to capacity. Banners with images of Kennedy, Lyndon Johnson, and Mayor Daley fluttered from the rafters, and the marching bands played lively, foot-stomping tunes.

At around 8:30 p.m., Daley escorted Kennedy from the motorcade into the building. When the mayor stepped to the podium, the roar inside the building grew louder and louder. The throng chanted, "We want Jack! We want Jack!" Spotlights shone bright beams of light over the crowd and into the arena rafters.

Young Paul Green sat in the first row of the balcony with a perfect view of the podium. Daley beamed with pride, especially when he introduced JFK as the next president of the United States.

When Kennedy strode to the rostrum, he basked in the cheers and applause for more than a minute before beginning his speech. He summed up the domestic proposals he had championed throughout the campaign.

He slapped again and again at Richard Nixon for his effort to ride "someone else's coattails" into the White House—a reference to President Eisenhower's last-minute campaigning for Nixon.

Kennedy said Nixon—not Eisenhower—was on the ballot. The election was about who was going to be their next commander in chief. And that, Kennedy said, was more important than ever. The world was in a dangerous place with nuclear weapons and the advance of communism. "I want to make it very clear that contrary to what you may have come to think this week, we are not electing a committee for president of the United States. I have seen pictures in the paper of the rescue squad. Nelson Rockefeller, Thomas E. Dewey, Cabot Lodge and I understand they are adding Alf Landon [GOP presidential nominee in 1936] to their strategy board this weekend on how to win their campaign," Kennedy quipped.

"I want to make it very clear that they are not all running for the presidency. Mr. Nixon is running. . . . You have all seen elephants in the circus, and you have seen how they grab the tail of the elephant in front of them, and they pull themselves around that way. Mr. Nixon grabbed that tail in 1952 and 1956, but now he is running, not President Eisenhower, but Mr. Nixon," he said.

Kennedy said the real issue in Tuesday's election was about "world freedom or world slavery, world peace or world war," and it could not be met by goodwill tours or kitchen debates with Nikita Khrushchev.

The United States had to stop the communist advance that had made inroads all over the world—including Cuba—under the Eisenhower-Nixon administration.

Kennedy said the vice president was apparently having trouble dealing with the pressures of the campaign. And if he couldn't withstand that, how could he deal with the pressure of the presidency?

He ended by reminding everyone that the campaign ended Tuesday and they had to make up their minds based on their own convictions.

"You make your judgment not merely about the two candidates, but you must make your judgment about yourselves, what you believe, what you stand for, what you see as your obligations to this country, what you see as your responsibilities as a citizen of this country," Kennedy said.

"I believe it is possible to build in this country an ornament of freedom, and I hope on November 8 that all of us are working together because that is what this country requires—all of us working together can begin a great effort to ensure that peace and ensure the United States will serve as the defender of peace," he said.

Kennedy stepped away from the platform and left behind the thundering applause. The bright lights were intoxicating, but the work in Chicago had just begun.

Dallas, Texas

While the rest of the Democratic team triumphed in Chicago, Lyndon Johnson was having a rough time in the Lone Star State. Johnson had been relegated there by the Kennedy team, kept well south of the Mason-Dixon Line. At some appearances, Johnson had been heckled and booed by both Republicans and Democrats.

The Dixiecrats thought Johnson a traitor to the South. He'd formed a ticket with Kennedy, a northern liberal who they believed would work to overturn Jim Crow.

Johnson and his wife, Lady Bird, were scheduled to speak at a luncheon at the Adolphus Hotel in downtown Dallas. They were met in the lobby by a crowd of fired-up Nixon supporters who blocked their way through the lobby, shouting, "We want Nixon! We want Nixon!"

A police officer attempted to disperse the crowd, but a defiant Johnson stopped him.

"I'm Senator Johnson. I don't want to go through here like this was another Cuba or Berlin," he declared.

It took the Johnsons fifteen minutes to elbow their way through the lobby to the banquet hall.

There was pushing and shoving, and the protesters mussed Lady

Bird's newly coiffed hair. Mrs. Johnson got into a sharp exchange with the wife of Edwin Bell, a Republican congressional candidate. Bell's wife was dressed in a red, white, and blue outfit that resembled those being worn by "the Nixon-Lodge Girls," supporters of the GOP campaign.

"Lyndon will win the election," Lady Bird snapped.

"Nixon will win," she shouted back.

"I'll bet you that Lyndon will win," Lady Bird said.

"I'm not a betting woman, but Nixon will win," Mrs. Bell drawled.

Once inside the banquet hall, Johnson shrugged off the demonstrators, telling two thousand supporters that he'd told the police officer to stand aside.

"When the time comes when I can't walk with my lady into the corridors of a hotel in Dallas without a police escort, I want to know it," he said.

Casper, Wyoming

Richard Nixon was on a campaign blitz all along the West Coast and Rocky Mountain states. He would push himself as hard as he could until Election Day. Nixon started in Casper, Wyoming, then moved on to Spokane, Washington, 630 miles away.

His plane had flown through a storm that had just dropped seven inches of snow on Wyoming. It forced the pilot to circle the Casper airport before visibility returned and the plane could land. The rough touchdown terrified several of the reporters aboard.

The plane finally skidded to a stop on the snow-covered runway.

Nixon went straight from the airport to a high school auditorium jam-packed with more than two thousand people. But a few thousand more either watched the talk on televisions in the high school gym or stood in hallways trying to catch a peek of Nixon walking by.

His voice was hoarse from speeches. Nixon told the cattle country crowd that Kennedy's farm policies would mean police state–type controls and require fifty thousand additional federal inspectors to enforce them.

He contended that JFK kept changing his mind on issues. "If he hasn't made up his mind at this point, he won't make up his mind as president, and I say we're going to vote for somebody who has made up his mind, and that is what I have done."

He was in and out in under forty-five minutes, then headed back to the airport and took off for another city. He only had to touch down in Alaska to keep his all-fifty-states promise, still rejecting his top aides' advice. He would be there on Sunday.

Then he'd be in Detroit on Monday night to field questions from voters in a four-hour nationally broadcast telethon. After that, he'd head back to California to watch the election returns.

It was ironic that Nixon's last major campaign stop on this stretch was a telethon where he'd answer questions from voters all over the nation. For three months, Theodore White noted—from July 25 until October 25—he made zero paid television campaign appearances. His television advisers wanted him to do more, but he ignored them.

Nixon wanted his television ads to feel more organic—not staged. He was so fearful of being accused of relying on slick Manhattan advertising firms on Madison Avenue that his television team moved their offices one block east to Vanderbilt Avenue.

Kennedy, though, had embraced television. A few nights earlier, JFK and his wife, Jackie, who had stepped away from the campaign trail as her pregnancy advanced, were asked questions by movie star Henry Fonda in a slick made-for-TV campaign program.

The three appeared from separate parts of the country—Fonda in New York, JFK in Los Angeles, and Jackie from their home in Washington, D.C.

While they waited for Kennedy to appear, Jackie shared family photos and snippets of home movies. Fonda asked softball questions about their lives.

After displaying a photo showing Jack reading a book, Jackie said she had been working with "Calling for Kennedy," a group that identified issues with "the most significance to women." Once such issues were identified, they'd put them on a form and she'd take those concerns to Jack, she said.

When JFK finally joined the interview, Jackie discussed the top issues the group had identified, then let her husband answer.

Jackie said almost every form listed "peace" as the top issue. She said one woman wrote that she'd like to see consistent, "not crisis-to-crisis planning."

"What can you tell [her], Jack?" Jackie asked.

Good question, Kennedy said. America wants to avoid war, he said, reminding the audience that he'd served in World War II and that his older brother was killed during the conflict.

That's why it's so important for him to keep the peace. Kennedy said no one wants another conflict. "So, if I'm elected President, we're going to work with all our energy, all of our effort, to maintain the peace. I think we're going to have to do better than we're now doing," he said, before moving into his pitch about America losing its international prestige. He talked about aid for students and a program to help the elderly pay for health care.

When he signed off, he sweetly assured Jackie he'd see her soon. He still had seventeen states to visit before ending his campaign.

Unlike Nixon, Kennedy also had Hollywood for celebrity backup.

In late October, Frank Sinatra, some of the Rat Pack, and several movie stars performed at the Governor's Ball, a Democratic Party function in Newark, New Jersey.

Police had to hold back a crowd estimated at somewhere between twenty-five and thirty thousand inside and outside the Newark Armory for the affair. Yes, in theory Adlai Stevenson was headlining the event. But the reality was this was in Sinatra's backyard—and he was more popular than ever with his music, movies, and high-profile association with JFK's campaign.

It was supposedly a formal event, and many attendees in gowns or tuxedos stood up on their chairs to get a better look at Hollywood actors Tony Curtis and his wife, Janet Leigh. But New Jersey native Sinatra stole the show singing seven big hits with a fourteen-piece orchestra.

The stars shone for Kennedy, all through his campaign. Lena Horne, Milton Berle, Gene Kelly, and Ella Fitzgerald were among the long list of other celebrities that made pitches for Kennedy or performed on his behalf.

Nixon had his share of Hollywood support. John Wayne and James Stewart were for Nixon, but they didn't go out to raise money or put on flashy shows like Kennedy's Hollywood friends did. No one knew if the celebrity support would translate into votes, but Kennedy wasn't taking any chances.

COUNTDOWN: **4 DAYS**

November 5, 1960
Oakland, California

Richard Nixon was ready for a last, desperate bomb blast to turn the election his way, and he had just the weapon: John F. Kennedy's health. Telling the world that his rival had a deadly disease could easily backfire on Nixon. Maybe it was already too late. Election Day was so close, maybe it wouldn't make a difference at all. Still, Nixon the gambler pushed his chips to the middle of the table. He was all in.

Voters wanted a president in good health. Both candidates had medical problems that, if made public, could cost them the election.

Kennedy didn't suffer only from Addison's disease. He had a bad back and persistent digestive problems—his family called it the "Kennedy stomach."

But it was more than that. In Robert Dallek's book, *An Unfinished Life*, he examined Kennedy's medical records, including the medications he was prescribed for stomach problems like irritable bowel syndrome, Addison's disease, and other issues.

He swallowed an assortment of hormones, steroids, painkillers, and stimulants each day. He upped the doses in times of stress.

Dallek wrote that Dr. Max Jacobson's injections of painkillers and amphetamines helped Kennedy stay off crutches during the campaign and that, in turn, protected JFK's image of being physically fit. How could he be sick? He looked so healthy.

It was the Addison's disease diagnosis that most concerned the Kennedy camp. Kennedy had to take prednisone, a hormone known to cause terrible mood swings and spur irrational decisions.

JFK's philandering was an equally potent weapon, but that was too seedy for Nixon to touch. The Addison's disease was Nixon's final ace.

Back in January, when JFK had announced his presidential candidacy, top UPI columnist Jack Anderson had approached him in a Senate hallway and asked him point-blank if he had Addison's disease. Kennedy had said no.

Anderson wasn't finished. A bronze skin tone was a symptom of the disease—was Kennedy's perennial suntan really due to illness? Kennedy, annoyed, snapped back, "Christ, it's the sun!"

A Lyndon Johnson surrogate had raised the question again before the Democratic National Convention. The Texas senator had just announced his interest in the presidential nomination when India Edward, co-chairwoman of Citizens for Johnson, publicly stated that Kennedy had Addison's—a potentially fatal disease.

His family had carefully covered up any mention of it. The public believed that JFK suffered pain and other physical problems because of failed back surgery to correct a war injury.

Kennedy's rapid-response team, led by his brother Bobby, quickly squashed the truth. They said JFK didn't have Addison's disease. It was a flat-out lie.

Nixon had known that Kennedy had the disease since 1954, when the vice president visited JFK in the hospital. Nixon disclosed the secret to his shrink, Dr. Arnold Hutschnecker.

Nixon hadn't wanted to go there, at least not yet. He was running a clean, dignified campaign. He was showing the public that he was the *new* Nixon, a statesman.

But his bad-luck streak resurrected Nixon's old, aggressive, slash-and-burn style of campaigning.

Raising the issue of Kennedy's disease could be a Pyrrhic victory. What if the Kennedy team knew he was under psychiatric treatment with Hutschnecker? Nixon hadn't gone once. No, he had been seeing the doctor since 1952.

Nixon waited until the last few days of the campaign, when he felt in his gut that the election was slipping away from him. If he timed it right, the Kennedy team—if they really knew Nixon's secret—wouldn't have time to respond. It could be a game changer. But he had to have someone else raise the issue.

Enter John Roosevelt, the youngest of Franklin Delano Roosevelt's four sons—and the only one who was a Republican and a Nixon supporter.

While speaking to the Michigan Lions Club in Mount Clemens on November 3, Roosevelt called for the candidates to disclose any medical issues they had that "might impair their ability to serve as president."

It was time for Nixon to get even more involved in the scheme. To amp up the pressure, he asked John Roosevelt to send telegrams the very next day to both campaigns, demanding that they release their medical records.

To make it look more realistic, Roosevelt's telegram to Nixon said the vice president should let the American people know if his knee had healed and if there were any lingering problems.

The telegram to Kennedy was a little more nefarious. Roosevelt recalled that Johnson's advisers said before the Democratic National Convention that JFK had Addison's disease. Yes, one of Kennedy's doctors had written a letter saying JFK was in good health. But it didn't address the specific allegations raised by Johnson's team. Roosevelt wanted to know if Kennedy suffered any "adrenal deficiency" as a result of Addison's disease.

Republican National Committee chairman and Senator Thruston Morton called on Kennedy to "make a full disclosure to the voters," stating that the earlier statement provided by Kennedy's doctors was not enough.

Morton reminded voters that President Eisenhower had his doctors release full details about his health a week before the election in 1956.

Others started jumping in, too, and with troubling questions. If Kennedy had Addison's, he'd have to take medication. Would the medicine affect his judgment in the White House? It was something voters needed to know before—not after—the election.

The Kennedy team snapped back.

"Anybody who has been with Senator Kennedy throughout his campaign should have no doubt as to the state of his health," said Pierre Salinger, JFK's press secretary.

Bobby Kennedy was livid. He couldn't believe that Nixon had the gall to raise the issue, especially so late in the game. If Nixon kept it up, they'd have to retaliate.

They knew all about Nixon's long relationship with Hutschnecker, a psychiatrist who had written *The Will to Live*, a bestselling self-help book in the early 1950s. All they had to do was a little detective work. The tip had been there, in plain sight, for years.

Nationally syndicated columnist Walter Winchell mentioned in 1955 that the vice president was seeing a shrink, but Winchell didn't know the doctor's name. It was a line in his column—a good tip—but the news media didn't follow up.

The Kennedys did. Joseph Kennedy called on Frank Sinatra for help in sniffing out the details.

Joe asked Sinatra if he knew a relentless private eye—someone who would follow leads to the ends of the earth, but discreetly.

Sinatra smiled. Sure, he knew somebody: Guenther Reinhardt. He called on the gumshoe, who jumped at the opportunity.

But he had to work fast. It was already September.

Reinhardt was a staunch anti-communist with a vast list of contacts. After days of telephone calls, the trail led him to Hutschnecker.

Just to be sure he had the right person, Reinhardt made an appointment. The meeting between Reinhardt and the doctor was recounted by David L. Robb in *The Gumshoe and the Shrink*.

During the visit, the investigator spoke in German to make the doctor feel comfortable. Reinhardt said he was working for a rich family that was having trouble with one of their children. Could he trust Hutschnecker to be discreet?

Hutschnecker said yes. And to prove his discretion, he bragged that he was treating a powerful member of the Eisenhower administration. The number two man.

And that was it. Reinhardt had what he needed. He turned the information over to Sinatra, who passed it along to Joe Kennedy.

Meanwhile, Nixon surrogates kept up the pressure for candidates to release their medical records. The issue gained traction.

The *New York Daily News* on Friday, November 4, published an editorial agreeing with John Roosevelt about the candidates sharing their medical records before the election.

"This confusing and contradictory evidence is alarming, to put it mildly, when you consider that the man under discussion may occupy the world's most important public office during the four years beginning January 20, 1961, if he lives that long."

They closed the editorial with "the people have the right to know everything the doctors know about the health or otherwise of both major Presidential candidates. The time is short before Election Day. How about action on the Roosevelt suggestions without a moment's needless delay?"

Nixon wouldn't let it go. Newspapers were starting to look at the issue, but it wasn't headline news yet—mostly short wire stories, buried on the inside pages. But the vice president hoped to change that on his way to a campaign stop in Oakland, California.

When the plane landed, Nixon said he'd release his medical records on Monday, November 7—the day before the general election—if Kennedy would agree to do the same. (Nixon made sure his psychiatric records would not be included. His medical records would cover everything else.)

Nixon press secretary Herb Klein said the candidate had asked his doctors to have the records available at 10:00 a.m. Monday, "if this is agreeable to Senator Kennedy."

But Salinger said Kennedy had provided medical reports from doctors at the Democratic convention, and that was enough.

Worried that the story might snowball, the Kennedy team took a step to stop Nixon dead in his tracks.

That night, Dr. Hutschnecker was home with his wife in Sherman, Connecticut, watching television when the phone rang. He looked at the time. It was 9:30 p.m.

When Hutschnecker answered, the man on the other end of the phone introduced himself as a reporter for the Associated Press.

Hutschnecker was surprised. His telephone number was unlisted. The "reporter" asked if he'd been following the news about the candidates releasing their medical records.

He responded that, yes, he had heard about it. Then the caller said that he had been informed that Hutschnecker was Nixon's doctor and that he wanted a statement about the vice president's health.

Hutschnecker was struck dumb for a moment, but soon told the caller that he had to be kidding. Not one legitimate doctor in the nation would disclose that kind of information without a patient's consent. And they'd never give out such personal information to a stranger.

Hutschnecker would neither confirm nor deny that Nixon was his patient.

But the caller kept asking questions, including who Hutschnecker would vote for on Tuesday. Finally, the doctor hung up the phone.

So, who made the call? Was it a reporter from the Associated Press? Was it someone from Kennedy's campaign? Hutschnecker didn't know.

When word got back to Nixon, he sighed. Kennedy had the goods on him.

Nixon had to decide what to do: Continue his crusade and risk exposure of his ongoing psychiatric care? Or drop the issue altogether?

From that moment on, not another word was said about medical reports.

COUNTDOWN: **2 DAYS**

November 7, 1960
Detroit, Michigan

Richard Nixon was running on fumes, barely able to smile. He hunkered into a chair in a Motor City television studio, ready to answer telephone calls from voters all over the nation.

He was nearing the end of his 7,000-mile circle that had begun before dawn in California and would end up there again sometime after midnight. The day had taken him to Alaska—the last of the fifty states that he had promised to visit—then on to Wisconsin and now Michigan.

Before the telethon, Nixon had held a three-thousand-person rally inside Ford Auditorium along the Detroit River. He was joined by his wife, Pat, and his two daughters, Tricia and Julie. He trumpeted his travels.

Nixon told his supporters that the momentum had shifted in the race. He could feel it at every campaign rally. He was going to push himself to the end, adding that "a great tide is running in our direction. It's running our way, and we'll just keep it going."

Seeking to dramatize what was at stake in the election, Nixon turned to the apocalypse to assure voters that Republicans were best qualified to safeguard the nation from nuclear disaster.

Traveling to all fifty states, Nixon said he discovered that peace and security was the connective tissue that united Americans in both parties. He said they wanted to know that leaders would do everything possible to protect our nation.

"We can have all the other things that make a good life, and it isn't going to make any difference if we have the nuclear disaster that would destroy civilization as we know it," he said.

After thirty minutes of light and darkness, Nixon zipped over to the WXYZ-TV studio for the four-hour telethon. The afternoon talkfest was being broadcast by ABC in more than 125 markets. Over one hundred telephones were installed and manned by two hundred people from the group Volunteers for Nixon. Questions were screened to avoid repetition, then passed along to a panel of celebrity supporters, including Robert Young, Lloyd Nolan, and John Payne.

They asked Nixon the viewers' questions—and they were all over the political landscape. Nixon reiterated his stand against federal aid to help pay teachers' salaries. He supported raising the minimum wage above $1.15 an hour.

At first, Nixon smiled only occasionally. Sometimes he seemed short-tempered. To a question about the state of the economy, Nixon snapped, "There isn't going to be a recession."

The vice president seemed to relax as the program ran on. He hammered at the joint themes of peace and economic well-being.

Nixon challenged Kennedy to tell voters in detail how he could fulfill his campaign promises without imposing new taxes or resorting to deficit spending.

And when it came to Cuba, Nixon said that Kennedy's proposal to topple the Fidel Castro regime was met with "shock and outrage" by America's international partners.

When the show finally wound up, the Nixon entourage hurried onto a flight to Chicago. The candidate would appear once more on national television, this time with President Eisenhower himself.

A Chicago police escort met the plane there and whisked them to WBBM-TV for their fifteen-minute finale. Eisenhower opened the broadcast with a passionate pitch to the nation's 100-million-plus eligible voters.

"I shall vote for Richard M. Nixon," he stated.

The vice president looked on, then calmly urged voters to elect the man "we think best can serve America."

He recounted the campaign of 1960. Nixon hit the obvious highlights: It was the first time any candidate had campaigned in all fifty states. (Of course, this was the first presidential election *with* fifty states.) It was the first time that two presidential candidates had a face-to-face debate—and it was televised live because of new technology.

Nixon said he didn't want to hash out the issues again. The public already knew where he stood.

But he did make one last sales pitch, leaning on his experience with Ike. Before casting their ballots for one candidate or the other, voters should compare the candidates' qualifications.

Nixon said he knew all about presidential responsibilities, having had a front-row seat for eight years. He had a great teacher: Eisenhower, who made "great decisions."

He said he'd watched as Eisenhower was urged after cabinet meetings to make immediate decisions. But the president would stop the discussion and say very quietly, "I don't think we should shoot from the hip on this one. I think I should think about it."

Then Eisenhower would walk from the Cabinet Room into the Oval Office. He'd sit there in silence while he weighed all the considerations and make "the decision which he thought was best for America and for the world," Nixon said.

He noted the administration's successes. They ended one war, avoided others. They kept the peace. Nixon said the nation was stronger now than when the administration took over. And he attributed the accomplishments to Eisenhower's great wisdom.

"I would like for you to have in mind these standards that I think all of us as Americans should consider as we vote tomorrow," Nixon said.

And he thanked the public—and his wife and children—for all the support they had given him over the years. Then he signed off and headed back home to California.

He was only forty-seven years old, but it seemed that Nixon had been around forever.

It had been a wild campaign. From his knee injury to the TV makeup debacle to struggling to keep his worst instincts in check, Nixon had seemed lost at times.

But Nixon was a battler. He never gave up. And despite the polls saying the voters were leaning toward Kennedy, Nixon knew he still had a fighting chance.

He'd given it his best.

Boston, Massachusetts

Jack Kennedy spent his last day of the campaign close to home. At every stop that day from Providence, Rhode Island, to Springfield, Massachusetts, the crowds grew larger and louder, chanting, "Give it to 'em Jack!" every time he slammed Nixon.

When Kennedy quipped that Nixon believed peace can be achieved by "parades and visits to the Soviet Union," the people cheered.

In the evening, standing at a podium in Boston Garden, he soaked in the applause from the overflow crowd of around seventeen thousand.

This was the penultimate event of the night, and the campaign. He was going out swinging.

His rival lacked the capacity to "lead this nation through the troubling and hazardous years which lie ahead," Kennedy had told a crowd earlier that day in Springfield.

To the Garden crowd, he pledged to "achieve peace through strength," out-hawking the Republicans. With the audience roaring at almost every word, Kennedy promised that he and his party would build up America's military power to the point where "no aggressor will dare attack—now or in the future."

For Kennedy, so many things had gone right. He had managed to keep all his flaws hidden from the public. And as the campaign had continued, his standing had skyrocketed. Journalists wanted to cover

Kennedy, not Nixon. Kennedy's staff made reporters feel welcome. In return, they protected him.

It was nothing like that with Nixon, who trusted only a few journalists.

Kennedy was a Harvard graduate, a war hero who'd won a Pulitzer Prize for his book *Profiles in Courage*. He was the cool kid in class, an intellectual with movie-star looks. JFK was wealthy, an articulate politician who could connect with the common man. Kennedy got inside tips from agency officials in Washington as well as his father's powerful friends—all of which helped keep his campaign one step ahead of Nixon's.

He proposed federal programs that could be expensive—like student loans and medical care for the elderly. But Kennedy made them sound like noble causes, programs that would improve the quality of life for so many Americans. The greatest country in the world could afford to care for its citizens.

Now, as Kennedy wrapped up his appearance at Boston Garden, he was ready to head for his final speech of the campaign at Boston's historic Faneuil Hall. It was the assembly hall where pre–Revolutionary War citizens first stood up to the British Empire's Sugar Act and Stamp Act, setting the principle that would come to be known as "no taxation without representation," the place where the seeds of the Revolutionary War were planted.

Kennedy reminded the crowd that the United States emerged from that war as the symbol of freedom and democracy to the world. In nearly two centuries, the nation had gone through so many "trials and tribulations." Yet, here it was, still standing, "the most powerful single country in the world."

But to keep it that way, the United States needed strong leadership, JFK said.

"If we succeed, freedom succeeds. If we fail, freedom fails. That is the sober and awesome responsibility which events and our own choice have put upon our shoulders," Kennedy said. When his speech ended, so did his campaign. Kennedy had much to be proud of. His brother, family, and friends had run one of the most skillfully engineered, innovative, and ruthless presidential operations in U.S. history.

In the final weeks, Kennedy had seized the initiative, hammering at the question of the immediate future, arguing that America was slowing down economically and militarily—and had lost its prestige in the world. He'd gained ground by becoming a hardliner on Cuba.

In the end, the exiles launched no invasion—at least not yet. And by pushing an administration that was unable to confirm publicly that it had taken steps to deal with the Cuba issue first, Kennedy was the beneficiary.

Still, there was that one brooding issue that stood between Kennedy and complete confidence: his religion. Was faith so important that voters would rather choose Nixon? No one could say.

COUNTDOWN: **1 DAY**

November 8, 1960
Ontario, California

Richard Nixon's Pan American 707 charter finally touched down in California in the early hours of the morning.

Fifteen thousand people met the plane at the Ontario International Airport—about 40 miles east of Los Angeles—eager to greet the vice president and his family.

It was Election Day at last. The polls wouldn't open for another several hours. This was the last rally of Nixon's long quest.

Supporters surrounded the airport terminal, waving banners and posters and chanting, "We want Nixon! We want Nixon!" Celebrities dotted the crowd, including Buddy Ebsen, Cesar Romero, and George Murphy.

When the aircraft doors opened, Nixon was surprised to see such a throng so early in the morning. He smiled and waved to the crowd. Local Republicans led Richard and Pat Nixon to a platform erected outside the terminal. Fireworks lit up the dark sky.

The vice president struggled to be heard over the shouts of "We want Nixon." His voice was hoarse, and he was exhausted after thirty-six sleepless hours. But he wanted to thank the people waiting there for him.

"I've seen a few larger crowds, but never any more enthusiastic and never at one o'clock in the morning," he said, smiling.

The polls gave Kennedy a slight edge, but Nixon said the momentum in the race was turning in his favor. The gloom of two weeks earlier had disappeared. Now the Nixon camp was confident their candidate could win.

He said Kennedy was strong in some regions of the country. So was Nixon, adding, he was unwilling to concede any state.

His statement would prove prophetic.

Gettysburg, Pennsylvania

President Eisenhower arrived just a little too early. A helicopter had whisked him from the White House to Gettysburg, Pennsylvania, where he was registered to vote. He planned to cast his ballot for Richard Nixon.

He showed up at the Barlow firehouse at 6:55 a.m. The doors were still locked. "You have to wait five minutes, Mr. President," said an election judge.

Ike was in a good mood. "I've got to make it legal," he said, laughing. "I don't want to come this far and lose my vote."

At 7:00 a.m. on the dot, the doors opened, and Ike walked inside. While he waited to vote, Eisenhower chatted with David McCleaf, an election inspector, who told the president about a proposed consolidation of several local school districts.

"My goodness, that's technical," Eisenhower said.

Then the president spotted eight-year-old John Harner, who was decked out in a big white hat loaded with Nixon-Lodge buttons.

"That's a nice looking hat you've got," Ike said to the boy.

When it was his turn, Eisenhower walked into the voting booth and closed the curtain behind him. About forty-five seconds later, he emerged.

Reporters outside asked him how he voted. Eisenhower held up his wristwatch with pictures of his four grandchildren on the crystal. "That's who I voted for," he said.

Eisenhower signed autographs for the election officials and firefighters. He said the next time he voted, maybe there wouldn't be so much fuss.

McCleaf smiled. "You'll be the same old Ike to us," he said.

Whittier, California

Richard Nixon spent the night at the Ambassador Hotel in Los Angeles with his family. After only a few hours of sleep, Nixon was ready to go. He and his wife got up early and headed out to vote.

They traveled by limousine to East Whittier. Their polling place was set up in a residence in the small town, less than a mile from Nixon's old family home. By 7:30 a.m., they were greeted by Mary McNey, who said her husband was out of town on business. Before they could vote, Nixon turned in the two absentee ballots he and Pat had originally planned to mail from their Washington, D.C., home.

When they emerged from the makeshift voting booth in the McNeys' living room, Nixon turned to Mary. "And now, we'd like to vote again if you don't mind," Nixon joked.

The campaign, finally, was over. And the candidate, fed up with all the press attention, especially from photographers, wanted to escape their scrutiny while the day played out.

The Nixons left the McNeys' house. Pat Nixon returned to the hotel in the black limousine. Her husband was whisked away in a white convertible.

Herb Klein, the vice president's press secretary, told reporters that Nixon would wait someplace quiet for the nation's verdict on his campaign.

Klein said he didn't know where Nixon went, but even if he did, he wouldn't say.

Boston, Massachusetts

John Kennedy and his wife, Jacqueline, looked stunning. Shortly after 8:30 a.m., the smiling couple arrived at their polling place: the West End branch of the Boston Public Library in Ward 3, Precinct 8.

When they stepped out together into the bright, chilly November morning, Kennedy wore a suit, but no coat or hat. His wife wore a fashionable loose-fitting six-button purple winter coat and a black leather hat.

JFK and Jackie voting in Boston, November 8, 1960
(Library of Congress, U.S. News & World Report Magazine Collection)

Reporters and photographers followed Jack Kennedy and his wife every step of the way. As they entered the building, they were questioned—like any other voter—by Evelyn Hiltz, a poll watcher. "Your names?" she asked.

"John F. Kennedy," he replied.

"Jacqueline Kennedy," she said.

The voting machines were in the basement. When their turn came, the Kennedys were directed to two of the six voting booths. Kennedy's wife hesitated in front of the voting machine, and her husband whispered a few words to her before she entered the polling booth.

After they voted, Kennedy told reporters what he'd said. "I just explained to her how to use the machines."

Good advice, from someone who'd need every vote he could get.

When they left the library, the couple jumped into a waiting car and headed to Logan International Airport for a quick flight to Hyannis Port, where the entire Kennedy clan was assembled.

Kennedy told reporters that he had no plans for the rest of the day. He said he was going to take it easy, spend time with his family.

And so, he did.

Johnson City, Texas

Lyndon Johnson and his wife, Lady Bird, arrived at 10:00 a.m. at the Pedernales Electric Cooperative headquarters in his hometown, about fifty miles west of Austin.

They slid their paper ballots into a voting box. Lyndon was voter number 99. Lady Bird was voter number 100. Both voted straight Democratic Party tickets.

As they left the building, Johnson smiled and held up his right hand and flashed the victory sign. Johnson planned to spend a few hours at his ranch, then head to the Driskill Hotel in Austin to watch the results come in.

He'd monitor the national and state races there.

Johnson didn't know how the night would play out, but he was sure he'd carry Texas. He knew nearly all of the Democratic Party officials in all 254 counties. Key people in every county and every critical precinct spread across the Lone Star State were under orders to keep him updated.

Few people understood Texas politics like he did. And if things got too close for comfort, Johnson knew who to call to put things right.

He was prepared for a long, stressful night. But if he won, it would be worth all the campaigning.

A day earlier, in a statewide television address, Johnson said all indications pointed to the Democrats carrying Texas.

"If so," he said, "I am deeply aware of the burden of responsibility that will fall upon me in the 1960s."

Hyannis Port, Massachusetts

Robert Kennedy and his staff were ready for action. His cottage in the Kennedy compound had been converted into the campaign headquarters and filled with the best and latest communication equipment money could buy, including four news agency teletype machines, extra television sets, and a bank of thirty telephones.

This was the first election in which each of the national television networks would use computers to tabulate votes and declare the winners in each state.

By early afternoon eastern time, all the polling places in the nation were open. Many states were reporting a heavy turnout. That was a good sign, since there were more registered Democrats than Republicans.

Bobby kept busy, talking to advisers in key places all over the country. Meanwhile, nearly three hundred journalists were setting up a giant press room at the Hyannis National Guard Armory, just down the road. With campaign advisers in the house and so many reporters nearby, Bobby's place was jumping.

The Kennedy team knew seven states with a total of 168 electoral votes were critically important to a victory: California, Pennsylvania, Illinois, Ohio, Texas, Virginia, and New Jersey. Both state and national polls said the same thing: The race was too close to call. This was probably going down to the wire. And that was okay—as long as JFK won. Bobby could hear his father's voice in his head: Kennedys always win. There is no second place.

COUNTDOWN: **22 HOURS**

Chicago, Illinois

All the pieces were in place. All Sam Giancana had to do was sit back and wait. If Jack Kennedy won, so would the Chicago Outfit, his sprawling crime syndicate.

Over the last year, Giancana had moved funds for the Kennedy campaign in the primaries and general election. How much? At this point, no one could really say.

But now he was using his muscle to ensure the rank and file in mob-controlled unions got to the polls and voted for Kennedy. In return, Giancana got a promise from Kennedy's old man that when his kid won, the Justice Department would go easy on the Outfit.

Giancana was the key. Joseph Kennedy had used Frank Sinatra to reach out to the ruthless mob boss, and over time, Joe and Giancana came up with a plan to help JFK.

When Giancana and the other four members of the Outfit's governing board voted on the agreement, Murray Humphreys was the only one to say no.

Humphreys was a fixer for the Outfit. According to the FBI, his role was to influence politicians, public officials, and union leaders to act on behalf of organized crime.

Still, despite his personal misgivings, Humphreys went along with the board's decision. For two weeks in October, he stayed in a Hilton Hotel suite in Chicago, setting up a nationwide effort to swing votes to JFK.

Years later, his wife, Jeanne Humphreys, recalled details for investigative reporter Seymour Hersh. She remembered two big meetings between union officials and her husband. The first was in July—right before the Democratic National Convention. The second was in October.

"We were stuck there—two weeks at a time," she said. "The people coming to the hotel were Teamsters from all over. The Chicago Outfit was coordinating the whole country. . . . They were coming in from everywhere, then fanning out across the country."

The union bosses made a pilgrimage to the suite in July "to get instructions from Murray. When we went back in October, it was just a follow up, to see that everything went the right way."

For Giancana, things couldn't be better. The FBI was still out to shut down organized crime, but at the same time, the CIA had hired him to kill Cuban leader Fidel Castro. And he had a deal now with Kennedy's father. Hell, he was even up close with one of Kennedy's women, Judith Campbell. If everything went the way it should, legal harassment would cease. He'd have protection from people in the highest branches of government, which would give him total power in his world. He'd be untouchable.

COUNTDOWN: **21 HOURS**

Tijuana, Mexico

On the most important day of his life, Richard Nixon ran for the border.

The vice president didn't want to spend all day analyzing results from counties and precincts. That would drive him crazy. He had done everything possible—and more—to win this election.

Now he had a few hours to cut loose and relax a bit, like Dr. Hutschnecker always advised. When Nixon heard that his military aide, Don Hughes, had never driven along the Pacific Coast Highway, the vice president decided to do something about it.

Nixon jumped into a white convertible with Hughes and Secret Service officer Jack Sherwood, with Los Angeles police officer John DiBetta behind the wheel. Nixon told the trio that no one was allowed to talk about the election.

And off they went, heading south. Nixon felt alive, on the open road with the wind blowing in his face.

About 90 miles out, they stopped for gas in Oceanside, California. When the gas station attendant recognized him, Nixon told him, "I'm only out for a little ride. It was the only way I could get some rest."

Nixon made a fifteen-minute stop to see his mother, Hannah, who lived nearby. Then they hit the open road again with no set destination. As they neared the Mexican border, Hughes said he had never been to Mexico, either. Nixon suggested they visit Tijuana, a raffish old party town just over the border.

Again, DiBetta followed the vice president's lead. When they stopped at a booth manned by the border patrol, DiBetta asked an agent for the best Mexican restaurant in town. He sent them to a place run by a German called the Old Heidelberg.

And inside, they ordered tacos, enchiladas, and beer. News traveled fast, and soon the mayor of Tijuana joined the party. The border agent was right. The food was great and, more important, Nixon finally relaxed.

He remembered that no one at home knew where he was. He had Hughes call Bob Finch in Los Angeles to let him know.

With a Tijuana police car escorting them, DiBetta hurried back toward the border, and the United States. The U.S. immigration agent was stunned when a convertible with the vice president inside pulled up to the checkpoint.

"Hello!" said Nixon, reaching out to shake the agent's hand.

"Are you all citizens of the United States?" the official asked.

"Yes. I am," Nixon replied. "I don't know about that man in the back."

As they headed north, Nixon asked to stop at one of his favorite places: the Mission San Juan Capistrano.

There were only a handful of other visitors. Nixon gave the men a tour of the old mission. They stopped inside the sanctuary and sat in silence.

Nixon would recall that for those few minutes, he had "an interlude of complete escape from the battles we had long fought together, and those still to come."

When they finished praying, the men scurried back to the convertible and headed to Los Angeles.

Nixon asked them to make one more stop, at a roadside ice cream stand. With a pineapple milkshake in hand, the vice president was ready to face the rest of the day.

COUNTDOWN: **20 HOURS**

Hyannis Port, Massachusetts

Jack Kennedy felt good, surrounded by family. And he looked surprisingly calm and relaxed for someone waiting for the results of an election that could make him the most powerful man in the world.

But his brother Bobby was a different story. He was busy. At times, Jack would walk inside his brother's house to watch him in action. He'd lean against the doorway as Bobby read through the teletype with the latest returns and rumors while telephones jangled.

This was Bobby's war room, and he was in total command. Calls came in from political leaders all over the country. Bobby answered with a terse "How are things going?"

JFK paced. He talked to his father. They walked from one home to another, but the road always seemed to take them back to Bobby's cottage.

Finally, Jack had enough. Everything was under control. He was tired. He decided to take a nap.

COUNTDOWN: **18 HOURS**

Los Angeles, California

By the time Nixon returned from his road trip, his family and friends were waiting in the Ambassador Hotel's Royal Suite. For one moment in time, the vice president had felt so carefree. Now, reality set in. Soon, the first polls would close on the East Coast. His heart hammered every time he thought about the results. His entourage was there for support—Pat and their two daughters; his mother, Hannah; and other family members. Nixon's longtime friend Bebe Rebozo and others were there, too. The vice president was anxious. What would happen? He didn't know. All he could do was wait.

COUNTDOWN: **17 HOURS, 45 MINUTES**

New York City

It was election night—and the nation's three television networks had brought out their big guns for election night coverage. Chet Huntley and David Brinkley were at the helm at NBC. Walter Cronkite was in the same role at CBS, and John Daly was the anchor for ABC.

The Huntley-Brinkley Report was the nation's most popular nightly news program. At 7:30 p.m. EST, Huntley opened its election coverage by saying that it was okay to do a little "dial-twisting" to check out the other networks. "But we hope and trust you'll be back."

Cronkite was an old-school broadcaster in the sonorous tradition of Edward R. Murrow. Both NBC and CBS decided to cover the election results from the beginning until they had a winner. ABC News, on the other hand, ran episodes of *Bugs Bunny* and *The Rifleman*, and broke in periodically with news updates. Later in the night, when the race heated up, ABC covered the election like the other networks.

Since this was the first time the networks were using computers to project winners, each had its own system.

CBS had a brand-new IBM 7090; NBC had an RCA 501; ABC had a Remington Rand Univac. They all expected the technology would enable them to call the race early—maybe by 8:00 p.m., or even earlier.

COUNTDOWN: 16 HOURS, 45 MINUTES

New York City

It was 8:00 p.m., and polls closed in some states on the East Coast. Results trickled in. The early returns showed that Kennedy was in the lead. But CBS made a bold prediction: Its IBM 7090 computer projected that Nixon would win in an Electoral College landslide. ABC's computer also predicted a Nixon victory. NBC said it was still too soon to tell.

Watching the election coverage at his brother Robert's house, Jack Kennedy was stunned. What the hell was going on? He was quickly assuaged by his pollster, Lou Harris, that CBS was flat-out wrong, that there were still hours to go before anyone knew for sure. Kennedy exhaled, but would stay on edge for the rest of the night.

COUNTDOWN: **15 HOURS, 45 MINUTES**

New York City

More polls closed, and CBS and ABC reversed themselves. Broadcasters at the two networks said they had jumped the gun. Now they were predicting a Kennedy victory. NBC agreed that Kennedy was ahead in the popular vote.

Nixon had been mulling over the new projections for the last half hour and thought it was still too early to say anything. It was only a little after 9:00 p.m. in the eastern United States. People were still voting in states in the Midwest, West Coast, and parts of the South.

But some GOP officials were expressing their frustration at the earlier computer projections.

Leonard Hall, one of Nixon's campaign managers, said, "I think we should put all of those electronic computers in the junk pile so far as election returns are concerned. This one is going down to the wire—a squeaker, a real close election."

COUNTDOWN: **15 HOURS, 30 MINUTES**

New York City

By 9:30 p.m. on the East Coast, all three networks had upped the odds of a Kennedy victory. Buoyed by their computers, the anchors proclaimed that JFK was on his way to a historic night.

In homes across the nation, families were gathered around their television sets. Kennedy supporters all over the nation cheered, while Nixon voters groaned. The networks would start calling states soon.

But Robert Kennedy was cautious. Yes, he and his advisers had gotten good reports from operatives in the field. The turnout, especially in big industrial cities, was heavier than expected. In fact, JFK was leading in New York and Pennsylvania.

But Bobby knew there were still a lot of votes to be cast and counted before any celebration started.

COUNTDOWN: **14 HOURS, 15 MINUTES**

Los Angeles, California

Nixon had isolated himself in his fourth-floor suite at the Ambassador Hotel. With a pen in one hand and a yellow legal pad in front of him, he had been doing the math. He'd scribble down numbers every time a state was called. It would take 269 electoral votes to win. All night, the vice president had been watching the returns from seven key states: New York, Pennsylvania, Ohio, Michigan, Illinois, Texas, and California. The vice president figured he had to win three of the seven to beat Kennedy. But then Nixon watched as Kennedy carried New York, with 45 electoral votes, and Pennsylvania, with 32 more. The numbers didn't leave much room for error.

COUNTDOWN: **13 HOURS, 45 MINUTES**

Hyannis Port, Massachusetts

With 21 percent of the nation's precincts having voted, Kennedy was 1 million votes ahead of Nixon. But it was the electoral votes that counted. By 11:00 p.m. big cities, like New York and Philadelphia, had given him large pluralities. That's why he carried New York

and Pennsylvania. JFK started to breathe easier. The television computers said he had 241 electoral votes. Indeed, everything looked like it was
going according to plan.

In Hyannis Port, Charles Von Fremd, a CBS News correspondent,
said JFK's sister, Eunice Shriver, reported her brother was so happy that he
was "smoking a big cigar." And Ray Scherer, an NBC News correspondent,
said Pierre Salinger, JFK's press secretary, was optimistic, too, calling the
returns from all over the country "very encouraging." But just as the Democrats were ready to celebrate, Nixon showed signs of life. He had already
landed Vermont, New Hampshire, Maine, and Indiana for 25 electoral
votes. Now he was the winner in four key states: Virginia, Oklahoma,
Florida, and Kentucky, adding 40 more electoral votes to his column. And
he suddenly showed surprising strength in New Jersey, Colorado, and
Ohio. He now had 65 electoral votes. Kennedy was only slightly ahead in
Michigan and Wisconsin, two union-heavy states he was supposed to win
easily.

JFK was leading in Illinois and Texas—but not by as much as expected. No, even with Lyndon Johnson on the ticket, broadcasters said
the Lone Star State was too close to call. In his suite at the Driskill
Hotel in Austin, Johnson walked the floor wearing his brick-red long-
john shirt, with a cup of hot chocolate in his hand and a walkie-talkie in
his ear. His eyes never left the television set.

COUNTDOWN: **13 HOURS, 15 MINUTES**

Hollywood, California

Frank Sinatra couldn't relax. It was getting close to midnight on the
East Coast. He knew most of the polls all over the country had either closed or were on the verge of closing. The election was too damn

close to call, and that made him nervous. He had worked so hard for his friend Jack.

At the home of Tony Curtis and Janet Leigh, Sinatra and a gaggle of stars and other movie people gathered to watch the election unspool on television.

Film producer Bill Goetz and director and screenwriter Billy Wilder were there, with comedian Milton Berle and other Hollywood Democrats who had worked for Kennedy.

The Kennedy compound took calls that evening from Henry Fonda in New York, and Sammy Davis Jr., who was performing that night at the Huntington Hartford Theatre in Hollywood. He interrupted his act several times to update the audience on the election returns.

COUNTDOWN: 12 HOURS, 45 MINUTES

Austin, Texas

At the Driskill Hotel, the crowd let out a loud cheer. The Texas Election Bureau had just given the state—with 24 electoral votes—to the Kennedy-Johnson ticket. A reporter asked Johnson about his plans.

"Going out and get some scrambled eggs and a glass of milk," he replied.

Nationally, Kennedy led Nixon by somewhere around 2 million votes. Despite the Democratic gains, Nixon's team said their chances were improving. And even though Texas had gone into the Democrat's column, the margin was smaller than expected.

The new returns gave Republicans some hope.

COUNTDOWN: **12 HOURS, 30 MINUTES**

Los Angeles, California

N ixon was making a comeback. It was 12:15 a.m. on the East Coast, and returns coming in from the West gave Nixon a boost. By winning Colorado, Washington, Oregon, Arizona, Idaho, and Utah, the vice president added 33 electoral votes to his column. Nixon also cut into Kennedy's popular vote advantage in California—a must-win for Nixon.

In the Midwest, Nixon grabbed Iowa and its 10 electoral votes, and now had 108 electoral votes. He was ahead in Wisconsin, and making it close in Michigan, where Kennedy had been favored because of the union vote.

Meanwhile, Kennedy was leading in Minnesota.

Yes, the odds were still in Kennedy's favor. But it still wasn't a sure thing. In state after state, the TV anchors said the race continued to tighten.

COUNTDOWN: **11 HOURS, 45 MINUTES**

Hyannis Port, Massachusetts

T ension grew in the Kennedy camp. They were no longer dreaming of a landslide. Now they didn't know if they'd win. Watching the returns in Bobby's cottage, Sargent Shriver was tense. Nixon was making gains in Illinois. Not a good thing, since Shriver was Illinois campaign manager for his brother-in-law.

Then the returns showed Nixon surging. Shriver was devastated. He thought that might cost JFK the race. He didn't want to face anyone.

So Shriver went back to his bedroom and almost cried himself to sleep.

Shriver wasn't the only one concerned about Illinois. So was Kennedy. A few hours earlier, Chicago mayor Richard Daley had called JFK with an update. Maybe it was more of a prediction. When he got off the phone, Kennedy told his friend Ben Bradlee that Daley had boasted, "With a little luck and the help of a few close friends, you're going to carry Illinois."

Kennedy didn't doubt Daley. But when Nixon captured Ohio and its 25 electoral votes, bringing the vice president's total to 133, JFK started to feel anxious.

Back in California, Nixon press secretary Herb Klein felt confident the vice president would carry Illinois. He was getting positive reports from operatives in the field.

But something strange was happening. The polls in Illinois had been closed for hours, but many Chicago precincts hadn't reported any results at all. What was going on?

COUNTDOWN: 10 HOURS, 45 MINUTES

Los Angeles, California

When Nixon won Wisconsin, he now had 145 electoral votes. California was still in play. So was Illinois. If he added those two states, Nixon would have a total of 204 electoral votes. And the popular vote margins were closing in many places. The campaigns realized the importance of the small states. Maybe Nixon visiting all fifty states hadn't been such a bad idea?

When Kennedy captured Delaware, Louisiana, and West Virginia, the place of his decisive victory over Humphrey in the Democratic presidential primary, it brought his total to 262 electoral votes. Kennedy was so close to victory, but the margins in key states like Michigan had made the outcome uncertain.

COUNTDOWN: **10 HOURS**

Hyannis Port, Massachusetts

By 2:45 a.m., they had all came in. Tens of thousands of votes from Chicago, delivered en masse—very suspicious. At least to Nixon campaign manager Leonard Hall. It meant that Mayor Daley and the Chicago machine were heavily involved in the returns. Not a good sign.

Meanwhile, Sargent Shriver heard someone rapping on his bedroom door, then a voice: The votes in Illinois had changed. JFK was in the lead.

Shriver got up from the bed, washed his face, and headed back to the war room.

COUNTDOWN: **9 HOURS, 30 MINUTES**

Los Angeles, California

The broadcasters had just received another batch of election returns. The ballots had been coming in fast and furious for hours.

The vice president tried to analyze the numbers, looking for trends, but his mind was groggy. It had been a grueling, demanding campaign. He'd had only a few hours of sleep in the last forty-eight.

There in his suite, it became clear to Nixon that, without a miracle, Kennedy would be the next president of the United States.

He had campaigned so damn hard. Nixon really *wanted* this. But reality set in.

He knew what he had to do. But first, he would talk to his wife and daughters.

When Nixon tapped on the door to his daughters' hotel room, Tricia and Julie were in bed, but Tricia was still awake. There was too much excitement for her to sleep. When Nixon informed her that he might have lost, she started to cry.

Then Nixon faced his wife. He said he wasn't going to concede defeat, but he wanted to go down to the ballroom to update his supporters. He'd just tell them the truth.

Pat was upset with her husband. With all the uncertainty surrounding the race, it was still too early to say anything less than uplifting. "I simply cannot bring myself to stand there with you while you concede the election to Kennedy," he recounted her saying in *Six Crises*.

But in the end, she couldn't let her husband face his supporters alone.

Now it was time—12:15 a.m. in Los Angeles and 3:15 in Hyannis Port. Nixon and wife headed to the grand ballroom of the Ambassador Hotel, where one thousand people were talking, drinking, and watching the results on the national newscasts.

Pat almost lost her composure when they entered the ballroom to the cheers of the GOP faithful. They stood arm in arm before the crowd, grinning to the chants of "We want Nixon! We want Nixon!" But Pat's eyes were beginning to glisten.

With his wife by his side—and millions of Americans watching at home—Nixon took the podium. Her husband needed her support, so Pat stood firm. She bit her lip to keep herself from crying.

"If the present trend continues, Senator Kennedy will be the next president of the United States," Nixon told his supporters.

There was a collective gasp in the ballroom. They couldn't believe it. How could this happen? As the crowd shouted, "No," Pat began to sob.

Pat Nixon hadn't cried during her husband's nationally televised address in 1952, when he denied allegations that he'd used an $18,000 political contribution for personal expenses—a claim that nearly led Eisenhower to boot him off the ticket. She had remained calm in 1958 when rioters booed and spat in her face on a trip to Lima, Peru, and Caracas, Venezuela, during one of her husband's goodwill tours. She hadn't cried then.

Richard and Pat Nixon telling supporters if the present trend continues,
Kennedy will win
(Copyright © Lawrence Schiller, All Rights Reserved)

But this was too much.

The couple scurried up four flights of stairs to their suite. Fourteen years of public life had brought them almost to the top of the world. Almost.

The pundits were perplexed by the speech. Huntley told Brinkley he wasn't sure if Nixon had just made a concession speech or not.

On CBS, Cronkite said the same thing, adding that Nixon "came as close as a man can, but did not actually concede."

Hyannis Port, Massachusetts

In the command center in Robert Kennedy's house, JFK's advisers were confused, then angry. Nixon didn't concede.

Press secretary Pierre Salinger urged Kennedy to seize the moment. Hold a news conference at the Hyannis National Guard Armory, where hundreds of journalists were waiting.

But Kennedy said no. He understood why Nixon issued that statement. The vice president had just won Wisconsin and continued to cut into Kennedy's lead in several key states, including Illinois. Nixon needed to take a break, hit the reset button, then make a decision when his head was clearer.

Kennedy said under the same circumstances he wouldn't have conceded the race.

He was disturbed by something else. Why did Nixon have Pat stand by his side? It was apparent that she was breaking down. It was a low-class thing to do, he said.

As he started to leave, Salinger tried to convince him to go to the Armory and make an on-air appearance.

JFK refused and said he was going to bed.

With that he said good night and headed out the door for the short walk home. It was a chilly, clear night with stars stretched across the black sky. Kennedy walked through his front door, then quietly up the stairs to his bedroom. Jackie was already asleep. Jack kissed her on her brow. She awakened and he smiled at her. "It looks like we're in," he whispered.

"Oh," she said, "is it really set?"

"I think so," Kennedy said. "Now, you'd better go back to sleep."

Moments later, he joined her.

COUNTDOWN: **7 HOURS, 45 MINUTES**

Hyannis Port, Massachusetts

By 5:00 a.m., Kennedy's national popular vote margin continued to slip, falling below 1 million. But while the popular vote tightened, JFK continued picking up electoral votes.

David Brinkley, like the other broadcasters, was dragging a little. None of them were used to covering a live news event for so many hours.

Robert Kennedy was tired, too. He had been working the phones day and night. This campaign would be a template for others to follow in the future. He knew he needed to get some rest. He told his father he'd be back in a little while. But the old man wasn't going anywhere. Joe had waited a lifetime for this. No bed for him. Not yet.

After what felt like hours, the Associated Press called Michigan for Kennedy. Joe knew that his son had surpassed the magic number: 269 electoral votes. He could go home now. His work was done.

COUNTDOWN: **5 HOURS, 26 MINUTES**

New York City

M any morning newspapers had headlines declaring Kennedy the winner. Others said JFK was ahead, but the race was still too close to call.

Ballots were still being counted in a number of states, including California and Illinois. Kennedy was ahead in both.

And then, at 7:19 a.m., Brinkley announced that the NBC Victory Desk had projected that Kennedy would win California. As a result, "Senator Kennedy was elected president of the United States."

COUNTDOWN: **3 HOURS, 15 MINUTES**

Hyannis Port, Massachusetts

I t was 9:30 a.m. when Ted Sorensen walked into Kennedy's bedroom and found JFK sitting at the edge of his bed in his white pajamas.

Nixon hadn't conceded yet, but that didn't matter. Kennedy had carried California, putting him well over 269 electoral votes, well over the threshold for the presidency, Sorensen said.

A few minutes later, Pierre Salinger interrupted Kennedy's bath to give him the same news. The three men talked for a while about the returns. Sorensen wanted to know when to schedule a press conference and claim victory. Kennedy said he wouldn't do anything until Nixon spoke.

"Well, that may be a long time, because Nixon claims he is not going to get up until 9 a.m. Pacific coast time, which would be noon [here]," Sorensen said.

Kennedy shrugged. "It's up to him; he can get up anytime he wants."

When his advisers left, Kennedy got ready. He shaved and put on his clothes. By 10:00 a.m., he came downstairs for breakfast with his family, then wandered into his yard with his daughter, Caroline.

She tried to keep up, then reached out her arms. "Piggyback!" she said. Kennedy laughed, picked her up, and carried her inside.

A few minutes later, he walked toward Bobby's cottage.

It was over, he thought. And it was starting. With each step, he felt more alive than he had in years.

COUNTDOWN: 1 HOUR

Los Angeles, California

Buckling into his seat on the chartered Boeing 707, Nixon was despondent. How could he have lost to Kennedy? He'd been Eisenhower's vice president for eight years. The country was at peace and the economy was in good shape and getting better. So, what happened? There were just too many things that didn't add up.

Nixon had rested well. The fog that engulfed him had lifted. And even though he was depressed because he lost, Nixon had regained his composure.

After breakfast, the family checked out of the hotel, waving goodbye to the reporters who were still there.

Nixon handed his press secretary a copy of a telegram he planned to send to Kennedy. Nixon still hadn't conceded the race. He still had too many questions.

Kennedy's popular vote lead continued to drop as the remaining vote counts trickled in. Hell, Nixon had received 49.6 percent of the national popular vote—and there were still many more votes to be counted in key states.

The networks said JFK won California, but Nixon wondered how they'd reached that conclusion. Election officials still hadn't counted more than 230,000 absentee ballots. And Nixon was still cutting into JFK's lead in Illinois and other states.

Everyone outside Nixon's inner circle was pushing him to concede defeat. But why should he? Why the hurry? This might end up being the closest race in U.S. history. It was clear already that certain states were ripe for a recount.

On the flight back to Washington, D.C., Nixon's campaign manager, Leonard Hall, told the vice president the Democrats stole the election. They had received reports of voter fraud in a number of key states, including Illinois, Texas, and Missouri. He pressed Nixon to do something about it, maybe even contest the election.

Nixon took a deep breath. He wasn't going to make a hasty decision on something that would divide the nation. No, he'd have to think about that, talk it over with GOP leaders. He didn't want to be a sore loser.

Nixon didn't know what the next phase of his life would look like. He was only forty-seven years old. Did he have a future in politics? Maybe he'd practice law again. After being vice president, though, that seemed like a big step down. He had a lot of decisions to make.

But before Nixon could move forward, he still had something painful to do. He had put it off for too long.

COUNTDOWN: **1 MINUTE**

Hyannis Port, Massachusetts

I t was early morning and the television networks had returned to their regular schedules, but if there was any election-related news, they cut into a program with updates.

Jack Kennedy had been taking walks around the compound, talking to family and close advisers. A squad of Secret Service agents had been dispatched to protect Kennedy and his family; they spread out across the compound.

When JFK returned to Bobby's cottage, one of the televisions was tuned to a game show called *Play Your Hunch*, hosted by entertainer Merv Griffin. No one in the house was watching.

And then, it happened.

At 12:45 p.m., the network interrupted the show with a bulletin. A hush fell over the room. Herb Klein, Nixon's press secretary, was there, holding a piece of paper.

Klein said he had a telegram that Nixon had sent to Jack's home. Then he read the message:

I want to repeat through this wire congratulations and best wishes I extended to you on television Tuesday night. I know you will have the united support of all Americans as you lead the nation in the cause of peace and freedom in the next four years.

And with that, the election was over. Cheers erupted in the room. After a long, bitter campaign, John Fitzgerald Kennedy was the president-elect.

Kennedy was appalled that Klein had announced the concession, and not Nixon. "He went out the way he came in," Kennedy said. "No class."

Kennedy planned to make a victory statement. But first, he rounded up his immediate family—his wife, parents, brothers and sisters and their spouses—to pose for photographers clustered at the compound. He knew this was a historic moment.

Then it was time for Jack Kennedy to address the nation. He took a motorcade to the Hyannis National Guard Armory. Inside, he moved to a makeshift platform, where hundreds of journalists and photographers from around the world were waiting.

Kennedy read telegrams he had received from Nixon and President Eisenhower, congratulating him on his victory. And then he made a pledge to the American people:

"I ask for your help in this effort and can assure you that every degree of mind and spirit that I possess will be devoted to the long-range interests of the United States and to the cause of freedom around the world," Kennedy said.

With his very pregnant wife standing beside him, JFK ended with a typical grace note. "So now my wife and I prepare for a new administration—and for a new baby."

Jack had done it. He had fulfilled his father's dream of putting a Kennedy in the White House. When he'd announced his candidacy in January, his critics said he was too young. Too inexperienced. He was a Roman Catholic, no less.

But with his younger brother's brilliant campaign strategy, and his father's money and unscrupulous connections, Kennedy had captured the Democratic presidential nomination and then the White House.

Jack Kennedy was a gifted communicator, able to articulate his vision for America. He believed in big government—federal aid for students so they could go to college, medical care for the elderly so they wouldn't struggle in their later years, and civil rights for all Americans. He delivered speeches that inspired a generation of young Americans to engage in their communities. He made being a politician cool, with his perennial suntan, sunglasses, and stylish wardrobe.

And to get himself to the end, he'd had to find ways to keep voters focused on all of that, and to hide his flaws from the public. That in itself took a lot of work, a lot of lies, a lot of people protecting him.

Now perhaps he could relax a little. Kennedy was glad. The election was over.

Maybe.

THE **CHALLENGE**

November 11
Washington, D.C.

Thruston Morton was sure Kennedy had stolen the presidency, and the Kentucky senator was hopping mad. Unlike Nixon, he refused to concede the election. And as the Republican Party national chairman, he was going to do something about it.

He asked Republican leaders in eleven states to look into allegations of voter fraud. Morton believed that could lead to recounts, which could overturn the results.

Morton said there were too many red flags, too many complaints filed by Republican voters all over the country not to investigate.

Most of the thousand fraud accusations came from Texas, Illinois, Michigan, Minnesota, Missouri, New Jersey, Nevada, New Mexico, Delaware, Pennsylvania, and South Carolina.

Morton seemed to have most GOP officials on board.

The RNC issued a news release saying: "We believe we owe it to the electorate to take every legitimate and reasonable step to ensure that the will of the people has in fact been correctly recorded."

The RNC said its investigators would confer with party leaders in the eight states "where the results were close and where complaints of widespread irregularities and election frauds have been the most frequent."

Herb Klein said Nixon had not been consulted about Morton's statement, and that the vice president accepted the decision of the voters.

But did he?

Before he conceded to Kennedy, Nixon had called Eisenhower to talk over the election with his boss. Years later in his memoir, Nixon said Ike had "urged" him to challenge the election. He had even offered to help raise money for recounts in Illinois and Texas.

Nixon said he decided against Ike's advice—even though there was evidence of substantial voter fraud.

Others said it was *Eisenhower* who had talked *Nixon* out of questioning the election loss.

Morton's push, however, gained traction inside GOP circles. While the issue was no more than a brief article buried inside daily newspapers, Republican officials all over the country knew about it. There was no internet or cable channels or partisan talking heads to explode the story overnight. The issue was a word-of-mouth phenomenon.

The vote margins were razor-thin in states and cities renowned for crooked elections, like Chicago. People began phoning in tips—and some in the Nixon campaign volunteered to look for suspiciously large pro-Kennedy results in eight states.

Maybe, or maybe not. The GOP decided to drill deeper into the precincts and moved forward with investigations, acting independently of Nixon.

November 14
Key Biscayne, Florida

All over the nation, headlines had blared "Kennedy Defeats Nixon." The news about the election was on every radio and television station. Nixon couldn't escape it.

Everywhere he looked, Kennedy's face was there, happy, smiling with his wife and family. Newspaper reporters were fawning over him, delighted to be in the presence of victory. It was all too much for Nixon to take.

And Nixon couldn't stop thinking about what Leonard Hall had said to him on the flight to Washington the day after the election: Fight. Contest the election. Top Republicans were joining the chorus. But

Nixon was exhausted and depressed. He had no energy or desire for more political warfare.

Nixon needed to get away. A few days after the election, he took his wife and daughters to a beachfront villa at the Key Biscayne Hotel to relax in the warm sunshine.

It wasn't all leisure. Three of his closest advisers came along with their wives: Herb Klein, Bob Finch, and Donald Hughes, his military aide, along with Nixon's secretary, Rose Mary Woods.

Klein had known Nixon for years. As a Navy veteran in his first reporting job, he had covered Nixon's first run for Congress back in 1946. He had either covered or worked on all his subsequent campaigns.

Key Biscayne, an island just off Miami, was an oasis of sandy beaches, nature preserves, and restaurants—a perfect place to unwind. The group shared quiet dinners and cocktails at Nixon's place, where they'd talk shop. Klein said that Nixon was "as low" as he'd ever seen him.

During one dinner at the Key Biscayne Hotel, Nixon admitted the election had taken a toll on him. GOP leaders had spent the past week flying in or calling, trying to convince him to challenge the election.

Some of Nixon's friends worried that a contested election would leave the country leaderless and divided at a critical time in the Cold War.

Still, party leaders pressed Nixon relentlessly. They believed Nixon was cheated in several states, including his home state of California. Although California was still in Kennedy's column, they believed the absentee ballot count would put Nixon over the top.

Kennedy had 330 electoral votes. If California, Illinois, and Texas flipped, then Nixon would be the winner. Or maybe the House of Representatives would step in to decide the election. They mapped out many different scenarios.

During dinner at the nearby Jamaica Inn on November 12, the maître d' approached Nixon's table. He told the vice president a man was on the telephone asking to speak to him. When Nixon picked up the line, it was Herbert Hoover, the former president. He told Nixon that he had just talked to Joe Kennedy. And Joe suggested that since JFK and Nixon were both in South Florida, the two rivals should meet. Nixon couldn't believe it and thought it was a cheap publicity stunt—and that's what he told Hoover. But now Hoover was upset. Joe Kennedy's suggestion was a "generous gesture" and should be treated as so. Nixon thought about it, then said, all right. He'd do it. When he got back to the table, the vice president told his guests about the conversation. Nixon said he was going to call President Eisenhower to tell him what happened. Hughes escorted Nixon to a public pay phone inside the restaurant.

Ike had also been feeling low since Kennedy's win. He felt it was a rejection of his own presidency. For the past eight years he had worked ceaselessly on behalf of the American people at great cost to his health and reputation . . . and this was what he got in the end.

Nixon put in a dime and dialed Eisenhower, who was in Augusta, Georgia, the site of the Masters Tournament, to unwind and play golf. While Nixon was talking to Ike, the maître d's phone rang again. This time it was JFK. Klein took the call.

As he talked to Kennedy, Klein got the feeling that the past few months had cost him, too. The president-elect "wandered in the conversation." He complimented Klein, saying he dressed "better than Pierre Salinger," his own press secretary. After more small talk, Klein said the vice president was on the phone with Eisenhower. Nixon would call him back, he said.

And Nixon did. Kennedy said he was at his family compound in Palm Beach and wondered if Nixon would meet with him. Nixon said yes, and offered to drive 80 miles north to Palm Beach. But Kennedy stopped him. JFK said he'd take his private plane to Miami International Airport, then a helicopter to Key Biscayne.

When Pierre Salinger disclosed the meeting to the media, he said that the reason was simple: Kennedy wanted to congratulate his opponent for a hard-fought campaign and resume cordial relations with Nixon.

No one knew what would happen when they saw each other. This was the closest race in U.S. history—and a bitter one at that. And Nixon supporters were pushing for him to contest the election. But when Kennedy traveled to Key Biscayne on Monday, the two greeted each other like a couple of tourists. "Gee, it's good to see you Jack," said Nixon, grasping Kennedy's hand and giving him a firm pat on the shoulder. "You have a nice tan already."

Kennedy laughed. "I'm afraid I've gotten you out of the sun today."

The two of them headed to Nixon's villa, number 69 at the Key Biscayne Hotel.

Nixon and Kennedy meet at Key Biscayne Hotel, November 14, 1960
(Richard Nixon Presidential Library)

They emerged after an hour. Kennedy told the assembled reporters they had talked about the transition to the new administration, as well as urgent foreign affairs.

But he said he didn't offer Nixon a cabinet post in his administration. And he doubted Nixon would have accepted such an offer.

Nixon sidestepped the question. "Only the president can properly make such a disclosure."

After Kennedy left, Nixon told reporters that he felt the president-elect was very gracious in coming to Key Biscayne instead of waiting for him to visit. Nixon called the meeting an excellent example of the way a democracy works. It was all about the peaceful transition of power.

When the reporters left, he recounted to his friends that Kennedy had offered him a cabinet position, but he'd turned him down, saying that he should instead be the "constructive opposition."

Nixon also said that he'd told Kennedy he would not contest the election.

Still, it was not over—thanks to GOP officials and a journalist who kept pushing the issue.

November 15
Washington, D.C.

Earl Mazo knew a great story when he saw one, and this was big—the juicy exclusive that he thought would finally win him his Pulitzer Prize for reporting. Mazo was one of the few journalists that Richard Nixon liked or trusted. Mazo believed the election had been stolen, and he was going to prove it.

He told his editors at the *New York Herald Tribune* he could give them a series about how the election was taken from Nixon. They said yes.

Mazo was short and pugnacious, with a thick, flat nose like a boxer and a shock of wavy black hair. He was outgoing but tough, a Polish Jew who'd grown up in the Deep South. He had learned how to fight to survive.

Mazo scaled the journalism ladder at newspapers in South Carolina, New Jersey, and then New York. In 1956 he became the chief political correspondent in the *Herald Tribune*'s Washington, D.C., bureau.

When he got to Washington, he began covering the Eisenhower administration. That's how he became friends with Nixon. He'd often travel to cover stories involving the vice president, including Nixon's terrifying trip to Venezuela in 1958. There, he wrote how the Secret Service saved the vice president from an angry mob that had surrounded his car.

The same year, Mazo decided to write a Nixon biography. As part of his research for *Richard Nixon: A Political and Personal Portrait*, Mazo spoke with national figures on both sides of the aisle.

Nixon liked Mazo's book and shared information with the reporter during the campaign. Now Mazo was on a mission to save Nixon's candidacy.

His first stories were fairly routine reports on GOP complaints about voter fraud:

Allegations of election irregularities in several states caused Republicans leaders today to closely examine returns in the presidential contest—and wonder if their concessions of victory to Sen. John F. Kennedy might have been premature.

One top-echelon figure in the party hierarchy told the Herald Tribune News Service that if "half the reports we've been getting can be run down quickly enough to be proven" it is "quite possible" Vice President Nixon would become President-elect instead of Kennedy.

Leonard Hall, chairman of the Nixon campaign was less optimistic. He said a mass of reports from "almost a dozen states" indicated there had been serious irregularities, especially in Texas and Illinois. But he said his off-hand view was that it may be too late to "catch enough of it" to switch the election result.

But Mazo didn't want to just report on what others said. He wanted to investigate the allegations. He thought the fraud had happened—and that ran counter to everything he believed in. He persuaded his editors to let him travel to the key states and started cataloging tips—those collected by GOP officials, and others he found himself.

The story was right there in front of him, but he had little time to run it down. Electors would certify the election on December 19. He'd have to push hard to get it in time.

November 16
Sacramento, California

California had landed in Jack Kennedy's column on election night, with a lead of nearly 35,000 votes. But with all but 20,000 of the 225,000 absentee ballots counted, the balance shifted—Nixon was leading the state by just over 13,000 votes.

California's 32 electoral votes now went to Nixon. That dropped Kennedy's electoral votes to 300, while Nixon's increased to 223. It was still not enough for a victory, but it gave hope to Republicans who were pressing for a recount in other states. Hell, Nixon's own wife was lobbying for him to contest the results.

Senator Thruston Morton was the public face of the effort. They would go to court if they had to, he promised. "I can say unequivocally that there have been shocking irregularities and fraud in this election," he would later say.

Many Republicans joined him, but the mainstream media played down the issue. There were stories, but they were buried on the inside pages of most newspapers.

Kennedy and his transition team were much more appealing, and Jacqueline Kennedy was due to give birth in weeks.

For many Americans, the election was over, and Kennedy had won, despite the tight race. At this point, Kennedy led the national popular vote by just under 200,000. But it wasn't the national vote that mattered—it was the razor-thin margins in eleven states, and what a change in the count might do to where their electoral votes went.

It was the holiday season. Thanksgiving and Christmas meant shopping, parties, visits. In places like Nashua, New Hampshire, and Greensboro, North Carolina, downtowns were decked with sparkling lights and Christmas trees.

The theaters offered up *The Magnificent Seven*, *Spartacus*, or *The Alamo*, and television would soon have the normal slate of specials like the Christmas episode on *The Andy Griffith Show*. Americans were happy to put the election behind them and think about peace on earth. "Rudolph the Red-Nosed Reindeer" replaced "High Hopes."

But a hard-core group of Republicans eyed California's reversal as a fighting chance for Nixon. And Morton and his colleagues were willing to push it as far as they could.

November 17
Washington, D.C.

J. Edgar Hoover's job was safe no matter who was elected. JFK said after the election that he would reappoint him as FBI director.

Hoover accepted, but had been in a sour mood for weeks. He summoned Philip Hochstein, editorial director of Newhouse newspapers, to his office.

Hoover launched into a long rant. He told Hochstein that Kennedy was not the president-elect, that the election had been stolen in a number of states, including New Jersey and Missouri.

The FBI director had access to secret electronic surveillance, and he'd heard enough to know about election corruption in places like Illinois.

Hochstein had a feeling that Hoover was trying to push him to investigate the fraud, but Hochstein didn't do it. It might be a big story, but it wasn't sexy. The majority of influential journalists had become friends with the Kennedys. They believed allegations of election fraud were nothing more than sour grapes—the GOP complaining about losing the election.

Was there fraud? Maybe. But many journalists believed there weren't enough irregularities to change the results. So why bother investigating?

November 18
Chicago, Illinois

The GOP in Illinois formed the Nixon Recount Committee. And on November 18, it held a coordinating meeting with groups from other states and announced the opening of a headquarters in Chicago.

Clearly the effort had picked up steam. The office handled inquiries from the Republican National Committee and the White House about recount actions underway in other states.

Harold Rainville, the Chicago office manager for Republican senator Everett Dirksen, said they were moving toward a recount, adding that Nixon was still cutting the vote margins in Missouri, Nevada, and New Mexico.

The Associated Press showed that Kennedy's lead in Illinois was now only 9,359 out of 4.7 million ballots cast.

William Fetridge, chairman of the Nixon Recount Committee, called a meeting to plan the anti-fraud battle.

The committee said more than $34,000 had been sent in from forty-four states to aid the drive.

A week earlier, Fetridge said, "people interested in fair play and honest elections" should contribute, even if only a dollar.

Republican leaders said that in all their years of poll watching, they had never seen more blatant fraudulent practices. They said Kennedy and the Democrats had stolen massive numbers of votes in the so-called river wards of Chicago. Those were blocs of working-class and low-income wards along the Chicago River that were the mainstay of the city's Democratic machine. Those neighborhoods regularly produced the machine's margins of victory.

The Democrats had rolled up "fantastic pluralities" for Kennedy. Republican investigators said they had found as many as forty-five fake voter registrations within just two apartment buildings in Ward 4. That single neighborhood gave Kennedy 25,770 votes, while Nixon got 7,120.

Other neighborhoods had one-sided totals. In Ward 2, JFK received close to 21,100 votes to Nixon's 5,450. And then there was Ward 24, where Kennedy collected some 24,000 votes to Nixon's just over 2,130.

Would Nixon get a recount in Illinois? Would Nixon be able to flip other states? No one knew for sure. But the Republican National Committee was pushing that narrative—and they weren't going to stop.

They were all in to find out the truth. It would be difficult, a long shot, maybe, but when the recounts were over, GOP officials said, Nixon would be declared the next president—especially if they could flip the 27 electoral votes in Illinois.

November 20
Washington, D.C.

Richard Nixon understood that challenging the results was a double-edged sword.

"From the evidence I examined, there was no question but that there was real substance to many of these charges," Nixon would write in his memoir, *Six Crises*.

But if the recounts and investigations weren't successful, Nixon would come across as a sore loser—and that could hurt him if he ran for office again.

Nixon also knew a switch of a few thousand votes from Democratic to Republican in places like Illinois or Missouri, where JFK carried the state by less than 10,000 votes, would give him 259 electoral votes to Kennedy's 263. That, plus a similar switch in any two of the three other states—New Mexico, Nevada, and Hawaii, where the vote was also very close—would reverse the election results. He could win this.

Chicago mayor Richard Daley was suspected of manipulating vote counts in Cook County, Illinois. So was Lyndon Johnson throughout Texas.

Money would be needed for the recounts—and possible court fights. Republican supporters were filling up the coffers.

But another scenario was emerging—one that focused on slates of unpledged electors who had won in the South. An unpledged elector is just what it sounds like—a person who hasn't sworn allegiance to any candidate.

Mississippi had eight unpledged electors. Alabama had six. If the recounts resulted in Nixon or Kennedy not collecting 269 electoral votes, the unpledged electors could throw the election to the candidate of their choice.

They were from segregationist states. They were likely unhappy with the federal government telling them to integrate their schools. So, in theory, the candidate who supported their position would get their electoral votes. Would that happen? No one knew. It all depended on what became of the recounts and the court fights.

Of course, if no one reached 269 electoral votes, the election could be thrown into the House of Representatives, and Congress would pick the next president. That had happened twice before: in 1801, when Thomas Jefferson defeated John Adams, and 1825, when Adams's son John Quincy Adams was selected over Andrew Jackson.

Many of Nixon's associates urged him to fight as long as there was hope—a chance that he could win. And even if the effort failed, disclosure of election irregularities would be big news. It might help GOP candidates in the 1962 and 1964 elections.

But Nixon was torn. He wasn't sure that contesting the election was the right thing to do for the country. He had already conceded. So, for now, Nixon would stay in the background.

November 23
Austin, Texas

Texas was a mess. Mazo was still collecting information, but he knew that the first part of his series would raise serious doubts about the outcome of the presidential race there.

He believed he had proof that the state's 24 electoral votes rightfully belonged to Richard Nixon, not John F. Kennedy—even though the Texas Election Board had already certified JFK as the winner.

As he examined the voter fraud complaints collected by the GOP in that state, he discovered what he would later call "many categories of alleged irregularities—from bald fraud to unintentional tally errors."

Part of the problem was the Texas ballot design. The Lone Star State had gone out of its way to make voting more complicated and confusing. Voters using paper ballots not only had to mark their choice for president but also had to *scratch out* the names of all the other candidates and the political parties they weren't voting for. This befuddled many voters, who failed to scratch out the outsider Constitution or Prohibition parties, which were also listed. Why would Texas election officials design the ballot that way? Mazo thought. It was a rhetorical question, of course. He was sure he already knew the answer.

Precinct judges had the power to decide whether ballots that were not fully marked should be counted. It made sense they would throw out more Nixon ballots than Kennedy ones—but only if you knew about the Texas political landscape.

From top to bottom, Texas had been controlled by Democrats forever and "Landslide Lyndon" Johnson was going to be the next vice president. House Speaker Sam Rayburn had been involved in Texas politics for decades. Both men had cut their teeth in the rough-and-tumble world of Texas elections, where the outcome of a race could change in a heartbeat. Johnson and Rayburn knew all the right people in every key precinct.

In Texas, Mazo uncovered evidence that some small places reported more votes than they had voters. For example, only 86 people turned out at Precinct 27 in Angelina County, but the vote reported—and approved all the way up to the state canvas board—was 147 for Kennedy and 24 for Nixon. And in Fannin County, 6,138 votes were cast. But only 4,895 people were registered to vote. Similar situations were reported all over Texas.

There were also reports of voter intimidation—people being coerced and intimidated by pistol-packing election officials. There were many cases of fixed machines. Somehow a machine in a GOP district in San Antonio tabulated every vote except those for Nixon-Lodge.

Republican officials said that at least 100,000 ballots might have been illegally counted—that mattered in a state that Kennedy carried by just over 46,000 votes. The plurality might be considered a landslide in a small state like Rhode Island. But in Texas—where nearly 2.3 million people voted—those ballots could be enough to flip the state for Nixon.

Mazo said the most egregious irregularity were the "throw outs," or disqualified paper ballots. It seemed that election judges in the precincts, practically all of whom were Democrats, varied widely as to what they considered grounds for voiding ballots.

So, in some precincts, notably where there was a heavy Republican presence, Mazo found that up to 40 percent of Nixon votes were disqualified. Meanwhile, in Democrat-dominated places like Starr County on the Mexican border, almost none of the ballots were thrown out. Also in Starr County, the GOP claimed that eighteen Republican voters had come forward saying that they voted a split ticket, which was not reflected in the totals for the county.

Something nefarious was going on, Mazo alleged. Throw out a handful of Nixon votes in this precinct, several hundred Nixon votes in another, it starts adding up—especially in a state with 254 counties, each with dozens and dozens of precincts.

Mazo said that based on the evidence, Republicans were demanding a recount of all ballots. That was the only way "the true results of this election can be determined legally and fairly," they wrote on a petition claiming an "illegal dilution" of votes for Nixon and Lodge.

Approximately half the nearly 2.3 million votes cast in Texas were on paper ballots. Republican leaders contended a recheck for uniform enforcement of the "negative vote" law would wipe out Kennedy's lead and give the state to Nixon by more than 50,000 votes.

Did the Kennedy-Johnson ticket really receive a swing of 100,000 votes, as the GOP claimed? In Texas, people had to pay a poll tax of more than a dollar before they could vote. It was used as a way to stop Black people from voting. But it also could be used as a way to track voter fraud. In Rayburn's Fannin County, the poll tax list showed 4,895 people paid the fee—yet 6,138 people voted on November 8. Kennedy carried the county by a three-to-one margin, collecting 4,282 ballots to Nixon's 1,844. (Twelve votes went to other candidates.)

Mazo said he found evidence of voters casting up to six ballots at once and precinct chiefs bribing voters.

But the clock was ticking. They had to do something before December 19, when the electors in each state convened to certify the results.

Almost as important, the GOP was too late to ask for a statewide recount. That's because the state election board—all Democrats—had already certified Kennedy as the winner, giving him the Lone Star State's 24 electoral votes.

Attorney General Will Wilson, a Democrat, was a member of the Texas Board of Canvassers, which certified Kennedy as the winner. He told Mazo that he "doubted anything could be done about the alleged irregularities." Maybe they could prosecute people for election fraud.

"I have found that elections are like cement. When they are set, they harden—and that's it," Wilson said.

Washington, D.C.

At first, President Eisenhower accepted the election outcome. But now he was beginning to have second thoughts. He had been staying at his cabin in Augusta, Georgia. Now he was back in Washington.

He began asking questions. After Postmaster General Arthur Summerfield expressed concern over possible voter fraud, Ike reached out to Attorney General William Rogers. Was anything being done to investigate the allegations? Yes, the election was over. But the voters deserved to know whether the vote was somehow rigged, Eisenhower said. Rogers said the FBI had been looking into voter fraud in Texas and Illinois, but they had stopped after Nixon objected to the investigation.

November 25
Washington, D.C.

Jack Kennedy wasn't watching the recounts. He was with his wife, who had given birth to a six-pound, three-ounce boy with a shock of black hair.

Kennedy wasn't there when his son was born. He was at the family compound in Palm Beach when he got the message: Jackie was in labor. He had to hightail it to Georgetown Hospital in Washington, D.C., to be by Jackie's side.

The president-elect smiled as he gazed at his son through a heavy glass window. His namesake was placed in an incubator, a normal procedure for babies born slightly prematurely. He'd be in there for a few days and would be released from the hospital on December 9.

Kennedy was still dragging almost two weeks after the election. He headed to his Georgetown home to get some sleep. As he left the hospital, he told reporters his wife was awake and lively. "She is fine," he said.

He told them the baby's name was John Fitzgerald Kennedy Jr. It was his first son. His daughter, Caroline, would turn three in just a couple days.

Most of America was looking forward to pictures and news of the Kennedy baby. The infant's arrival again relegated the GOP election recount efforts to the inside sections of newspapers.

November 30
Washington, D.C.

With under three weeks remaining before the Electoral College met, the GOP was still pushing for statewide recounts. They had already started in Chicago.

JFK's press secretary, Pierre Salinger, said the president-elect wasn't worried.

But Democrats thought there was no damn way this was going on without Nixon's backing.

It was frustrating. Kennedy and top Democratic leaders knew the GOP was casting doubt on Kennedy's legitimacy. That would resonate with some Americans. They would believe that Kennedy wasn't the real president—that somehow, he'd bought the office just like he had bought the Democratic presidential nomination. That was the real danger.

Proving widespread voter fraud was a dangerous game at a dangerous time. With the Soviet Union making inroads all over the world, would a divided America be able to stop the advance?

Some Democratic Party leaders felt it was like a coup—the GOP was trying to seize power and undermine the democratic process, even though Kennedy had won.

At the beginning, part of the Republican strategy was to take small developments and rumors and embellish them. But now new and relevant details seemed to emerge almost every day. Would it be enough?

There were some people hoping it would. A few newspapers in the South had started an editorial campaign to persuade southern electors to reverse their support for Kennedy when the Electoral College met, thus putting the election in the hands of U.S. House members.

The Mobile Press Register Inc., which published two newspapers, said that might lead to the election of a southern Democrat who believed in states' rights.

Could that really happen? If it did, there'd certainly be chaos when the Electoral College met on December 19. Nobody wanted it to play out that way. Or did they?

December 4
Chicago, Illinois

When Earl Mazo got to Illinois he discovered it was just as bad as Texas.

And it didn't take long before he reported some of the tricks being used to inflate numbers in Cook County.

Election rolls were supposed to keep track of registered voters. But they were rigged so the names of the dead would still appear, allowing others to vote in the deceased's name.

Now Mazo had company. Since the election, the *Chicago Tribune* had been reporting on widespread voter fraud in the city. Their findings could be summarized by that newspaper's editorial board: "The election of November 8 was characterized by such gross and palpable fraud as to justify the conclusion that [Richard Nixon] was deprived of victory."

In another editorial, the conservative newspaper said the U.S. district attorney in Chicago should investigate the disappearance of a ballot box critical to an election fraud probe.

The missing records were for Ward 2, Precinct 50. Nearly eighty votes were cast—even though that precinct only had twenty-two registered voters. The box was being kept in a locked vault. When the safe was opened, the box was gone. Election judges were supposed to look for suspicious activity at the polls. But it was often difficult to find Republicans to volunteer for the job. So, Democrats would pretend to be Republicans to fill those vacancies.

Newspapers all over the country began to look more closely at the allegations. The *Newark Ledger-Dispatch* in an editorial quoted Mazo's reporting:

> Take for example, a couple of incidents turned up only yesterday, while certain Cook County ballot boxes were being checked in Chicago as part of the Republican initiated "discovery" procedure leading to a probable vote recount. Two boxes were empty. The ballots that had vanished from them had added up to a majority of about 500 votes for Senator Kennedy. Furthermore, 50 ballot boxes were brought to the inspection room without seals, and 23 with broken seals. All ballots have been in custody of the Democratic-controlled Election Board since election night. . . . The chairman said the seals probably dropped off or were broken accidentally when workmen moved the boxes.

Every day, it seemed like Mazo was uncovering more stories of suspicious activity surrounding the results of the election.

This wasn't a fishing expedition. This was evidence. Mazo argued that the integrity of the nation's election system was at stake.

But time was on the Democrats' side—and they knew it. They only had to run out the clock.

December 6
Washington, D.C.

Mazo kept investigating. Then he got a call from Richard Nixon. The vice president wanted to see him.

Mazo had just published the fourth installment in his series. He knew he had more than enough material for twelve installments. His editors were behind him. His stories were being picked up by newspapers all over the country—and generating buzz.

He had been doing some of the best reporting of his career. In Chicago, he had obtained lists of voters in precincts that seemed suspicious. And when he started checking their addresses, he found they were cemeteries where the names on tombstones were registered and had voted.

There was no question in his mind that the election was "stolen like mad . . . in Texas and Illinois."

He wondered why Nixon wanted to see him. He hadn't heard from him since he began his series. Maybe the vice president was going to praise him for his hard work.

Mazo made his way to Capitol Hill and Nixon's office. But when he sat down in the vice president's office, Nixon looked glum.

"Earl, those are interesting articles you are writing," Nixon said. "But no one steals the presidency of the United States."

He said he wanted Mazo to stop writing more stories on election fraud. At first, Mazo thought Nixon was kidding. He wasn't. He was dead serious.

Nixon said it had gone too far. The nation needed to know who was the new president, especially at the height of the Cold War. Mazo explained that the election fraud he uncovered would make a difference. He might be elected president.

But Nixon said it didn't matter. The cost was too high.

"Our country cannot afford the agony of a constitutional crisis—and I damn well will not be a party to creating one just to become president or anything else," Nixon said.

He didn't want to undermine the new administration. And it could take years in the court system to settle the issue. And then what? The nation's enemies would gain ground. No, Nixon didn't want to take that chance.

Mazo took a deep breath. He thanked the vice president and left his office. Even though Nixon urged him to stop, Mazo wasn't going to give up.

He told his editors about his exchange with the vice president. And that he was going to keep going.

But then Nixon called Mazo's bosses at the *Herald Tribune* and implored them to stop Mazo's investigation. And they did.

Mazo's reporting on the subject was over. His chance for a Pulitzer was gone.

Six years later, Nixon would respond to a letter written by Mazo offering advice. Then Nixon brought up voter fraud. He said he hoped someday "some enterprising reporter in the future" would "write a story about the voter fraud of 1960." He said such a story "might have great national impact."

December 8
Chicago, Illinois

Just because the vice president told Mazo to stop didn't mean the GOP didn't keep trying.

The Republicans filed a lawsuit to keep Kennedy from getting Illinois's 27 electoral votes.

But circuit court judge Thomas Kluczynski, who had been appointed by former Democratic governor Adlai Stevenson, rejected a GOP demand that the Chicago and Cook County election canvassing boards revise their vote tallies to correct alleged irregularities.

The Republicans had charged that a recount of Chicago paper ballots showed Nixon picking up more than 5,500 votes from ballots that were improperly thrown out; according to the tally of the Democratic-dominated election board, Nixon gained less than 1,000 votes.

Kluczynski paid no attention to the Democratic or Republican figures. He merely ruled that the canvassing boards had already certified the election results and could not be reconvened.

On the basis of the latest figures, Kennedy won Illinois by only 8,858 votes out of nearly 4.8 million cast.

One of the attorneys for the Chicago Nixon Recount Committee said they'd decide in a few days whether to appeal.

Meantime, they presented their case to the State Election Board, where they hoped to get an impartial hearing. But the board certified the state's 27 electoral votes to Kennedy.

Morton said they didn't know whether they'd appeal. It could take two years for the courts to decide on voter fraud cases in Illinois and Texas. By then, it would be far too late to reverse the election outcome and make Vice President Nixon the chief executive.

"As a realist, I don't think there is a chance," he said.

December 10
Austin, Texas

Two days later, in Texas, Republicans went to court, too. The Republicans filed a federal lawsuit asking a judge to order a recount of more than 1 million paper ballots. They claimed that could change the outcome of the election in Texas.

The Democrats tried to stop it. But a federal district court judge signed a temporary restraining order prohibiting certification of Texas's 24 electoral votes pending a hearing on a Republican lawsuit challenging the validity of the November 8 general election.

The GOP said the suit was filed to protect "both the GOP presidential electors and all Nixon voters in the state."

U.S. district court judge Ben Connally held a three-and-a-half-hour pretrial conference on the lawsuit. Republican attorneys argued that some election judges threw out ballots that were improperly marked, but other judges did not. They wanted a recount of all 1,277,184 paper ballots cast in Texas's 254 counties to find out how many were marked improperly but still counted.

Texas's twenty-four electors were pledged to Kennedy. And attorneys for the electors argued that it was not in the jurisdiction of the federal judge because the GOP didn't exhaust all the state courts. The Republicans argued that Connally did have jurisdiction because the Fourteenth Amendment of the Constitution provides for equal rights for citizens and protects the right to vote.

But Connally dismissed the lawsuit, saying there was insufficient evidence of civil rights violations—violations that could change the outcome.

The Texas canvassing board met and, relying on Connally's decision, said it had no authority to order a recount. And it added that none of the allegations, even if true, would have changed the outcome. So, the board certified the victory of the Kennedy-Johnson ticket.

It was the end of the road for the GOP in Texas. And soon it was the end in Illinois and other states. Without any paths left to rectify the wrongs GOP leaders saw in those big, close states, it was over.

It didn't mean that election fraud didn't happen. All sides agreed that it did. It was a question of the extent of the fraud: Would it have been enough to overturn the results in key states like Texas and Illinois? And if a few select states were lawfully restored to Nixon, could the course of history have gone a different way?

To this day, the questions remain unanswered.

December 19
Washington, D.C.

They began arriving at state capitals all over the nation—a ritual dating back to the birth of the United States. And when they were finished, a new president would be chosen.

Under the U.S. Constitution, electors were the ones who actually selected a president. Yes, the popular vote mattered, but only in the sense that if a presidential candidate carried a state, he'd pick up its electoral votes. That was the theory. Of course, things didn't always go as planned.

And with this contentious election, no one really knew what would happen at statehouses where 537 electors would cast their ballots. A candidate needed 269 to win. (This would be the only election with that threshold, since it was the first election for Hawaii and Alaska, which had become states since 1956, but the last before the District of Columbia participated.)

It was a crazy system and every four years it seemed that some people would call for it to be scrapped. They'd ask why it wasn't the popular vote that determined the outcome of presidential elections—just like in gubernatorial, senatorial, and mayoral races. But as soon as the presidential race faded from the nation's collective memory, so did efforts to reform the system.

It was a compromise made at the birth of the nation. The Founding Fathers debated whether the people or Congress should pick a new president.

They came up with the Electoral College, where each state would be given a certain number of electors based on its population. A populous state like New York had 45, the most in the nation, while sparsely populated ones like Alaska, Wyoming, and Vermont had three.

It got complicated at the state level, where political parties would choose a separate slate of electors. If a Republican presidential candidate won a state, the GOP slate would go to the Electoral College meeting.

But there was a wild card: Nothing in the Constitution said an elector had to vote for the party's candidate. And this year, some electors in southern states had already publicly stated they'd support Senator Harry Byrd of Virginia, a staunchly conservative seventy-three-year-old who seemed like he had been around forever.

Would other electors do the same thing? As the day wore on, it became clear that the electors were sticking to the script. And by the time they finished, Kennedy had 303 electoral votes to Nixon's 219. Byrd collected 15.

And so, it was finally over. Kennedy was officially the thirty-fifth president of the United States, an anticlimactic end to a dramatic presidential election.

In a few days, it would be Christmas and the nation had already turned its attention to the holidays. In Palm Beach, Florida, John Kennedy would spend the time at the Kennedy mansion, surrounded by family and friends.

A fourteen-foot-high Christmas tree stood near the fireplace, adorned with seven angels and topped with a lighted Santa Claus. The base of the tree was covered with a silver spangled blanket.

Jack was there with his newborn son, John Jr., and daughter, Caroline. It was a house filled with laughter and promise. Good days were ahead.

For Nixon, the future was uncertain. He had spent fourteen years in Washington, as a congressman, senator, and vice president.

But soon, he'd be out of work. In a way he'd be starting over. He was too young to retire. But he had been around for so long, would there be a political future for him?

As the year came to an end, that was a question he knew he'd eventually have to address.

January 6, 1961
Washington, D.C.
The Count

Richard Nixon greeted his fellow lawmakers inside the Senate Chamber in the U.S. Capitol. He smiled like a man on his way to the dentist. It was going to hurt, but it had to be done.

With senators following him, the vice president walked slowly to the other end of the Capitol, passing through the Great Rotunda, their footfalls echoing off the marble floors. They reached the House of Representatives Chamber, another roomful of lawmakers.

Nixon stepped inside and was greeted with a rousing, bipartisan ovation. He smiled and headed over to sit next to House Speaker Sam Rayburn, on the upper level of the rostrum.

Under the Constitution, it was Nixon's job as president of the Senate to preside over a joint session of Congress for the formal counting of the electoral votes.

The ballot-counting ceremony dated all the way back to George Washington. The ritual symbolized the peaceful transfer of power in the United States from one administration to another.

Nixon tried to put aside his disappointment—at least for one day. He watched as the senators and representatives found their seats, arranged in a semicircle on tiered platforms facing the front of the room.

The "People's House" was magnificent. The House Speaker's rostrum had lower, middle, and upper tiers, each filled with people responsible for different tasks: the sergeant at arms, the journal clerk, and the parliamentarian, who oversees the processes and rules.

Behind the rostrum stood Ionic columns made of black Italian and white Alabama marble, and an American flag flanked by two bronze fasces. In front of the rostrum were two lecterns—one for Democrats, the other for Republicans.

The chamber's lower walls were paneled in walnut, with light gray marble pilasters. A gallery for visitors and the press corps ringed the chamber on the upper level.

Nixon lifted the gavel and banged it against the desk, calling the session to order. A hush fell over the room.

First, Nixon wished House Speaker Rayburn a happy seventy-ninth birthday. There was no love lost between the two men. During one midterm election, Nixon was believed by Johnson and the Democrats to have called them "the party of treason." And Rayburn considered Nixon "a crook."

Congressional pages carried in two shiny boxes of inlaid wood. The certified electoral votes had been kept inside since they were sent to Washington by each state's officials.

The actual vote counting was done by tellers. As they scanned each paper, they took turns announcing the results out loud. Members of the House and Senate scribbled down notes and added up the numbers for themselves.

Everything went smoothly until the roll call reached Hawaii. There were two slates of electoral votes for the state. The tellers threw the issue in Nixon's lap.

Hawaii had only just become a state in August 1959 and was holding its first presidential election. Turnout had topped 93 percent, and the state's result was close.

On Election Day, Nixon carried the state by just 141 votes. A recount wasn't done by the time the electors met on December 19. So the issue fell to the vice president. Now Kennedy led Nixon by 115 votes. Nixon settled the dispute by certifying the Kennedy electors.

It all had to hurt. Kennedy won Hawaii by less than two-tenths of one percentage point. And Kennedy had barely edged Nixon in the nationwide popular vote, winning 34,226,731 ballots to Nixon's 34,108,157.

The fraud cases went nowhere. When Senator Everett Dirksen, the minority leader from Illinois, asked the FBI to investigate voter fraud in his state, he was told they'd forward his complaint to the new attorney general: Bobby Kennedy.

Standing on the rostrum after the count was complete, Nixon told his colleagues that this was the "first time in 100 years that a candidate for the presidency announced the results of an election in which he was defeated, and announced the victory of his opponent."

He paused.

"I don't think we can have a more striking and eloquent example of the stability of our Constitutional system and of the proud tradition of the American people of developing and respecting and honoring institutions of self-government," Nixon told the joint session.

Nixon congratulated Kennedy and Lyndon Johnson, who were in the audience, wishing them the best as "you work in a cause that is bigger than any man's ambition, greater than any party—it is the cause of freedom and justice and peace for all mankind. And it is in that spirit that I now declare that John F. Kennedy has now been elected president of the United States and Lyndon Johnson vice president of the United States."

The members of Congress cheered and gave Nixon a standing ovation—even Rayburn, who rarely applauded from the rostrum. But today, Rayburn smiled at Nixon and said, "That was a damn fine speech, Dick. I will miss you here. Good luck."

The final presidential tally: 303 electoral votes for Kennedy, 219 for Nixon, and 15 of the unpledged electors for Harry Byrd, the segregationist senator from Virginia.

Nixon was praised for the way he'd handled the joint session. It didn't heal the deep personal wound; he would carry that for the rest of his life.

But he set an example for all to follow: Democracy works when there is a peaceful transition of power after an election—especially from one political party to another. Peaceful transitions require all lawmakers and citizens to uphold democratic institutions and norms, including the rule of law, despite their personal interests. Without that common agreement, democracy dies.

The standard Nixon set would come perilously close to collapsing during another joint session of Congress sixty years later. But on that January 6, 1961, Nixon reaffirmed the democratic tradition, and set an example for history.

January 20, 1961
Washington, D.C.
Inauguration Day

John F. Kennedy stood at the podium, squinting a little in the brilliant winter sunshine. He wore neither hat nor coat. He stood slim and tall on a bitterly cold day in the nation's capital.

Hundreds of thousands of people huddled in front of the pillared platform erected on the steps of the U.S. Capitol for Kennedy's inauguration ceremony. Tens of millions watched the festivities on their televisions or listened to their radios.

Dolly Bellavance and John Latvis from Nahua, New Hampshire, where Kennedy had made the first stop of his campaign on a snowy day almost exactly a year earlier, were there in spirit. So were Franklin McCain, Ezell Blair Jr., Joseph McNeil, and David Richmond, the students who had sparked a national movement when they sat down at a whites-only lunch counter in Greensboro, North Carolina, back in February.

The Reverend Martin Luther King Jr. and his wife, Coretta, watched from their home in Atlanta, Georgia. Kennedy's telephone call to Coretta Scott King seemed to translate into votes.

Kennedy landed 68 percent of the Black vote, up from the 1956 Democratic presidential ticket's showing of 58 percent. But that was still lower than in 1952, when 79 percent of Black voters supported Democrats.

The young president would have to prove himself to King. He'd have to show him that civil rights were a priority in the Kennedy White House.

Frank Sinatra was there in Washington, D.C. He'd spent one night that week at Bobby Kennedy's Virginia home, called Hickory Hill. The Kennedys seated him at a piano and had him sing song after song, until he finally told Bobby to "get him a drink."

Sinatra and Kennedy's brother-in-law Peter Lawford arranged a glittering inauguration gala for twelve thousand people, but a howling snowstorm meant only three thousand could attend. The fortunate few saw Gene Kelly dance, Ella Fitzgerald and Nat King Cole sing, and other Hollywood entertainers and actors like Sidney Poitier give speeches.

Sammy Davis Jr. was conspicuously absent. He was asked by Kennedy—at the request of his father—to stay away. Davis had married May Britt in November, and the Kennedys believed his appearance would still be too controversial. (Davis would become a big Richard Nixon supporter in the early 1970s.)

Frank Sinatra escorted Jacqueline Kennedy to the presidential box at the gala that night. Her husband took a microphone and said he was "indebted to a great friend, Frank Sinatra."

"You cannot imagine the work he has done to make this show a success," JFK said.

Would their friendship continue once Kennedy took office? And what about Sam Giancana, the mob boss who'd helped Kennedy's campaign? Would new attorney general Bobby Kennedy go easy on the mob? And then there was Cuba. With no action to take down Castro before the election, Kennedy's campaign received a boost, especially when he took a hard-line stance against the Cuban dictator. Now he had inherited the plans Nixon hadn't been able to talk about publicly. And Fidel Castro would hand the new president his first international crisis. How would he handle it?

As cold winds whipped across the inauguration platform that morning, Judith Campbell watched from her home in Los Angeles. She and Kennedy still talked, and occasionally met each another—even during the busy campaign. How would Kennedy behave as president?

So many people on the platform that day had high hopes for the new commander in chief. Richard Nixon and his wife, Pat, sat on one side of Kennedy, while President Eisenhower sat on the other with the new first lady.

Former president Truman was on the platform. In the row behind them were Joseph P. Kennedy and his wife, Rose, and the Kennedy sisters. Joe raised his high silk hat and beamed at Pat Nixon.

The eighty-six-year-old Pulitzer Prize–winning poet Robert Frost was there to recite one of his works.

The moment came for Kennedy to take the oath of office. He placed his left hand on the Bible held by Earl Warren, the chief justice of the United States. And when JFK swore to "preserve, protect and defend the Constitution of the United States, so help me God," Kennedy officially became the thirty-fifth president of the United States. A thunderous roar rose from the crowd.

Nixon was still bitter about the election. A few thousand more votes

JFK taking the oath of office, January 20, 1961
(John F. Kennedy Presidential Library)

in key states and *he* would have been in Kennedy's place today. As he told a friend before the ceremony, "We won but they stole it from us." But Nixon buried his disappointment and moved swiftly to Kennedy's side to shake his hand and offer his congratulations.

Kennedy turned and looked out over the massive crowd on the snow-covered plaza before him. It was 22 degrees—so cold that with every breath, the spectators released small misty clouds of smokelike vapor.

JFK's face was a mask. He didn't show any emotion—and that reflected the gravity of what had just transpired. He was now the most powerful man in the free world. Powerful and reckless. Brilliant and self-absorbed.

Kennedy knew that the inaugural ceremony could be a defining moment in a president's term. He'd written a short, clear speech devoid of

Richard Nixon congratulating John F. Kennedy
(New York Daily News/Getty Images)

partisan rhetoric, focused on foreign policy. Every sentence was worked, reworked, and polished.

He took the podium, with tens of millions of people watching, and delivered the speech of his life.

Kennedy warned "friend and foe alike" that the generation of Americans now taking power was "unwilling to witness or permit the slow undoing of those human rights to which this nation has always been committed."

Then he pledged: "Let every nation know whether it wishes us well or ill, that we shall pay any price, bear any burden, meet any hardship, support any friend, oppose any foe to assure the survival and the success of liberty."

He addressed other issues in broad sweeping phrases, a policy of peace through negotiation, backed by a strong military. He dedicated himself and his new administration to the two shining goals of freedom and peace in the world, as it was then, at a new precipice of unknown challenges.

"I do not shrink from this responsibility—I welcome it," Kennedy said.

His voice was firm and emphatic. Cheers thundered up from the crowd. And he warned enemies not to underestimate the power of the United States.

"To those nations who would make themselves our adversary, we offer not a pledge but a request: that both sides begin anew the quest for peace, before the dark powers of destruction unleashed by science engulf all humanity in planned or accidental self-destruction," Kennedy declared.

"So let us begin anew—remembering on both sides that civility is not a sign of weakness, and sincerity is always subject to proof. Let us never negotiate out of fear. But let us never fear to negotiate," he said.

And then, he encouraged Americans to get involved in the country's future, saying, "And so, my fellow Americans: ask not what your country can do for you—ask what you can do for your country."

Kennedy's inaugural address was an emotional appeal for peace— and a warning to America's adversaries—at a time of great uncertainty.

Almost a year earlier, at a dinner party a few days after Kennedy had announced his candidacy for the Democratic presidential nomination, he was a guest at his friend Ben Bradlee's house. Another journalist, James Cannon, was there, too—and he recorded the dinner conversation.

Kennedy described his career choices, including why he decided to run for president. He said he could never see himself as a lawyer, dealing with wills and trusts. That was too boring.

After he entered politics, he wanted to see how high his ceiling was. He had been a member of the House and the Senate. But president, that's where the real power was, he said.

"The presidency is the source of action. . . . All the things you're interested in doing, the president can do," he said, adding, "The presidency is the place to be . . . if you want to get anything done."

And he described himself as a new age politician. He was an introvert and didn't like shaking hands or talking to voters. "I'd rather read a book on a plane than talk to the fellow next to me," he said.

But he admitted that there were parts of campaigning that he enjoyed, including making speeches.

"It's stimulating. Life is a struggle and you're struggling in a tremendous arena. It's like playing Yale every Saturday in a sense. How could anything be more interesting than this sort of checkerboard chess struggle of the next seven months?" he said.

Now, just a year later, it all was his. He was the center of action. The Cubans. Soviets, gangsters, assassins. After everything he had been through on the campaign trail, Kennedy was a hardened political veteran.

He was older, tougher, and more purposeful. He was prepared.

He felt strong. In the past, he'd depended on family and friends to make it all happen. They had helped to create him, but he was the man on top now.

It was time for Jack Kennedy to stand on his own.

Epilogue

The 1960 presidential election changed everything. It was the first to be conducted largely on television. The first to feature debates between the two major-party candidates. The first where both candidates were born in the twentieth century. American presidential politics would never be the same.

Television would grow to play an ever greater role in how we choose our leaders—in both so-called earned media, where politicians make news that television and print reporters cover, and "paid" media, where candidates spend ballooning sums of money to sell themselves on television like soap or cereal. Perhaps the single biggest event in the next presidential campaign in 1964 was the "Daisy" ad, which showed a little girl picking petals off a flower counting from one to ten—which then transitioned to the countdown to the detonation of a nuclear bomb. It aired only once, but made the central point of Lyndon Johnson's campaign: that Barry Goldwater was too extreme and too trigger-happy to be president.

The legacy of debates between the two major party candidates is spottier. Despite the excitement over the Nixon-Kennedy debates—and tens of millions of Americans watched them—there were no presidential debates in the next three election cycles. In the wake of the Kennedy assassination, President Johnson had no interest in sharing a platform with an opponent like Barry Goldwater, whom he dismissed as a right-wing extremist. And after his experience in 1960, Nixon was not about to repeat the exercise against Vice President Hubert Humphrey in 1968, or South Dakota senator George McGovern in 1972. It wasn't until

1976 that the nominees of the two major parties faced off again. Gerald Ford, who was never elected to national office and became president when Nixon resigned after Watergate, agreed to debate former Georgia governor Jimmy Carter, who enjoyed a big lead in the polls.

Since then, there have been debates in every presidential election year. I was selected to moderate the third debate between Hillary Clinton and Donald Trump in 2016, and the first debate between Trump and Joe Biden in 2020. They became such a staple of the election process that the bipartisan Commission on Presidential Debates was formed in 1987. Over the years, it grew in authority so that it came to dictate to the presidential nominees how many debates would be held, the dates and locations, and even the moderators. Despite complaints, no candidate ever refused to participate—that is, until 2024, when the candidates once again seized control of the debates and shut out the commission. But in a media world with more platforms than ever—and smaller, spread-out audiences—presidential debates are one of the few events, including entertainment and sports, that still attract viewers in the tens of millions.

There is another, less savory aspect of 1960 that has had the biggest and most disruptive impact: the possibility that one side might try to steal an election and the growing acceptance of the argument that a loser can reject the results and refuse to engage in the peaceful transfer of power.

As we have recounted in this book, Richard Nixon and some of his Republican supporters at least considered taking that position in 1960—based on firmer evidence of election fraud than any seen before or since—before rejecting the idea as too destabilizing and too dangerous at the height of the Cold War. But since that moment more than sixty years ago, what was once unthinkable has become a rallying cry for tens of millions of Americans.

Timothy Naftali, who directed the Richard Nixon Presidential Library and Museum from 2006 to 2011, believes the former president never got over his defeat in 1960. In a podcast just before the 2020 election, Naftali said that "1960 deepened Nixon's sense of self-pity. It deepened his dark sense of American politics. It confirmed his belief that the best don't usually persevere and succeed. And I think it enabled his dark side more than he had allowed it to be enabled in the fifties. I think he began to believe that he could do anything, and it would be right."

Evan Thomas, a respected journalist who wrote *Being Nixon: A Man Divided*, has a similar take: "Nixon's paranoia went up a great deal after he lost in 1960, partly because he felt the Kennedys had used dirty tricks to defeat him. He felt the Kennedys were better at dirty tricks than he was in 1960. And he was probably not wrong about that."

Nixon would not make the same mistake again. When he ran for president in 1968, he ended up in another razor-thin, all-night election against Hubert Humphrey. Once again it came down to a handful of key states, including Illinois. John A. Farrell writes in his definitive biography, *Richard Nixon: The Life*: "At 6 am, when the newscasters reported that Mayor Daley [still the Democratic Party boss and mayor of Chicago] was holding back votes in Chicago, Pat went into her bathroom and threw up."

But this time would be different. My father, CBS correspondent Mike Wallace, was part of that network's election coverage. He covered Nixon for much of the 1968 Republican primaries, and he developed good sources. Dwight Chapin, Nixon's personal aide, or "body man," recounted in a 2007 interview with Naftali what happened that night. "Around 1:30 or 2:00 in the morning, the phone rang in the suite at the Waldorf [the Waldorf-Astoria in New York City, where Nixon and his top advisers were watching the returns]. This is election night, and it was Mike Wallace calling for John Mitchell [Nixon's campaign chairman]. And John—I went and got John. John came, got on the phone, and he said, 'Mike, that's right.' He said, 'That's right.' He said, 'You tell the mayor when they bring in a box of ballots, we'll bring in a box of ballots. They bring in a box, we'll bring in a box.' And Mitchell had withheld, down in southern Illinois, many boxes of ballots through the campaign organization."

I remember my father telling me what happened after that phone call.

He reported on the air to CBS anchor Walter Cronkite and the nation exactly what Mitchell said—that downstate Republican election judges were holding back their returns until the Daley machine in Chicago reported its results. Finally, Daley gave up and released the vote totals in precincts he controlled. This time, Nixon ended up carrying Illinois by 134,960 votes. And in an almost poetic reversal, it was Illinois's 26 electoral votes that put Richard Nixon over the top and into the White House.

And then, of course, there was Watergate. Running for reelection, President Nixon was still consumed with the Kennedys. On April 15, 1971, Nixon met with chief of staff Bob Haldeman and national security adviser Henry Kissinger in the Oval Office. The Watergate tapes record their conversation. "Kennedy was cold, impersonal, he treated his staff like dogs, particularly his secretaries and the others," the president said. "His staff created the impression of warm, sweet, nice to people, reads lots of books, a philosopher, and all that sort of thing. That was a pure creation of mythology."

"We have created no mythology," Nixon complained to his top aides. "For Christ's sake, can't we get across the courage more? Courage, boldness, guts? Goddamn it."

But the lesson Nixon took from his 1960 defeat was about much more than image. It was also about the absolute need to win, whatever the methods and whatever the cost.

The Committee for the Re-Election of the President—which was widely mocked with the acronym CREEP—financed a dirty-tricks operation against the Democrats, run by a friend of Dwight Chapin's, a young lawyer named Donald Segretti. His team forged a letter, supposedly written by Democratic front runner Senator Edmund Muskie of Maine, that disparaged French Canadians, a sizable voting bloc in New Hampshire. Segretti called this "ratfucking." After several other dirty tricks, Muskie ended up dropping out of the race.

And then there was the separate operation to break into the offices of the Democratic National Committee on June 17, 1972—offices located in the Watergate office building. Five men were arrested. A criminal trial and a Senate investigation would later uncover their assignment was to photograph campaign documents and install listening devices in DNC telephones. Money that the men were carrying was later tracked back to the Committee for the Re-Election.

In 1983, years after Nixon resigned the presidency, he sat down for a series of interviews with Frank Gannon, one of his former White House staffers. Gannon asked, "What was Watergate?"

"Let's start with what Watergate was not," Nixon responded. "No election was affected or stolen by it, as some believe the election of 1960 was stolen."

Gannon asked later, "Do you think that you were elected president of the United States in 1960?"

"Well, many objective observers believe that I was," Nixon said. "I haven't the evidence to prove that I was not or was. I will say this, however. There was no question, and these are facts, that there was immense fraud in Chicago, and it was all on that side, not on our side."

But if 1960 was an election that may—repeat *may*—have been stolen, and the losing candidate in the end refused to contest it, the presidential election of 2020 turned that set of events on its head. Sixty years later, in 2020, there was no evidence of voter fraud, no evidence of dirty tricks. But the loser of that election kidnapped American politics for years with claims that somehow he was the real winner.

Donald Trump has a long history of claiming he was robbed of victory. From 2004 to 2006, his reality show *The Apprentice* went up against *The Amazing Race* at the Emmys in the category of Outstanding Reality Competition Program. It lost each time. Years later, Trump tweeted, "The Emmys are all politics, that's why, despite nominations, *The Apprentice* never won—even though it should have many times over."

On election night in 2012, when President Obama was reelected, Trump said that the contest was a "total sham" and that the United States is "not a democracy." And in an eerie foreshadowing of what he would say after losing in 2020, Trump tweeted this: "We can't let this happen. We should march on Washington and stop this travesty. Our nation is totally divided."

In February 2016, Trump was the candidate, and the tirades continued. After he lost the Iowa caucuses to Senator Ted Cruz, Trump claimed "fraud" and demanded "either a new election should take place or Cruz results nullified."

By October, Trump was routinely warning about "rigged" elections and urging supporters to "watch your polling booths. . . . We can't lose an election because of—you know what I'm talking about."

Donald Trump talked about this so much in the final month of the campaign that I felt compelled as the debate moderator to ask him about it in his third and final face-off with Hillary Clinton on October 19.

I noted that both his running mate, Mike Pence, and his daughter Ivanka said he would accept the result of the election, and then continued: "I want to ask you here on the stage tonight, do you make the same commitment that you'll absolutely accept the result of the election?"

"I'll look at it at the time," Trump answered, and then complained about "millions of people that are registered to vote that shouldn't be registered to vote."

I was shocked at the answer and pressed on. "But sir, there is a tradition in this country, in fact, one of the prides of this country is the peaceful transition of power. And no matter how hard-fought a campaign is that at the end of the campaign, that the loser concedes to the winner. . . . Are you saying you're not prepared now to commit to that principle?"

Trump's response was short and stunning. "What I'm saying is that I will tell you at the time. I'll keep you in suspense, okay?"

In 2020, President Trump raised the issue of voter fraud again, months before the election. But this time, he had a different concern. In the midst of the worst pandemic to hit the United States in a century— and public health advisories urging Americans to "socially distance" to avoid catching COVID-19—a number of states loosened their rules about mail-in voting.

As early as April 7—just weeks after the coronavirus hit the United States hard—Trump said, "Mail ballots are a very dangerous thing for this country, because they're cheaters. They go and collect them. They're fraudulent in many cases."

The president kept up a steady drumbeat through the spring and early summer. On July 19, a broiling day in Washington, I sat down with Trump for an interview on a patio just outside the Oval Office. And once again, we discussed our democracy.

The president said, "I think mail-in voting is going to rig the election. I really do."

"Are you suggesting that you might not accept the results of the election?" I asked.

The president sounded the same note as in the 2016 debate. "I have to see," he answered.

I tried again. "Can you give a direct answer: Will you accept the election?"

Trump replied, "I'm not going to just say yes. I'm not going to say no."

Of course, we got our answer around 2:30 a.m. on November 4, in the middle of election night. The race was still far too close to call, with millions of votes still to be counted. But earlier, Fox News had projected Joe Biden would carry Arizona, the first state either party had won in 2016 to be put in the other party's column in 2020.

President Trump appeared before a crowd of supporters in the East Room of the White House. Though the loss of the state was the choice of the voters, he flipped the script. "This is a fraud on the American people. This is an embarrassment to our country," Trump declared. "We were getting ready to win this election. Frankly, we did win the election."

There was no systemic fraud—and certainly nothing that would change the results. Nine days after the election, the nation's Cybersecurity and Infrastructure Security Agency concluded, "The November 3rd election was the most secure in American history."

On December 1, Attorney General William Barr met with the president in the Oval Office. "Our mission is to investigate and prosecute actual fraud," Barr said he told Trump. "The fact is, we have looked at the major claims your people are making, and they are bullshit."

The issue of fraud in the 2020 presidential election was adjudicated exhaustively. The Trump team and allies filed more than sixty lawsuits challenging the results in states across the country. They lost nearly all of the cases, winning on only one technical issue.

The U.S. Supreme Court—with a 6 to 3 conservative majority, including three justices named by Trump—rejected challenges filed by the president's team and supporters in five states Biden won. And it threw out a lawsuit brought by seventeen Republican state attorneys general—and supported by 106 GOP members of Congress—challenging Biden victories in four states.

But if there is a single moment that crystallizes the difference and the devolution from 1960 to 2020, it is the events of January 6. This is the day set by the Electoral Count Act of 1887 for Congress to meet in joint session to count the electoral votes of each state and for the vice president to certify the winners of the election.

Remember, this was the day on January 6, 1961, when Richard Nixon presided over the official declaration of his own defeat. But sixty years later, it played out very differently.

President Trump summoned a crowd of tens of thousands of angry supporters to a rally at the Ellipse, just across from the White House. "We will never give up. We will never concede," he told them. He urged them to walk down Pennsylvania Avenue to the Capitol, where the official counting of the electoral votes was just starting. He said he would march with them. And he gave the crowd their marching orders: "And we fight. We fight like hell. And if you don't fight like hell, you're not going to have a country anymore."

Trump had been pressuring his vice president, Mike Pence, for days—saying he could reject electoral votes for Biden and overturn the election. He told the crowd that day, "Mike Pence is going to have to come through for us. And if he doesn't, that will be a sad day for our country because you're sworn to uphold our Constitution."

But while the president was still speaking, Pence put out a statement: "It is my considered judgment that my oath to support and defend the Constitution constrains me from claiming unilateral authority to determine which electoral votes should be counted and which should not."

Thousands of people stormed the Capitol, shutting down the counting of electoral votes mandated by the Constitution—trashing the citadel of American democracy, and even setting up gallows outside while chanting "Hang Mike Pence."

Watching the riot play out on television in the White House, Trump tweeted this: "Mike Pence didn't have the courage to do what should have been done to protect our Country and our Constitution."

The election of 1960 will be remembered for many things. The turning of a generational page in our politics. Impressive technological advances in how we see and judge who we choose to lead us. The crumbling of one pillar of religious bigotry. A step forward in the journey to racial equality.

But in the end, what stands out is that in 1960, with the most powerful position in the world at stake, and with the difference between victory and defeat on a razor's edge, Richard Nixon chose to do the right thing—what was best not for himself, but for his country.

As we have learned so painfully, that choice is not always guaranteed.

Acknowledgments

Why 1960? Ever since the chaos of the 2020 election—a president refusing to concede his defeat, the failure to conduct a normal transition, the bogus attempts to contest the election, and then the deeply shocking January 6 attack on the Capitol—I have found myself thinking back to all the elections I've covered over the past half century.

We knew the rules of democracy in America: Somebody won, somebody lost, both sides acknowledged it, and we moved on. It wasn't something we discussed. That's just the way it was.

But 2020 shattered that. And I'm not sure we will ever return to the same unspoken confidence that our political leaders will accept those rules and abide by them.

Somehow, that brought me back to 1960. It was the first presidential campaign I truly became engaged in (my mother told me that back in 1952, I kept saying, "I like Ike"). But at the ripe old age of thirteen, I was fascinated by the Nixon-Kennedy contest. I read about it in the papers, watched it on television, and sat beside my parents in front of the TV set for all four of the debates.

I was rooting for Nixon. And "rooting" is the right word. It was like the way you support a sports team. And looking back, I think I was just pulling for the underdog. Kennedy was so rich and glamorous. Nixon was neither of those things. But he was serious and earnest.

After the election, I remember hearing stories about possible fraud—especially how Mayor Daley held back the vote in his Chicago precincts until the downstate numbers came in. But Nixon was a good loser (remember I was thirteen). He accepted his defeat—was there on the inaugural stand and was one of the first to congratulate Kennedy after he took the oath of office.

I think that's where I learned the rules. And after the deeply disappointing events of 2020, that's where my thoughts kept returning—to the presidential campaign of 1960. That was an election that may truly have been stolen. But the losing candidate accepted defeat. That was the paradigm—until Donald Trump turned all that on its head in 2020.

What struck me in researching and then writing this book is that the events of 1960 were even more dramatic, more highly charged than I understood back then. The campaign corruption and voter fraud were even more egregious. The pressure on Nixon from some Republican leaders to contest the election was real. Some scholars told me they suspect Nixon was egging that on behind the scenes. But in the end, he did the right thing.

I couldn't imagine a sharper contrast to the events of 2020.

To tell this story, I got the Countdown team back together. Mitch Weiss is a Pulitzer Prize–winning investigative reporter for the Associated Press. He has a remarkable ability to dig up facts and find the indelible anecdote that puts the reader in the middle of the action. It was a powerful experience to immerse ourselves in 1960 and the coverage of it, from contemporary accounts to more recent works, to bring this year to life.

Lori Crim is my treasured researcher. She's been by my side for the Countdown books and two presidential debates. When I left Fox News for CNN in 2021, I asked one staffer to come with me—Lori.

I wouldn't have even considered taking on another Countdown book without Mitch and Lori. And I was thrilled and honored when they signed up.

Then there are the folks I have called my Sherpa guides and consiglieres in the previous Countdown books. Larry Kramer is my longtime manager. Claudia Cross and Frank Weimann of Folio Literary Management know the publishing industry. They take care of everything on the business side—but do so much more, providing wise counsel and invaluable perspective.

Part of that counsel was the decision to take this latest Countdown project to the esteemed Dutton Books. Publisher Christine Ball made us feel like we had a safe and supportive new home. Editor in chief John Parsley made this book so much better—sharpening our storytelling and coming up with new ideas to explore. And we had the backing of the great team they have assembled. I want to thank Amanda Walker, Sarah Thegeby, Stephanie Cooper, Nicole Jarvis, Ella Kurki, David Howe, Melissa Solis, and Erica Rose.

Along the way, there were people who helped us put this book together. I want to thank Tim Naftali, a celebrated historian who ran the Richard Nixon Presidential Library and Museum for five years. He gave me thoughtful guidance and set me up with the library's extensive collection of oral history interviews. When we were writing about the Greensboro Four, we came across Anne Moebes, who opened up the collection of her late photojournalist father, Jack Moebes. And then there is Maryrose Grossman, an archivist at the John F. Kennedy Presidential Library and Museum, who went above and beyond in helping us find just the right photographs of JFK and his family to help tell our story.

As I worked on this book, I never forgot about my real job. I want to thank CNN for its support and understanding. I am deeply grateful to Chairman and CEO Mark Thompson, Senior Vice President of Communications Emily Kuhn, and Senior Communications Manager Alex Manasseri. I also want to thank the team that does double duty on my two shows, *Who's Talking to Chris Wallace?* and *The Chris Wallace Show*, that sometimes had to pick up the slack, especially executive producer Javier de Diego.

Finally, Mitch and Lori and I again thank our families for their understanding while we took time from them to work on this book. You put up with a lot of "I'll be right down," after yelling from downstairs that it was time for dinner.

Once again, I want to conclude by expressing my deep gratitude to two members of my family. My daughter Catherine, who spent more than a decade in publishing, came up with the Countdown format for writing history. It is a great way to turn the dusty past into a page-turning thriller. Thank you for sharing the idea with me, instead of one of your other writers.

And then, there is my dear wife, Lorraine. Lord knows, you put up with a lot. But you make every day a joy and an adventure. I can't wait to see what happens next.

Notes

COUNTDOWN: 312 DAYS

1 family holiday in Jamaica: *Sacramento Union*, December 27, 1959.

2 "presidency of the United States": John F. Kennedy statement, January 2, 1960.

3 "the nomination and the election": John F. Kennedy statement, January 2, 1960.

3 "in a series of primary contests": John F. Kennedy statement, January 2, 1960.

5 "separation of church and state?": *Baltimore Sun*, January 3, 1960.

COUNTDOWN: 298 DAYS

7 "It's almost one o'clock": *Miami News*, January 16, 1960.

7 "opponents worked for two years": *Salt Lake Tribune*, November 5, 1958.

8 "my hair down with anyone": Alsop, *Nixon & Rockefeller*, 200–201.

9 that you had the "best hand": Kornitzer, *The Real Nixon*, 146.

9 "playing became tops," Stewart said: Kornitzer, *The Real Nixon*, 146.

9 "with a pair of deuces": *Life*, November 6, 1970.

9 "and jungles of the Solomons": Costello, *Facts about Nixon*, 52.

9 "Jerry Voorhis is a Communist": Costello, *Facts about Nixon*, 55.

10 distributed at campaign rallies: Costello, *Facts about Nixon*, 65.

10 "right down to her underwear": Rather, *The Palace Guard*, 140.

11 candidate on December 26, 1959: *New York Times*, December 27, 1959.

12 "was we didn't know it": Aitken, *Nixon: A Life*, 12.

12 "would entail a massive struggle": *Time*, January 4, 1960.

13 "been kicked in the groin": White, *The Making of the President 1960*, 77.

13 treating him for "stress": Robb, *The Gumshoe and the Shrink*, 16.

13 "nation in the years ahead": Associated Press, December 27, 1959.

13 "one war, avoiding others": *Austin American-Statesman*, January 30, 1960.

14 "eight years of direct experience": Campaign Brochure, *Why America Needs Richard Nixon*, 1960.

14 "right decisions for America": Campaign Brochure, *Why America Needs Richard Nixon*, 1960.

14 unless it was mandatory: Gellman, *Campaign of the Century*, 157.

14 New Hampshire, Ohio, and Oregon primaries: Associated Press, January 10, 1960.

15 "do not make major mistakes": *Miami Herald*, January 16, 1960.

15 "youth, inexperience, wealth, and religion": Nixon, *Six Crises*, 306.

COUNTDOWN: 289 DAYS

19 **"going to get coffee?":** *Nashua Telegraph*, January 25, 2010.

19 **"they're for the next president":** *Nashua Telegraph*, November 23, 2013.

19 **after JFK's handshake:** *Nashua Telegraph*, November 23, 2013.

20 **talk about any subject:** *Nashua Telegraph*, January 25, 1960.

20 **"to be heard," Kennedy said:** John F. Kennedy statement, January 25, 1960.

20 **"course of freedom succeeds":** Video of John F. Kennedy campaigning in Nashua, New Hampshire.

21 **ham and cheese sandwich:** *Portland Press Herald*, January 26, 1960.

22 **"Isn't he handsome?":** *Nashua Telegraph*, January 25, 1960.

22 **in front of a paint store:** *Boston Globe*, January 26, 1960.

22 **"he's got to work":** *Boston Globe*, January 26, 1960.

COUNTDOWN: 282 DAYS

24 **they went on until dawn:** David Richmond oral history, 1992.

25 **"take some action now":** Associated Press, October 23, 1994.

25 **majority supported the boycott:** History.com, January 10, 2023.

25 **southern bus depot:** WUNC, January 10, 2014.

25 **25,000 square feet of retail space:** *Smithsonian*, February 2010.

27 **pencils for a homework assignment:** *Our State*, January 21, 2011.

27 **The store closed at 5:30:** *New York Times*, February 14, 1960.

27 **"We don't serve colored here":** *Chattanooga Daily Times*, February 15, 2010.

27 **"You just served me":** *Chattanooga Daily Times*, February 15, 2010.

28 **"payment on my manhood":** *Atlanta Constitution*, January 29, 1995.

29 **like "a Mack truck":** *News & Observer*, January 27, 1980.

29 **"so long to do this":** WUNC, January 10, 2014.

COUNTDOWN: 276 DAYS

31 **frequent guests at their home:** Exner, *My Story*, 19.

31 **later in her memoir:** Exner, *My Story*, 86.

33 **concept had been Lawford's idea:** Exner, *My Story*, 86.

34 **She sighed, but said yes:** Exner, *My Story*, 87–88.

34 **escorted Teddy to the door:** Exner, *My Story*, 88–89.

34 **"We're just finishing up":** Exner, *My Story*, 89–90.

34 **"Well, we'll change that":** Exner, *My Story*, 89–90.

35 **"That little rascal":** Exner, *My Story*, 93.

35 **"mentioned that Jack was married":** Hersh, *Dark Side of Camelot*, 294.

COUNTDOWN: 274 DAYS

37 **overthrow his government:** Associated Press, February 11, 1960.

37 **"conspiracy against the Revolution":** Radio Progreso broadcast, August 17, 1959.

37 **five-man military tribunal:** UPI, February 11, 1960.

38 **thirty-thousand man professional army:** Paterson, *Contesting Castro*, 60.

39 **closed after Castro seized power:** Paterson, *Contesting Castro*, 226–27.

40 **exports depended on sugar:** Foreign Agriculture Economics, March 1962.

40 **its sugar for Russian fuel:** Associated Press, February 14, 1960.

COUNTDOWN: 273 DAYS

42 **"if you don't get started?":** Dallek, *An Unfinished Life*, 242.

42 **"for the next six months?":** Dallek, *An Unfinished Life*, 242.

43 **father's decision, Dalton resigned:** Goodwin, *The Fitzgeralds and the Kennedys*, 760; Dallek, *An Unfinished Life*, 242.

43 **"I'll just screw it up":** Thomas, *Robert Kennedy: His Life*, 59.

43 **"absolute catastrophic disaster":** Dallek, *An Unfinished Life*, 172.

44 **Bobby created and instructional guide:** Smith, *Bad Blood*, 65.

44 **of the life-threatening disease:** "Addison's Disease," Mayo Clinic, February 3, 2024.

45 **"intellectual blood bank":** White, *The Making of the President 1960*, 50.

45 **"how it sounded to the ear":** Sorensen, *Kennedy*, 60.

46 **"newspapermen around this town":** Pierre Salinger oral history, July 19, 1965.

46 **even bought a plane:** Sorensen, *Kennedy*, 100.

47 **"your gun like a man":** Dallek, *An Unfinished Life*, 269.

COUNTDOWN: 267 DAYS

49 **"nonpolitical posture of statesman":** White, *The Making of the President 1960*, 64.

50 **"(Soviet) war making capability":** *Lansing State Journal*, February 16, 1960.

50 **"free business and free labor":** *Lansing State Journal*, February 16, 1960.

50 **as much as fifteen pounds:** *Lansing State Journal*, February 16, 1960.

50 **"damaging to the country":** *Windsor Star*, February 15, 1960.

51 **"between issues and personalities":** *Windsor Star*, February 15, 1960.

51 **"same tired politics":** Associated Press, February 14, 1960.

51 **to "out-Nixon Nixon":** Associated Press, February 13, 1960.

51 **"reason for ours to change":** Associated Press, February 13, 1960.

51 **"what the times call for":** Costello, *Facts about Nixon*, 4.

53 **with building his tenacity:** *New York Times*, November 14, 2014.

53 **"vivacious woman with Titian hair":** Nixon, *RN*, 23.

53 **"someday, I'm going to marry you!":** Nixon, *RN*, 23.

54 **called her his "Irish gypsy":** Associated Press, March 12, 2012.

54 **"happiness we know is ours":** Associated Press, March 12, 2012.

54 **filled with mayflowers in the car?:** Associated Press, March 12, 2012.

55 **"loves you all the time":** Swift, *Pat and Dick*, 48.

55 **"tablecloth with someone to serve":** Swift, *Pat and Dick*, 48.

56 **undeveloped 35mm film:** *New York Times*, February 1, 1976.

56 **"and he came from California":** White, *The Making of the President 1960*, 66.

56 **around 350,000 to 15 million in 1952:** Ponce de Leon, *That's the Way It Is*, 6.

57 **Nixon recalled in *Six Crises*:** Nixon, *Six Crises*, 113.

57 **"we're going to keep it":** UPI, September 24, 1952.

58 **"press and the political establishment"**: *Atlantic*, September 22, 2012.
58 **"You're my boy"**: *Boston Globe*, September 29, 1952.
58 **"me into that house yet"**: Frank, *Ike and Dick*, 142.

COUNTDOWN: 263 DAYS
62 **"stand on his own feet"**: Scripps-Howard, April 7, 1960.
62 **street along Nantucket Sound**: Storey, *White House by the Sea*, 190.
62 **"all his kids' lives"**: Kessler, *Sins of the Father*, 111.
63 **"those monkeys"**: Scripps-Howard, April 7, 1960.
63 **"trying to avoid war"**: Scripps-Howard, April 7, 1960.
63 **"it any other way"**: Scripps-Howard, April 7, 1960.
63 **"that approach remorseless perfection"**: *Saturday Review*, March 26, 1960.
64 **"want any losers around here"**: Bedell-Smith, *Grace and Power*, 37.
65 **between $200 and $400 million**: Associated Press, November 10, 1957.
65 **Columbia Trust Company**: Dallek, *An Unfinished Life*, 9.
65 **youngest bank president in America**: Dallek, *An Unfinished Life*, 18.
65 **unseat Representative Peter Tague**: Hersh, *Dark Side of Camelot*, 35–39.
65 **Tague was reelected**: Hersh, *Dark Side of Camelot*, 35–39.
66 **"ashore the way the Pilgrims"**: Whalen, *Founding Father*, 66.
66 **killed in the shootout**: Eisenberg, *Meyer Lansky*, 108.
66 **plunged into the Great Depression**: *Time*, October 24, 2019.
67 **"burdens than one can bear"**: Kessler, *Sins of the Father*, 322.
68 **"strongly influenced by the Jews"**: Kessler, *Sins of the Father*, 161–62.
68 **could get in London**: Koskoff, *Joseph P. Kennedy*, 136–37.
68 **"that has gone to smash"**: Goodwin, *The Fitzgeralds and the Kennedys*, 693.
69 **"gangland style" in the head**: Hersh, *Dark Side of Camelot*, 52–53.
69 **$8 million months later**: Hersh, *Dark Side of Camelot*, 47.
70 **"can be elected president"**: *Time*, April 18, 1960.

COUNTDOWN: 247 DAYS
71 **"the way to the White House"**: Author interview with Dolly Bellavance, January 10, 2024.
72 **that many seriously injured**: *Time*, March 14, 1960.
73 **"receive arms for our defense"**: *New York Times*, March 6, 1960.
73 **homes had a television set**: Jordan, *The Americans*, 798.
74 **"country, and our age, demand"**: John F. Kennedy statement, Dover, New Hampshire, March 7, 1960.
74 **"all over the country"**: John F. Kennedy statement, Dover, New Hampshire, March 7, 1960.
74 **"take victory for granted"**: John F. Kennedy statement, Dover, New Hampshire, March 7, 1960.
74 **"primary contests with indifference"**: John F. Kennedy statement, Dover, New Hampshire, March 7, 1960.

75 **set by Eisenhower in 1956:** Associated Press, March 17, 1956.
75 **"vote-getting ability of Dick Nixon":** *Baltimore Sun*, March 10, 1960.

COUNTDOWN: 229 DAYS

77 **"Jack, and play fair!":** Humphrey, *Education of a Public Man*, 151.
78 **"economic conditions even worse":** Humphrey, *Education of a Public Man*, 12.
78 **"banks began to fail":** Humphrey, *Education of a Public Man*, 12.
78 **"picket, indeed to destroy":** Humphrey, *Education of a Public Man*, 27.
78 **"take care to do justice":** Humphrey, *Education of a Public Man*, 6.
79 **"bright sunshine of human rights":** Humphrey, *Education of a Public Man*, 77.
79 **"mama's recipe for beef soup":** *Marshfield (WI) News-Herald*, March 25, 1960.
80 **"many cold people":** O'Donnell and Powers, *Johnny, We Hardly Knew Ye*, 172.
81 **"My time is now":** Collier and Horowitz, *The Kennedys*, 236.
82 **"against a chain store":** Humphrey, *Education of a Public Man*, 152.
82 **blindness and other physical ailments:** Humphrey, *Education of a Public Man*, 56.
83 **rickety bus in Wisconsin:** Pietrusza, *1960*, 90.
83 **"some Hollywood production":** Dallek, *An Unfinished Life*, 249.

COUNTDOWN: 227 DAYS

85 **soak up the Florida sun:** *Clio*, June 21, 2018.
89 **"date in Washington very soon":** Exner, *My Story*, 107.
90 **"his hips like a stripper":** Exner, *My Story*, 108.
90 **"on a sentimental journey":** Exner, *My Story*, 108.
91 **"Hey, Frank, look who's here":** Exner, *My Story*, 116.
91 **"diamonds and rubies":** Exner, *My Story*, 116.
92 **Eden Roc hotel:** Exner, *My Story*, 121.
92 **"Yes, that's fine":** Exner, *My Story*, 122.
92 **"man of 'position'":** Exner, *My Story*, 122.

COUNTDOWN: 223 DAYS

93 **more than forty were arrested:** History.com, January 25, 2022.
94 **eleven were arrested:** Associated Press, March 8, 1960.
94 **"nations of the world":** UPI, April 12, 1960.
95 **"seats in the rear":** King, *Autobiography of Martin Luther King, Jr.*, 8.
95 **"grave injustice":** King, *Autobiography of Martin Luther King, Jr.*, 7.
95 **"rather than a natural order":** King, *Autobiography of Martin Luther King, Jr.*, 3.
96 **"bring great, intangible gains":** King, *My Life with Martin Luther King, Jr.*, 183.
96 **away the moral high ground:** James McNeil oral history, 1978.
96 **"on some kind of prank":** Franklin McCain and Jibreel Khazan (Ezell Blair Jr.) oral history, 1979.
96 **"white people have there now":** Franklin McCain and Jibreel Khazan (Ezell Blair Jr.) oral history, 1979.
98 **address the Alabama delegation:** George Wallace oral history, 6.

98 **"living antithesis of Earl Warren":** *Birmingham Post-Herald*, June 27, 1957.
98 **a thank-you note:** Pietrusza, *1960*, 292.
98 **outraging Black leaders:** *Daily Times*, December 11, 1959.

COUNTDOWN: 218 DAYS

99 **returns trickle in:** White, *The Making of the President 1960*, 94.
99 **"filled with beautiful people":** Humphrey, *Education of a Public Man*, 151.
100 **"politics in the United States":** CBS News, June 11, 2015.
101 **"selection of their presidential nominee":** John F. Kennedy's television advertisement, April 1960.
101 **Senate voted on McCarthy:** *New York Times*, May 26, 1972.
101 **"He gave to everybody":** Goodwin, *Remembering America*, 82.
101 **"Son-of-a-bitch":** Goodwin, *Remembering America*, 83.
102 **"sell Jack like soap flakes":** Davis, *Kennedys*, 151.
102 **"anything else would be gravy":** *Sheboygan (WI) Press*, April 6, 1960.
102 **"a sort of warmup":** *Argus Leader* (Sioux Falls, SD), April 6, 1960.
102 **"might have won it":** *Argus Leader* (Sioux Falls, SD), April 6, 1960.
103 **"him over the Catholic thing":** Bradlee, *Conversations with Kennedy*, 115.
103 **"What does it all mean?":** White, *The Making of the President 1960*, 94.

COUNTDOWN: 217 DAYS

105 **"in Wisconsin in November":** *Daily Tribune*, April 6, 1960.
106 **congressman in the late 1940s:** White, *The Making of the President 1960*, 62–63.
107 **"of 'Peace and Prosperity'":** *Denver Post*, April 18, 1960.
107 **"critical of Vice President Nixon":** *Tampa Tribune*, April 7, 1960.
108 **"appeal to Wisconsin voters":** *Journal Times* (Racine, WI), April 6, 1960.
108 **"blaze of national publicity":** *Times-Tribune*, April 11, 1960.

COUNTDOWN: 216 DAYS

109 **"is that his real name?":** Hersh, *Dark Side of Camelot*, 300.
110 **Chicago's highly profitable "numbers rackets":** Roemer, *Man Against the Mob*, 293.
110 **"might get whacked, too":** Roemer, *Man Against the Mob*, 2.
111 **do much business with Giancana:** Hersh, *Dark Side of Camelot*, 134.
111 **several times a day:** Exner, *My Story*, 125.
111 **rendezvous countless times:** Exner, *My Story*, 127.
112 **Georgetown at 7:30 p.m.:** Exner, *My Story*, 128.
112 **"You look fantastic":** Exner, *My Story*, 129.
112 **cold soup, meat, and potatoes:** Exner, *My Story*, 130.
112 **"Not at all":** Hersh, *Dark Side of Camelot*, 303.
113 **so much money:** Hersh, *Dark Side of Camelot*, 303.
113 **which palms to grease:** Hersh, *Dark Side of Camelot*, 95–101.
114 **"almost immediately amorous":** Exner, *My Story*, 131.
114 **journalist Inga Marie Arvad:** Hersh, *Dark Side of Camelot*, 124–25.
115 **loved Jack's possessiveness:** Exner, *My Story*, 132.

COUNTDOWN: 192 DAYS

118 **the secret flyovers continued:** *Leader-Telegram*, May 12, 1960.

118 **drifted over Soviet airspace:** *Leader-Telegram*, May 12, 1960.

120 **"our houses in California":** Kitchen debate transcripts, July 25, 1959.

COUNTDOWN: 191 DAYS

123 **30 percent over Humphrey:** *Chattanooga Times*, April 3, 1960.

123 **"as pale as ashes":** Pietrusza, *1960*, 109.

124 **"found out you're Catholic":** Pietrusza, *1960*, 109.

125 **kind of government assistance:** Pietrusza, *1960*, 113.

125 **"to feed hungry people":** Kennedy statement, Charleston, West Virginia, April 11, 1960.

126 **a judge approached Humphrey:** Humphrey, *Education of a Public Man*, 157–58.

126 **"going to carry the state":** Humphrey, *Education of a Public Man*, 157–58.

127 **all over the Mountaineer State:** Kessler, *Sins of the Father*, 379–80.

127 **flocks to support JFK:** Kessler, *Sins of the Father*, 379–80.

127 **"good for the candidate":** Humphrey, *Education of a Public Man*, 159.

127 **warned not to mention religion:** Manchester, *One Brief Singing Moment*, 102.

128 **"president or not":** *St. Louis Post-Dispatch*, April 19, 1960.

128 **"make church conformity compulsory":** *Star Tribune*, April 20, 1960.

128 **"fly his last mission":** O'Donnell and Powers, *Johnny, We Hardly Knew Ye*, 167.

128 **"Church speaks for me":** John F. Kennedy statement, April 21, 1960.

128 **"an issue in the campaign":** Associated Press, April 22, 1960.

129 **"it once and for all":** *Chattanooga Daily Times*, April 23, 1960.

129 **The news release added:** Scripps-Howard, April 30, 1960.

129 **brought him $35,000:** Leamer, *Kennedy Men*, 424.

129 **"rented it for a day":** Haught, *Fascinating West Virginia*, 65.

130 **Kennedy carried his county:** Kessler, *Sins of the Father*, 376.

130 **"owners for Jack's campaign":** Summers and Swan, *Sinatra*, 272.

130 **"where that came from":** Summers and Swan, *Sinatra*, 272.

130 **Humphrey was during World War II:** Leamer, *Kennedy Men*, 426.

131 **"vote in the primary?":** Dallek, *An Unfinished Life*, 255.

131 **"much less buy an airplane":** Associated Press, April 27, 1960.

COUNTDOWN: 186 DAYS

133 **apology to the Soviet Union:** Associated Press, May 26, 1960.

134 **"anxious to draft Rockefeller":** *Portland Evening Express*, April 22, 1960.

135 **"superb job as vice president":** Associated Press, April 23, 1960.

136 **"wants another Pearl Harbor":** *Buffalo News*, May 11, 1960.

136 **"any gap in its intelligence":** *Sault Star*, May 16, 1960.

COUNTDOWN: 183 DAYS

137 **Convair 240 aircraft:** Leamer, *Kennedy Men*, 431.

138 **"you found me attractive?":** Kessler, *Sins of the Father*, 378.

138 **"I got into the blondes":** *Daily Mail*, April 29, 2020.

139 **waited for the election results:** Bradlee, *Conversations with Kennedy*, 27.

139 **opened a bottle of champagne:** Bradlee, *Conversations with Kennedy*, 27.

139 **$34,000 on television ads alone:** White, *Making of the President 1960*, 110.

COUNTDOWN: 179 DAYS

141 **letter to the media:** Hersh, *Dark Side of Camelot*, 107.

141 **Senator Kennedy's D.C. office:** Hersh, *Dark Side of Camelot*, 107.

143 **distribute the photograph—or else:** Hersh, *Dark Side of Camelot*, 107–9.

144 **"country before the people":** *Baltimore Sun*, May 14, 1960.

144 **"previous appearances here":** *Baltimore Sun*, May 14, 1960.

144 **"I want to touch him":** *Baltimore Sun*, May 14, 1960.

144 **"the Presidency itself":** *Baltimore Sun*, May 14, 1960.

144 **"looks like Tricky Dick":** Gellman, *Campaign of the Century*, 131.

145 **created by Christian zealots:** Gellman, *Campaign of the Century*, 131.

COUNTDOWN: 150 DAYS

147 **landing the Republican presidential nomination:** *Time*, June 24, 1940.

148 **exposed the United States to danger:** *Wisconsin State Journal*, June 10, 1960.

148 **"vice president to state his":** Associated Press, June 10, 1960.

148 **up local media attention:** Gellman, *Campaign of the Century*, 111–14.

150 **"stand-pat attitude":** Gellman, *Campaign of the Century*, 180.

150 **"using the words themselves":** *New York Times*, June 15, 1960.

151 **"disagree without being disagreeable":** Associated Press, June 12, 1960.

COUNTDOWN: 127 DAYS

153 **"forceful conservative as Lyndon B. Johnson":** *Orlando Evening Star*, June 3, 1960.

154 **"patriotism that rises above partisanship":** *New York World-Telegram and the Sun*, June 3, 1960.

154 **"potential nominee in his party":** Associated Press, June 1, 1960.

154 **"time to a personal campaign":** *Orlando Evening Star*, June 3, 1960.

154 **"think this is remarkable":** *Orlando Evening Star*, June 3, 1960.

155 **"known to politicians":** *Detroit Free Press*, June 29, 1960.

155 **"Democratic opponents personally":** *New York Times*, June 22, 1960.

156 **"regrets to Mr. Khrushchev, are you?":** *Daily Press*, May 29, 1960.

156 **"purpose of partisan advantage":** *Kansas City Times*, May 31, 1960.

156 **"among warring and divergent forces":** *Kansas City Times*, May 31, 1960.

COUNTDOWN: 122 DAYS

159 **into a hot auditorium:** *Los Angeles Times*, July 11, 1960.

161 **Democratic platform committee:** King, *Autobiography of Martin Luther King, Jr.*, 143.

161 **"fruitful and rewarding":** Martin Luther King letter to Chester Bowles, June 24, 1960.

161 **"un-American and immoral":** King letter to Bowles, June 24, 1960.

162 **"Stop it. Stop it please":** Scripps-Howard, July 11, 1960.

162 **"American anywhere in this country":** John F. Kennedy remarks, NAACP Rally, July 10, 1960.

162 **"facilities including lunch counters":** John F. Kennedy remarks, NAACP Rally, July 10, 1960.

163 **"save the soul of America":** *St. Louis Argus*, July 15, 1960.

163 **"it's stand-up for justice":** *St. Louis Argus*, July 15, 1960.

COUNTDOWN: 121 DAYS

165 **1,521 delegates, die-hard Democrats:** Associated Press, July 11, 1960.

165 **explosion of flashbulbs:** Reuters, July 13, 2010.

166 **"classically as Addison's disease":** *Des Moines Register*, July 5, 1960.

166 **"contrary is malicious and false":** UPI, July 5, 1960.

166 **filed under another letter:** *New York Times*, May 3, 1973.

167 **cozied up to Adolf Hitler:** Smith, *Bad Blood*, 72.

168 **illegal in thirty-one states:** ABC News, April 18, 2014.

168 **"let 'em get to you":** *Hollywood Reporter*, July 12, 2010.

168 **"I could to help out":** *The Age*, July 13, 1960.

169 **was looking for Kenny O'Donnell:** Exner, *My Story*, 163.

170 **"home and think this over":** Exner, *My Story*, 166.

COUNTDOWN: 119 DAYS

172 **"hoodlum connections of Kennedy":** FBI file on John F. Kennedy, 1960.

173 **"man's wife during World War II":** FBI file on John F. Kennedy, 1960.

173 **"In the interest of brevity":** FBI file on John F. Kennedy, 1960.

COUNTDOWN: 118 DAYS

175 **for a handful of others:** *New York Times*, July 14, 1960.

176 **"a pitcher of warm piss":** White, *Making of the President 1960*, 176.

176 **"morning at ten [signed] Jack":** Martin, *Hero for Our Time*, 174.

177 **"persuade him to accept":** Watson, *Chief of Staff*, 35.

177 **"wants to talk to you":** Miller, *Lyndon*, 312.

177 **"Power is where power goes":** White, *Making of the President 1960*, 174.

177 **"vice presidents don't do much":** Smith, *Bad Blood*, 70.

179 **"He wants it":** Schlesinger, *Robert Kennedy*, 218.

180 **"be president of the United States?":** Reston, *Lone Star*, 194.

180 **"where he could help me":** Mooney, *Lyndon Johnson Story*, 161.

180 **"you stay hated":** O'Neill, *Man of the House*, 83.

181 **Texas senator said no:** White, *Making of the President 1960*, 433–34.

182 **"well that it won't be":** Salinger, *With Kennedy*, 72.

183 **"know how they could":** Hersh, *Dark Side of Camelot*, 129.

183 **"presidency doesn't mean a thing":** Hersh, *Dark Side of Camelot*, 130.

184 **elections turned in his favor:** *Des Moines Register,* February 14, 1960.

184 **more votes were discovered:** Associated Press, November 9, 1960.

184 **Stevenson by eighty-seven votes:** *Des Moines Register,* February 14, 1960.

185 **worked for, they said:** White, *Making of the President 1960,* 175.

185 **"harshest racial plank in history":** *News and Courier,* July 24, 1960.

COUNTDOWN: 117 DAYS

187 **energy to pull it off:** Associated Press, July 16, 1960.

188 **"appeasement of Southern bigots":** Gellman, *Campaign of the Century,* 88.

188 **"satisfy his own personal ambition":** Gellman, *Campaign of the Century,* 88.

188 **"I accept your nomination":** JFK Democratic Party acceptance speech, July 15, 1960.

188 **crowd of sixty thousand people:** Associated Press, July 16, 1960.

COUNTDOWN: 109 DAYS

191 **Nixon was exhausted:** *Time,* August 1, 1960.

192 **"kind of artist, aren't you?":** Associated Press, June 27, 1960.

192 **over the age of sixty-five:** *Sunday Star,* July 24, 1960.

193 **to meet with Rockefeller privately:** White, *Making of the President 1960,* 198–200.

COUNTDOWN: 107 DAYS

195 **Greensboro had lost $200,000:** *News & Observer,* (Raleigh, NC), January 27, 1980.

195 **Woolworth's store was desegregated:** UPI, July 25, 1960.

196 **summer vacation from school:** Greensboro Public Library Oral History Project, 1979.

196 **integration through peaceful protest:** Greensboro Public Library Oral History Project, 1979.

COUNTDOWN: 104 DAYS

199 **the last vestiges of segregation:** Associated Press, July 26, 1960.

200 **glowing stories about Nixon:** Politico, October 28, 2022.

200 **Soviet missile capabilities:** *Pittsburgh Press,* May 22, 1960.

200 **early and run out of gas:** White, *Making of the President 1960,* 103–4.

200 **steady and focused:** UPI, July 28, 1960.

200 **ambassador to the United Nations:** Nixon, *RN,* 216.

201 **Nixon's biggest supporters:** Nixon, *RN,* 216.

201 **"real stature before the nation":** Gellman, *Campaign of Century,* 206–7.

201 **"It's out of the Soviet Union":** Associated Press, May 27, 1960.

202 **"ever before in our history":** UPI, July 27, 1960.

202 **"will be glad to do so":** Associated Press, July 28, 1960.

202 **"all of us are united":** *Press and Sun-Bulletin* (Binghamton, NY), July 29, 1960.

202 **"succeed Dwight D. Eisenhower":** *Kansas City Times,* July 29, 1960.

204 **"We want Dick!":** *Richmond News Leader,* July 28, 1960.

205 **"the survival of civilization":** Nixon Presidential Nomination Acceptance Speech, July 29, 1960.

205 **"November the eighth"**: Nixon Presidential Nomination Acceptance Speech, July 29, 1960.
206 **"work cut out for him"**: UPI, July 29, 1960.
206 **"minus into a plus"**: Associated Press, July 29, 1960.
206 **"still stood out prominently"**: UPI, July 29, 1960.
206 **"seemed to make him quiver"**: UPI, July 29, 1960.
206 **"hardly boring at all"**: *Lansing (MI) State Journal*, July 29, 1960.

COUNTDOWN: 95 DAYS
209 **arms, and guns to Cuba**: Associated Press, February 14, 1960.
209 **Latin American Youth Conference**: UPI, August 6, 1960.
210 **the property of Cuba**: Associated Press, August 8, 1960.
210 **"advance of communism in our country"**: Associated Press, August 8, 1960.
210 **foothold in the Western Hemisphere**: Associated Press, August 8, 1960.

COUNTDOWN: 94 DAYS
213 **but Nixon would win**: Nixon, *RN*, 217.
213 **"doesn't count—but win"**: Schlesinger, *Robert Kennedy and His Times*, 218.
213 **kind of thing for years**: Hersh, *Dark Side of Camelot*, 110–12.
214 **allegations of "sexual misconduct"**: DeLoach, *Hoover's FBI*, 30, 37–39.
214 **"only little girls giggled"**: *Chicago Tribune*, June 10, 1959.
215 **Chicago mayor Richard Daley**: Hersh, *Dark Side of Camelot*, 132–34.

COUNTDOWN: 77 DAYS
217 **"The Meaning of Communism to Americans"**: *Fort Worth Star-Telegram*, August 25, 1960.
217 **"The Scientific Revolution"**: Study paper by Richard Nixon.
218 **D.C. in the middle of August**: Associated Press, August 9, 1960.
218 **"he is vitally interested"**: Richard Nixon news conference, August 1, 1960.
218 **maturity to run the country**: White, *Making of the President 1960*, 308.
219 **Nixon had participated in**: Dwight Eisenhower press conference, August 24, 1960.
219 **I don't remember**: Eisenhower press conference, August 24, 1960.
219 **"recall a single one"**: *Evening Sun*, August 29, 1960.

COUNTDOWN: 65 DAYS
221 **called *hemolytic Staphylococcus aureus***: Associated Press, September 5, 1960.
221 **"the pace of economic advance"**: Associated Press, September 5, 1960.
221 **"excellent physical condition"**: *Arizona Daily Star*, August 30, 1960.
222 **swing through fourteen states**: Associated Press, September 2, 1960.
223 **"You never had it so good"**: John F. Kennedy speech, September 5, 1960.
225 **"sit down for them"**: John F. Kennedy speech, September 5, 1960.
225 **"bearcat at campaigning"**: Associated Press, September 6, 1960.

COUNTDOWN: 60 DAYS

227 **throat and taking deeper breaths:** Silvestri, *Becoming JFK*, 96.

227 **over the next ten weeks:** Dallek, *An Unfinished Life*, 277.

228 **"one stroke of the pen":** John F. Kennedy speech on the twenty-fifth anniversary of the signing of the Social Security Act, August 14, 1960.

228 **"It's not the *pope* . . . it's the *pop*":** John F. Kennedy Presidential Library, October 2, 2011.

228 **"What just took place?":** Harry Truman news conference, August 20, 1960.

228 **"Isn't that enough?":** Harry Truman news conference, August 20, 1960.

229 **"ticket to carry Texas":** Reston, *Lone Star*, 197.

229 **"your speeches, wherever you go":** Shesol, *Mutual Contempt*, 60.

COUNTDOWN: 58 DAYS

231 **renounce his Catholic beliefs:** Associated Press, September 9, 1960.

231 **would make the best president:** John F. Kennedy, "The Religious Issue in American Politics" speech, April 21, 1960.

231 **dignify it with a response:** White, *Making of the President 1960*, 259.

232 **"good omen":** Dwight D. Eisenhower remarks at the opening of the Republican campaign, September 12, 1960.

233 **"freedom throughout the world"** Associated Press, September 12, 1960.

233 **"should be taken for granted":** Associated Press, September 12, 1960.

234 **"hard day for me":** Remarks of Senator John F. Kennedy, September 12, 1960.

235 **"a religious issue does exist":** John F. Kennedy speech at Greater Houston Ministerial Conference, September 12, 1960.

235 **"the coast of Florida":** John F. Kennedy speech at Greater Houston Ministerial Conference, September 12, 1960.

237 **"without regard to geography, religion":** Question and Answer, Greater Houston Ministerial Conference, September 12, 1960.

COUNTDOWN: 56 DAYS

This chapter is based on CIA files about the operation to hire organized crime figures to kill Fidel Castro. It also draws on books and newspaper stories and magazine pieces about fixers like Robert Maheu and organized crime figures like Sam Giancana, who were involved in the plot to assassinate Castro.

239 **"as a result of Castro's action":** Memo for deputy director of Central Intelligence Agency, Robert Maheu, June 24, 1966.

241 **"requiring gangster-type action":** "Subject: Robert A. Maheu," CIA files.

241 **"high-ranking member of the 'syndicate'":** "Subject: Robert A. Maheu," CIA files.

COUNTDOWN: 51 DAYS

243 **address the United Nations:** Associated Press, September 20, 1960.

244 **difference in a tight race:** White, *Making of the President 1960*, 284.

244 **"mankind hold her in disdain"**: Associated Press, September 20, 1960.

245 **Harlem over the bill**: *Smithsonian*, September 18, 2020.

245 **"surrender or even to war"**: Associated Press, September 22, 1960.

245 **"what he was espousing"**: UPI, September 21, 1960.

245 **first in the world**: Associated Press, September 21, 1960.

245 **"on their part, no deviation"**: Nixon comments in Flint, Michigan, September 20, 1960.

245 **"personal attacks and insults"**: UPI, September 23, 1960.

245 **"up for a stronger America"**: John F. Kennedy speech in Denver, Colorado, September 23, 1960.

COUNTDOWN: 45 DAYS

This chapter is based on CIA files about the meeting between CIA fixer Robert Maheu and top mob leaders Sam Giancana, Santo Trafficante Jr., and Johnny Roselli. It's also based on books by Maheu and others about the operation to kill Fidel Castro.

COUNTDOWN: 44 DAYS

252 **"like death warmed over"**: Don Hewitt oral history, October 8, 2002.

252 **stay calm under pressure**: Robb, *Gumshoe and the Shrink*, 61–64.

252 **Nixon's face turn white**: Matthews, *Kennedy and Nixon*, 148.

253 **owned at least one set**: Britannica, 2024.

253 **hours of television every day**: White, *Making of the President 1960*, 280.

253 **"on to other things"**: Matthews, *Kennedy & Nixon*, 213.

254 **"Kitner saying we accepted"**: Pierre Salinger oral history, July 19, 1965.

254 **"the blood of young lambs"**: Leamer, *Kennedy Men*, 449–51.

255 **"job in the debate"**: H. R. Haldeman oral history, August 13, 1987.

255 **leading up to the debate**: Pietrusza, *1960*, 328.

255 **deciding who'd go first**: Associated Press, September 25, 1960.

256 **would watch the first debate**: Associated Press, September 25, 1960.

256 **"it by the hostile press"**: Herbert Klein oral history, February 20, 2007.

256 **Ambassador East Hotel in Chicago**: White, *Making of the President 1960*, 283.

257 **himself of the "assassin image"**: White, *Making of the President 1960*, 285.

257 **microphone for a sound check**: Robb, *Gumshoe and the Shrink*, 178.

258 **he was trying to conceal**: Gellman, *Campaign of the Century*, 330.

258 **"Kick him in the balls"**: Leamer, *Kennedy Men*, 451.

259 **history, to that point**: Television Academy Foundation News, September 24, 2010.

259 **"progress that we're making"**: Presidential Debate Transcript, September 26, 1960.

259 **"him before he even died"**: Dallek, *An Unfinished Life*, 286.

260 **"grant me the same"**: Debate Transcript, September 26, 1960.

262 **"foreign policy or communism"**: Manchester, *One Brief Shining Moment*, 117.

263 **"bitch just lost the election"**: Matthews, *Kennedy & Nixon*, 155.

COUNTDOWN: 43 DAYS

265 **changed in just a few hours:** Klein, *Making It Perfectly Clear*, 102–3.

265 **"was not in top shape":** Jamieson, *Packaging the President*, 153.

268 **"audience that was the nation":** Friedenberg, *Rhetorical Studies of National Political Debates*, 21.

268 **Nixon was the clear choice:** Dallek, *An Unfinished Life*, 286.

268 **"par before the next debate":** Nixon, *Six Crises*, 341.

268 **"I thought my husband was brilliant":** Associated Press, September 27, 1960.

269 **"determined and overly aggressive father":** Robb, *Gumshoe and the Shrink*, 183.

269 **"issue and not the head":** Robb, *Gumshoe and the Shrink*, 183.

COUNTDOWN: 26 DAYS

271 **the governor told Kennedy's advisers:** Hersh, *Dark Side of Camelot*, 175–78.

271 **General Eisenhower's London staff:** *Washington Post*, June 5, 2021.

272 **NAACP from operating in Alabama:** Associated Press, June 30, 1958.

272 **never let it happen again:** Associated Press, November 5, 1958.

272 **along a senior official from the CIA:** Hersh, *Dark Side of Camelot*, 176.

272 **"old man know about it?":** Hersh, *Dark Side of Camelot*, 176.

273 **"I'll meet him anywhere, anytime":** Hersh, *Dark Side of Camelot*, 177.

274 **"I believed Nixon would win":** Hersh, *Dark Side of Camelot*, 177.

COUNTDOWN: 15 DAYS

275 **trying to buy the election:** Associated Press, February 16, 1960.

275 **"no job for a playboy":** Gellman, *Campaign of the Century*, 343.

275 **"with the gloves off":** Bochin, *Richard Nixon: Rhetorical Strategist*, 51.

276 **half minutes to rebut:** *Miami Herald*, October 7, 1960.

276 **pre-debate small talk:** Associated Press, October 8, 1960.

276 **"helps the situation one bit":** Presidential Debate Transcript, October 7, 1960.

276 **the Communist Chinese mainland:** Presidential Debate Transcript, October 13, 1960.

277 **"tied behind his back":** Nixon, *Six Crises*, 328.

278 **"should be sustained and assisted":** Scripps-Howard, September 23, 1960.

278 **"communist rule to an end":** Scripps-Howard, September 23, 1960.

279 **"militant communist satellite":** Kennedy speech, Cincinnati, Ohio, October 6, 1960.

280 **"can we keep the peace?":** Presidential Debate Transcript, October 21, 1960.

COUNTDOWN: 13 DAYS

281 **Lillian Smith for dinner:** Associated Press, May 5, 2020.

281 **by less than a week:** King, *My Life with Martin Luther King, Jr.*, 177–78.

282 **Magnolia Room:** Associated Press, October 20, 1960.

282 **"until something is done":** Associated Press, October 20, 1960.

282 **"counters but the lunch counter":** Associated Press, October 20, 1960.

282 **four months on the chain gang:** UPI, October 25, 1960.

282 **"while he was in prison":** Eleanor Roosevelt diary, United Feature Syndicate, November 14, 1960.

283 **issues if elected president?:** King, *Autobiography of Martin Luther King, Jr.*, 148.

283 **"do something about it":** Presidential Debate Transcript, October 7, 1960.

284 **"the advancing Negro race":** Associated Press, October 21, 1960.

284 **"and the city of Atlanta":** Associated Press, October 21, 1960.

284 **further demonstrations would be punished:** Associated Press, May 5, 2020.

284 **"freedom of our people":** King, *Autobiography of Martin Luther King, Jr.*, 146.

284 **Nixon remained silent:** *New York Times*, April 14, 1987.

285 **"deserve to win":** *New York Times*, April 14, 1987.

285 **secure her husband's release:** Levington, *Kennedy and King*, 85.

285 **came up with a plan:** Matthews, *Kennedy and Nixon*, 171.

285 **headed to the hotel:** Leamer, *Kennedy Men*, 459–61.

286 **had already moved on:** Levington, *Kennedy and King*, 85.

286 **They'd vote for Nixon:** Dallek, *An Unfinished Life*, 293.

286 **"upon principle and not expediency":** Levingston, *Kennedy and King*, 91.

286 **Sunday before the election:** Wofford, *Of Kennedy & Kings*, 24.

287 **Democratic presidential ticket:** James Meriwether, "Worth a Lot of Negro Votes," December 2008.

287 **"have not grown weary":** National Peace Corps Association, 2022.

COUNTDOWN: 12 DAYS

289 **beachhead, and move inland:** UPI, October 30, 1960.

290 **from behind the Iron Curtain:** Associated Press, October 23, 1960.

290 **"apparent from the start":** *Miami Herald*, October 20, 1960.

290 **Guatemala's ambassador to the United States:** UPI, October 25, 1960.

290 **"a fake invasion":** UPI, October 26, 1960.

290 **Castro rounded up everyone involved:** Associated Press, October 23, 1960.

291 **execution by firing squad:** *New Yorker*, May 28, 2012.

292 **"threatened by Communist activities":** Kennedy statement, October 20, 1960.

COUNTDOWN: 11 DAYS

The scenes, including color, describing Richard Nixon's Victory Train tour are drawn from various sources, including numerous newspaper stories filed by reporters traveling with Nixon, as well as books like *The Making of the President 1960*.

294 **and cutting criticisms:** Associated Press, October 25, 1960.

294 **to go before Election Day:** White, *Making of the President 1960*, 296.

294 **a Black man to the cabinet:** *Time*, October 24, 1960.

294 **minority cabinet appointment again:** White, *Making of the President 1960*, 297.

294 **a more aggressive campaign:** White, *Making of the President 1960*, 297.

295 **New York's Waldorf Astoria Hotel:** White, *Making of the President 1960*, 298.

295 **estimated at 1 million people:** Associated Press, October 20, 1960.

296 **"Nixon and Governor Rockefeller":** John F. Kennedy speech, Al Smith dinner, October 29, 1960.

296 **the sixteen-car train cut:** *Marion (OH) Star*, October 27, 1960.

296 **He'd played piano and violin:** *Newsday*, October 27, 1960.

297 **"clothing store, in the drugstore":** Richard M. Nixon statement, Marietta, Ohio, October 25, 1960.

297 **"an old jalopy":** Nixon statement, Marietta, Ohio, October 25, 1960.

298 **the hard economic facts of life:** White, *Making of the President 1960*, 302.

298 **"any more talk about it":** *Time*, November 7, 1960.

298 **"goon squads":** Associated Press, October 28, 1960.

298 **"we'll take care of you":** Associated Press, October 28, 1960.

299 **"going to stop me either":** Richard M. Nixon remarks, Danville, Illinois, October 28, 1960.

COUNTDOWN: 7 DAYS

301 **parade two weeks earlier:** *Baltimore Sun*, November 3, 1960.

301 **had both advised against it:** Safire, *Before the Fall*, 622–23.

301 **experience to run the country:** Gellman, *Campaign of the Century*, 241–42.

301 **asked the president to help:** White, *Making of the President 1960*, 308–9.

301 **remarks about his administration:** Gellman, *Campaign of the Century*, 243–44.

303 **"Which do you choose?":** Associated Press, October 18, 1960.

303 **"malicious propaganda":** Associated Press, October 18, 1960.

303 **the last week of the campaign:** Gellman, *Campaign of the Century*, 397.

304 **crowd of ten thousand people:** Associated Press, November 3, 1960.

304 **was "immeasurably stronger" than:** Associated Press, November 3, 1960.

304 **"the brightest in our history":** Associated Press, November 3, 1960.

304 **"This is the greatest day in the campaign":** Nixon speech, New York Coliseum, November 2, 1960.

COUNTDOWN: 5 DAYS

305 **waving from decorated floats:** Associated Press, November 5, 1960.

305 **Cook County Democratic Party:** NBC Chicago, November 20, 2013.

306 **Truman or bald like Eisenhower:** *Daily Herald*, October 25, 2013.

307 **ride "someone else's coattails":** Associated Press, November 5, 1960.

307 **"how to win their campaign":** UPI, November 4, 1960.

307 **"world peace or world war":** UPI, November 4, 1960.

308 **"as the defender of peace":** John F. Kennedy speech, Chicago, November 4, 1960.

308 **both Republicans and Democrats:** UPI, November 4, 1960.

308 **"We want Nixon!":** UPI, November 4, 1960.

308 **"was another Cuba or Berlin":** *Lubbock Avalanche-Journal*, November 4, 1960.

309 **supporters of the GOP campaign:** Associated Press, November 4, 1960.

309 **"Lyndon will win the election":** Associated Press, November 5, 1960.

309 **"but Nixon will win":** Associated Press, November 5, 1960.

309 **police officer to stand aside:** UPI, November 5, 1960.

309 **"I want to know it":** *Fort Worth Star-Telegram*, November 5, 1960.

309 **started in Casper, Wyoming:** Associated Press, November 5, 1960.

309 **peek of Nixon walking by:** *Casper Morning Star*, November 5, 1960.

310 **"is what I have done":** Richard M. Nixon speech, Casper, Wyoming, November 4, 1960.

310 **four-hour nationally broadcast telethon:** UPI, November 8, 1960.

310 **paid television campaign appearances:** White, *Making of the President 1960*, 312.

310 **one block east to Vanderbilt Avenue:** White, *Making of the President 1960*, 312.

311 **"not crisis-to-crisis planning":** Interview with Henry Fonda, November 2, 1960.

311 **Newark Armory for the affair:** *Record* (Newark), October 27, 1960.

312 **and his wife, Janet Leigh:** *Record* (Newark), October 27, 1960.

312 **performed on his behalf:** Summers and Swan, *Sinatra: The Life*, 274.

COUNTDOWN: 4 DAYS

313 **"Addison's disease, and other issues.":** Dallek, *An Unfinished Life*, 75–76, 398–99.

314 **swings and spur irrational decisions:** *Los Angeles Times*, September 5, 2009.

314 **"Christ, it's the sun!":** John F. Kennedy taped conversation at dinner party, January 5, 1960.

314 **his shrink, Dr. Arnold Hutschnecker:** Robb, *Gumshoe and the Shrink*, 92–93.

315 **"might impair their ability to serve as president":** *Times-Herald*, November 4, 1960.

315 **release their medical records:** Robb, *Gumshoe and the Shrink*, 94.

315 **as a result of Addison's disease:** UPI, November 4, 1960.

315 **"full disclosure to the voters":** UPI, November 7, 1960.

316 **"the state of his health":** UPI, November 6, 1960.

316 **news media didn't follow up:** Robb, *Gumshoe and the Shrink*, 55.

316 **help in sniffing out the details:** Robb, *Gumshoe and the Shrink*, 107.

317 **trouble with one of their children:** Robb, *Gumshoe and the Shrink*, 45–46.

317 **"if he lives that long":** *New York Daily News*, November 4, 1960.

317 **campaign stop in Oakland, California:** Robb, *Gumshoe and the Shrink*, 196.

317 **"agreeable to Senator Kennedy":** Associated Press, November 6, 1960.

318 **It was 9:30 p.m.:** Robb, *Gumshoe and the Shrink*, 196–99.

COUNTDOWN: 2 DAYS

319 **again sometime after midnight:** Associated Press, November 8, 1960.

319 **"we'll just keep it going":** Associated Press, November 8, 1960.

320 **Lloyd Nolan, and John Payne:** Associated Press, November 8, 1960.

320 **"There isn't going to be a recession":** Associated Press, November 8, 1960.

321 **"as we vote tomorrow":** Associated Press, November 8, 1960.

322 **"Give it to 'em Jack!":** Associated Press, November 7, 1960.

322 **"visits to the Soviet Union":** Associated Press, November 7, 1960.

322 **"hazardous years which lie ahead":** Associated Press, November 8, 1960.

323 **"no taxation without representation":** John F. Kennedy speech, Boston, Massachusetts, November 7, 1960.

323 **"put . . . upon our shoulders":** JFK speech, Boston, November 7, 1960.

COUNTDOWN: 1 DAY

325 **Cesar Romero, and George Murphy:** UPI, November 8, 1960.

325 **Fireworks lit up the dark sky:** *Los Angeles Mirror,* November 8, 1960.

325 **"one o'clock in the morning":** Associated Press, November 8, 1960.

326 **"far and lose my vote":** Associated Press, November 9, 1960.

326 **"My goodness, that's technical":** Associated Press, November 9, 1960.

326 **"That's a nice looking hat you've got":** Associated Press, November 9, 1960.

326 **"That's who I voted for":** Associated Press, November 9, 1960.

326 **"be the same old Ike to us":** Associated Press, November 9, 1960.

327 **"again if you don't mind":** Associated Press, November 9, 1960.

328 **"Your names?":** Associated Press, November 8, 1960.

329 **Lyndon was voter number 99:** Associated Press, November 8, 1960.

329 **"upon me in the 1960s":** Associated Press, November 8, 1960.

COUNTDOWN: 23 HOURS, 45 MINUTES

330 **a bank of thirty telephones:** Associated Press, November 8, 1960.

330 **the winners in each state:** Associated Press, November 6, 1960.

330 **Armory, just down the road:** Associated Press, November 9, 1960.

330 **Virginia, and New Jersey:** Associated Press, November 8, 1960.

COUNTDOWN: 22 HOURS

332 **"fanning out across the country":** Hersh, *Dark Side of Camelot,* 145.

COUNTDOWN: 21 HOURS

332 **decided to do something about it:** Nixon, *Six Crises,* 377–79.

333 **"I could get some rest":** UPI, November 8, 1960.

333 **called the Old Heidelberg:** Nixon, *Six Crises,* 378.

333 **tacos, enchiladas, and beer:** Associated Press, November 9, 1960.

333 **"that man in the back":** Pietrusza, *1960,* 398.

334 **"fought together, and those still to come":** Nixon, *Six Crises,* 378.

334 **pineapple milkshake in hand:** UPI, November 9, 1960.

COUNTDOWN: 20 HOURS

334 **rumors while telephones jangled:** Associated Press, November 8, 1960.

COUNTDOWN: 18 HOURS

335 **Ambassador Hotel's Royal Suite:** *Birmingham Evening Mail,* November 9, 1960.

COUNTDOWN: 17 HOURS, 45 MINUTES

335 **was the anchor for ABC:** *Portland Press Herald,* November 8, 1960.

335 **"trust you'll be back":** *New York Times,* October 29, 2016.

COUNTDOWN: 16 HOURS, 45 MINUTES

336 **still too soon to tell:** Associated Press, November 9, 1960.

COUNTDOWN: 15 HOURS, 45 MINUTES

337 **they had jumped the gun:** Associated Press, November 9, 1960.
337 **"a real close election":** *Time*, November 16, 1960.

COUNTDOWN: 15 HOURS, 30 MINUTES

337 **on his way to a historic night:** *Time*, November 16, 1960.

COUNTDOWN: 14 HOURS, 15 MINUTES

338 **and Pennsylvania, with 32 more:** *Time*, November 16, 1960.

COUNTDOWN: 13 HOURS, 45 MINUTES

339 **he had 241 electoral votes:** White, *Making of the President 1960*, 21.
339 **"smoking a big cigar":** CBS News, November 8, 1960.
339 **walkie-talkie in his ear:** *Austin American*, November 9, 1960.

COUNTDOWN: 13 HOURS, 30 MINUTES

339 **"very encouraging":** NBC News, November 8, 1960.

COUNTDOWN: 13 HOURS, 15 MINUTES

340 **election unspool on television:** Summers and Swan, *Sinatra*, 273–75.
340 **the audience on the election returns:** PopHistoryDig.com, August 21, 2011.

COUNTDOWN: 12 HOURS, 45 MINUTES

340 **"and a glass of milk":** *New York Times*, October 29, 2016.
340 **somewhere around 2 million votes:** *Time*, November 16, 1960.

COUNTDOWN: 12 HOURS, 30 MINUTES

341 **a must-win for Nixon:** *Time*, November 16, 1960.
341 **"its 10 electoral votes.":** Network news coverage, November 8, 1960.

COUNTDOWN: 11 HOURS, 45 MINUTES

342 **"you're going to carry Illinois":** Bradlee, *Conversations with Kennedy*, 33.

COUNTDOWN: 9 HOURS, 30 MINUTES

344 **she started to cry:** Nixon, *Six Crises*, 386.
344 **"concede the election to Kennedy":** Associated Press, November 9, 1960.
344 **"next president of the United States":** Associated Press, November 9, 1960.
344 **She hadn't cried then:** Associated Press, November 9, 1960.
345 **"but did not actually concede":** *New York Times,* October 29, 2016.
346 **"said he was going to bed.":** Salinger oral history, July 19, 1965.

COUNTDOWN: 5 HOURS, 26 MINUTES

347 **"president of the United States":** NBC News, November 9, 1960.

COUNTDOWN: 3 HOURS, 15 MINUTES

348 **"which would be noon here"**: Pierre Salinger oral history, July 19, 1965.

348 **"anytime he wants"**: Salinger oral history, July 19, 1965.

348 **"Piggyback!" she said**: *Evening Star*, November 9, 1960.

COUNTDOWN: 1 MINUTE

350 *Hunch*, **hosted by entertainer Merv Griffin.**: *New York Times*, October 29, 2016.

350 **"freedom in the next four years"**: Associated Press, November 9, 1960.

350 **"out the way he came in"**: Salinger, *With Kennedy*, 76.

351 **"freedom around the world"**: John F. Kennedy acceptance speech, November 9, 1960.

THE CHALLENGE

NOVEMBER 11

353 **"in fact been correctly recorded"**: Associated Press, November 11, 1960.

354 **for recounts in Illinois and Texas**: Nixon, *RN*, 224.

354 **results in eight states**: Associated Press, November 27, 1960.

NOVEMBER 14

355 **"as low" as he'd ever seen him**: Herbert Klein oral history, February 20, 2007.

355 **him to challenge the election**: Klein oral history, February 20, 2007.

355 **would put Nixon over the top**: UPI, November 12, 1960.

355 **approached Nixon's table**: Gellman, *Campaign of the Century*, 441.

356 **guests about the conversation**: Nixon, *Six Crises*, 403–4.

356 **"wandered in the conversation"**: Herbert Klein oral history, February 20, 2007.

357 **"have a nice tan already"**: *Miami News*, November 14, 1960.

358 **"make such a disclosure"**: *Miami News*, November 14, 1960.

358 **instead be the "constructive opposition"**: Gannett News Service, November 15, 1960.

NOVEMBER 15

359 **GOP complaints about voter fraud**: Herald Tribune Service, November 11, 1960.

359 **"to switch the election result"**: Herald Tribune Service, November 11, 1960.

NOVEMBER 16

360 **state by just over 13,000 votes**: *New York Times*, November 17, 1960.

360 **"and fraud in this election"**: Associated Press, December 1, 1960.

360 **by just under 200,000**: *New York Times*, November 17, 1960.

NOVEMBER 17

361 **reappoint him as FBI director**: Associated Press, November 11, 1960.

361 **newspapers to his office**: Summers, *Official and Confidential*, 275.

NOVEMBER 18

362 **opening of a headquarters in Chicago:** Scripps-Howard, November 18, 1960.

362 **Missouri, Nevada, and New Mexico:** Scripps-Howard, November 18, 1960.

362 **out of 4.7 million ballots cast:** *Chicago Tribune*, November 19, 1960.

362 **forty-four states to aid the drive:** *Chicago Tribune*, November 19, 1960.

362 **even if only a dollar:** UPI, November 12, 1960.

362 **river wards of Chicago:** *Chicago Tribune*, November 12, 1960.

362 **while Nixon got 7,120:** *Chicago Tribune*, November 12, 1960.

NOVEMBER 20

363 **"many of these charges":** Nixon, *Six Crises*, 412.

364 **selected over Andrew Jackson:** *Prologue*, Summer 2012.

NOVEMBER 23

365 **"to unintentional tally errors":** *Boston Globe*, December 6, 1960.

365 **they weren't voting for:** *Cedar Rapids Gazette*, July 23, 1973.

365 **were reported all over Texas:** Farrell, *Richard Nixon*, 295.

365 **pistol-packing election officials:** *Decatur Herald*, December 5, 1960.

366 **votes for Nixon and Lodge:** Herald Tribune Service, December 5, 1960.

367 **Nixon objected to the investigation:** Gellman, *Campaign of the Century*, 444.

NOVEMBER 25

368 **through a heavy glass window:** Associated Press, November 25, 1960.

368 **the hospital on December 9:** UPI, December 6, 1960.

368 **"She is fine," he said:** Associated Press, November 26, 1960.

NOVEMBER 30

368 **president-elect wasn't worried:** Associated Press, November 27, 1960.

369 **Democrat who believed in states' rights:** UPI, November 19, 1960.

DECEMBER 4

369 **just as bad as Texas:** *Boston Globe*, December 4, 1960.

370 **"was deprived of victory":** *Chicago Tribune*, December 11, 1960.

370 **"workmen moved the boxes.":** *Norfolk Ledger Dispatch*, December 9, 1960.

DECEMBER 6

371 **"mad . . . in Texas and Illinois":** *Washington Post*, November 17, 2000.

371 **"presidency of the United States":** Mazo, *Richard Nixon*, 249.

372 **"become president or anything else":** Boller Jr., *Presidential Anecdotes*, 327.

372 **to stop Mazo's investigation:** London *Times*, July 30, 1968.

372 **"have great national impact":** Richard Nixon letter to Earl Mazo, February 1, 1966.

DECEMBER 8
372 **to correct alleged irregularities:** Newton, *Mafia at Apalachin*, 169.
373 **"think there is a chance":** UPI, December 12, 1960.

DECEMBER 10
373 **"Nixon voters in the state":** *Chicago Tribune*, December 8, 1960.

JANUARY 6, 1961
377 **"the party of treason":** *Buffalo News*, November 9, 1954.
377 **considered Nixon "a crook":** Gellman, *Campaign of the Century*, 8.
380 **two shiny boxes of inlaid wood:** Associated Press, February 6, 1960.
378 **"victory of his opponent":** UPI, January 6, 1961.
378 **"institutions of self-government":** Congressional Record, January 6, 1961.
379 **"miss you here. Good luck":** Nixon, *Six Crises*, 416.

JANUARY 20, 1961
380 **Black voters supported Democrats:** *Pantagraph*, November 14, 1956.
380 **told Bobby to "get him a drink":** Summers and Swan, *Sinatra*, 278.
380 **request of his father—to stay away:** Summers and Swan, *Sinatra*, 281.
381 **"indebted to a great friend, Frank Sinatra":** Associated Press, January 20, 1961.
381 **"You cannot imagine . . . show a success":** Associated Press, January 20, 1961.
381 **her home in Los Angeles:** Exner, *My Story*, 197.
382 **"they stole it from us":** *Washington Post*, November 17, 2000.
383 **"nation has always been committed":** John F. Kennedy inaugural speech, January 20, 1961.
385 **"want to get anything done":** John F. Kennedy taped conversation at dinner party, January 5, 1960.
385 **"the fellow next to me":** Widmer, *Listening In*, 38.
385 **"this sort of checkerboard chess":** Widmer, *Listening In*, 41.

EPILOGUE
389 **"and it would be right":** "Sixty/Twenty: The Election of 1960 and Its Echoes Today," End of the Road, October 29, 2020.
389 **"probably not wrong about that":** CNN, March 19, 2018.
389 **"her bathroom and threw up":** Farrell, *Richard Nixon*, 345.
389 **"ballots through the campaign organization":** Dwight Chapin interview with Tim Naftali, April 2, 2007.
390 **"courage, boldness, guts? Goddamn it":** *Vanity Fair*, July 14, 2014.
390 **voting bloc in New Hampshire:** *New York Times*, February 27, 1972.
390 **dropping out of the race:** Bernstein and Woodward, *All the President's Men*, 126–27.
391 **"what Watergate was not":** Richard Nixon interview with Frank Gannon, June 13, 1983.

391 **"should have many times over"** X, September 12, 2012.

392 **"nation is totally divided":** X, November 12, 2012.

392 **"take place or Cruz results nullified":** X, February 3, 2016.

392 **"what I'm talking about":** *Washington Post*, October 1, 2016.

393 **"They're fraudulent in many cases":** *New York Times*, October 4, 2020.

393 **"the most secure in American history":** Cybersecurity & Infrastructure Security Agency, November 12, 2020.

394 **"and they are bullshit":** Barr, *One Damn Thing After Another*, 6.

394 **on only one technical issue:** Politifact, Poynter Institute.

394 **supporters in five states Biden won:** Associated Press, February 22, 2021.

394 **Biden victories in four states:** CBS News, December 11, 2020.

394 **"to have a country anymore":** Donald J. Trump speech, January 6, 2021.

395 **"our Country and our Constitution":** X, January 6, 2021.

Bibliography

BOOKS

Aitken, Jonathan. *Nixon: A Life*. Washington, DC: Regnery, 2007.

Alsop, Stewart. *Nixon and Rockefeller: A Double Portrait*. Garden City, NY: Doubleday, 1960.

Ambrose, Stephen E. *Nixon: The Education of a Politician, 1913–1962*, vol. 1. New York: Simon & Schuster, 1987.

Anderson, Jack, and James Boyd. *Confessions of a Muckraker*. New York: Random House, 1979.

Barr, William. *One Damn Thing After Another: Memoirs of an Attorney General*. New York: William Morrow, 2022.

Bartlett, Donald L., and James Steele. *Howard Hughes: His Life and Madness*. New York: W. W. Norton, 1978.

Bedell-Smith, Sally. *Grace and Power: The Private World of the Kennedy White House*. New York: Random House, 2004.

Bernstein, Carl, and Bob Woodward. *All the President's Men*. New York: Simon & Schuster, 1974.

Black, Conrad. *Richard M. Nixon: A Life in Full*. New York: PublicAffairs, 2007.

Bochin, Hal W. *Richard Nixon: Rhetorical Strategist*. Westport, CT: Greenwood Press, 1990.

Boller, Paul F, Jr. *Presidential Anecdotes*. New York: Oxford University Press, 1981.

Bradlee, Benjamin C. *Conversations with Kennedy*. New York: W. W. Norton, 1975.

Bruno, Jerry, and Jeff Greenfield. *The Advance Man*. New York: William Morrow, 1971.

Caro, Robert A. *Master of the Senate*. New York: Alfred A. Knopf, 2002.

Collier, Peter, and David Horowitz. *The Kennedys: An American Drama*. San Francisco: Encounter Books, 2002.

Costello, William. *The Facts About Nixon*. New York: Viking Press, 1960.

Dallek, Robert. *An Unfinished Life: John F. Kennedy, 1917–1963*. Boston: Little, Brown, 2003.

———. *Lone Star Rising: Lyndon Johnson and His Times, 1908–1960*. New York: Oxford University Press, 1991.

Davis, John H. *The Kennedys: Dynasty and Disaster*. New York: McGraw-Hill, 1985.

DeLoach, Cartha D. *Hoover's FBI: The Inside Story by Hoover's Trusted Lieutenant*. Washington, DC: Regnery, 1995.

De Toledano, Ralph. *One Man Alone: Richard Nixon*. New York: Funk & Wagnalls, 1969.

Eisenberg, Dennis. *Meyer Lansky: Mogul of the Mob*. New York: Paddington Press, 1979.

Exner, Judith. *Judith Exner: My Story*. New York: Grove Press, 1977.

Farrell, John A. *Richard Nixon: The Life*. New York: Doubleday, 2017.

Fay, Paul. *The Pleasure of His Company*. New York: Harper & Rowe, 1966.

Ferrell, Robert H., ed. *The Eisenhower Diaries*. New York: W. W. Norton, 1981.

Frank, Jeffrey. *Ike and Dick: Portrait of a Strange Political Marriage*. New York: Simon & Schuster, 2013.

Friedenberg, Robert V. *Rhetorical Studies of National Political Debates*. Westport, CT: Praeger, 1994.

Gellman, Irwin. *Campaign of the Century: Kennedy, Nixon, and the Election of 1960*. New Haven, CT: Yale University Press, 2021.

Goodwin, Doris Kearns. *The Fitzgeralds and the Kennedys*. New York: Simon & Schuster, 1987.

———. *Lyndon Johnson and the American Dream*. New York: St. Martin's Press, 1991.

Goodwin, Richard N. *Remembering America: A Voice from the Sixties*. New York: Harper & Row, 1988.

Halberstam, David. *The Fifties*. New York: Villard, 1993.

Hamilton, Nigel. *JFK: Reckless Youth*. New York: Random House, 1992.

Haught, James A. *Fascinating West Virginia*. Charleston, WV: Gazette, 2008.

Hersh, Seymour M. *The Dark Side of Camelot*. Boston: Little, Brown, 1997.

Humphrey, Hubert H. *The Education of a Public Man: My Life in Politics*. Garden City, NY: Doubleday, 1976.

Jamieson, Kathleen Hall. *Packaging the President: A History and Criticism of Presidential Campaign Advertising*. New York: Oxford University Press, 1996.

Jordan, Winthrop D. *The Americans: A History*. Boston: Houghton Mifflin, 1991.

Kennedy, John F. *Profiles in Courage*. New York: Harper, 1956.

Kennedy, Robert F. *The Enemy Within*. New York: Ishi Press International, 1960.

Kessler, Ronald. *The Sins of the Father: Joseph P. Kennedy and the Dynasty He Founded*. New York: Warner Books, 1996.

King, Coretta Scott. *My Life with Martin Luther King, Jr.* New York: Holt, Rinehart and Winston, 1969.

King, Martin Luther, Jr. *The Autobiography of Martin Luther King, Jr.* New York: Warner Books, 1998.

Klein, Herbert G. *Making It Perfectly Clear: An Inside Account of Nixon's Love-Hate Relationship with the Media*. Garden City, NY: Doubleday, 1980.

Kornitzer, Bela. *The Real Nixon: An Intimate Biography*. New York: Rand McNally, 1960.

Koskoff, David E. *Joseph P. Kennedy: A Life and Times*. Englewood Cliffs, NJ: Prentice-Hall, 1964.

Lasky, Victor. *JFK: The Man and the Myth*. New York: Macmillan, 1963.

Leamer, Lawrence. *The Kennedy Men: 1901–1963: The Laws of the Father*. New York: William Morrow, 2001.

Levington, Steven. *Kennedy and King: The President, the Pastor and the Battle over Civil Rights*. New York: Hachette Books, 2017.

Lincoln, Evelyn. *My Twelve Years with Kennedy*. New York: D. McKay, 1965.

Maier, Thomas. *The Kennedys: America's Emerald Kings*. New York: Basic Books, 2004.

Martin, Ralph G. *A Hero for Our Time: An Intimate Story of the Kennedy Years*. New York: Macmillan, 1983.

Matthews, Christopher J. *Kennedy and Nixon: The Rivalry that Shaped Postwar America*. New York: Touchstone, 1997.

Mazo, Earl. *Richard Nixon: A Political and Personal Portrait*. New York: Harper & Brothers, 1959.

Miller, Merle. *Lyndon: An Oral Biography*. New York: Ballantine, 1981.

Mooney, Booth. *The Lyndon Johnson Story*. New York: Farrar, Straus, 1964.

Morris, Roger. *Richard Milhous Nixon: The Rise of an American Politician*. New York: Henry Holt, 1990.

Newton, Michael. *The Mafia at Apalachin, 1957*. New York: McFarland, 2014.

Nixon, Richard M. *RN: The Memoirs of Richard Nixon*. New York: Grosset & Dunlop, 1978.

———. *Six Crises*. Garden City, NY: Doubleday, 1962.

O'Brien, Lawrence. *No Final Victories: A Life in Politics from John F. Kennedy to Watergate*. Garden City, NY: Doubleday, 1974.

O'Donnell, Kenneth, and David Powers. *Johnny, We Hardly Knew Ye*. New York: Little, Brown, 1972.

O'Neill, Tip. *Man of the House: The Life and Political Memoirs of Speaker Tip O'Neill*. New York: Random House, 1987.

Paterson, Thomas G. *Contesting Castro: The United States and the Triumph of the Cuban Revolution*. New York: Oxford University Press, 1994.

Pietrusza, David. *1960: LBJ vs. JFK vs. Nixon: The Epic Campaign that Forged Three Presidencies*. New York: Union Square Press, 2008.

Ponce de Leon, Charles L. *That's the Way It Is: A History of Television News in America*. Chicago: University of Chicago Press, 2015.

Quirk, Robert E. *Fidel Castro*. New York: W. W. Norton, 1995.

Reston, James. *Lone Star: The Life of John Connally*. New York: HarperCollins, 1989.

Robb, David L. *The Gumshoe and the Shrink: Guenther Reinhardt, Dr. Arnold Hutschnecker, and the Secret History of the 1960 Kennedy/Nixon Election*. Solana Beach, CA: Santa Monica Press, 2012.

Roemer, William F., Jr. *Man Against the Mob: The Inside Story of How the FBI Cracked the Chicago Mob by the Agent Who Led the Attack*. New York: Ballantine, 1989.

Safire, William. *Before the Fall: An Inside View of the Pre-Watergate White House*. New York: Doubleday, 1975.

Salinger, Pierre. *With Kennedy*. Garden City, NY: Doubleday, 1966.

Schlesinger, Arthur M. *A Thousand Days*. Boston: Houghton Mifflin, 1965.

———. *Robert Kennedy and His Times*. Boston: Houghton Mifflin, 1978.

Shesol, Jeff. *Mutual Contempt: Lyndon Johnson, Robert Kennedy, and the Feud that Defined a Decade*. New York: W. W. Norton, 1997.

Silvestri, Vito N. *Becoming JFK: A Profile in Communication*. Westport, CT: Praeger, 2000.

Smith, Jeffrey K. *Bad Blood: Lyndon B. Johnson, Robert F. Kennedy and the Tumultuous 1960s*. North Charleston, SC: Author-House, 2012.

Solberg, Carl. *Hubert Humphrey: A Biography*. New York: W. W. Norton, 1984.

Sorensen, Theodore C. *Kennedy*. New York: Harper & Row, 1965.

Storey, Kate. *White House by the Sea: A Century of the Kennedys at Hyannis Port*. New York: Scribner, 2023.

Summers, Anthony. *Official and Confidential: The Secret Life of J. Edgar Hoover*. New York: G. P. Putnam's Sons, 1993.

Summers, Anthony, and Robbyn Swan. *Sinatra: The Life*. New York: Alfred A. Knopf, 2005.

Swift, Will. *Pat and Dick: The Nixons, an Intimate Portrait of a Marriage*. New York: Threshold, 2014.

Thomas, Evan. *Robert Kennedy: His Life*. New York: Simon & Schuster, 2002.

Watson, W. Marvin. *Chief of Staff: Lyndon Johnson and His Presidency*. New York: Thomas Dunne, 2004.

Whalen, Richard J. *The Founding Father: The Story of Joseph P. Kennedy*. New York: New American Library, 1964.

White, Theodore H. *The Making of the President 1960*. New York: Atheneum, 1961.

———. *The Making of the President 1964*. New York: Atheneum, 1965.

Wicker, Tom. *One of Us:. Richard Nixon and the American Dream*. New York: Random House, 1991.

Widmer, Ted. *Listening In: The Secret White House Recordings of John F. Kennedy*. New York: Hyperion, 2012.

Wofford, Harris. *Of Kennedys and Kings*. New York: Farrar, Straus and Giroux, 1980.

ARCHIVES AND DOCUMENTS

John F. Kennedy Presidential Library and Museum.

Why America Needs Richard Nixon, campaign brochure, 1960.

"Castro Gives Details of Counterrevolution," Radio Progreso, August 17, 1959.

James McNeil oral history, Greensboro Public Library.

Franklin McCain and Jibreel Khazan oral history, University of North Carolina Greensboro and Greensboro Public Library.

John F. Kennedy's television advertisement, Wisconsin Public Television, April 1960.

Kitchen debate transcripts, *New York Times*, July 25, 1959.

Richard M. Nixon Presidential Library.

FBI files on John F. Kennedy, 1960.

CIA Documents: The John F. Kennedy files.

Commission on Presidential Debates.

Congressional Record, January 6, 1961.

Index

Note: Italicized page numbers indicate material in photographs or illustrations.

About the Authors

Chris Wallace is anchor of CNN's *The Chris Wallace Show* and host of *Who's Talking to Chris Wallace?* on Max. Prior to CNN, Wallace was the anchor of *Fox News Sunday* for eighteen years, where he covered every major political event. Throughout his five decades in broadcasting, he has interviewed numerous U.S. and world leaders, including seven American presidents, and won every major broadcast news award for his reporting, including three Emmy Awards, the duPont–Columbia Silver Baton, and the Peabody Award. He is the *New York Times* bestselling author of *Countdown 1945: The Extraordinary Story of the Atomic Bomb and the 116 Days That Changed the World* and *Countdown bin Laden: The Untold Story of the 247-Day Hunt to Bring the Mastermind of 9/11 to Justice.*

Mitch Weiss is a Pulitzer Prize–winning investigative reporter and *New York Times* bestselling author who's part of the Associated Press global investigative team. He has launched projects exposing police misconduct, government corruption, war crimes, clerical abuse, and a politically connected cult with thousands of followers. He is the critically acclaimed author or coauthor of ten books.